CAMBRIDGE STUDIES IN
ANGLO-SAXON ENGLAND

14

THE 'LATERCULUS MALALIANUS' AND THE SCHOOL OF ARCHBISHOP THEODORE

CAMBRIDGE STUDIES IN
ANGLO-SAXON ENGLAND

GENERAL EDITORS
SIMON KEYNES
MICHAEL LAPIDGE

ASSISTANT EDITOR: ANDY ORCHARD

Cambridge Studies in Anglo-Saxon England is a series of scholarly texts and monographs intended to advance our knowledge of all aspects of the field of Anglo-Saxon studies. The scope of the series, like that of *Anglo-Saxon England*, its periodical counterpart, embraces original scholarship in various disciplines: literary, historical, archaeological, philological, art historical, palaeographical, architectural, liturgical and numismatic. It is the intention of the editors to encourage the publication of original scholarship which advances our understanding of the field through interdisciplinary approaches.

Volumes published

1 *Anglo-Saxon Crucifixion Iconography and the Art of the Monastic Revival* by BARBARA C. RAW

2 *The Cult of the Virgin Mary in Anglo-Saxon England* by MARY CLAYTON

3 *Religion and Literature in Western England, 600–800* by PATRICK SIMS-WILLIAMS

4 *Visible Song: Transitional Literacy in Old English Verse* by KATHERINE O'BRIEN O'KEEFFE

5 *The Metrical Grammar of* 'Beowulf' by CALVIN B. KENDALL

6 *The Irish Tradition in Old English Literature* by CHARLES D. WRIGHT

7 *Anglo-Saxon Medicine* by M. L. CAMERON

8 *The Poetic Art of Aldhelm* by ANDY ORCHARD

9 *The Old English Lives of St Margaret* by MARY CLAYTON and HUGH MAGENNIS

10 *Biblical Commentaries from the Canterbury School of Theodore and Hadrian* by BERNHARD BISCHOFF and MICHAEL LAPIDGE

11 *Archbishop Theodore: Commemorative Studies on his Life and Influence* by MICHAEL LAPIDGE

12 *Interactions of Thought and Language in Old English Poetry* by PETER CLEMOES

13 *The Textuality of Old English Poetry* by CAROL BRAUN PASTERNACK

THE 'LATERCULUS MALALIANUS' AND THE SCHOOL OF ARCHBISHOP THEODORE

JANE STEVENSON

Research Fellow, Department of British Cultural Studies
University of Warwick

CAMBRIDGE
UNIVERSITY PRESS

Published by the Press Syndicate of the University of Cambridge
The Pitt Building, Trumpington Street, Cambridge CB2 1RP
40 West 20th Street, New York, NY 10011-4211, USA
10 Stamford Road, Oakleigh, Melbourne 3166, Australia

First published 1995

Printed in Great Britain at the University Press, Cambridge

A catalogue record for this book is available from the British Library

Library of Congress cataloguing in publication data

Stevenson, Jane.
The 'Laterculus Malalianus' and the school of Archbishop Theodore.
p.   cm. – (Cambridge studies in Anglo-Saxon England; 14)
Includes Latin text and English translation of the Laterculus Malilianus.
Includes bibliographical references (p.   ) and index.
ISBN 0 521 37461 8
1. Laterculus Malalianus. 2. England – Church history – 449–1066.
3. Monasticism and religious orders – England – Canterbury – Education – History
4. St Augustine's Abbey (Canterbury, England) – History.
5. Theodore of Canterbury, Saint, 602–690.
I. Laterculus Malalianus. English & Latin.
II. Title. III. Series.
BR749.S74   1995
274.22'3402 – dc20   94-33347 CIP

ISBN 0 521 37461 8 hardback

for Michael and Winifred

Contents

Preface	*page*	ix
List of abbreviations		xi
1	Introduction	1
2	The contents of the *Laterculus*	5
3	Date and origin of the *Laterculus*	8
4	The nature of the *Laterculus*	21
5	Sources of the *Laterculus*	56
6	The Latinity of the *Laterculus*	74
7	Translational technique of the *Laterculus*	87
8	Manuscripts	94
9	Conclusion	114
	Text and Translation	117
	Commentary	162
	Appendix: Variant and anomalous biblical texts	230
	Bibliography	237
	Index of biblical sources	245
	General Index	248

Preface

It is both a duty and a pleasure to thank the various people who have given generously of their time in reading and commenting on my various drafts. Henry Chadwick, Michael Lapidge, Dáibhí Ó Cróinín, Elizabeth Jeffreys, Andy Orchard, Winifred Temple, Neil Wright, David Dumville and Richard Sharpe have all been extremely helpful. Lesley Abrams and Simon Keynes both answered queries about charters, for which I am most grateful. Michael Lapidge collated the Vatican manuscript on my behalf, and also allowed me to use his *Biblical Commentaries* pre-publication. I owe a particular debt to David Dumville, for his generous loan of his complete set of photographs of the Vatican MS of the *Laterculus*, which formed the basis of my edition. I would also like to thank Carmela Vircillo Franklin for giving me xeroxes of her edition and commentary on the *Passio S. Anastasii*, and Elizabeth Jeffreys for sending me most of the *Studies* volume months before it came out. Peter Davidson performed the traditional duties of an academic spouse by checking references in the final stages. Earlier versions of the main arguments in the Introduction were presented as papers to the Cambridge Classics Faculty seminar on the transmission of Latin texts in the Middle Ages, and the seminar which was held in the Department of Anglo-Saxon, Norse and Celtic to mark the 1300th anniversary of the death of Archbishop Theodore in 1990. I am indebted to participants at both these occasions for illuminating comments and helpful information. The substance of the work for this book was done during my tenure of a Drapers' Research Fellowship at Pembroke College, Cambridge, and I am grateful both to the Master and Fellows of Pembroke and to the Department of Anglo-Saxon, Norse and Celtic at Cambridge for their support of my endeavours. I also received consistent support and assistance from the Literary and Linguistic Computing Centre in

Cambridge, for which I am most grateful. I owe particular thanks to Rosemary Rodd for all her help. The Department of History, University of Sheffield, did all they reasonably could to speed the final stages. The dedication expresses my abiding gratitude for, respectively, fourteen and thirty-four years of education and encouragement.

Abbreviations

AASS	*Acta Sanctorum quotquot toto orbe coluntur*, 69 vols. (Antwerp, Paris and Rome, 1643–1895)
AB	*Analecta Bollandiana*
ANT	*The Apocryphal New Testament*, trans. M.R. James (Cambridge, 1924)
Archbishop Theodore	*Archbishop Theodore: Commemorative Studies on his Life and Influence*, ed. Michael Lapidge, Cambridge Studies in Anglo-Saxon England 11 (Cambridge, 1995)
ASE	*Anglo-Saxon England*
BCL	M. Lapidge and R. Sharpe, *A Bibliography of Celtic-Latin Literature, 400–1200* (Dublin, 1985)
BHG	*Bibliotheca Hagiographica Graeca*, ed. Société des Bollandistes and F. Halkin, 3rd ed., Subsidia Hagiographica 8 (Brussels, 1957)
Biblical Commentaries	*Biblical Commentaries from the Canterbury School of Theodore and Hadrian*, ed. Bernhard Bischoff and Michael Lapidge, Cambridge Studies in Anglo-Saxon England 10 (Cambridge, 1994)
BOT	*Bedae Opera de Temporibus*, ed. C. W. Jones (Cambridge, MA, 1943)
BZ	*Byzantinische Zeitschrift*
CSEL	Corpus Scriptorum Ecclesiasticorum Latinorum (Vienna)
CCSL	Corpus Christianorum Series Latina (Turnhout, 1954–)
ChLA	*Chartae Latinae Antiquiores*, ed. A. Bruckner, R. Marichal *et al.* (Olten and Lausanne, 1954–)

CLA	E.A. Lowe, *Codices Latini Antiquiores: a Palaeographical Guide to Latin Manuscripts prior to the Ninth Century*, 11 vols. and suppl. (Oxford, 1934–71; 2nd ed. of vol. II, 1972)
CMCS	*Cambridge Medieval Celtic Studies*
CSCO	Corpus Scriptorum Christianorum Orientalium (Rome, Louvain, etc., 1903–)
Script. Armen.	Scriptores Armeniaci
Script. Syr.	Scriptores Syri
CSEL	Corpus Scriptorum Ecclesiasticorum Latinorum (Vienna, 1866–)
ECC	J.N.D. Kelly, *Early Christian Creeds*, 3rd ed. (London, 1972)
ECD	J.N.D. Kelly, *Early Christian Doctrines*, 5th ed. (London, 1977)
EEMF	Early English Manuscripts in Facsimile, ed. P.A.M. Clemoes *et al.* (Copenhagen, 1951–)
EHR	*English Historical Review*
GCS	Die griechischen christlichen Schriftsteller der ersten drei Jahrhunderte
HBS	Henry Bradshaw Society Publications (London)
HTR	*Harvard Theological Review*
JEH	*Journal of Ecclesiastical History*
JTS	*Journal of Theological Studies*
LXX	Septuagint
MGH	Monumenta Germaniae Historica
AA	Auctores Antiquissimi
PLAC	Poetae Latini Aevi Carolini
SSRM	Scriptores Rerum Merovingicarum
ODB	*The Oxford Dictionary of Byzantium*, ed. A.P. Kazhdan *et al.*, 3 vols. (New York and Oxford, 1991)
PG	Patrologia Graeca, ed. J.-P. Migne, 161 vols. (Paris, 1857–66)
PL	Patrologia Latina, ed. J.-P. Migne, 221 vols. (Paris, 1844–64)
Sawyer	P. H. Sawyer, *Anglo-Saxon Charters: Annotated List and Bibliography*, Royal Historical Society Guides and Handbooks 8 (London, 1968)

SChr Sources Chrétiennes, ed. J. Daniélou *et al.* (Paris)

SettSpol *Settimane di studio del Centro italiano di studi sull' alto medioevo*

SP *Studia Patristica* (Bonn)

Studies *Studies in John Malalas*, ed. E. Jeffreys *et al.*, Byzantina Australiensia 6 (Sydney, 1990)

Tjäder J.-O. Tjäder, *Die nichtliterarischen lateinischen Papyri Italiens aus der Zeit 445–700*, 2 vols. (Lund and Stockholm, 1982)

TLL *Thesaurus Linguae Latinae* (Munich, 1900–)

TU *Texte und Untersuchungen zur Geschichte der altchristlichen Literatur*, ed. O. von Gebhardt and A. Harnack (Bonn, 1883–)

ZcP *Zeitschrift für celtische Philologie*

1

Introduction

At the end of the last century, Mommsen edited a series of *Chronica Minora* in the Monumenta Germaniae Historica.[1] These included a chronicle which he called *Laterculus Malalianus*, which covers the historical period of the gospels, and is based in part on the work of John Malalas, author of a sixth-century Byzantine world-chronicle. The word *laterculus* in Classical Latin means 'a brick', or 'a tile' or something of the sort, but in the early Middle Ages it came to mean a list, sometimes a computus (a table for calculating the date of Easter), and is often used as equivalent to *fasti*.[2] Mommsen grouped several imperial lists together in *Chronica Minora*, and used *laterculus* as the generic name for them. So my text is defined, superficially, as an imperial list – a definition which I should say here and now is almost entirely irrelevant to it. The classification of *Laterculus Malalianus* is based on a very minor aspect of the text, which is that it ends

[1] *Chronica Minora III*, ed. T. Mommsen, pp. 424–37. There is also an earlier edition of the *Laterculus* by Cardinal Angelo Mai, printed in PL 94, 1161–74. The text of the *Laterculus*, and its references to Rome and to the Irish have been noticed by a number of writers. Its existence was noted by Kenney, *Sources for the Ecclesiastical History of Ireland*, p. 518, n. 71, by R. E. McNally, 'Isidorean Pseudepigrapha in the Early Middle Ages', *Isidoriana*, ed. M. C. Díaz y Díaz (Leon, 1961), pp. 305–16, at 309 and *Scriptores Hiberniae Minores I*, 189, and in *Bedae Opera Didascalica I*, ed. C. W. Jones, CCSL 123A, xiv. None of these writers gave the work much thought, and all of them assumed that its origins were in Rome itself. There are also two notes on the *Laterculus* by L. Traube, 'Chronicon Palatinum', *BZ* 4 (1874), 489–92, repr. as an article in his *Vorlesungen und Abhandlungen* III, 201–4; and one by T. Mommsen, 'Lateinische Malalasauszüge', *BZ* 4 (1895), 487–8.

[2] In computistical texts, it is sometimes used synonymously with 'computus', as in Paris, Bibliothèque Nationale, lat. 16361, 242r: 'Apud hebreos niman et aput syros et caldeos. Apud grecos autem arithmus et altera ratione cyclus. Apud egiptos laterculus. Apud macedones calculus. Apud latinos compotus uocatur.' (quoted in *BOT*, p. 15, n. 3).

with a list of Roman emperors, from Augustus to Justin II. The second half of the title, *Malalianus*, simply means 'connected with John Malalas'.

The *Laterculus* has always been categorized as a chronicle-text, its name linking it specifically with the chronography of the consular lists, or of the calculation of Easter. And, of course, it is based in part on the *Chronographia* of Malalas. But some two-thirds of its length is completely independent of Malalas, and although its Malalian structure is a correlation of the gospels and Roman imperial history, its independent content is basically exegetical. I hope to show below that the historical element is no more than a component of the exegesis. Its manuscript context, also, sets it among exegetical and computistical writings.

Laterculus Malalianus is preserved in two manuscripts. The most important is now Vatican City, Biblioteca Apostolica Vaticana, Pal. lat. 277, written probably in Rome in the early eighth century. The second manuscript is in Leiden, Bibliotheek der Rijksuniversiteit, Voss. Misc. 11, and is an early ninth-century copy of the earlier manuscript, possibly made at Weissenburg. But I will argue that the text itself was composed in Canterbury at the end of the seventh century. It therefore assumes an interest and importance out of all proportion to its modest length. Because of the formidable achievements of Bede, learning and culture in early Anglo-Saxon England are firmly associated in most peoples' minds with Northumbria, and in particular, with Bede's school at Jarrow. Yet, as Bede himself acknowledged, it was Canterbury which was the principal school of Christianity and Latin literacy in Anglo-Saxon England.[3] The reason why this is not a truth universally acknowledged is that, until very recently, the activities of Canterbury have been almost entirely opaque to scholarly investigation. The recent uncovering of work at Theodore's school, of which this book is a part, is a redressing of the balance, which should in future make it possible to assess the total intellectual achievement of the Anglo-Saxons, both north and south of the Humber. It is even true to say that the intellectual achievement of Jarrow, far from being the first and only school of England, was directly derivative from Canterbury. Benedict Biscop, who was later to found Wearmouth and Jarrow, was on

---

[3] This is not exclusively a modern perception. A tenth- or eleventh-century Aquitanian monk called Gausbertus placed Theodore and Hadrian at the head of the entire Insular contribution to continental learning and literature. He was edited by L. Delisle, 'Notices sur les manuscrits originaux d'Adémar de Chabannes', *Notices et extraits des manuscrits de la Bibliothèque Nationale et autres bibliothèques* 35 (Paris, 1890), 241–357, at 311–12.

his third visit to Rome when he was entrusted by the pope in 668 with the task of conveying the elderly monk Theodore of Tarsus, the newly-created archbishop of Canterbury, together with his companion Hadrian, from Rome to England, where they arrived in 669. Benedict lived with Theodore and Hadrian in Canterbury for two years, as abbot of St Paul's (later St Augustine's), before Hadrian was ready to take over this responsibility. He then returned to his native Northumbria and founded there a school which was, briefly, the light of the west. And Bede, who was its chief glory and the reason that we are so well informed about the educational achievements of Northumbria, spoke in the highest terms of the education which Theodore and Hadrian offered at Canterbury. He said of Albinus, Hadrian's successor, 'in tantum studiis scripturarum institutus est, ut Grecam quidem linguam non parua uero parte, Latinam uero non minus quam Anglorum, quae sibi naturalis est, nouerit'.[4] Bishop Tobias of Rochester, another Canterbury alumnus, is also described by Bede as knowing both Greek and Latin.[5] And although Aldhelm, our main surviving witness to the school of Canterbury, does not seem ever to have learned Greek, his extraordinary learning stretched far and wide across the field of Latin literature, Classical and Christian, in a way which Bede himself could not match, and he is witness to the existence of a remarkable library in southern England. It is also worth noting that the Canterbury archives appear to have been one of Bede's most significant historical resources. Abbot Albinus was both the instigator of Bede's *Historia ecclesiastica*, and one of Bede's chief informants, as Bede's Preface bears witness. But the achievement of Theodore and Hadrian was a matter of reportage only until Bernhard Bischoff and Michael Lapidge began to uncover the Canterbury origins of parts of the early medieval glossary tradition.[6] Now, building on this achievement, Theodore's œuvre, his poems, the Penitential, and other traces of his activity, have come under new scrutiny. The text edited in the present volume, *Laterculus Malalianus*, is a contribution to this collective endeavour. It is a historical exegesis of the life of Christ, and is the sole surviving complete text from seventh-century Canterbury. Its characteristics are therefore of the highest

---

[4] Bede, *Historia ecclesiastica* V.20 (ed. Colgrave and Mynors, p. 530).

[5] *Ibid.*, V.8 (p. 474).

[6] The full results of this are published in their edition of the *Biblical Commentaries*. Both have made some preliminary remarks, in Bischoff, 'Wendepunkte', pp. 206–9, and in Lapidge, 'The School of Theodore'.

significance. The first thing to be said about it is that it vindicates Bede's claim that Greek was taught at Canterbury to that first generation of students.[7] It proves that Greek texts were available, and used, in Anglo-Saxon England. And it also shows that Canterbury was almost the only western school in the seventh century to teach the exegetical methods of the school of Antioch. The *Laterculus* implies the need for a thorough re-examination of the entire basis of Anglo-Saxon Christian culture, and also calls into question fundamental assumptions about what is Irish and what is English.

[7] See for example Bede, *Historia ecclesiastica* V.8 and V.20 (ed. Colgrave and Mynors, pp. 474 and 530).

2

The contents of the *Laterculus*

The first half of the *Laterculus* (chs. 2–11) follows the *Chronographia* of John Malalas almost exactly, with one or two minor additions, and an introduction. It may help the reader here if I briefly describe what the *Chronographia* is: it is a universal history, beginning with Adam, and going down to the reign of Justinian, conforming to a familiar type of early Byzantine historical writing. Its author, about whom nothing is known, was probably a rhetor of Syrian extraction, connected with Antioch, though he seems also to have spent time in Constantinople. In his forward sweep through the history of the world, he devotes one of his eighteen books (bk 10) to the life and times of Jesus. It is this book which forms the basis of the first half of the *Laterculus*. This is what it contains. The text begins with the Annunciation, and a discussion of the various important events which have fallen on this date (25 March). Most of this material is additional to Malalas. Then the text returns to straight translation from the *Chronographia* for an account of the division of historical time: the reader is told that there were 3,000 years between Adam and Phalech, and 2,967 years from Phalech to the birth of Christ, which of course makes 6,000 years from the creation of Adam to the Crucifixion. Most of this is straight from Malalas, and very odd it is too: the only addition is a gratuitous, parenthetic remark about the stupidity of the Irish. The next event mentioned is the visit of the Magi, first to Herod, and then to Christ at Bethlehem, followed by the flight into Egypt. Here again, the writer inserts additional material, which he claims to have derived from Epiphanius, the fourth-century iconoclast bishop of Constantia in Cyprus. The author, following Malalas once more, then treats of the return to Jerusalem, Augustus's dream of an unknown Jewish divinity, the succession of Tiberius, the baptism of Christ, the death of John the

Baptist, the Crucifixion, and the Resurrection. His account follows the chronology of the biblical narrative in sequence. Each of these significant events is given its date, often very elaborately. Here is an example of the writer's technique:

in the sixth month of the forty-first year of that Caesar, in the month of Distrus (that is, according to the Latins, March), on the twenty-fifth day of the month (which is the eighth of the kalends of April, which is called Xanthicus according to the Greeks) ... the archangel Gabriel was sent to bear witness to blessed Mary...[1]

The second half of the *Laterculus*, which is original prose rather than translation or paraphrase, is rather different in its contents. Ch. 12 goes back to Christ's birth, and begins a recapitulation of the life of Christ treated typologically rather than historically, and displaying a marked Antiochene bias. Thus the *Laterculus* is written in the form of two parallel structures of historical fact and spiritual significance. Although it is not very long, it is a work of considerable learning. The bipartite structure, odd though it may seem, can be paralleled quite easily in the Antiochene exegetical tradition, with its avoidance of undue dependence on allegory, and its concern with both literal and historical truth and typological significance. The most specific model for the plan of the work as a whole appears to be Theodore of Mopsuestia's commentary on the minor epistles of St Paul, which similarly begins its exegetical discussion of each epistle by setting it in its political and temporal context. Another possible model is the greatest hymn of the Byzantine church, the 'Akathistos' ('un-sitting'), a long hymn to Mary sometimes attributed to Romanos the Melodist, and probably composed in the sixth century. The first half of the 'Akathistos' covers the historical events of Mary's career, while the second half explores the theological and spiritual significance of her actions and experiences. The contents of the *Laterculus* may be set out schematically as follows:

ch. 1. Introduction.
ch. 2. The date of the Annunciation and the various important events which fall on that date (25 March).

---

[1] Interestingly, the *Canones Theodori*, ch. 143, based on Theodore's verbal *iudicia*, suggest the appropriate time for an annual autumn council, and use both the Greek and the Roman calendar to do it in exactly the same way: 'Bis in uno anno concilia episcopi fiant id est quarta septimana post pentecosten. Secundo .xii. die mensis Hyperberethei id est .iiii. idus .viii.bris iuxta Romanos' (ed. Finsterwalder, p. 250).

ch. 3. The division of time: 3,000 years from Adam to Phalech and 2,967 years from Phalech to Augustus.

ch. 4. The ages of the world, their total length to the Passion of 6,000 years.

ch. 5. The visit of the Magi to Herod.

ch. 6. The Nativity, the visit of the Magi, the flight into Egypt.

ch. 7. The Holy Family in Egypt, Middle Eastern historical information.

ch. 8. The return to Jerusalem, Augustus's dream of an unknown Jewish divinity.

ch. 9. The succession of Tiberius, the baptism of Christ, the death of John the Baptist.

ch. 10. The Crucifixion.

ch. 11. The Resurrection.

ch. 12. Christ's birth from a virgin reverses the judgement on Adam and Eve. Discussion of Christ's prophecy of the destruction of the temple which was built in forty-six years. Historical note on which temple this was.

ch. 13. The temple stands for Christ's body. Embryological discussion, forcing a numerological relationship between the period from the Annunciation to Christ's birth (276 days) and the number 46, breaking it down as 6×40 (240) $+ 6 \times 6$ (36). The perfection of the number 6.

ch. 14. Old Testament foreshadowings of the life of Christ.

ch. 15. Explanation of the gifts of the Magi.

ch. 16. The circumcision of Christ and its foreshadowing in the circumcision of Moses's son which saved his family from death.

ch. 17. Adam and Eve were created as perfect adults, with full adult understanding.

ch. 18. Christ's baptism, the temptation in the desert and the relationship of Christ and Adam.

ch. 19. The *ordines Christi*: Christ in his human lifetime performed the functions of each of the grades of the ecclesiastical hierarchy.

ch. 20. The mocking of Christ, the paradox of man's mistreatment of God and God's mercy to man.

ch. 21. Typological reflections on the crucifixion.

ch. 22. Pentecost and the true validity of Christian priesthood.

ch. 23. Return to a discussion of the six ages and the approaching world sabbath.

ch. 24. A warning that one should not attempt to guess its exact duration.

ch. 25. List of emperors from Augustus onwards, employing only relative chronology and based mainly on Malalas.

It will be seen that the Latin author's text from ch. 12 onwards recapitulates chs. 2–11, working through the life of Christ in chronological order for a second time, but from a completely different perspective and drawing on a different set of data.

7

3

Date and origin of the *Laterculus*

My reasons for deducing that the *Laterculus* was written by Archbishop
Theodore are essentially circumstantial. To begin with, this is a seventh-
century text, written in Latin by a man whose education in the Greek
patristic tradition is both wide and deep, and whose knowledge of Latin
(both the language and its literature) is relatively superficial. This in itself
is a highly anomalous state of affairs. There were numbers of Greeks active
in the west in the seventh century, but they seldom wrote in Latin.
Furthermore, the very few Latin works which the author of the *Laterculus*
can be shown to have known are paralleled in the known contents of the
library at Canterbury.[1] There are only two Latin poets who can be shown
to have impressed him, both Christian writers: Caelius Sedulius and
Faltonia Betitia Proba. Proba's *Cento* was very little read in the early
Middle Ages, but it *was* known to Aldhelm, who was partly trained in the
school at Canterbury. Furthermore, Caelius Sedulius was one of Aldhelm's
favourite authors. There are also two passages which suggest that the
author of the *Laterculus* had read Gildas. Gildas was very well known to
Aldhelm, but on the other hand there is little or no indication that he was
read at all outside the Celtic west and England in the early Middle Ages.

Another fact which can be deduced about the author of the *Laterculus* is
that he was probably familiar with the city of Rome, because he refers to a
great church dedicated to the Virgin, which had just been built on the
Capitol. This must refer to Aracoeli, built on the Capitol some time in the
second half of the seventh century.[2] Although it might seem plausible that

---

[1] Lapidge, 'The School of Theodore', pp. 54–5.

[2] R. Krautheimer, *Rome: Profile of a City, 312–1308* (Princeton, NJ, 1980), p. 285: 'to the
North, perhaps using the ruins of the Temple of Juno, the monastery and church of
S. Maria in Capitolio had been set up by the eighth century or earlier.' No remains of

the building of a new church in Rome would be the kind of news which would get around, the chances of this are considerably reduced by the nature of Aracoeli itself. The churches mentioned in the *itineraria* (which functioned as early medieval 'Michelin guides' for pilgrims) are *martyria*, like St Anastasius *ad aquas salvias*.[3] Because of the Classical Roman prohibition against allowing corpses to remain within the city walls, the pilgrim-churches of early medieval Rome form a ring around the city. Aracoeli, not associated with a high-profile martyr, and located in the heart of old Rome within the walls, is relatively unlikely to have attracted the attention of outsiders. The later, notorious Anglo-Saxon enthusiasm for going on pilgrimage to Rome took some time to get started. Only a very few Anglo-Saxons, notably Benedict Biscop, Wilfrid, King Cædwalla, and possibly Aldhelm,[4] are known to have visited Rome in the period from 650 to 680.[5] These facts about the development of pilgrimage in Anglo-Saxon England are, of course, only relevant if the case for this text's origins in England can be made. Although the earliest manuscript is north Italian, and there was a plethora of Greek monks in later seventh-century

---

this church survive to clarify the question of its date, because it was rebuilt in the twelfth century, and rebuilt yet again in the thirteenth, each time in a larger and more impressive form, thus obliterating the original basilica (*ibid.*, pp. 286–7).

[3] For example, the mid-seventh-century text *De locis sanctis martyrum quae sunt foris ciuitatis Romae*, in *Itineraria*, ed. Geyer *et al.*, pp. 314–22, and another mid-seventh-century text (not surviving) which lies behind a similar description of the Roman *martyria* in William of Malmesbury's *Gesta Regum* (*ibid.*), pp. 324–8. See also R. Valentini and G. Zucchetti, *Codice topografica della Città di Roma*, 4 vols. (Rome, 1940–53) II, 101–53.

[4] *Aldhelmi Opera*, ed. Ehwald, p. 494: the letter of an anonymous student to Aldhelm includes the phrase 'quia tu Romae aduena fuisti', but there is no way of establishing whether his pilgrimage was made in youth, middle, or old age.

[5] The pilgrimage was a dramatic feature of Anglo-papal relations in the eighth century, on the witness of both Bede and Boniface. See, for instance, Bede's comment on the year 725 in his *Chronica Maiora* (*Chronica Minora III*, ed. Mommsen, pp. 223–333, at 320): 'his temporibus multi Anglorum gentis, nobiles et ignobiles, uiri et feminae, duces et priuati, diuini amoris instinctu de Britannia Romam uenire consueuerant'; and also W. Levison, *England and the Continent in the Eighth Century* (Oxford, 1946), pp. 34–44. But this flood of eager pilgrims seems very much a feature of the confident and consolidated church of the mid- and late eighth century, which, on the evidence of the earliest manuscript, is too late a date for the author of the *Laterculus*. Venturesome Anglo-Saxon Christians of the seventh century were more likely to cross the sea to Ireland, like Wihtfrith and Heahfrith, or to the monasteries of Gaul, like the future abbess Hild, than to go as far as Rome.

Rome, there are a number of reasons for insisting that the *Laterculus* is Insular in origin. One small pointer is in the eighth-century manuscript itself, the reading *suminantur* for *ruminantur*. The considerable similarity of *s* and *r* in Insular minuscule hands suggests that the exemplar from which this text was copied was of Insular origin; and since the manuscript is not very far removed in time from the original text, this original may itself have been written in the British Isles. I have already mentioned the significance of the author's possible use of Gildas. But a far stronger piece of evidence for an English origin is that the author goes out of his way, on two separate occasions, to be rude about the Irish, saying in his preface, 'iam ne nos fallant multiloquio suo Scottorum scolaces', and in ch. 4, 'In sex milia autem annorum concordant omnes apparuisse Dominum; quamuis Scotti concordare nolunt, qui sapientia se existimant habere, et scientiam perdederunt.' The peevish tone of these comments is comparable with Aldhelm's gibes at Irish scholarship. The point here is that the *Laterculus* was written in the later seventh century, at which time nobody but the English concerned themselves to any great extent about the Irish. Certainly, there is some conspicuous Hibernophobia in continental circles in the eighth and ninth centuries,[6] but in the seventh, there were not enough *peregrini* about to have excited any particular reaction.[7] And there is only one testimony of an expedition to Rome from seventh-century Ireland that I know of, Cummian's dispatch of three monks to go to Rome and find out how they calculated Easter, a journey which took nearly three years there and back.[8] It is just possible that this small band of Irishmen contrived to incense a Greek writer living in Rome, but the possibility

[6] See for example Bischoff, 'Theodulf und der Ire Cadac-Andreas', *Mittelalterliche Studien* (Stuttgart, 1966) II, 19–25, and also Theodulf's poem *Ad Carolum regem*, ed. E. Dümmler, MGH, PLAC 1 (Berlin, 1881), 483–9, which describes at some length (lines 214–34; pp. 488–9) an Irishman 'quae tamen ignorat, omnia nosse putat'.

[7] The Irish presence on the Continent began towards the end of the sixth century with the foundation of Annegray, Fontaines, Luxeuil and Bobbio by Columbanus, and of Péronne by Fursa. In all these cases, a small core of Irish monks was balanced by much larger numbers of continental recruits. Apart from the perennial battle over the calculation of the date of Easter, on which Columbanus has left us two important epistles (*Epistolae* I and III, ed. Walker, pp. 1–13 and 22–5), there is no evidence that the eccentricities of Irish scholarship attracted the attention of their continental neighbours at this time. It was the Carolingian era, which saw the influx of a larger number of Irish scholars than the market could easily bear, which led to the development of pronounced anti-Irish sentiments in some Frankish quarters.

[8] *BOT*, pp. 97–8. The text of his letter is in PL 87, 969–78.

seems a remote one. Whom would such a writer be seeking to defend against the heterodox views of the *Scotti*? As Cummian himself very fair-mindedly pointed out, the Irish seemed a remote and eccentric group from a Mediterranean perspective.[9]

To sum up, the author of the *Laterculus* was educated in the Greek tradition, familiar with Rome, disliked the Irish, and flourished in the later seventh century. This seems to point straight to Theodore of Tarsus, who was certainly educated in the eastern empire, was living at Rome in the 660s, and is pictured by Aldhelm in his letter to Heahfrith as locked in battle with Irish students, like an old boar surrounded by hounds, suggesting with some force that he was well aware of contemporary controversies between Irish and English scholars.[10] Furthermore, the Latin sources of the *Laterculus*, such as they are, were all known to Aldhelm; and the biblical commentaries known to originate in seventh-century Canterbury show a very considerable overlap in the Greek authorities used. Whenever the *Laterculus* and the Theodorian commentaries happen to coincide in their comments,[11] they are in agreement.

We must also give some attention to what is known of Theodore and his school, to see how the *Laterculus* fits in with the known facts. Although there is no complete schooltext (other than the *Laterculus*) from Canterbury, Theodore, as befitted an archbishop active in England for over twenty years, has left various literary evidence of his interests. This may be divided into three categories: writings by Theodore himself, texts worked up from lecture notes by his pupils, and, more distantly, writings influenced by the Canterbury school. The first category is rather small. It includes one or two formal letters, short octosyllabic poems and probably the synodal *acta* over which Theodore had presided, notably the Council of Hatfield recorded by Bede.[12] In the second category are three closely-related penitentials, all of which are direct reflections of Theodore's teaching, in one case (the penitential written by the 'discipulus Umbrensium') redacted by a person who specifically identifies himself as a pupil at

---

[9] *BOT*, pp. 89–93, at 92: 'the Britons and the Irish . . . are on the edge of things and, if I may say it, but a pimple on the face of the earth' (PL 87, 974).

[10] Aldhelm, *Epistola ad Ehfridum* (*Aldhelmi Opera*, ed. Ehwald, p. 493).

[11] For example, that the new bodies received by all human beings at the Resurrection will be thirty years old (ch. 16).

[12] See *Archbishop Theodore*, which contains separate essays on all aspects of Theodore's œuvre.

Canterbury, and the *Biblical Commentaries*. The fact that the greatest bulk of Canterbury teaching which has survived is the work of pupils rather than of the master himself seems characteristic of this school, probably for good reason. Brooks stressed that Theodore was 'a very old but outstandingly able man'.[13] His achievement in England was prodigious, and his actions were marked by ruthless speed and decisiveness, probably in the ever-present fear that he might drop dead before his organisational reforms could be completed.[14] It is awe-inspiring, in view of his other commitments, that he should have also been putting in long hours in the Canterbury classrooms as well; but the penitentials[15] and commentaries, to say nothing of the *Laterculus*, show clearly that this was the case. Since all this is so, Theodore may perhaps be likened to a lecturer who seldom had time to work his notes up into a book; the result is that the main testimonies to his interests and activities, except, probably, the *Laterculus*, were assembled by amanuenses. The third category includes the works of Aldhelm, the only identifiable seventh-century alumnus of the Canterbury school to leave a surviving œuvre of substantial size, possibly some of the early Southumbrian, particularly Kentish, charters, medical *dicta* mentioned by Bede, and probably the base-text of the Corpus-Epinal-Erfurt group of Latin–Old English and Latin–Latin glosses. Of these, only the commentaries on the Pentateuch and gospels give any clue to Theodore's

---

[13] Brooks, *Early History of Canterbury*, p. 71.

[14] One testament to his energy is the fact that he made a visitation over the whole of England soon after his arrival in the country: 'moxque peragrata insula tota, quaquauersum Anglorum gentes morabantur' (Bede, *Historia ecclesiastica* IV.2, ed. Colgrave and Mynors, p. 352). This must have been a gruelling test of physical stamina for a man in his late sixties.

[15] The place of Theodore in the development of the system of private penance in the west might bear more investigation than it has yet received. As is well known, he drew on the Hiberno-Latin penitential tradition to which the earliest witness is the British writer Gildas (whose *De excidio* is drawn on in the *Laterculus*). But it has long been observed by orientalists that, to quote Murray, 'the Syriac churches seem to have been the first to introduce private confession, apparently in a form not unlike that which the Irish monks were to develop' (*Symbols of Church and Kingdom*, p. 202). It may be that Theodore's confidence in the legitimacy and utility of Celtic private penance was strengthened by his acquaintance with similar procedures in Syria, since he was evidently not normally welcoming to Celtic innovations. The Syriac penitential tradition is discussed by W. de Vries, *Sakramententheologie bei den syrischen Monophysiten* (Rome, 1940), pp. 181–210, and *Sakramententheologie bei den Nestorianern* (Rome, 1947), pp. 265–80.

exegetical interests and, like the *Laterculus*, they have been found to be not only Greek, but strongly Antiochene in their terms of reference.

The *Laterculus* draws on a formidable range of Greek and Syriac sources. Theodore is the only native Greek speaker known to have worked in these islands in the seventh century: moreover, he came from Tarsus, an economically and politically important city on the trade-routes from Edessa (the home of Ephrem) and Antioch (the home of John Malalas).[16] The *Laterculus* displays to a much greater extent the pronounced Antiochene exegetical tendencies that Bischoff noted as an unexpected attribute of Bede's exegetical work, which he attributed to his second-hand acquaintance with Canterbury traditions, and which are also found in the commentaries associated with Theodore's school,[17] and to some extent in Aldhelm.[18]

Other aspects of the known career and interests of Theodore fit in with the contents of this text. It displays a knowledge of Greek medicine, which was known to be an interest of Theodore.[19] In particular, the embryological theory of the *Laterculus*, which puts the acquisition of limbs and thus human shape at the forty-fifth day, accords well with the penalties assigned in the penitentials dependent on Theodore, which give the fortieth day as the point where abortion is treated as homicide.[20] The difference might be accounted for by erring on the side of severity, given the difficulty of actually calculating dates and the tendency, in the circumstances, of the mother to underestimate. Other aspects of Canterbury studies reflected in the *Laterculus* are Roman law, evidenced in ch. 20, and an interest in chronology, although this is not really a historical text. Theodore lived in Rome for some time before the pope seconded him to Canterbury, which would give a context for this writer, who is otherwise almost wholly eastern in his background, being *au fait* with new

---

[16] For further notes on his background and education, see *Biblical Commentaries*, pp. 6–41.

[17] Bischoff, 'Wendepunkte', pp. 207–9, and Lapidge, *Biblical Commentaries*, pp. 243–9.

[18] Mayr-Harting, *The Coming of Christianity*, p. 208.

[19] Lapidge, 'The School of Theodore', p. 50, and discussion below, pp. 147–55.

[20] *Iudicium de penitentia Theodori*, ch. 147, ed. Finsterwalder, p. 280. 'Mulieres qui abortiuum faciunt ex eodem sententiam iudicentur antequam animam habent et postea, id est post .xl. dies acceptatione seminis ut homicida peniteat.' Note that the phrase 'antequam animam habent' implies something like the Galenic distinction between the embryo as a sort of vegetable growth up to the thirtieth or fortieth day, depending on sex, and its gradual transformation thereafter into a fully human foetus.

building in Rome itself.[21] Another of Theodore's well-attested talents was as a rhetorician and rhetorical, or homiletic, skills are evident in this text, such as the enlivening aside to the reader or hearer, in the second person (ch. 18) and the epanalepsis of ch. 23. Nicholas Brooks in his book on the early history of Canterbury put forward the suggestion that Theodore may specifically have encouraged the use of written English, noting that he was familiar with English weights and measures and that his pupil Tobias is said by Bede to have been trained in the Saxon language as well as Latin and Greek.[22] In addition, the earliest Latin–Anglo-Saxon glossaries seem to have had their origin in seventh-century Canterbury. This interest in, and concern for, the vernacular is more comprehensible from a man of the eastern empire than from a westerner. Theodore was a man of wide and sophisticated linguistic background, whose language skills may even have included Syriac. In the churches of the east, it was normal for the vernacular to be the language used for both the Bible and the liturgy, be it Syriac, Coptic, Ethiopic or Armenian. These tongues were, and remain, the liturgical languages of their respective Christian communities. The interactions between Greek, Latin, Syriac and other languages in the eastern empire may be contrasted with the west, where there was no vernacular as sophisticated as Syriac or Armenian and consequently a more rigid attitude to Latin *versus* 'Barbarian' tongues.[23] This more flexible linguistic background may have helped the elderly Theodore, who had already suffered one major upheaval in his life when he moved from Asia Minor to Italy, to see Old English not as an unavoidable evil but as something interesting in itself and with considerable expressive potential.

The *Laterculus*, far from suggesting that its author was naive or incompetent, as the choice of the somewhat unsatisfactory Malalas as a base-text

---

[21] '[Théodore] semble avoir habité Rome assez longtemps, où il acquit sa conaissance du Latin': Mango, 'La culture grecque et l'Occident', p. 686.

[22] Bede, *Historia ecclesiastica* II.8 (ed. Colgrave and Mynors, p. 274): 'Tobiam pro illo consecrauit, uirum Latina Greca *et Saxonica* lingua atque eruditione multipliciter instructum' (see also V.23, *ibid.*, p. 556). Brooks, *The Early History*, pp. 95–6.

[23] The attitude of the Roman empire to the linguistic centrality of Latin was brought out by Augustine, *De ciuitate Dei* XIX.7: 'at enim opera data est, ut imperiosa ciuitas non solum iugum, uerum etiam linguam suam domitis gentibus per pacem societatis imponeret' (ed. Dombart and Kalb II, 671; 'the imperial city was at pains to impose on conquered people not only her yoke, but also her language, as a bond of peaceful society'). This attitude was taken over by the western church, which had a very similar need for such a strong centralising force.

might initially have seemed to indicate, stands revealed as a work of considerable subtlety and originality, using the rigorous methods of the Antiochene school of exegesis and an almost entirely eastern set of motifs and examples, in order to expound a theological position that would only be acceptable in the west. This combination makes sense in terms of the peculiar circumstances of Theodore of Tarsus, though probably in few others. If this attribution is accepted, the *Laterculus* bears out the high opinion of Theodore's character, good sense and scholarship held by Bede and subsequent writers. It is wholly consistent with the picture of him built up by the surviving contemporary sources and also has a good deal to contribute to it.[24]

THE GREEK EAST AND THE ANGLO-SAXONS

The overwhelmingly eastern mental background of this, the only surviving complete text from Archbishop Theodore's school, is a matter of very considerable importance and some surprise, though the surprise is mitigated by Bischoff's demonstration as long ago as 1954 that the glossarial material from Theodore's school draws largely on Greek and Syriac sources, some named.[25] The element of surprise in this is that an eastern stratum in Southumbrian learning after Theodore's time has not been generally perceived. But such a stratum may in fact exist, for a number of historiographic reasons have combined to conceal it.

There is the inevitable problem with scholarly demarcations, first of all. Very few people have combined interest and expertise across the various fields involved. The present writer is no exception: I am completely unacquainted with any Semitic language and dependent on the findings of Semitic scholars and the availability of works in translation. Looking at things the other way, there is no reason why students of near and middle eastern Christianity should think of engaging in a study of Anglo-Saxon or Anglo-Latin. Another factor is less pragmatic, but has to do with the history of ideas. The strong pro-Germanic bias of Anglo-Saxon studies in the last two centuries generated a climate of thought about the shape of the early medieval world which was not calculated to bring oriental parallels

---

[24] The evidence for Theodore's biography, and the historical context of the eastern empire and its centres of learning, are fully discussed by Lapidge, *Biblical Commentaries*, pp. 5–82.

[25] Bischoff, 'Wendepunkte', pp. 208–9.

leaping to the eye. Thus the historiography of early Anglo-Saxon Christianity, following the immensely powerful and convincing lead given by Bede, has categorized it as 'Roman'; a concept which was not until very recent years perceived to require further examination. In addition, an essentially unworkable but entrenched contrast has dominated the study of early England and early Ireland. There has long been a strong, though not very securely supported, belief that Ireland was intimately in contact with the wellsprings of Egyptian monasticism and with the east in general;[26] and therefore a tendency to equate traces of eastern thought with Celtic influence,[27] even though the evidence for early Irish contact with eastern thought, aside from their familiarity with Cassian, is actually quite thin.

The evidence of the *Laterculus* and the Canterbury commentaries combines to suggest a completely different conclusion; that, as far as the seventh century is concerned, Canterbury may have been simultaneously a direct link with Rome, *and* much the most direct source for eastern ideas, the Antiochene exegetical tradition and possibly even the transmission of apocrypha. Perhaps the Irish students whom Aldhelm envisaged snarling like a pack of dogs at Theodore's heels could actually have gained, in this stronghold of ecclesiastical *Romanitas*, the kind of exotic education that the schools of Ireland have long been believed to have provided, enriched by Greek thought, apocrypha, Classical poetry and mythology and even Syriac themes and exegetical techniques. It is too easily forgotten in making the equation between Greek and Celt, Roman and Saxon, that the pope, his court, and several important monastic communities at Rome were Greeks. We have Stephen of Ripon's word for it that when Bishop Wilfrid, during Theodore's archiepiscopacy, went to plead his cause at Rome, he found the papal court (Agatho, a Greek, was pope at the time) talking Greek amongst themselves.[28]

---

[26] On which see J. A. Raftery, 'Ex Oriente . . .', *Journal of the Royal Society of Antiquaries of Ireland* 95 (1965), 143–204.

[27] The opposition of Celt and Saxon has recently been described, not without sarcasm, by P. Sims-Williams, 'The Visionary Celt: the Construction of an Ethnic Preconception', *CMCS* 11 (1986), 71–96, at 74: 'somehow. . .the occidental Celts were privileged by special links with the Oriental peripheries, in language, institutions, art, folklore, and varieties of Christianity'.

[28] *The Life of Bishop Wilfrid, by Eddius Stephanus*, ed. B. Colgrave (Cambridge, 1927), p. 112 (ch. 51): 'tunc inter se graecizantes et subridentes, nos autem celantes, multa loqui coeperunt' ('then they began to talk Greek among themselves, and to smile covertly, saying many things which they concealed from us').

The search for eastern influence on Anglo-Saxon writings has already begun. Bernhard Bischoff made a start in 'Wendepunkte', pointing out the influence of Antiochene thought and of Theodore himself on the exegesis of Bede. J. Rendel Harris, many years earlier, made a tentative list of points of contact between Ephrem's commentary on the Diatessaron and Bede's exegesis of Luke.[29] Henry Mayr-Harting extended this by pointing out that Aldhelm had access to Greek information presumably derived from Canterbury. He further noted, 'From the fifth century onward, reflection on the physical suffering of Christ was a marked feature of Byzantine and Syrian devotion ... one cannot help seeing the influence of this kind of piety in the Book of Nunnaminster, mediated to it through some Spanish or Gaulish channel.'[30]

The *Laterculus*, incidentally, is noteworthy for the vividness of its reflections on Christ's physical sufferings. Perhaps the suggested Spanish and Gaulish channels might be replaced by direct influence from Canterbury traditions. Michael Lapidge, in addition to his work on the Canterbury glossaries, pointed out in his translation of Aldhelm that the underlying exegetical justification for the position of the aristocratic nuns he addressed in *De uirginitate* was eastern, not western, and based particularly on Basil of Caesarea. Patrick Sims-Williams has written on the influence of Ephrem in Anglo-Saxon England,[31] with particular reference to the Book of Cerne. The exotic features of the latter prayerbook have normally been taken as a reflection of Irish influence on English private prayer.[32] Irish influence there undoubtedly is, but the eastern antecedents of some prayers in English books should not be glibly defined as 'Irish symptoms'.

THE STUDY OF GREEK AT CANTERBURY

A context for such a work as the *Laterculus* at Canterbury is provided by several Anglo-Latin texts based on Greek originals and associable with this centre. We also have the witness of Bede that some of his contemporaries, notably Tobias the bishop of Rochester and Albinus the abbot of St Peter's

---

[29] *Fragments of the Commentary of Ephrem*, ed. Harris, pp. 98–9.

[30] Mayr-Harting, *The Coming of Christianity*, p. 188.

[31] 'Thoughts on Ephrem'.

[32] K. Hughes, 'Some Aspects of Irish Influence on early English Private Prayer', *Studia Celtica* 5 (1970), 48–61.

(later St Augustine's), Canterbury, knew Greek as well as they knew Latin. Since Bede himself learned enough Greek during the course of his life to be able to read parts of the Greek New Testament, he is unlikely to have been deceived by a mere smattering of knowledge on the part of these men. The Greek texts which have been held for one reason or another to have been at Canterbury (excluding, for the moment, the sources for the *Laterculus* and the *Biblical Commentaries*) are various. They include a version of Epiphanius's exegetical tract on the Twelve Stones (Epiphanius is quoted in the *Laterculus*),[33] a Greek litany composed in the time of Pope Sergius (687–701) translated in the eighth-century English prayerbook London, BL Royal 2.A.XX, a prayer in the same manuscript,[34] and a Latin translation of a Greek acrostic quoted by Aldhelm.[35] This poem is a prophecy of Christ attributed to the Sybil, and the acrostic, 'Christus filius Dei' is neatly imitated without detriment to the translation of the content of the verses.[36] It may be worth noting that an interest in Sybilline prophecy is also found in the *Laterculus*, which gives the story of Augustus's dream from Malalas.[37] A Persian saint, Miles of Susa, was included in the Old English Martyrology. Since the only surviving accounts of this saint are in Syriac and Greek, it has been suggested that Theodore was responsible for introducing the knowledge of his cult into England.[38] The version of the *Passio S. Anastasii* (another Persian saint) which Bede described as 'male de greco translatum et peius a quodam imperito emendatum'[39] may

---

[33] P. Kitson, 'Lapidary Traditions in Anglo-Saxon England, Part I: the Background and the Old English Lapidary', *ASE* 7 (1978), 9–60.

[34] *An Ancient Manuscript of the Eighth or Ninth Century, formerly belonging to St Mary's Abbey, or Nunnaminster, Winchester*, ed. W. de G. Birch (London, 1889), p. 109: 'eulugomen patera cae yo, cae agion pneuma, cae nym, cae ia, cae isenas nenon, amin; adiuro te Satanae diabulus ælfae'. Note the interesting combination of Latin and abominably-spelt but mostly recognizable Greek with the Old English word *ælf* ('malignant spirit') used of Satan.

[35] Brooks, *Early History of Canterbury*, p. 96.

[36] W. Bulst, 'Eine anglo-lateinische Übersetzung aus dem Griechischen', *Zeitschrift für deutsches Altertum und deutsche Literatur* 75 (1938), 105–11.

[37] B. McGinn, 'Teste Dauid cum Sibylla: the Significance of the Sybilline Tradition in the Middle Ages', in *Women of the Medieval World: Essays in Honour of John H. Mundy*, ed. J. Kirshner and S. F. Wemple (Oxford, 1985), pp. 7–35, at 17–21.

[38] Lapidge, 'The School of Theodore', p. 49, and see *Das altenglische Martyrologium*, ed. G. Kotzor, 2 vols., Bayerische Akademie der Wissenschaften, Abhandlung, phil.-hist. Klasse, n.s. 88 (Munich, 1981) II, 251 and 370.

[39] Bede, *Historia ecclesiastica* V.26 (ed. Colgrave and Mynors, pp. 568–70).

well have been brought into England by Theodore.[40] There is also an *Oratio Effremis* in another early English prayer book, the ninth-century *Book of Cerne*, written in rhyming verse (a genre which was cultivated at Canterbury),[41] and genuinely based, though at some distance, on Ephrem.[42] Dionisotti noted that 'a lost version of the *Hermeneumata Ps-Dositheana* [a Greek-Latin glossary] came to southern England, probably with Theodore of Tarsus'.[43] In another area, Thompson noted that Oxford, Oriel College MS 42 contains a set of conciliar canons and papal decrees copied by William of Malmesbury, which was composed at Rome about the turn of the fifth and sixth centuries.[44] William described his exemplar as 'uetustissimus' and, as Thompson comments, Canterbury springs to mind as a likely source for this type of text.[45] It is also interesting in this context that Ruth Kozodoy has made a strong case[46] for regarding the fragmentary and very unusual stone cross at Reculver in Kent as seventh-century. She argues that the body-forms and other details suggest 'a context for the Reculver carving between the sixth and seventh centuries in date, *and between Byzantine-Italian* and Irish-English in milieu'.[47] So this surviving

---

[40] Meyvaert and Franklin, 'Bede's Version', p. 384. The martyrdom of Anastasius is the only incident which Bede records from the seventh-century war between Byzantium and Persia (*Chronicon maius*, *s.a.* 539–40, ed. Mommsen, MGH, AA 13 (Berlin, 1898), 223–331, at 310–11). He also notes the translation of the head of Anastasius to Rome. Why should this have struck him as important, unless Canterbury maintained an interest in Anastasius?

[41] Lapidge, 'The School of Theodore', pp. 46–7.

[42] Sims-Williams, 'Thoughts on Ephrem', pp. 208–10.

[43] Dionisotti, 'On Bede, Grammars and Greek', p. 140. See also G. Baeseke, *Der 'Vocabularius Sti Galli' in der angelsächsischen Mission* (Halle, 1933), pp. 80–1, and Lapidge, 'The School of Theodore', pp. 54–5, who observes that a text of the *Hermeneumata* was among the works excerpted and glossed in Theodore's school at Canterbury.

[44] PL 56, 359–742.

[45] R. Thompson, 'The Reading of William of Malmesbury', *RB* 85 (1975), 362–402, at 384–6.

[46] R. Kozodoy, 'The Reculver Cross', *Archaeologia* 108 (1986), 67–94.

[47] *Ibid.*, p. 78. Kozodoy's date for the Reculver cross is disputed by Dominic Tweddle in *The Golden Age of Anglo-Saxon Art, 966–1066*, ed. J. Backhouse *et al.* (London, 1984), pp. 40–1, on the grounds that, 'there was very little stone sculpture in south-east England before the ninth century, and certainly nothing which can compare in technical skill with the Reculver fragments.' Clearly, this fragmentary sculpture poses the usual problems of a unique object.

fragment of Kentish sculpture may show the same mixture of characteristics found in the literary remains of the school of Canterbury.

The style of the *Laterculus* is in keeping with that of the only named
alumnus of the seventh-century Canterbury school, Aldhelm, and shares
the same kind of literary devices. It also displays the same kind of
gratuitous animosity displayed against Irish scholars and scholarship,
which is significant, since there is no seventh-century context other than
England in which any writer can be shown to go out of his way to cry down
Irish intellectual attainments. The style of the *Laterculus* is a powerful
argument in itself for associating it with the Southumbrian school rather
than with the Northumbrian school of Benedict Biscop and Bede. In any
case, the only Northumbrian to use Greek texts was Bede, his knowledge
did not extend much beyond the Greek New Testament and he is rather
late as a possible author for the *Laterculus*. Furthermore, the historical
naiveties of Malalas would hardly have impressed Bede, arguably the
greatest historian and chronographer of his age. The *Laterculus* is too
sophisticated in some ways and too silly in others. In short, every aspect of
the *Laterculus* suggests that it was written in Canterbury either by Archbishop Theodore himself, or translated and assembled by pupils as a class
activity, with Theodore controlling the content, or put together from
notes taken by his pupils. The last possibility is suggested by the
commentaries and the penitentials, but is counteracted by the basically
continental character of the author's Latinity.

4

The nature of the *Laterculus*

John Malalas is not, by twentieth-century standards, a reliable or authoritative writer. Are we to conclude that the preservation and use of this rather inadequate chronographer casts an unfortunate light on the much-praised school of Canterbury? This would probably be unfair. It is often stated that chronicles and histories are different types of text. In practice, modern students, perhaps especially those whose area of study includes such notable historians as Bede, find chronicles not simply different, but deeply unsatisfactory. There has been relatively little effort to understand the nature and purpose of a chronicle as such. Fortunately, the *Chronographia* of Malalas has recently been the subject of such a study. Croke argues:

The very pattern of content (wars, inventions, cosmic phenomena, natural disasters, imperial births, deaths and marriages, etc.) also had a long tradition, reflected originally in the local records of city states, then in chronicles as diverse as those of Apollodoros, the Parian marble, Phlegon and Jerome. There is, for the most part, a serious unifying element, namely that of public religious ceremonial or events of religious significance. Most of the events traditionally recorded in chronicles from Classical Athens to the time of Justinian and which form the backbone of Malalas's work were the great civic and imperial occasions. Even earthquakes and other prodigies gave rise to elaborate ceremony and ritual which is why they find a place in such a chronicle.[1]

Croke further comments, 'Chronicles in particular were works of reference and polemic while histories were for instruction and edification.' The particular polemic purpose which Elizabeth Jeffreys and the group of Australian classicists who have recently published a collective volume of

[1] Croke, 'Early Byzantine Chronicles', in *Studies*, p. 37. See further B. Croke, 'City Chronicles of Late Antiquity', in *Reading the Past in Late Antiquity*, ed. G.W. Clarke *et al.* (Canberra, 1990), pp. 165–204.

21

studies on Malalas have identified in the *Chronographia* is to do with world ages. The chronographic thesis set out in bk 10 implies that the sixth millennium had long since passed by 529. Malalas underlines this in bk 18 (§ 8), where he digresses into a chronological summary not immediately relevant to his narrative. His message is that there was no need for his contemporaries to fear that recent disasters such as the earthquake of 526 heralded the end of the world. His work was thus designed to allay the fears of the Antiochenes by showing them to be founded on a fallacious chronology: local chronographic theory suggested that the fateful year AM (Annus Mundi) 6000 was rapidly approaching.[2] In other words, he was a man with a radical thesis to put forward, not an ill-informed, naive or gullible one. His work was carefully researched, neither aimless nor incoherent, but 'informed by an overriding chronographical argument'.[3] The argument was ultimately unpersuasive, in that very few subsequent chronographers accepted it, but it was both serious, and in his own context, an intelligent solution to a genuine problem. It can hardly be accidental that chronographic data form a very large part of the material which the author of the *Laterculus* has chosen to extract from Malalas's work. Bk 10 of Malalas's chronicle is of obvious utility for teachers faced with the gigantic task of simultaneously inculcating Christian learning, Classical culture, and a sense of historical context, into a group of intelligent Anglo-Saxons whose own cultural traditions were utterly foreign to all these things. Bk 10 anchors the gospel narrative to a specific context in historical time, and provides an overview of the temporal relationship between the Incarnation, the seventh century, and the entire history of the world. Its demotic language and simplicity might have struck anyone in Theodore's position as positive recommendations. Croke emphasizes the chronographic meticulousness of Malalas's treatment of the historical life of Christ:

In describing the events of Christ's lifetime Malalas is especially punctilious. For the Incarnation, birth, the preaching and beheading of John the Baptist, the events of Thursday of Holy Week, the Crucifixion, resurrection, ascension and Pentecost, he records the precise hour, day of the week, day of the month (including, sometimes, the lunar month), consulship and year of Antioch. This

---

[2] Croke, 'The Chronology of Christ', in *Studies*, p. 18. See also S.A. Harvey, 'Remembering Pain'.

[3] Croke, 'Early Development', p. 27.

concentration of detailed dating is unusual for the Chronicle and again under-scores the significance of accurate chronology in describing crucial cosmic events.[4]

In a context of Antiochene, that is, historically-oriented, theological writing, so detailed an account of what from a Christian point of view were the most important few days in the history of the world had an obvious utility. The original text is frequently repetitive and laboriously explana-tory; the interpolations made into it by the author of the *Laterculus* are even more so. The most salient characteristic of the *Laterculus* is its pedagogic tone: the patient repetition of information (especially dates, frequently given Roman style, *and* with the days of the months, the months themselves given in both Latin and Greek) in different forms, the parenthetic explanations, all betray the patient teacher working at an elementary level; and imply an unsophisticated audience whom the author does not expect always to grasp his meaning at the first attempt. Another pointer in the same direction is the considerable use of words like *inquit* to indicate quotation and the occasional use of first and second person.

CHRONOGRAPHY

A set of linked issues pervades both the Malalian and original sections of the *Laterculus*: the *sex aetates mundi*, numerology, the intrinsic perfection of the number 6 (which is mentioned more than once, and discussed below in the section on exegesis), and the explication of the approaching World Sabbath. Jeffreys and others have argued that these chronographic data are the central purpose of Malalas's work.[5] The author appears to be anxious lest the Eusebian data derived from Malalas which form his ch. 3 be used to predict the future and to assign a length of 1,000 years to the seventh World Day which was inaugurated by the Incarnation, an anxiety which was shared by the more reputable writers on this issue, including August-ine and Bede, as well as by Malalas himself.[6] The scheme in Malalas's *Chronographia* is bizarre in a number of ways. It conflates two separate sets of temporal categorization, the division of time into three parts, and the division of time into a World Week. Neither is treated conventionally. The tripartite system used by many chronographers from St Paul onwards

---

[4] Croke, 'Chronology of Christ', p. 12. [5] *Studies*, p. 27.

[6] Augustine, *De ciuitate Dei* XXII.30 (ed. Dombart and Kalb II, 865–6); Bede, *Epistola ad Pleguinam*, ch. 14 (*BOT*, p. 313).

divided the history of the world into three sections: an age of natural law, an age of Judaic law (inaugurated by Moses' reception of the Ten Commandments), and an age of Christ.[7] Malalas's purely chronological division of pre-Christian history which sets the mid-point at Phalech (who was deemed to have lived exactly at the halfway point between Adam and the Passion) is paralleled only in the *Commentarii in Genesin* of the early-sixth-century Greek theologian, Procopius of Gaza, and the second-century Julius Africanus.[8] Even his date of 3000 AM for Phalech is unusual: it is that used by Julius Africanus, and not the pseudo-Eusebian one usually used in the Byzantine world (which was 2980 AM).[9] The use of the World Week in the *Chronographia* is also distinctly unusual. There is an enormous literature, primary and secondary, on the World Week. The bare bones of the idea, fleshed out by generations of erudite chronographers, combined the Psalmist's statement that a day in the sight of the Lord was as a thousand years (Ps. XC.4, see also II Pet. III.4) with the Genesis myth that the Lord laboured for six days and rested on the seventh.[10] Millennia and ages rapidly became inseparable in Christian thought; and it followed that the world as we know it was to last 6,000 years, with the eternal Sabbath beginning thereafter. Landes, in his comprehensive article on chronography and apocalyptic, has shown that chronographers repeatedly recalculated the arithmetical data of the Bible so as to place the generation in which each one wrote somewhere early in the second half of the fifth millennium – thus, a good ten to fifteen generations away from the earliest point when the end of the world might be expected. The underlying motive, Landes has suggested, was probably to provide a safely distant focus for any public anxiety there might be, and thus to defuse the potentially dangerous adoption of unofficial, and perhaps irresponsible, chronographers.[11] Byzantine ecclesiastics were less possessed by millennial fears than their Latin counterparts, and some Byzantine chronographers bravely carried the Eusebian Annus Mundi (which set Year One at 5500

---

[7] See Luneau, *L'histoire du salut*, p. 47, and *BOT*, p. 345.

[8] See the Commentary, below, p. 173–4, n. 28.

[9] Jeffreys, *Studies*, p. 113.

[10] Cf. *Biblical Commentaries*, p. 386 (Gn-Ex-EvIa 5).

[11] Landes, 'Lest the Millennium be Fulfilled'. N. Cohn, in *The Pursuit of the Millennium*, 3rd ed. (London, 1970), pp. 21–40, has shown in the context of the later Middle Ages the amount of unrest and disruption which could be caused by socially irresponsible millenarians who brought their message to troubled and unstable parts of Europe.

BC) into its seventh millennium, tacitly refuting the common, though not universal, assumption that the world would come to an end after 6,000 years, and that therefore any calculation which extended time past the year 6,000 had thereby proved itself inaccurate.

However, Malalas's radical thesis that the year 6000 passed in the year of the Passion was completely out of step with established Byzantine chronography.[12] There were two important calculations of the age of the world operative in Malalas's time. The earlier of the two put the Creation at 5500 BC, the later put it at 5199 BC. This naturally equates the Christian era with the Sabbath of Genesis, and requires the Apocalypse to be the beginning of a new World Week, not the end of this one. There is a certain speciousness in the claim of the *Chronographia* and the *Laterculus* that 'all agree that the Lord appeared in 6,000 years' (ch. 4), since the two most familiar calculations of the date of Creation, 5500 and 5199 BC, which put the Incarnation 500–800 years before the end of the sixth millennium, are markedly different in their implications from Malalas's 5,967, which puts it right at the end: both the earlier calculations are carefully designed to place the chronographer's own present moment safely within the *first half* of what readers were likely to construe as the last millennium, not, as Malalas's calculations suggest, well into the seventh. The *Laterculus* is, in fact, the only subsequent work to be impressed by Malalas's theory of time. All other writers who draw on Malalas's work ignore this element of it.

While millenarianism was not quite such a problem in the eastern empire as it was in the west, this is not to say that it was not a problem at all. Croke and Jeffreys have argued that Malalas's work is chronologically tendentious, aimed at a specific millenarian problem in his own time.[13] The two points at which Malalas is extraordinarily careful about time-markers are book 10, the account of Christ's life on earth, and the beginning of Justinian's reign (bk 18, § 8), where it is not presented as

---

[12] Julian of Toledo, in the preface to his *De comprobatione sextae aetatis* (ed. Hillgarth, *Opera*, pp. 142–212, at 145), noted that the Jews believed the Messiah would come in the year 6000 (see Laistner, *Thought and Letters*, p. 168). This Jewish tradition is also commented on by Robbins, *The Hexemeral Literature*, p. 27, and by Luneau, *L'Histoire du salut*, p. 41. Though this evidence is obviously later than Malalas's *Chronographia*, it suggests that his original idea may have been influenced by the Jews, who were a significant element in the culture of Byzantine Syria.

[13] Croke, *Studies*, p. 18, and E.M. Jeffreys, 'Malalas's Use of the Past', in *Reading the Past in Late Antiquity*, ed. Clarke *et al.*, pp. 121–46.

part of an ongoing discussion, but as a digression. For the significant events of Christ's lifetime, Malalas gives the hour, day of the week, day of the month (sometimes also the lunar month), consulship and year. This dating suggests that he attaches great importance to the significance of accurate chronology in dating crucial cosmic events (though some of his dates, derived from different sources, are subtly but pervasively contradictory).[14] The point he is making in returning to this chronographic punctiliousness in the year 529 is to emphasize that the sixth millennium had long since passed by that date. Therefore, by implication, recent natural disasters, such as the earthquake of 526, should not be understood as symptoms of the approaching end of the world and the coming of the kingdom of God.[15] This was particularly relevant in the context of Antioch, Malalas's native city, since Syrian monophysites had raised considerable local anxiety by precisely this apocalyptic interpretation of events.[16]

The chronographic framework expressed in bk 10 of Malalas's *Chronographia* is so anomalous that it is very important for us to ask why the author of the *Laterculus* accepted it as it stood. There are several indications in the *Laterculus* that the school where it was written, which I would argue to have been of Canterbury, was not innovative in the field of chronography. The *Laterculus* demonstrates direct, first-hand knowledge of only two chronographic theories: that of Malalas, which the author accepts without reservation, and one known to the *Scotti*, which he rejects. This, while it naturally tends to suggest that the author is working in a centre with easy access to Irish works, and hence supports the thesis that the *Laterculus* was written at Canterbury, is problematic in that there is no surviving seventh-century Irish chronographic text which can be brought forward as corroborative evidence. The only original chronographer who is known to have flourished in early medieval Britain is Bede, whose work appeared a generation too late to have been accessible to the author of the *Laterculus*. Bede boldly placed AM 1, the first year of Creation, at 3952 BC, thus setting the birth of Christ in the fourth millennium, but he is not known to have done so earlier than 703. He gives no sources for this innovatory chronography, other than independent calculation based on the Massoretic text of the Bible provided by Jerome, though it may be relevant to note that many of his earlier works made considerable use of the work of Irish

14 Croke, *Studies*, p. 12.   15 *Ibid.*, p. 18.
16 S.A. Harvey, 'Remembering Pain'.

scholars, often without acknowledgement.[17] Bede's work may thus be dependent on one or more lost Hiberno-Latin works; or there may have been an entirely independent Irish chronography – since all the *Laterculus* says is that the Irish *concordare nolunt*, it gives no clue to the scale of the disparity between this rejected version and that commended by Malalas. Since the Irish are known to have been interested in universal history, the nature of the world and computus in the seventh century,[18] it is more than possible that there was also an Irish chronographer active at that time. Thus, we have Bede as a rather too late, clearly-attested specialist chronographer in the Northumbrian school of Jarrow at the end of the century (who taught Bede is unknown), and a possible, though unproven, interest in chronography in seventh-century Ireland, which certainly possessed a suitable intellectual climate in which such an interest might develop. But there is no indication whatsoever that any Southumbrian writers laboured effectively in this particular field. The reproduction in the *Laterculus*, without further discussion or the introduction of alternative versions, of this unheard-of muddle between the Three-Age and the Six-Age system of dividing time is a mark of robust indifference to the specialist demands of historical and chronographic investigation. It contrasts strangely with Bede's fascination with the *sex aetates mundi*, which he mentioned more than forty times.[19] The writings of the principal scholar whom we know to have been associated with Theodore and Hadrian's Canterbury, Aldhelm, evince no very great interest in or specialist knowledge of history, or indeed of chronography. He claimed in his letter to Geraint of Wales that the British Easter was derived from a table by Sulpicius Severus which, as Jones notes, is completely implausible.[20] Bede read this letter and did not accept the Sulpician origin of the British Easter, but merely referred, in his précis of the letter, to their *dubii circuli*.[21] Specifically, Aldhelm was wrong about this because 'it is inconceivable that an Easter-table with *lunae*

---

[17] His work is discussed by Landes, 'Lest the Millennium', pp. 174–8.

[18] See, for example, M. Smyth, 'The Physical World in Seventh-century Hiberno-Latin Texts', *Peritia* 5 (1986), 201–34, and D. Ó Cróinín, *The Irish Sex Aetates Mundi* (Dublin, 1983).

[19] *BOT*, p. 345: 'Bede often seems to have been more enthusiastic about the notion of the Six Ages of the World than any other writer'.

[20] *Ibid.* Cf. Aldhelm, *Epistola ad Geruntium* (*Aldhelmi Opera*, ed. Ehwald, pp. 480–6, at 483).

[21] Bede, *Historia ecclesiastica* III.4 (ed. Colgrave and Mynors, p. 224); and see V.18 (p. 514).

xiv-xx (which the Celtic table had) would be created anywhere after the Nicene Council'.[22] Sulpicius Severus was writing about seventy years later than the Council of Nicaea; so this suggests a certain lack of historical sophistication on Aldhelm's part, which was particularly unfortunate since he was attempting to express an authoritative correction of the British point of view.

Further evidence for a difference in the approach to chronography between the Northumbrian and Southumbrian schools is in the area of dating. The *Laterculus*, following Malalas, dates events in the lifetime of Christ with reference to the consular lists and/or the regnal year, for example: 'in anno autem XV regni eiusdem Tiberii Caesaris sub consolatu Siluani et Neri'. Bede also dated by regnal years, but he introduced the concept of *anno Domini* dating as well, which provided a more coherent, and less purely local, dating scheme.[23]

Outside of the *Laterculus*, which, as a historical text, is a special case, there is a number of witnesses to dating practices in seventh-century Southumbria, the most significant of which is the practice of dating by indiction. An indiction is a fifteen-year cycle, beginning each year on 1 September rather than 1 January, which had its origin in the cycle of imperial tax-assessment.[24] Since the indiction only tells you where you are within a fifteen-year period and does not number the cycles, it is inadequate and impractical for chronography. The early medieval papacy preferred to date by indiction, which was unlikely to cause problems in a context of frequent letter-writing, the careful keeping of archives, and regular contact with Constantinople. For example, Gregory the Great dated his letters to Augustine by the year of the reigning emperor and the indiction. Bede rarely used indictions, almost always in his transcriptions of other writings.[25] It is therefore interesting that the Council of Hatfield, with Theodore as its president, was dated by indiction. As Kenneth Harrison noted,

---

[22] *BOT*, p. 101.

[23] Harrison, *Framework*, pp. 82–98.

[24] Though Bede, *De temporum ratione*, ch. 48 (*BOT*, p. 268) believed it to begin on 24 September, adding a further complication.

[25] Harrison, *Framework*, p. 98: 'although Bede's attitude to the Indiction is not made explicit in the *Historia*, it is possible to infer something about his thoughts. Throughout we discover the Indiction only in official documents – with one exception, and that in a Papal context.'

Theodore was following the rule laid down by Justinian, and continued by Gregory the Great, that documents should be dated by the Indiction of 1 September, that is, ... as to the beginning of the administrative year, at least, Theodore was not likely to depart from the usage of Constantinople and Rome.[26]

Several early Kentish charters, conspicuously those which have Theodore as a witness, date by indiction and the year of the local monarch, as do also the very earliest Kentish charters, Æthelbert's charters of 604 and 605, presumably under the influence of Augustine.[27] There are also two dubious seventh-century Glastonbury charters, witnessed by Theodore, of which one specimen has both a date by indiction and a curious Vetus Latina reading of I Tim. VI.7 which is similar to the type of Pauline text found in the *Laterculus*.[28] The important fact about the indictional dating found in this group of texts associated with Canterbury is that while being historically inadequate, it is the form of dating used by the papacy.[29] It therefore carries the double inference of a lack of interest in chronology for its own sake and a desire to maintain Roman orthodoxy even in small and unimportant matters. This can be compared with the *Laterculus*'s treatment of a similar, and equally minor issue, the date of the vernal equinox. Though Greek astronomers had established beyond any reasonable doubt that the vernal equinox was as early as 18 March, the Roman church maintained the traditional date of 25 March (this is germane to the calculation of the date of Easter). We find that the *Laterculus* dates the equinox to 25 March, even though this date was no longer accepted in the Greek church. Jones points out that Theodore seems to have introduced the concept of beginning the year on 1 September to Canterbury. He also comments that there seems to have been surprisingly little record-keeping

---

26 Harrison, *Framework*, p. 41.

27 Birch, *Cartularium Saxonicum*, nos. 3–6 (Sawyer, nos. 1–4); then 28 (Sawyer, no. 10), 35 (Sawyer, no. 13), 36 (Sawyer, no. 7) and 43 (Sawyer, no. 51); which are all witnessed by Theodore. The authenticity of these charters is, of course, far from certain.

28 Robinson, *Somerset Historical Essays*, pp. 48–53 (Sawyer, nos. 227 and 230). The reading (p. 51) is shared with various early writers, including Cyprian and Pelagius, and also with the Book of Armagh (the readings in the *Laterculus* quite often agree with those of the Book of Armagh). Dr Lesley Abrams (pers. comm.) has suggested that the charter (Sawyer, no. 227) which quotes Paul in an unusual version is a forgery concocted to provide better title to the land with which it is concerned, but based to some extent on a genuine, pre-existing document.

29 Harrison, *Framework*, pp. 39–41.

at Canterbury throughout the seventh century, suggesting a basic lack of interest in history.[30]

The list of emperors extracted from Malalas's *Chronographia* and appended at the end of the *Laterculus* stretches from Augustus to the sixth century and, like Malalas, employs only relative chronology: so-and-so reigned for six years, two months. This does include emperors not mentioned in the (lacunose) surviving copy of Malalas's work, but makes no attempt to correct Malalas's occasional grave errors in calculating regnal length. Both the *Chronographia* and the *Laterculus*, assign nine years to Vitellius, for example; Valerian appears in the *Laterculus* twice; and the later emperors, many of whom ruled jointly for at least part of their reigns, have been presented as consecutive emperors, severely distorting their chronology.[31] Malalas himself issued an emphatic caveat on this point:

One must not add up the years of the earlier emperors according to the number mentioned above for their reigns, because two used to reign at the same time; equally fathers would crown their children from infancy and reign with them. The chronicler must thus record how many years each emperor reigned, but readers of chronicles must pay attention simply to the sum of the years that have elapsed in the case of the reigns of all the emperors mentioned above.[32]

Unfortunately, Malalas offered the reader no possible way of calculating 'the sum of the years that elapsed'. And the *Laterculus*, by excerpting the simple regnal data without any comment of this kind, creates a natural but misleading impression that one simply followed on from the other. In consequence, the *Laterculus* gives only a rough idea of Roman imperial chronology. It makes no distinction between emperors of the west and the east after the division of the Roman *imperium* took place, and both it and the original *Chronographia* are exceedingly unreliable in detail. It is only fair to say that history, and in particular chronological dating from a fixed point, was rather a new discipline in the seventh century, following the lead given by the computist Victorius of Aquitaine. As C.W. Jones noted,

---

[30] Jones, *Saints' Lives and Chronicles*, p. 46.

[31] J. L. Nelson noted in 'Symbols in Context', *The Orthodox Churches and the West*, ed. D. Baker (Oxford, 1976), pp. 97–119, at 98, that there were more inaugurations of co-emperors than of 'new' emperors between 450 and 1000; thirty-six as against twenty-seven. Thus the figures in the *Laterculus*, even if they were entirely correct, would be very misleading.

[32] *Chronographia* XVIII.8 (trans. Jeffreys *et al.*, p. 429).

Victorius stimulated the creation of history in two ways, He included the name of the consuls of each year in a separate column; after there were no more consuls to record, this column cried aloud for some other historical item to fill the vacant place. His notion of a list of consuls was pagan Roman, but Christian computists had adopted it in Easter-tables even before his time, because events in the life of Christ were often dated by the consular lists.[33]

But while one should not castigate the *Laterculus* unduly, it is quite evidently not a text belonging to the vanguard of historical thought in its time. It is therefore doubly unfortunate that it has hitherto been classed as a chronicle rather than an example of exegesis, since it has thus been judged by its worst rather than its best aspects.

THEOLOGY AND EXEGETICAL METHOD

Theodore's position as a representative of the eastern church active in the far west requires to be set carefully in the appropriate historical context before it will really be possible to see how the *Laterculus* fits in. The middle decades of the seventh century were a highly complex period in the history of the church.[34] By the time Theodore was appointed to Canterbury, eastern and western churches faced each other across an apparently unbridgeable gap of mutual hostility and incomprehension.[35] They did, of course, share the same basic tenets, but they did not share the same language, in either the literal, or the metaphoric sense. Aspects of practice and organization differed widely – bishops, for instance, enjoyed a far less exalted position in the east than in the west – and they were also mutually separated by a number of important theological issues which had never been satisfactorily resolved, and which must now briefly be discussed. In 451, the Council of Chalcedon had reached conclusions which Pope Leo the Great completely endorsed (and for which he bore a good deal of responsibility). The Council had explicitly formulated the view, generally known as dyophysite, or orthodox, that Christ had two natures (δύο φύσεις), divine and human, in one person (ὑπόστασις).[36] This, unfortu-

---

[33] *BOT*, p. 118.

[34] See, for example, P. A. B. Llewellyn, 'The Roman Church in the Seventh Century: the Legacy of Gregory I', *JEH* 25 (1974), 363–80.

[35] Herrin, *Formation of Christendom*, pp. 250–9.

[36] The text of the Chalcedonian definition is translated in Kelly, *ECD*, pp. 339–40. The fifth-century historian Socrates, writing of the controversy between the Arians and

nately, resulted in immediate schism in the east, and the development of the monophysite heresy, which held that the divine and human natures of God united into one divine nature at the Incarnation. The first attempted solution to the eastern schism, the Fifth General Council held in Constantinople in 553 under Justinian, was an almost total failure. Moreover, Justinian's attempts to manage the crisis included the peremptory deposition of one pope, and the arrest of his successor. This unfortunate episode, often known as the 'Three Chapters' controversy, illustrates another of the most salient problems between the east and the west. The early Byzantine emperors had a marked tendency to act as if it were they who held ultimate jurisdiction over the faith of Christendom, a position which was in general accepted by the leaders of the eastern churches, and vehemently opposed by a succession of popes. Papal politics in the sixth and seventh centuries were dominated by the struggle of successive popes to establish the principle that laymen, even the emperor himself, should *not* adjudicate in theological matters.[37]

In 634, the emperor Heraclius made a second attempt to mend the damaging schism between monophysites and the orthodox, by coming up with a compromise position, monotheletism: the thesis that Christ had two natures, but only one 'will'.[38] This was in effect a political solution to a theological problem, of marked ungainliness, and has the melancholy distinction of being the only heresy designed by a committee – like most committee recommendations, it pleased very few people. Constans there-

Athanasians in the fourth century, remarked that 'the situation was exactly like a battle by night, for both parties seemed to be in the dark about the grounds on which they were hurling abuse at each other' (*Historia ecclesiastica* I.23, quoted by Kelly, *ECD*, p. 239). This eminently sane comment applies equally well to this later conflict between monophysites, dyophysites and monotheletes.

[37] W. Ullmann, *A Short History of the Papacy in the Middle Ages*, 2nd ed. (London, 1974), p. 54, and Llewellyn, *Rome in the Dark Ages*, pp. 146–56. Rome was not the only ecclesiastical centre to defend this position. In the 380s Ambrose, bishop of Milan, mounted a vigorous defence of the principle of ecclesiastical authority (see R. Krautheimer, *Three Christian Capitals: Topography and Politics* (Berkeley and Los Angeles, CA, 1983), pp. 71–92).

[38] The monothelete solution attempted to give equal weight to Christ's manhood and his divinity, but suggested that His perfect sinlessness meant that he had only one will, a divine one. This of course implies that Jesus, the son of Mary, lacked the highest and most important characteristic of humanity, a free and independent will to action, which was anathema to the pro-Chalcedonians (Herrin, *The Formation of Christendom*, pp. 213–14).

fore issued his *Typos*: a document which prohibited further discussion of the issue, as a threat to the security of the state (then facing the first, traumatic incursion of the Muslims).

The pope, of course, was the natural leader of the opposition.[39] Martin I convened a synod at Rome, the Lateran Council of 649,[40] attended by both Greek and Latin religious leaders.[41] Both Martin and the most articulate of his supporters, the Greek mystical theologian Maximus the Confessor, were arrested on a charge of treason,[42] taken to Constantinople to stand

---

[39] The spiritual authority of St Peter was important to both the eastern and western churches from very early times (see, for example, below, pp. 202–3, n. 132, and 222, n. 222 and J. J. Taylor, 'Eastern Appeals to Rome in the Early Church: a Little Known Witness', *Downside Review* 89 (1971), 142–6); the problem for the early medieval papacy was engineering the transformation of this abstract respect into concrete political power.

[40] This synod was not an aberrant policy on Martin's part, but in line with the policies of his predecessor. The initiative for holding such a synod went back to his predecessor Theodore, as E. Caspar demonstrated, 'Die Lateransynode', *Zeitschrift für Kirchengeschichte* 51 (1931), 75–137. See also Riedinger, *Concilium Lateranense*.

[41] See Sansterre, *Les Moines grecs et orientaux à Rome* I, 115–27, and note also this response of Maximus the Confessor to his interrogator: Διατί ἀγαπᾷς τοὺς 'Ρωμαίους καὶ τοὺς Γραικοὺς μισεῖς; 'Αποκριθεὶς ὁ τοῦ Θεοῦ δοῦλος, εἶπε· Παραγγελίαν ἔχομεν, τοῦ μὴ μισῆσαι τινα. 'Αγαπῶ τοὺς 'Ρωμαίους, ὡς ὁμοπίστους· τοὺς δὲ Γραικούς, ὡς ὁμογλώσσους ([he asked:] '"why do you love the Romans and hate the Greeks?" The servant of God replied, saying, "It is commanded of us not to hate anybody. I love the Romans, because we are of the same faith, I love the Greeks, because we share the same language"': PG 90, 128).

[42] The charge of treason is one which has to be taken seriously. Maximus, according to one of his biographies, had once been the secretary of the emperor Heraclius (PG 90, 67–110, at 72), but had abandoned his public career for a monastic life. Whether this is true or not, he was the director of the organized resistance to monotheletism in North Africa in the 640s, with the full support of the exarch, Gregory of Africa, and other leading dignitaries (Richards, *The Popes and the Papacy*, p. 185). The significance of this is that Gregory of Africa rebelled *c.* 646, and proclaimed himself emperor in Africa on a religious orthodoxy/anti-monothelete platform, and it was only his death at the hands of the invading Arabs which enabled Constans II to regain control over the province. Constans II had good reason to accuse Maximus of political sabotage. It is profoundly unlikely that he was such a simple, naive old monk that he was a mere tool in Gregory of Africa's hands (see further Stratos, *Byzantium in the Seventh Century* III, 58–73, 120–5 and 194–6). At his trial (*Vita ac certamen*, ch. 19: PG 90, 89) the prosecutor accused him directly of betraying Byzantine Africa to the Arabs: καὶ δὴ κατεφλυάρει τοῦ ὁσίου, ὡς εἴη πόλεις μεγάλας προδεδωκός, 'Αλεξάνδρειαν φημὶ καὶ Αἴγυπτον καὶ Πεντάπολιν, τῶν ἡμετέρων μὲν, φησιν, ἀποσπάσας ὁρίων, τοῖς δὲ τῶν Σαρακηνῶν ἤδη προσθέμενος. . . ('he

trial, and exiled in conditions of appalling hardship.[43] Thus, while some individual Greeks (notably the heroic Maximus) were obviously on the side of Roman orthodoxy, the western church remained suspicious of Greeks in general. Moreover, even in the case of a Greek whose theology could be reckoned impeccably Roman, there were basic differences in practice which might still cause trouble. It is against this background of 200 years of increasingly negative interaction between the papacy and the Greek churches that we must see Vitalian's initial reluctance to appoint a Greek to Canterbury, a less petty attitude than it might at first appear. The theological position actually adopted by Theodore is remarkable alike for subtlety and tact. Pope Vitalian hesitated to appoint Theodore as archbishop of the English lest he introduce Greek positions or practices into the English church, on the evidence of Bede, who says of Theodore that Hadrian was sent along with him, 'ne quid ille contrarium ueritati fidei Graecorum more in ecclesiam cui praeesset introduceret'.[44] Vitalian need not have worried. Theodore's knowledge was equalled only by his adroitness. Before discussing the evidence for his admirably diplomatic attitude, we should recognize that he was known in his lifetime as one of the great experts on doctrine in western Christendom. There is a letter written by Pope Agatho to the Emperor Constantine IV, dated 27 March, 680, in which Theodore is cited as an expert on the monothelete conflict which separated Constantinople and Rome, and which Agatho was labouring to bridge:

εἶτα ἠλπίζομεν ἀπὸ Βρεττανίας Θεόδωρον τὸν σύνδουλον ἡμῶν καὶ συνε-πίσκοπον, τῆς μεγάλης νήσου Βρεττανίας ἀρχιεπίσκοπον καὶ φιλόσοφον,

---

raved at the holy man that he had betrayed mighty cities, Alexandria that is, and Egypt, and Pentapolis, which, he said, "you have taken outside our borders, and made them possessions of the Saracens'"). On the principle that an opportunistic and fast-moving force like the seventh-century Muslim army would find their territorial ambitions very substantially expedited by civil war in the territory they aspired to, Maximus's accuser may well have had more of a point than his biographer was prepared to admit.

[43] The martyrdom of Martin I was described by his friend and contemporary, Theodore Spoudaios: see R. Devreesse, 'Le texte grec de l'hypomnesticon de Théodore Spoudeé, le supplice, l'éxil et la mort des victimes illustres du monothélisme', *AB* 53 (1935), 49–80. See also PG 87, 105–212, a Latin account of Martin's trial, together with his own letters, and the papal privileges he granted.

[44] Bede, *Historia ecclesiastica* IV.1 (ed. Colgrave and Mynors, p. 330).

μετὰ ἄλλων ἐκεῖσε κατὰ τὸν τόπον διαγόντων, ἐκεῖθεν τῇ ἡμετέρᾳ ἑνωθῆναι μετριότητι.[45]

We can hardly be surprised that the octogenarian Theodore was not to be prised loose from the church which he had virtually rebuilt in order to undertake such a long, dangerous and exhausting journey. It is a measure of his status in the western church that Agatho should have thought of asking him, at such an age. The eventual decision to entrust the Anglo-Saxon church to Theodore was justified in every respect. He showed the greatest sensitivity to the issue of introducing non-Roman practices, as we can see from the writings of the pupil who calls himself *discipulus Umbrensium*, who redacted a version of Theodore's penitential judgements: 'Ergo hoc Theodorus ait pro magna tantum necessitate, ut dicitur, consultum permisit qui numquam Romanorum decreta mutare a se sepe iam dicebat uoluisse.'[46]

Theodore did, of course, make use of Greek penitential writers, most notably of Basil the Great on the subject of Christian marriage. Anglo-Saxon practice, which permitted partners to divorce in order that one of them might enter a monastery, was sharply divergent from the precepts of the western fathers.[47] Theodore states: 'Potest tamen alter alteri licentiam dare accedere ad seruitutem Dei in monasterium et sibi nubere, si in primo connubio erit, secundum Grecos, et tamen non est canonicum.'[48] 'Mulieri non licet uirum dimittere licet sit fornicator, nisi forte pro monasterio. Basilius hoc iudicauit.'[49] This is dependent on Basil's three letters on the canons to Amphilocius of Iconium, which acquired canonical status in the eastern church, but not in the west.[50] Note that this Greek ruling, based

---

[45] PL 87, 1215–48, 1226. 'We were hoping, therefore, that Theodore, our co-servant and co-bishop, the philosopher, and archbishop of Great Britain, would join our enterprise, along with certain others who remain there up to the present day.'

[46] *Canones Theodori* V.2, ed. Finsterwalder, p. 295: 'Therefore Theodore, as was said [above] said this: he permitted the custom "in great necessity"; he who often used to say that he wished the decrees of the Romans should never be changed by him.'

[47] See Lapidge, 'A Seventh-Century Insular Latin Debate Poem', at 14–15.

[48] *Canones Theodori*, ed. Finsterwalder, p. 327: 'According to the Greek Fathers, one marriage partner may give the other permission to enter into God's service in a monastery, and marry [again] him- or herself, if it was a first marriage; and yet this is not canonical.'

[49] *Ibid.*: 'It is not permissible for a woman to reject her husband unless he is an adulterer, unless perchance she should enter a monastery. Basil has declared this.'

[50] See M. Brett, ' Theodore and the Canon Law', in *Archbishop Theodore*, pp. 120–40.

on a work generally accepted as canonical in the eastern church, is introduced with remarkable tentativeness. Basil's ruling offers the Anglo-Saxons a way out of a problem which they had created for themselves, yet Theodore is extremely diplomatic in presenting it. He certainly is very far from appearing to imply that Greek practice is necessarily better than Latin. He made it clear that he was unwilling to interfere with local custom even when it did not meet with his approval. Another judgement states, 'Non licet uiris feminas habere monachos neque feminis uiros. Tamen nos non distruamus quia consuetudo est in hac terra.'[51] The most public statement of Theodore's theological beliefs occurred when he presided over the Council of Hatfield in 679. It confirms the impression of his loyalty to the Holy See by adhering point for point to the position taken by Rome.[52] Under the presidency of Theodore, the Anglo-Saxon church acknowledged the Father, Son and Holy Spirit as a Trinity consubstantial in unity and specifically acknowledged the procession of the Holy Ghost from the Father *and* the Son (the so-called *filioque* clause, which was not accepted in the Greek church).[53]

There is more to this judgement at Hatfield than meets the eye. The problem with the *filioque* clause was that the First Council of Constantinople (381) and the Council of Chalcedon (451), which, in their turn, issued the definitive creeds of orthodox Christianity, had agreed on the wording that the Holy Spirit proceeds from the Father. The addition 'and from the Son' was accepted by almost all parties in and after the fourth century as orthodox *doctrine*, and was actually inserted into the Creed in the west, following the example of St Augustine. Since the Creed was recited during Mass in the east from the sixth century on,[54] its precise wording was a highly visible and sensitive issue.[55] It must also be said that disagreement on the *filioque* clause was not a mere matter of words. It

---

[51] *Iudicia*, § 198 (*Canones Theodori*, ed. Finsterwalder, p. 283): 'It is not proper for nuns to control monks, or monks nuns. However, we do not seek to alter this, since it is the custom in this land.'

[52] Bede, *Historia ecclesiastica* IV.17 (ed. Colgrave and Mynors, p. 386).

[53] The history of the *filioque* clause is described in *ECC*, pp. 358–67. The significance of this for Theodore has been discussed by Lapidge, 'The School of Theodore and Hadrian', p. 51, and *Biblical Commentaries*, pp. 139–46.

[54] B. Capelle, 'L'introduction du symbole à la messe', *Travaux liturgiques de doctrine et d'histoire*, 3 vols. (Louvain, 1955–67) III, 60–81.

[55] See also the concluding pages of H. Chadwick, 'Theodore of Tarsus and Monotheletism', in *Archbishop Theodore*, pp. 88–95, esp. 93–5.

related also to an understanding of trinitarian theology which was fundamentally different in east and west. As Kelly puts it, 'It was a cardinal
premise of [Augustine's] theology that whatever could be predicated of
one of the Persons could be predicated of the others. So it was inevitable
that he should regard the denial of the double procession as violating the
unity and simplicity of the Godhead.'[56] Augustine's eloquently expressed
views on this issue set the tone for the whole of medieval western trinitarian thinking. On the other hand, the Greek Fathers held that the distinctions made between the persons of the Trinity resulted from the Father's
standing as 'cause' (τò αἴτιον) to the other two persons.[57] So the Father
alone was the source of deity, and the Son and the Holy Spirit derived from
him, one by generation, and the other from procession.[58]

It should be clear that the *filioque* clause was a species of theological
time-bomb, which lay latent among the myriad potential causes of dissension from the fourth century to the eighth, when it was finally exploded by
the tactless insistence of Charlemagne that it should be proclaimed and
supported by all of Christendom.[59] In the seventh century (as indeed in the
eighth) the papacy was anxious to minimize the trouble which a stand on
this clause would inevitably bring with it. Rather significantly, the *filioque*
clause was proclaimed, and anathemas pronounced on the primitivists who
rejected it, by the Council of Hatfield in 679 and later by the Third
Council of Toledo in 688. But even though Pope Agatho seems deliberately to have set in motion provincial synods,[60] on the strength of which
he would be in a position to speak as the indisputable voice of western
orthodoxy at the Sixth General Council at Constantinople in 680/1,[61] his

[56] *ECC*, p. 359.
[57] See Gregory of Nyssa, *Quod non sint tres dii* (PG 45, 115–36, at 133).
[58] As Henry Chadwick observed to me (pers. comm.), Syriac thinkers were not unani-
mously on the side of the Greeks in this respect. Dadishoʻ of Qatar, a theologian of
strongly dyophysite, or orthodox, views flourishing in the seventh century, speaks of
the *filioque* clause *en passant* as a credal statement, without perceiving any necessity to
argue the case for it.
[59] Herrin, *The Formation of Christendom*, pp. 439–40.
[60] Apart from the Council of Hatfield, under Archbishop Theodore, there was also a synod
at Milan under Archbishop Mansuetus of Milan, and Agatho's own synod at Rome,
in 680.
[61] Richards, *Popes and Papacy*, noted that 'copies of the anti-Monothelete decisions of the
synods of Milan and Hatfield were also sent East' (p. 199), that is, together with the
proceedings of the pope's own synod. But the unity of the western church, though
politically highly desirable, was always a fragile phenomenon. The century-old bugbear

own synod at Rome on 27 March 680[62] cannily *refrained* from putting the *filioque* clause in its confession of faith.[63] The implication of this seems to be that the papacy was anxious to defend and maintain the Augustinian position on trinitarian theology within the west, and therefore encouraged provincial councils and synods to take a firm line on the *filioque* clause. But in dealing with Constantinople, Agatho, who was in the middle of engineering the enormously delicate business of bringing the monothelete controversy to a mutually acceptable end, carefully refrained from wrecking his own diplomatic initiative by introducing an entirely separate *casus belli*.

In the light of this dissension, it is interesting to observe that the theology of the *Laterculus*, insofar as it is expressed, is quite clearly aligned with that of Augustine rather than that of Gregory of Nyssa. Ch. 22 contains the sentences: 'ascendit Christus ad patrem et descendit spiritus sanctus ad plebem. qui discendit, ipse et ascendit super caelos, ut adimpleret omnia', and emphasizes the unity of the Trinity, since Jesus and the Holy Spirit are here expressed as being two aspects of the same Godhead, and the actions of one are the actions of the other. A later statement, 'quidquid enim operatur pater, unum est cum filio et spiritu sancto', repeated twice with the Son and the Holy Ghost, respectively, as the subject (ch. 24), also emphasizes the unity of the Trinity, as also does ch. 18, but more importantly, ch. 24 makes it quite clear that this

---

of the Three Chapters (anathematized by the Lateran Council of 649, and by Theodore at Hatfield) was still causing trouble at the time of Agatho's attempts to unite the western church. He was seeking in the 680s to amass conciliar condemnation of the Three Chapters from the entire western church to add to that of Constantinople, as a point of rapprochement. But when he sought such a decree from Spain, Julian of Toledo, acting as spokesman, *defended* the Three Chapters (*Apologeticum de tribus capitulis*: *Opera*, ed. Hillgarth, pp. 128–39), and his views were subsequently approved by the Council of Toledo in 688 (see R. Collins, *Early Medieval Spain* (London, 1983), p. 79).

[62] Which was attended, and signed, by Wilfrid of York on behalf of the English church. Wilfrid had gone to Rome, in his characteristically leisurely fashion, in order to submit his private grievances to the adjudication of the pope. But to judge from the terms in which he signs, he was at some point *en route* given the status of an official delegate from the English church to the Roman synod. See R. L. Poole, *Studies in Chronology and History* (Oxford, 1934), p. 54, and F. M. Stenton, *Anglo-Saxon England*, 3rd ed. (Oxford, 1971), p. 137.

[63] Text in PL 87, 1215–58, at 1220.

author, like Augustine, believed that whatever could be predicated of one of the persons could be predicated of the others. Thus, we seem in the *Laterculus* to have further evidence for a man who used a deep and extensive knowledge of the Greek theological tradition to express a set of orthodoxly Roman viewpoints. If Theodore was indeed one of the monks associated with producing the *acta* of the Lateran Council of 649, this would be explicable. The principal architect of the Roman position, Maximus the Confessor, was asked at his subsequent trial why he loved the Romans and hated the Greeks. He denied, naturally, that he hated anybody, but stated that, 'I love the Romans since we are of the same faith, and the Greeks because we have the same language.'[64] As Thunberg says, 'here Maximus clearly underlined that he shared a fellowship of faith with Rome that he did not have with "the Greeks" (of Constantinople)'.[65] Similarly, Maximus asserted that the Roman church 'has the keys of the faith and of the orthodox confession'.[66] His position, as a writer who was culturally Greek, but theologically Roman, closely resembles that of the author of the *Laterculus*. It is one which is explicable in terms of the career of Theodore of Tarsus.

One of the difficulties which the text of the *Laterculus* presents is the disjunction between its Romanist theological position and the Greco-Syrian texts which plainly go to shape it. This is most acute in the case of Theodore of Mopsuestia who, as I suggest in the section on exegetical method below, probably provides the stylistic model for the *Laterculus* as a whole, and who also offers parallels for many of this writer's distinctive ideas. Theodore of Mopsuestia was born *c.* 350 and died *c.* 428. He was a fellow-pupil of John Chrysostom under Libanius, the great rhetor of Antioch, and then under the distinguished exegete and scholar Diodore of Tarsus. After some initial hesitation on his part, he was ordained bishop *c.* 383 and remained in his Cilician see of Mopsuestia until his death. He was respected and admired in his own time. Unfortunately, the heresiarch Nestorius was subsequently alleged to have been one of his pupils, and in retrospect it seemed that Theodore's formulations had set Nestorius on his path of error. His opinions on Christology and sin were first proscribed at

---

[64] PG 90, 128.

[65] L. Thunberg, *Man and the Cosmos: The Vision of Maximus the Confessor* (Crestwood, NY, 1985), p. 25.

[66] PG 91, 140.

the Council of Ephesus in 431 (which also condemned Nestorius).[67] It was the Council of Chalcedon in 451 which laid down the doctrine of two natures (φύσεις) in Christ, one divine, the other human, united in a single person. The Chalcedonian judgement split the church into pro- and anti-Chalcedonians, since many Christians were unable to accept the principle of a human nature in Christ, implying as it did that he was less than perfect and had even had the capacity to sin. Theodore's statements were reviewed in this new light, and found wanting. In the sixth century, when the believers in a single will in Christ (the monophysites) and the orthodox communion were at loggerheads, Justinian attempted to bring the disputants closer together by uniting them in the condemnation of three writers whose works were incompatible with the formulations of Chalcedon, and who were thought to be Nestorian in tendency – who included Theodore of Mopsuestia.[68] This ruling, the 'Three Chapters', was made law at the Second Council of Constantinople (553). It met with considerable resistance from contemporary popes, who were happy neither with the condemnation of Theodore nor with Justinian's high-handed methods, and aroused resistance in the west generally (even, two generations later, in Columbanus, one of the earliest Hiberno-Latin authors).[69]

But if western theologians were unhappy at the principle of condemning a writer retrospectively in this fashion, some branches of the eastern church were outraged. The east Syrian church, especially the school of Edessa, was deeply reluctant to accept the judgements of the Second Council of Constantinople and of Chalcedon on this issue. For the Edessenes, Theodore remained a great teacher, and the effect of Justinian's action (aimed at unifying the monophysites and the orthodox) was profoundly to alienate these Syrians. Narsai (*ob.* 502), one of the principal scholars of the Edessene school, refers to Theodore of Mopsuestia as 'the doctor of doctors'. Indeed, the school of Edessa adopted the work of

---

[67] See *ECD*, pp. 301–9. Theodore of Mopsuestia stated his position on the nature of Christ most clearly in *De incarnatione*, PG 66, 969–94, at 972. See further Greer, *Theodore of Mopsuestia*, pp. 48–65.

[68] *ODB* III, 2044. These works came to be known as the Three Chapters. This is discussed in detail by P. T. R. Gray, *The Defense of Chalcedon in the East (451–553)* (Leiden, 1979), esp. pp. 44–79.

[69] Columbanus, *Epistola* V (ed. Walker, pp. 36–57).

Theodore as the main source of instruction in biblical exegesis.[70] His contemporary Ibas (*ob.* 457), who became bishop of Edessa, was known as 'The Translator' because of his translation of Diodore of Tarsus and Theodore of Mopsuestia into Syriac.

There is a 'continuous relationship' between the school of Antioch itself, and the east Syrians.[71] The exegetical method of the Antiochene school founded by Diodore and Theodore of Mopsuestia was ultimately dependent on Jewish models.[72] Theodore's teaching proceeded by summarizing and paraphrasing the biblical text in order to bring out the gist of the argument, and surrounding his discussion with historical and circumstantial introductions to fill in and explain the background to the composition.[73] His method, therefore (though based on Jewish techniques for the exegesis of the Old Testament), was highly distinctive, and involved the use of historical information which was not in itself the province of any particular theological party. It was consequently quite possible to make use of Theodore of Mopsuestia's work without accepting his distinctive theological formulations. One of the points made by the Edessenes in Theodore of Mopsuestia's defence was that he had been condemned for not writing in terms of a theological formulation on the nature of Christ which was not created until twenty-four years after his death. A theme of their writing is therefore that the Council of Nicaea, and the Nicene Creed which it issued, were uniquely authoritative and binding on all Christians, and that the theological fine-tuning of subsequent councils was not of quite the same status. Since none of Theodore of Mopsuestia's formulations can be shown to contradict the letter or spirit of the Nicene Creed, he must therefore be acceptable as a Christian teacher.

Clearly, Theodore of Tarsus did not take this position, which was unacceptable to Rome: in the public statement of the Council of Hatfield, he insists that the Anglo-Saxon church acknowledges the five universal councils: Nicaea, Constantinople, Ephesus, Chalcedon, and the Second Council of Constantinople, as well as the Lateran Council.[74] He thus

---

[70] Beggiani, *Early Syriac Theology*, pp. 5–6.

[71] Drijvers, *East of Antioch*, p. 13.

[72] W. A. Meeks and R.L. Wilken, *Jews and Christians in Antioch in the First Four Centuries of the Common Era* (Missoula, MT, 1978), p. 21.

[73] Young, *Nicaea to Chalcedon*, p. 203.

[74] Bede, *Historia ecclesiastica* IV.17 (ed. Colgrave and Mynors, p. 386).

publicly acknowledged the validity of the three councils which condemned Theodore of Mopsuestia.[75]

Interestingly, in the less *ex cathedra* context of his penitential writing, Theodore appealed to Nicaea in particular. The *discipulus Umbrensium* reports, 'Theodorum dixisse non credimus contra Nicenae concilium et sinodi decreta', and quotes another judgement 'iuxta Nicene concilium'.[76] Not much can be made of this. Theodore was publicly committed to the Roman church. At the same time, he manifestly accepted the techniques, values and objectives of the Antiochene exegetical school, which meant falling over the works of Theodore of Mopsuestia at every turn. These contradictions are reconcilable if one is careful to distinguish methodology from content.

The Christology of the *Laterculus* will bear a good deal of investigation. It appears that, despite the author's devotion to the exegetical techniques of the Antiochene school, his understanding of Christ and the Trinity bypassed the thought of Theodore and the Antiochenes altogether and was rigorously orthodox. He was conspicuously at pains to assert the complete consubstantiality of the Trinity, notably in ch. 24, where he headed off a too literal reading of Matth. XXIV.36 simply by a statement of orthodox trinitarian doctrine, avoiding the potential heresies, of which the most obviously dangerous here was Theodore of Mopsuestia's distinction between Christ's activities as man and as God, which was almost certainly familiar to him, and appears at one point to have been actually used by him (ch. 18).[77] However, the apparent Nestorian leanings of this one phrase in ch. 18, which speaks of Christ 'putting on' humanity like a garment ('homo, quem sumpserat propter ueterem Adam'), may be mitigated if we note that the *Te Deum*, one of the most widely accepted Latin prayers of all, includes the line 'tu ad liberandum suscepturus hominem', a phrase which the theologically vigilant could equally well accuse of Nestorian tendencies. In both cases, the use, respectively, of *sumo* and *suscipio* in this context should be taken as acceptably within the limits of orthodox dyophysitism, and within the spirit of the Chalcedonian formulation.[78]

---

[75] It is noteworthy that the Greek monks who attended the Lateran synod of 649 (see below, p. 88) also anathematized Theodore of Mopsuestia.

[76] *Iudicia* V.6 and 14 (ed. Finsterwalder, *Die Canones*, p. 296).

[77] Greer, *Theodore of Mopsuestia*, pp. 48–63 and 127–36.

[78] It may be worth observing that Pope Martin, the recently-dead hero of the papal struggle against monotheletism, maintained a somewhat more relaxed attitude towards

Archbishop Theodore's unique position as an eastern-trained thinker
working in an entirely western context, reflected at every turn in the
Biblical Commentaries (which are also pronouncedly Antiochene in tone and
content), is very closely paralleled in the *Laterculus*, which combines a
wholly Antiochene/Syrian exegetical technique with a Christology and
trinitarian theology which tacitly repudiate the peculiarities of Antiochene
thought and firmly maintain positions consistent with the Athanasian
creed and theological orthodoxy. The author held fast, one might say, to
what he found good in his native traditions, their methods and approach,
yet diplomatically avoided muddling the nascent English church with the
schismatic subtleties of Antioch, Edessa or Constantinople.

It is perhaps significant that Theodore of Mopsuestia became an important source for the Insular churches. Ramsay demonstrated that Theodore's
Commentary on the Psalms underlies several Insular works on the Psalter,
both Irish and Anglo-Saxon, written in the ninth and tenth centuries.[79]
The mid-sixth-century Latin writer Junilius drew extensively on Theodore
of Mopsuestia: his work is cited by Aldhelm, and is preserved in a
manuscript written in southern England in the early eighth century.[80] A
very possible route into Insular exegetical circles for this proscribed author
(and others associated with him) is offered by the school of Theodore.

EXEGETICAL METHOD

The exegesis of the Antiochene school has as its main principles the use of
historical method, and typology. Typology is quite different from
allegory.

This [typological exegesis] was not allegorising. It was the practice of *theoria*,

Nestorians, on the evidence of the Syriac Life of Maximus ('An Early Syriac Life of
Maximus the Confessor', § 24, ed. S. Brock, *AB* (1971), 299–346, at 281), which
mentions an African monastery containing eighty-seven Nestorian monks of Nisibene
origins who were hospitably received by him at Rome, identified by the (hostile) author
with the inmates of the monastery of St Saba on the Aventine, one of the three oriental
monasteries in seventh-century Rome. This on the face of things implausible story may
receive some corroboration from the discovery of a group of Nestorian monks living
'in monasterio qui appelatur Boetiana', in Rome (Duchesne, *Liber Pontificalis* I, 348)
during the pontificate of Donus (676–8).

[79] 'Theodore of Mopsuestia', p. 421.
[80] London, BL Cotton Tiberius A.xv (*CLA* II, no. 189). This is discussed by Laistner, 'The
Influence of Antiochene Exegesis', and by Lapidge, *Biblical Commentaries*, pp. 248–9.

insight, which enabled the Christian to see what could not be seen by people living in the old dispensation.

Typology based on historical fact is permitted [in the Antiochene school], allegory is not . . . typological linking of one event with another must presuppose the historical reality of both events.[81]

The use of typology is the creation of a comparison between two events in the light of an eschatological theory of history. Human history is patterned, with a beginning and an end. In accordance with the overall pattern of fulfilment and redemption which hinges historically on the life of Christ, events from pre-Christian history can be related meaningfully to events in the life of Christ. But this depends on the principle that the pre-Christian event has its own reality.[82] One of the earliest writers to articulate this principle is Justin Martyr, in his *Dialogue with the Jew Trypho*.[83] The Antiochene school was not simply indifferent, but actually hostile, to allegory. Diodore of Tarsus's works included a tract, now lost, called τίς διαφορὰ θεωρίας καὶ ἀλληγορίας (*What is the difference between theoria and allegory?*), mentioned in the Byzantine lexicon known as the *Suda*,[84] and Theodore of Mopsuestia himself wrote a tract (also lost) against Origen on the difference between allegory and history.[85] Theodore of Mopsuestia himself uses typology only very restrainedly, preferring to rely for the most part on establishing the historical context of the writing in question, and on analysing the author's aims, methods, intentions and presuppositions in a highly rationalistic way.

'Antiochene' exegesis, as Theodore of Mopsuestia developed it, keeps close to the literal meaning of the text: it is alert to historical and textual questions: when was the author writing? In what historical context? What else is known about the subject of the narrative? Is there any evidence that we have an exact version of the original words? This set of questions is related on one hand to the Classical pagan tradition of textual criticism,

---

81 Wallace-Hadrill, *Christian Antioch*, pp. 35–6 (and discussion on pp. 33–5). See also B. de Margerie, *Introduction à l'histoire de l'éxèse: les pères grecs et orientaux* (Paris, 1980), pp. 189–94.

82 Greer, *Theodore of Mopsuestia*, pp. 108–9.

83 *Dialogus cum Tryphone*, § 114, in *Iustini Philosophi et Martyris Opera*, ed. J. Otto (Jena, 1876), pp. 404–5: Ἔσθ' ὅτε γὰρ τὸ ἅγιον πνεῦμα καὶ ἐναργῶς πράττεσθαί τι, ὃ τύπος τοῦ μέλλοντος γίνεσθαι ἦν, ἐποίει ('sometimes the Holy Spirit caused something which was to be a type of the future to be performed openly').

84 *Suidae Lexicon*, ed. Adler II, 247.

85 R.M. Grant, *A Short History of the Interpretation of the Bible* (London, 1965), pp. 39–40.

which interrogated school-texts such as Homer and Vergil in very similar ways,[86] and on the other to Talmudic scholarship as it was practised by the rabbis of Byzantium and Persian Syria. Typology was used more lavishly and with a greater dependence on Jewish exegesis of the Talmud (*midrashim*) by the Syriac Christian writers than it was by Theodore of Mopsuestia and his disciples who wrote in Greek, and in this respect, the *Laterculus* seems closer to the Syrians than to the surviving Greek Antiochene writings (discussed further below).

There are ten significant typological motifs in the *Laterculus*.

(1) the Crucifixion is linked with the Crossing of the Red Sea on the same day (ch. 2)

(2) Christ is paralleled with Adam (ch. 3)

(3) the creation of Christ at the end of the sixth millennium is paralleled with the creation of Adam on the sixth day (ch. 4)

(4) the Flight into Egypt is paralleled with Isaiah's reference to the Lord moving on a light cloud (ch. 7)

(5) the Annunciation is contrasted with the Temptation of Eve, and virgin earth with the Virgin (ch. 12)

(6) the promise to Jacob is referred to Christ (ch. 14)

(7) the Crucifixion is paralleled with the redemption of Moses by the blood of his son's circumcision (ch. 16)

(8) Christ's forty-day fast is connected with the prophecy concerning Jesus the high priest (ch. 18)

(9) the taking of Christ is paralleled with Joseph sold to the Ishmaelites (ch. 20)

(10) Christ's victory over death and the redemption of mankind is linked with Exodus (ch. 21).

This is quite an extensive list of typological motifs for so short a text, especially since they are all in the original sections of the work, and not taken over from the *Chronographia*. All of them are also to be found within texts of the Antiochene tradition, as may be seen from many passages of the Commentary (below, pp. 162–229). By contrast, allegory is used on only one occasion, to deal with the problematic parallelling of Christ's body and the temple at Jerusalem in St John's Gospel (John II.19), where it is directly dependent on the figurative diction of Jesus himself. This passage is also the only part of the *Laterculus* to draw on Latin exegesis in the Alexandrian tradition, that of St Augustine (see below, p. 196).

The other salient exegetical concern of this writer is with the inner

[86] N.G. Wilson, *Scholars of Byzantium* (London, 1983), p. 29.

meaning of numbers, in particular, the number 6. This belief that numbers carry important messages is often associated with Jewish thought (e.g. *gematria*, adding up the numerical value of the letters in a word to arrive at a hidden meaning), but is also found in a great number of Christian writers of the patristic age, both east and west.[87] One very early Christian instance is in the Epistle of Barnabas, in which the 318 servants of Abraham are identified as Jesus, on the grounds that the Greek letters which make up 318 (τιη) represent the cross (tau), and the first two letters of Jesus' name.[88] An interest in numerology was not peculiar to the Jews. It is also characteristic of the Neoplatonic tradition which derives from Pythagoras and his followers, as Henry Chadwick points out, discussing a second-century Neoplatonist called Nichomachus of Gerasa:

To Nichomachus, Pythagoreanism is not simply a mathematically based philosophy. It has the merit of offering a synthesis of science and religion, combining exact mathematical theory with a belief that the harmony apparent in the cosmos is the same that binds together soul and body in man.[89]

It is this Neoplatonic, Pythagorean interest in numerology which accounts for Augustine's passion for numbers: Augustine admired Plato immensely. Thus, Augustine's *De ciuitate Dei* II.30 and 31 are on 'The Perfection of the Number Six', and 'The Seventh Day of Completeness and Rest'.[90] The number 6 attracted a great deal of attention, as a 'perfect' number, and particularly interested St Augustine. Augustine's technique of reducing numbers to their factors in a search for hidden meaning, witnessed not only in the essay on the relationship between the building of the temple and the formation of Christ's human body copied in the *Laterculus*, but also in his treatment of the 153 fish of the Miraculous Draught,[91] is the only allegorical method of exploring a text used in the *Laterculus*. It is perhaps worth observing that it is a highly specialized type of allegory with its roots in Neoplatonism, and that therefore this pseudo-scientific background, which assumes that the significance attached to particular numbers is real and not arbitrary, makes it acceptable to an Antiochene-

---

[87] H. Meyer, *Die Zahlenallegorese im Mittelalter* (Munich, 1975).

[88] *Barnabae epistola*, ch. 9, in *Patrum Apostolicorum Opera*, ed. R.M. Dressel (Leipzig, 1857), pp. 18–21.

[89] H. Chadwick, *Boethius: The Consolations of Music, Logic, Theology and Philosophy* (Oxford, 1981), p. 72.

[90] *De ciuitate Dei*, ed. Dombart and Kalb II, 350–2.

[91] *De diuersis quaestionibus lvii* (PL 40, 39–40).

trained scholar. Number symbolism also appears in the *Biblical Commentaries* (PentI 76; this reference system is the one used in the *Biblical Commentaries*).

Thus, the exegetical techniques used in the *Laterculus* show a preference for the historical, literal and rationalistic over the allegorical or mystical. They are profoundly suggestive of a writer who was trained in the Antiochene tradition.

MEDICINE

One of the relatively few pieces of personal information which Bede gives us about Archbishop Theodore is that he was well informed about medicine. This is confirmed by the *Canones Theodori*, as well as by the *Biblical Commentaries*. We also find evidence of an interest in medicine in the *Laterculus*, in ch. 13, which deals with embryology, and ch. 19, which presents Christ as a *medicus*. Before discussing this evidence for Theodore's medical interests in detail, it is probably helpful to put it in context by outlining the development of Greek medical theory and practice.

The first great name in Classical medicine is Hippocrates, who flourished in the fifth century BC (born *c.* 460). A scholar in the Greek empirical tradition, he set Greek medicine on the path which it was subsequently to follow: one of detailed, accurate observation of symptoms, and a holistic treatment of the patient which paid great attention to such matters as diet and environment. The combination of medicine and philosophy is clearly marked as a part of the Hippocratic tradition: Plato states in his *Phaedrus* that the doctors of the Hippocratic school held the view that an understanding of the body was impossible without an understanding of nature as a whole.[92]

The second most important figure in the history of Greek medicine is Galen, who flourished in the second century AD, and died at Rome about AD 200.[93] Galen was both a physician and a philosopher, and by creating a theoretical basis for medical praxis (the well-known 'theory of humours') did much to make medicine intellectually respectable.

Although the early Byzantine world is often thought of as essentially derivative, parasitic on the knowledge of the ancients, this is not the case

---

[92] *Phaedrus* 270 c–e, ed. and trans. L. Robin (Paris, 1954), pp. 80–1.
[93] *ODB* II, 816.

with medicine. Practical medicine was at a high level by medieval standards, and Byzantine doctors used their written sources carefully, supplementing the classic accounts with contemporary experience.[94] Early Byzantine medicine split into two schools: first, that of Alexandria, which flourished until the Arab entry into Alexandria in 642, and was remarkably creative: 'it did not merely continue what had been done and known before. Out of the works of Galen it created a medical system that was to endure for a thousand years. It was still heathen, though some of its teachers became Christian.'[95] Meanwhile, a Christian medical school developed at Constantinople, which was less creative in its approach. Richard Walzer has pointed out that although Galen himself was a pagan, his philosophy of the human body came to play a considerable role in Christian theology. He was not merely accepted, but admired, by Christian thinkers: so much so that he was virtually accepted as a Father of the Church by a contemporary, heretical (Adoptionist) splinter-group of Roman Christians of markedly academic tendencies, who were attempting to rationalize Christianity in philosophical terms.[96] Galen was thus the founder of two divergent medical traditions, one of which was firmly incorporated within the tradition of Christian thought (the other, ultimately, was the point of origin for the great tradition of Arabic medicine, as well as feeding back into Christian medical theory).

The reason why the acceptability of Galen to the Christians is historically significant is that the teaching of philosophy and medicine as allied disciplines became part of a Christian syllabus of higher education in late antiquity. In the fourth century, the vast corpus of Galenic and Hippocratic texts was newly ordered and systematized by Oribasius, the personal physician of the emperor Julian the Apostate, and a man of considerable learning. His work helped to make medical writing intellectually respectable; and he is one of the first people to be referred to as an *iatrosophist*: a philosopher of medicine.[97] In the sixth century, his encyclopaedic

---

94 *ODB* II, 1327–8.
95 Temkin, 'Byzantine Medicine', p. 97. See also J. Longrigg, 'Superlative Achievement and Comparative Neglect: Alexandrian Medical Science and Modern Historical Research', *History of Science* 19 (1981), 155–200.
96 R. Walzer, *Galen on Jews and Christians* (Oxford, 1949), p. 77, and see Temkin, 'Byzantine Medicine', p. 106.
97 *ODB* III, 1533. The writings of Oribasius may have been available at least in part at Canterbury: his *Synopsis* and *Euporistes* were used in England at the end of the ninth

approach was continued by other writers, including Alexander of Tralles
(brother of the mathematician Anthemius who designed Hagia Sophia for
Justinian), Aetius of Amida (*fl. c.* 530–60)[98] and Paul of Aegina (*ob.* after
642).[99] The attraction of intellectuals into medicine in the sixth century is
also shown by the fact that John Philoponus, a monophysite and also a
scientist of brilliant originality, wrote medical works in addition to his
commentaries on Aristotle.[100]

The figure of the physician-philosopher, the *iatrosophist*, is increasingly
common in later sixth- and seventh-century Byzantium.[101] The more
intellectual tradition of Alexandrian medicine, exemplified in the sixth
century by John Philoponus, seems to have merged with the Christian
medical tradition of Constantinople in the early seventh century, when
Stephanus of Alexandria was summoned by the Emperor Heraclius shortly
before the Persian conquest of Alexandria in 617 to head the new imperial
university in Constantinople.[102] Thus, medical studies in Constantinople
in the early part of the seventh century were not only intellectually
rigorous and philosophically respectable, there was a long-standing tradition of considering such an interest appropriate for churchmen. An

century (see M.L. Cameron, 'The Sources of Medical Knowledge in Anglo-Saxon
England', *ASE* 11 (1983), 135–55, at 147–8).

[98] *ODB* I, 30–1. He worked in both Alexandria and Constantinople, and wrote an
encyclopaedia, the *Tetrabiblion*, which covers subjects including pharmacy, dietetics,
general therapeutics, hygiene, bloodletting, fever and urine lore, gynaecology and
obstetrics. (Theodore of Tarsus touches on all these subjects in the course of his works.)

[99] ODB III, 1607.

[100] For the career of John Philoponus, see *ODB* III, 1657 and S. Sambursky, *The Physical
World of Late Antiquity* (London, 1962), pp. 154–75. His medical writings are
discussed by M. Meyerhof, 'Joannes Grammatikos (Philoponos) von Alexandrien und
die arabische Medizin', *Mitteilungen des deutschen Institut für Ägyptische Altertumskunde in
Kairo* 2 (1931), 1–21, and briefly by Temkin, 'Byzantine Medicine', p. 105.

[101] L.G. Westerink, 'Philosophy and Medicine in Late Antiquity', *Janus* 51 (1964),
169–77, p. 169.

[102] *Ibid.*, pp. 174–5. For the history of Stephanus, see *ODB* III, 1953. He may have been
born at Athens *c.* 550/5, and died at Constantinople *c.* 620 (though W. Wolska-
Conus, 'Stéphanos d'Athènes et Stéphanos d'Alexandrie', *Revue des Etudes Byzantines* 47
(1989), 5–89, at 82–9, identifies him with Stephen of Athens, and considers these
dates a little early). He was closely associated with John Philoponus. His summons by
Heraclius to Constantinople is under dispute; rejected by some authorities and
accepted by others. The main concern here is that he was a distinguished Alexandrian
medical theorist, who ended his days at Constantinople, where Michael Lapidge has
argued in *Biblical Commentaries* that Theodore was educated (pp. 41–64).

interesting minor figure, Meletius, author of *On the Fabric of Man* (Περὶ τῆς τοῦ ἀνθρώπου κατασκευῆς),[103] was a monk in the monastery of the Holy Trinity in Asia Minor. He was not only a monk and physician, but also a surgeon. His treatise was put together from a variety of sources, including the works of Galen and the theological works of Nemesius, Gregory of Nyssa, Gregory Nazianzus and Basil the Great. The latest writer whom he cites is Maximus the Confessor. Thus, he was writing no earlier than the mid-seventh century, though Byzantinists normally date him to the ninth.[104] But the arguments for dating his work are far from absolute. It is thus not impossible that he was a contemporary of Archbishop Theodore. Even if he was not, his combination of interests, and the fact that he cites medical and theological writers side by side in the same work, tell us something about the parameters of theological and philosophical enquiry in the early Byzantine world which illuminates the scholarly monk-physician with whom we are immediately concerned. Another writer who is certainly earlier than Theodore, since his work is used in the *Biblical Commentaries*, Severian of Gabala (*ob. c.* 408), wrote an exegetical work in the Antiochene style (Gabala is in Roman Syria, some fifty miles south of Antioch), the *Orationes in mundi creationem*, which frequently explain the biblical creation in terms of Greek medical science.[105] Again, this suggests that Theodore was working within a tradition, and was not as unusual in his combination of interests as he appears in a purely western context.

Since it should now be clear that a seventh-century monk of scholarly inclinations trained in the Greek east might very reasonably be interested in medicine, let us now examine the evidence for the medical interests of Archbishop Theodore himself. Theodore's interest in medicine is one of the very few pieces of personal information which Bede had about him. This appears in Bede's account of the miracles of John of Beverley (*ob.* 721), a pupil of Theodore's. John visited a nunnery at *Wetadun* (Walton), and was told about a nun there who had recently been bled and who had, we may surmise, suffered a violent septicaemic infection: her arm had swelled grotesquely and she was in intense pain. The story continues,

Interrogans autem ille, quando flebotomata esset puella, et ut cognouit, quia in

---

[103] Ed. J.A. Cramer, *Anecdota Graeca* III (Oxford, 1836).
[104] *ODB* II, 1333.
[105] His work is printed in PG 56, 429–500.

luna quarta, dixit: 'Multum insipienter et indocte fecistis in luna quarta flebotomando. Memini enim beatae memoriae Theodorum archiepiscopum dicere, quia periculosa sit satis illius temporis flebotomia, quando et lumen lunae et reuma oceani in cremento est.'[106]

The practice of phlebotomy as a general aid to health is part of the Galenic medical tradition.[107] The concept of good and bad days for such a practice is also well enshrined in Greek tradition, which often associated it with the Egyptians (whom the Greeks, as early as Plato, tended to view as the guardians of arcane and ancient wisdom). 'Egyptian days' are mentioned in Anglo-Saxon calendars as unlucky days for bloodletting.[108] The concept of the 'Egyptian days' is related in some way to another Greek medicomagical product, the 'Sphere of Pythagoras', or 'Sphere of Petosiris', as it is also known. This was a mantic device for establishing the fate of a patient by combining the number of the day of the moon on which he or she fell ill with another number derived from a numerical evaluation of the letters forming the patient's name.[109] The 'Sphere of Pythagoras' was developed some time between the second century BC and the first century AD. It clearly lent itself to the development of the concept of 'Egyptian days', in that the figure results in two sets of numbers grouped under 'Life' and 'Death'. Interestingly, Theodore's own grounds for asserting that the fourth day of the moon is unlucky in itself are not magical, but rationalistic, given that the Greek medical tradition assumed the direct influence

---

[106] Bede, *Historia ecclesiastica* V.3 (ed. Colgrave and Mynors, p. 460): 'Then he asked when the girl had been bled and, on hearing that it was on the fourth day of the moon, he exclaimed, "You have acted foolishly and ignorantly to bleed her on the fourth day of the moon; I remember how archbishop Theodore of blessed memory used to say that it was very dangerous to bleed a patient when the moon is waxing and the Ocean tide flowing." '

[107] It may seem strange that Theodore, as a bishop, was concerned with bleeding patients. In fact, Talbot (*Medicine in Medieval England*, pp. 51–2) has demonstrated that the principle that clerics should not shed blood is first articulated as late as the Lateran Council of 1215, though Galen admits that in his day there was already a cleavage between physicians, who give consultations, but do not dirty their hands, and surgeons. The Greek distaste for any kind of manual work tended to put surgical operations on a lower level, but no religious principle was involved (p. 54). The Byzantine writer Meletius, mentioned earlier, was both a monk and a surgeon.

[108] Grattan and Singer, *Anglo-Saxon Magic*, pp. 38–43, at 43.

[109] Thorndike, *A History of Magic and Experimental Science* I, 683.

51

of the environment on the patient.[110] The 'Sphere of Pythagoras' itself is attested very early in an Anglo-Saxon context: it appears in an eighth-century Anglo-Saxon manuscript from Echternach (Paris, BN Lat. 11411, fol. 99).[111] It may well have come to England with Archbishop Theodore.

The *Canones Theodori* also give evidence of Theodore's medical interests: 'Leporem licet comedere, et bonus est pro desinteria et fel eius miscendum est cum pipro pro dolore.'[112] Greek medicine paid considerable attention to diet from the time of Hippocrates onwards, and recorded the health-giving properties of various foodstuffs. The use of parts of animals as medicine forms a whole subclass of early medieval medical writing. The seventh-century Alexandrian writer Paul of Aegina listed about 600 botanical and 170 animal products in medical use in his own time;[113] and a Latin work of similar scope, the *De medicina de animalibus*, by Sextus Placitus Papyriensis, entirely devoted to this topic, appears in Anglo-Saxon England, translated into Old English as part of a text called *Medicina de quadrupedibus*.[114] In addition to this evidence for Theodore's knowledge of dietetic medicine, there is also some evidence for his knowledge of pharmacy. Lapidge has pointed out that a collection of medical recipes now preserved in St Gallen, Stiftsbibliothek 44, includes a recipe for an 'antidotum teodori', followed immediately by an 'antidotum adrianum quod est optimum multis infirmis': as he observes, the appearance of a Theodore and a Hadrian *together* in such a context is strongly suggestive that the entry derives from the school of Canterbury.[115]

By far the most extensive testimony to Theodore's medical interests is in the *Biblical Commentaries*, which endorse and extend the range of knowledge and skills attested in the evidence we have already considered. Three

---

[110] The classic account is Hippocrates, *On Airs, Waters and Places* (Πέρι ἀέρων ὑδάτων τόπων), ed. and trans. W.H.S. Jones (Cambridge, MA, 1923), pp. 70–137.

[111] For a description of the manuscript and its contents, see Lapidge, 'A Seventh-Century Insular Latin Debate Poem', pp. 1–3 and 8. The contents are a strange mixture, including the B- and C-Texts of the *Hisperica Famina* (Hiberno-Latin), with Old Breton glosses, the 'Sphere of Pythagoras', a medical recipe from the *Prognostica Galieni*, and the Anglo-Latin poem, 'Ad deum meum': the material may, on the grounds of the Old Breton glosses, have been put together in Brittany.

[112] *Iudicium de penitentia Theodori*, § 122, in *Canones Theodori*, ed. Finsterwalder, p. 279.

[113] *ODB* III, 1607.   [114] Grattan and Singer, *Anglo-Saxon Magic*, p. 30.

[115] Lapidge, 'The School of Theodore', p. 50.

entries relate to aspects of female physiology, PentI 72,[116] PentI 113[117] and, most interesting, PentI 131: 'Dicunt matres abscintio cum uino mixto ungere papillas et sic amouere a lacte.'[118] One note (PentI 156) is in the same area of 'medicina ex animalibus' as the advice on eating hares in the *Canones Theodori*: 'ideo quia medici dicunt carnes haedorum meliores esse omni carne causa lasciuiae eorum'.[119]

Several entries are much more technical in content. EvII 15 is a very detailed account of the various types of fever known to medical science.

Pyratus graece, latine febris. Yrinosus graece, latine aquosus, quia de aqua uel de aera uenit. Amphironosus graece, latine febris cotidiana. Triteris graece, latine terciane febres quae de felle iecoris fiunt. Tytarteus graece, latine quartana febris quae de splene uenit. Sinoichus graece, latine iugis febris quae nocte et die praeter .vi. horas fit.[120]

EvII 13, on the four different kinds of leprosy, is another note of the same type. EvII 43 defines a 'lunatic'.[121] EvII 73 discusses the case of the deaf and dumb.[122] The tone of this last comment is interestingly rationalistic,

---

[116] *Biblical Commentaries*, pp. 316–18: 'Natural pitch, found in the Dead Sea, can only be broken up with menstrual blood.' This information is derived from Josephus.

[117] *Ibid.*, p. 324: 'The menstrual flow ... begins to occur in young girls in their fourteenth year.'

[118] *Ibid.*, p. 328: 'They say that mothers smear their nipples with wormwood mixed with wine, and thus they wean their infants from milk.' This has a close parallel in Augustine, *Enarrationes in Psalmo xxx*, *Sermones* II. 12 (CCSL 38, 210), as noted in *Biblical Commentaries*, p. 460.

[119] *Ibid.*, p. 332: 'Physicians say that the flesh of kids is better than all flesh because of their promiscuity.'

[120] *Ibid.*, p. 398: '*pyratus* (πυρετός) in Greek, "fever" in Latin. *Yrinosus* in Greek, "watery" (ὕδερος) in Latin, since it arrives either from water or air. *Amphironosus* (ἀμφημερινός) in Greek, in Latin, "quotidian fever". *Triteris* (τριταῖος) in Greek, in Latin "tertian fevers", which arise from the bile of the liver. *Tytarteus* (τεταρταῖος) in Greek, in Latin, "quartan fever", which arises from the spleen. *Sinoichus* (σύνοχος) in Greek, in Latin "intermittent fever", which persists night and day except for a six-hour remission.' On the medical sources of this information, see *ibid.*, pp. 509–11.

[121] *Ibid.*, p. 404: 'A lunatic is someone whose brain diminishes and changes as the moon waxes and, with a demon entering through his nostrils, makes him demented. Otherwise lunatics are said to be those who, with the moon waxing, full or waning, fall down and prostrate themselves.'

[122] *Ibid.*, p. 408: 'Some commentators say that these illnesses come from an evil spirit; physicians, however, do not think in these terms but say that they arise from contracted and dormant veins.'

and like the remark on blood-letting recorded by Bede, seems to demonstrate the professionalism of Theodore's commitment to medicine rather than to the religious approach to the problem of sickness one might naturally tend to assume in an early medieval bishop. Similarly, the comment on lunacy is clinical, and can probably be derived ultimately from Galen.[123] Two consecutive entries, PentI 192 and 193, relate to the pharmacopoeia: balm and myrrh are both described as 'suitable medicine'. PentI 357 relates to another aspect of medicine: a useful piece of hardware, the clyster, which Theodore (following a whole series of Greek and Latin writers) claims was invented after observing the ibis, which allegedly aids its digestion by squirting water up its anus with its beak. In sum, these entries suggest a quite extensive practical acquaintance with the art of medicine.

It is now time to turn to the *Laterculus*, and to see how it fits in with this picture of Theodore as a clerical iatrosophist. In the *Laterculus*, the most conspicuous section relating to medical matters is in chs. 12–13, which are mainly devoted to embryological theory. The context of this discussion is the exegesis of John II.19, with its statement that 'the temple' was built in forty-six years. If this number is deemed allegorically relevant to the person of Christ, as the context suggests, then, since Christ traditionally lived only thirty-three years, embryological theory offers a way out of the impasse which this creates. A detailed discussion of the text and its sources is presented below in the Commentary (pp. 196–200). In summary, the background to this theory of human conception is to be found in Oribasius, Περὶ διαμορφώσεως ('On the shaping of the embryo'). However, rather than using Oribasius directly, the author of the *Laterculus* is clearly following in close detail Augustine's *De annis quadraginta sex aedificandi templi*, in his *De diuersis quaestionibus lxxiii*.[124] This gives a precisely comparable account of the temple which took forty-six years to build with the first forty-six days of the formation of Christ's body in Mary's womb. Apart from close resemblances of phrase, other corroborative details

---

[123] Talbot, *Medicine in Medieval England*, p. 76, quotes the thirteenth-century medical writer Gilbertus Anglicus on mania and melancholia, which he considered 'due to disturbances of the anterior and middle cell of the brain by which imagination or reason were diminished', a thesis which he derived from Galen via Arabic medical writers. The theory seems to spring from the same concept of pressure fluctuation within the brain itself.

[124] PL 40, 11–100, at 39.

include the precise date of 276 days from conception to birth, based on a calculation of the number of days from the Annunciation on 25 March to birth on 25 December, and found in no other writers, and the assertion that the conception and the Passion of Christ both took place on 25 March, which is also stated in ch. 2 of the *Laterculus*. This is the only occasion in the entire *Laterculus* in which the author turns to allegory for an explanation of any aspect of the life of Christ. It is also the only instance where he can be shown to be dependent on the work of a theologian in the Latin tradition. It is therefore particularly interesting that the *Biblical Commentaries* include a note (PentI 131, quoted above) which may derive from Augustine's *Enarrationes*, and which also deals with a gynaecological question: how babies are weaned. This tends to strengthen both the thesis that Theodore was interested in matters concerned with gynaecology and conception, and that he trusted Augustine as a source of medical information, even though he (rather curiously) did not draw on him as a theologian.

There are no other passages in the *Laterculus* which deal with medical theory. However, the beginnings of chs. 14 and 19 both present Christ as, metaphorically, a doctor. This was an image dear to Ephrem Syrus, and is not so common in the west. It may perhaps be connected with the potentially high status attached to the healer in the Byzantine world: while doubtless Byzantium had her share of quacks, the highly educated, theologically inclined *iatrosophists* who combined care for body and soul in a single enterprise must have made this a much more sympathetic way of viewing the figure of Christ. The works of Grattan and Singer, Talbot and, more recently, M.L. Cameron, have made it clear that the Old English medical works depend quite heavily on Greek sources. It has already been observed that some of the works of Oribasius were apparently available in ninth-century England. Talbot has also found evidence for the use of Paul of Aegina and Alexander of Tralles, sixth-century Byzantine writers, and other, earlier medical writers in Anglo-Saxon England.[125] The Greek 'Sphere of Pythagoras' was in England by the eighth century. There may be a case for suggesting that Theodore introduced quite substantial quantities of Greek medical material into the Canterbury curriculum, and that texts of Greek and Latin medical authorities may have been translated into Old English from an early period.

[125] *Medicine in Medieval England*, p. 18.

5

Sources of the *Laterculus*

The *Laterculus* is dependent for about half its length on Malalas's *Chronographia*; these sections are literal translation. In the rest of the *Laterculus*, all the authorities named are Greek or biblical, with the exception of Ephrem. Malalas himself in the course of book 10 acknowledged dependence on the Greek historians Clemens, Theophilus, Timotheus and Eusebius;[1] and these names are carried over into the Latin text, although no further material of any kind is drawn from them. There are references to dates *secundum Gregus* (ch. 2) and *secundum Athineos* (ch. 8). We also have biblical references, 'sicut euangelista testatur' (ch. 2) and 'ut Lucas euangelista narrat' (ch. 8). The two authorities mentioned by name are 'beatus Epyfanius Cyprius episcopus' (ch. 7) and Ephrem: 'et haec quidem etiam sanctus Ephrem commemorat similiter' (ch. 19). In general, the ideas and to some extent the language of the sections of the *Laterculus* which are not based directly on Malalas's *Chronographia* can be connected

---

[1] Timotheus is otherwise unknown. The whole problem is discussed by Croke and Jeffreys, in *Studies*, pp. 36 and 194–5 respectively.

The *Historia ecclesiastica* of Eusebius has come down to us, the works of the other three historians mentioned have not. The Clement and Theophilus may be Clement, bishop of Alexandria and Theophilus, bishop of Antioch (author of *Ad Autolycum*), but no historical work has survived from either writer to set beside his exegetical œuvre.

Another possible Theophilus is the twenty-first bishop of Alexandria who flourished in the later fourth century. According to the *Chronica* of Hydatius (a fourth-century Spanish bishop) Theophilus 'a primo consulatu Theodosii Augusti laterculum per centum annos digestum de pasce obseruatione conscribit' ('compiled a chronological table concerning the observance of Easter which extended one hundred years from the first consulate of Augustus Theodosius'). Such a document may also have included annalistic notes. See R.W. Burgess, *The Chronicle of Hydatius and the Consularia Constantinopolitana* (Oxford, 1993), p. 74.

with Greek and Syriac writers of the Antiochene school, as I will suggest below. The author's thought in the section of this work which is independent of Malalas is subtle and far-ranging. His simple expository phrases may wear their learning lightly, but his knowledge of the Greek patristic tradition was deep and extensive, as was his knowledge of the Bible. In addition, he was well versed in the Latin poetry of Proba (and perhaps Vergil) and Caelius Sedulius. Theodore of Mopsuestia, the great Antiochene, appears to have been a major influence, and so was Epiphanius. The Syrian doctors, Ephrem, Narsai and Jacob of Sarug, who were trained in the Antiochene tradition, also afford several useful parallels. John Chrysostom and Irenaeus were other theologians who may also have been read by this writer, and Theodoretus, Cyril of Alexandria, Theophilus, Hippolytus and others offer occasional parallels on particular topics. Every one of these writers was eastern, and wrote either in Greek or in Syriac;[2] most of them were Antiochene in tendency. Outside of exegesis, the author of the *Laterculus* also drew on the historians Josephus and Eusebius, and the medical writers Galen and Oribasius.[3] In short, the content of his thought seems to be almost entirely formed by Greek writers of one kind or another. He was not, however, entirely ignorant of Christian Latin literature. Apart from the two poets mentioned above, his phraseology was influenced by Latin bible-texts, even though he sometimes seems to have been translating directly from the Septuagint. The only point at which the actual content is dependent on a Latin text is the passage from Augustine discussed above.

MALALAS

The *Laterculus* is partly based, as I have said, on the *Chronographia* of John Malalas. Malalas was an Antiochene, who flourished in the late sixth century. His name is derived from the Syriac word *malal*, which means

---

[2] The works of the great Syrian doctors were rapidly translated into Greek, and similarly, much Greek literature, theological and otherwise, was translated into Syriac. See Brock, 'Greek into Syriac and Syriac into Greek'.

[3] The *Synopsis* and *Euporistes* of Oribasius were certainly in England by the end of the ninth century, because they were known to the compiler of 'Bald's Leechbook' (*c.* 900): M.L. Cameron, 'The Sources of Medical Knowledge in Anglo-Saxon England', *ASE* 11 (1983), 135–55, at 147–8. See now also M.L. Cameron, *Anglo-Saxon Medicine* (Cambridge, 1993).

'eloquent', or 'endowed with the power of speech', and seems to imply 'rhetor' or 'preacher'.[4] The name may suggest that Malalas's origins lay with the Semitic rather than the Greek sector of the Antiochene population. His *Chronographia* is a universal chronicle in eighteen books, from the creation of the world to, probably, AD 565, written in demotic Greek.[5] The exact point at which the *Chronographia* originally ended is not at all clear. There seem to have been two editions of his work, the second updating and revising the first and, unfortunately, we have only one surviving manuscript, the twelfth-century Oxford Bodl. Baroccianus 182. This is not only lacunose, but has obviously been abbreviated here and there,[6] and the end is missing completely.[7] But bk 18 is so full of circumstantial detail about the reign of Justinian, especially as his activities affected Antioch, that the writer was clearly speaking of events within his own lifetime. A fuller text of the second half of the chronicle was translated into Old Church Slavonic, and survives in this translated form. Fragments of the original Greek text are also quoted here and there in Byzantine encyclopaedists and historians, and this makes it possible to reconstruct something more like the original text than the Baroccianus manuscript by itself would permit.[8] *Laterculus Malalianus* itself is the earliest manuscript witness to the text of Malalas, by a considerable margin.

John Malalas's *Chronographia* has a number of claims to scholarly attention. It is the earliest of the various Byzantine annalistic histories, and exerted considerable influence. It is also the earliest extensive text in colloquial Byzantine Greek, either because Malalas was aiming at a wide and relatively uneducated audience, or because he was incapable of a more elevated style. It should be remembered that a chronicle is not the same

---

[4] It is from Syriac (*malal*) in the nominal form, which means 'endowed with power of speech', 'eloquent', hence the Greek form Μαλάλας. Alternatively, it could derive from the participle adjective of the *peal* form, which similarly means 'endowed with speech and reason'. See Haddad, *Aspects of Social Life in Antioch*, p. 89, n. 2.

[5] *ODB* II, p. 1295.   [6] See Bidez, 'Sur diverses citations'.

[7] J. B. Bury, 'Malalas: the Text of the *Codex Baroccianus*', *BZ* 6 (1897), 219–30.

[8] The full Greek text is edited by Dindorf, and is also in PG 97, 9–806. Bks IX-XII are ed. Schenk von Stauffenberg, *Die römische Kaisergeschichte bei Malalas*, and the second half of the Old Church Slavonic version is translated by Spinka and Downey, *Chronicle of John Malalas, Books VIII-XVIII*. Furthermore, the recent translation into English by E. M. Jeffreys and others gives in its notes references to all the other witnesses to the text of Malalas.

thing as a history. Malalas's selection of facts relates to the interests of himself and his contemporaries, rather than to the analysis of political or religious events. He is invaluable, therefore, for the social history of sixth-century Antioch and Constantinople, but his understanding of the past is profoundly coloured by the preconceptions of his own time, and his use of his sources is almost entirely uncritical.[9]

Malalas's sources are an interesting study in themselves. The *Chronographia* may be divided into three main sections, marked off from one another by the type of source available to the author. The first few books are an uneasy amalgam of Greek myths and the Old Testament. Then, for Roman and Christian history, he drew mainly on Christian historians like Eusebius and Julius Africanus, together with other chronographers, some of whom are now no more than names. As he got nearer his own time, he also used the 'City Chronicles' of Antioch and Constantinople. In the last section, from AD 490 or so onwards, he relied heavily on oral sources, and consequently retains a lasting importance for modern Byzantinists. As it happens, the source-criticism of the first section of the *Chronographia* was the subject of Richard Bentley's spectacular academic début in 1691, when he was 29, which is known as the *Epistola ad Joannem Millium*. Bentley's particular interest was in exhuming half-digested fragments of Classical Greek drama from the earlier, mostly legendary, books. The whole exercise is an impressive example of the mileage a great scholar can get out of an apparently bizarre and unpromising source.[10] As these comments imply, Malalas's qualities as a historian do not inspire much confidence in his education and abilities. He used his sources very uncritically and often not at first hand. Although he occasionally attributes a statement to Josephus, Eusebius or other historians, these citations are

---

[9] The nature of his work is described by A. Cameron, *Circus Factions* (Cambridge, 1975), p. 139: 'we should not be misled into treating their [the chroniclers'] selection of facts and emphasis as an accurate reflection of the political and religious realities of the day' – still less, it should be added, as an accurate reflection of pre-sixth-century history in the earlier parts.

[10] Bentley, *Epistola ad Ioannem Millium*, ed. G. P. Goold (Toronto, 1962). Goold comments snidely in his Introduction that 'the *Epistola ad Ioannem Millium* was called forth by one of those unhappy productions which, mediocre themselves, have had the ill luck to attract the inspection of genius' (p. 7), and that '[Bentley's] notes are not so much a commentary on the old chronicler as a set of dazzling dissertations pegged upon a random set of appalling howlers' (p. 9).

frequently obtained through intermediate sources.[11] But it has already been argued (above, pp. 21–2) that the features of his text which render it unacceptable as history conform precisely to the expectations and proper form of its actual genre, the chronicle. The fact that his text fails rather badly when read as history should no more be held against it (or its author) than the equivalent failure of Gildas' *De excidio Britanniae*.

The *Laterculus* is very different in scope from the *Chronographia*. Bk 10 of Malalas's eighteen books deals with the life and times of Christ, and it is part of this book which is reproduced by the Latin author. Bk 10 could be described as a reasonably intelligent synchronism between the gospels and the *fasti consulares*: that is, the biography of Jesus Christ is derived from a synthesis of all four gospels,[12] and anchored historically to the reigns of Roman emperors, consuls, procurators of Syria and other major political figures of imperial history. What the author of the *Laterculus* does is to translate Malalas's historical account of the life of Christ from his birth to his assumption into heaven, which forms the first half of his own text, and then to desert the *Chronographia* completely in order to discuss the significance of the events he has just described. The *Laterculus* then ends with a list of the Roman emperors as a sort of appendix, giving the lengths of their reigns, and extending from Augustus to Justin II. The list is extracted from the historical account of these emperors in bks 10 to 18 of Malalas's chronicle. The text of the *Chronographia* used by the author of the *Laterculus* (which is one of the earliest witnesses to Malalas's work) has some aspects in common with the Codex Baroccianus, the only complete manuscript of the *Chronographia*. In particular, the names of consuls and other historical figures appear in garbled, but often similar, versions in both, suggesting that the distortion of the names went back at least to the seventh century, and possibly to Malalas himself. However, Codex Baroccianus is somewhat lacunose, whereas the *Laterculus* seems to have drawn on a text which was complete, or nearly so, to judge by the other witnesses to the missing bits of the *Chronographia*, and the inclusion in the *Laterculus*

---

[11] Downey, *A History of Antioch*, pp. 38–9.

[12] It is also possible that Malalas's source was a gospel-harmony. The tradition of creating a gospel-harmony goes back to the second century, and is particularly associated with the Syrian writer Tatian. Gospel-harmonies were still in use, in both east and west, in the sixth century. The celebrated Codex Fuldensis is an example of a Latin harmony. See O. C. Edwards, 'Diatessaron or Diatessara?', *SP* 15 [= *TU* 129] (Berlin, 1984), 88–92.

of the names and reign-lengths of emperors who are missing in the Baroccianus *Chronographia*.

The Bible is, of course, the author's primary resource. His Bible-text is interesting and problematic. It appears to be separable into several layers. Some of its readings are pure Vulgate, as we now know it. Some are Vetus Latina, or possibly assignable to an early stage of the development of the Vulgate, and agree with readings found in such writers as Augustine and Cassiodorus.

Old Testament

The author makes surprisingly extensive use of the Old Testament, mainly in the service of his fascination with Old Testament typology, but also as a source of imagery. The Psalms are drawn on several times in the *Laterculus*. The version used is apparently 'iuxta LXX' (that is, Gallican), again as one might expect, since it was the text used at Rome. This is demonstrable from, for example, the reference to 'sicut gigans per uiam', which is a near-quotation from Ps. XVIII.6, which reads 'exsultauit ut gigans ad currendam uiam suam' in the 'iuxta LXX' version and is quite different in the 'iuxta Hebraeos'. This, however, leaves unresolved the question of whether the author is always thinking of a Latin version of the Psalms, or sometimes of the Septuagint, since the Latin translation preferred by Rome was from the Septuagint in the first place. There is some reason to think that Greek versions may lie behind the writer's usage in citations from other parts of the Bible. However, the Vetus Latina was often closer to the Septuagint than the Vulgate and this effectively obscures the question of whether the writer was actually translating from the Septuagint at times. But a few of the citations are quite startlingly anomalous, in ways that suggest that the writer was paraphrasing from memory.

All this greatly complicates any attempt to reconstruct the writer's Bible-text. But even when a writer is paraphrasing from memory, he is quite likely to retain words and structures from the version he knows most intimately, even if he elides or inverts parts of the original sentence. It may therefore be significant that non-Vulgate phrases, even in loose quotation or paraphrase, may be found to be shared with Vetus Latina or early 'mixed' Bible-texts, though the sentence in the *Laterculus* has been so thoroughly re-cast that it resembles no one version in detail.[13]

The version of Num. XXIV.17 in ch. 15 appears at first sight to be an unsupported and wildly divergent reading. 'Ascendit homo in Israhel' is a translation of the Septuagint, found also in some Vetus Latina texts. However, both the Vetus Latina and Septuagint continue in a different way, with the sons of Seth and the leaders of Moab, so this would appear to be a paraphrase. But on the other hand, Leo the Great quoted this verse in his *sermones* in the form 'orietur stella ex Iacob, et exsurget homo ex Israel, et dominabitur gentium',[14] which is closer than any other to the version in the *Laterculus*; this may or may not be a coincidence. This reading of Num. XXIV.17 is not the only quotation to support the possibility of a rather recondite Vetus Latina text. There are other, common Vetus Latina readings, such as *terra* rather than *puluis* in Gen. III.19 (which, again, follows the Septuagint's γῆ).

This writer twice appears (whether deliberately or unconsciously) to alter the text of the Bible in accordance with the point he wished to make. With his quotation of Isaiah LX.6, 'omnes a Saba uenient ferentes aurum, thus, *et murra*', either he or his source-text made an unauthorized addition of myrrh to the gold and incense in order to strengthen the typological connexion of this passage with the visit of the Magi (this may have been an inadvertent trick of memory). Although many exegetes, for example Eusebius, linked this verse typologically with the Magi, none that I know of quotes the verse with *et murra*, though some early Greek versions, witnessed by the Codex Siniaticus and the text used by Hesychius in his commentary on Isaiah,[15] have 'gold, silver and a precious stone' (λίθον τίμιον).

New Testament

The basic structure of the *Laterculus* offers a synoptic account of Christ's history on earth which utilizes the historical information of gospels and Acts very fully; and the New Testament is therefore drawn on extensively in a variety of ways.

---

[13] See below, pp. 238–44.

[14] Leo the Great, *Sermo* XXXIV (PL 34, 137–463, at 245).

[15] *Hesychii interpretatio Isaiae*, ed. Faulhaber, p. 186.

The kinds of minor textual changes found in the *Laterculus* may be illustrated with respect to New Testament as well as Old Testament citations. Matth. XXVII.19, 'nihil tibi et iusto illi, multa enim passa sum hodie per uisum propter eum', is quoted accurately (ch. 10) except for a change from plural to singular, 'multum enim passa sum', not found in any other witness known to me. A similar case is in ch. 15, where the *Laterculus* adds an internal gloss as he did with Zechariah: 'uox in excelso, hoc est in Rama'. Jeremiah XXXI.15 gives 'uox in excelso' (Vulgate), the Vetus Latina of Jeremiah agrees with both versions of Matth. II.15 in giving 'uox in Rama'.[16] The *Laterculus* quotation is closer to the Matthew versions, but even so, has replaced 'ploratus et ululatus multus' with 'pluratus et *luctus magnus*', and 'quia non sunt' with '*quoniam* non sunt'. Once again, this variant appears to be completely unsupported. But the writer's acceptance of the problematic *neque filius* in Matth. XIV.26 seems to suggest that the writer was not, at least consciously, given to rewriting the Bible to suit his own purposes. It is not impossible that the Bible-text he drew on varied considerably from those that have survived.

A certain lack of scruple in bending the sacred text to one's immediate purpose is to be found in ch. 16, where 'donec occurramus omnes in unitatem fidei et agnitionis filii dei, in uirum perfectum, in mensuram aetatis plenitudinis Christi' (Eph. IV.13) is cut from *omnes* to *in uirum*, considerably altering the meaning. In this case, quotation from memory might be responsible for the anomaly. However, a similar tendency to paraphrase the biblical texts is found in the Latin version of Theodore of Mopsuestia's commentary on the Minor Epistles, for example in the 'quotation', 'quem scripsit Moyses in lege et prophetae, inuenimus Messaiam, qui est Christus', which in fact conflates the words of Andrew in John I.41 and Philip in John I.45.[17] We similarly find what is either careless paraphrase or otherwise unattested Vetus Latina text in the *Miraculum S. Anastasii*, written by a Greek monk at the monastery of St Anastasius in Rome, a generation after Theodore.[18]

---

[16] *Versiones antiquae*, ed. Sabatier II, 698 and III, 11.

[17] Theodore of Mopsuestia, *Commentary on the Minor Epistles*, ed. Swete I, 54. See also I, 81 and II, 152.

[18] For example, the Vulgate's 'petite et dabitur uobis, quaerite et inuenietis, pulsate et aperietur uobis' (Luke IX.3) is transformed in ch. 7 into 'quaerite et inuenietis, petite *et accipietis*, pulsate et aperietur uobis'. For further discussion of this text, see below, p. 91.

Apocrypha

It is noteworthy that the author seems to share the eastern churches' relatively relaxed attitude towards apocrypha, since he quotes (ch. 7) an apocryphal story of the Holy Family in Egypt allegedly from Epiphanius of Cyprus.[19] The details given of the deaths of James the Lord's brother (ch. 2) and of John the Baptist (ch. 9) are extra-biblical, and must draw ultimately on apocrypha, though quite possibly through the medium of the martyrologies (or in the case of James, the Christian historians). Similarly, the name Procla given to the wife of Pontius Pilate (ch. 10) is derived from the widely circulated second-century apocryphon, the *Acts of Pilate*.

Conclusions

It may be seen that this writer's treatment of his biblical sources is bold, confident and bordering on the unorthodox. His misquotations might suggest that he quoted from memory some of the time. The details of change of vocabulary or construction cannot be pressed into any particular pattern, except that there is a tendency to agree with Ambrose and Augustine, who are witnesses both to the Vetus Latina and to an earlier stage of the Vulgate text, against later Vulgate texts. The versions preferred, where a distinction can be drawn, are consistently closer to the Septuagint and the Greek New Testament than to Jerome. The strangest variants in the *Laterculus* are from the minor prophets, Numbers and Isaiah: his versions of the gospels, Acts and the Pauline Epistles appear to fall into the Vetus Latina/early Vulgate category without significant anomalies. It may be worth raising the question of whether his occasional independence of Latin versions might be due to his quoting from memory of the Greek Bible and making extempore translations into Latin, but this is a possibility there is no clear way of testing. There is no justification in the Septuagint text for, for example, his conspicuous mistreatment of Zechariah. In any case, the writer's knowledge of the Latin Bible is evidently extremely good. There are many points aside from his deliberate

---

[19] The story is also found in the gospel of Pseudo-Matthew (*ANT*, p. 75) and elsewhere, though not in the surviving works of Epiphanius. See discussion in the Commentary below, pp. 182–4, n. 63.

quotations where his phraseology is consciously or unconsciously reminiscent of a biblical verse.

It will be evident from this list that the degree of variation from any known standard of text in these citations is such that no firm conclusions can be drawn. Nonetheless, there are some interesting correspondences. The *Laterculus* is sometimes found to agree in a reading with one or other member of the Insular family DELQR[20] and also with the Irish Vetus Latina text, Codex Usserianus Primus (r).[21] It is also extremely interesting to find that an apparent quotation from Amos in ch. 20 is shared only with the sixth-century British writer, Gildas, whose quotations from the Prophets were taken from a notably archaic version based directly on the Septuagint. There is some degree of affinity with Spanish Bibles, C (Cavensis) and T (Toletanus), and also an important reading in Genesis shared only with Isidore of Seville. Most interestingly of all, the Bible-text of the *Laterculus* is compatible with that of gospel-texts particularly associated with Canterbury, the two sixth-century Bibles linked with St Augustine (OX) and the Codex Aureus (*aur.*). It is particularly noteworthy in Matth. XXIV.36, where the variant reading adopted in the *Laterculus* (ch. 24) conspicuously affects the meaning, that O, X and *aur.* all share the reading *neque filius*.

GREEK SOURCES AND ANALOGUES

The *Laterculus* appears to lean to a surprisingly great extent on the founding father of Antiochene exegesis, Theodore of Mopsuestia. The precise extent of this is difficult to determine, for the anathematizing of Theodore and his œuvre a century after his death inevitably led to the destruction of much of his work. Theodore of Mopsuestia provides by far the closest model for the overall structure of the *Laterculus*, which at first

---

[20] These sigla refer, respectively, to the Book of Armagh, London, BL Egerton 609, the Lichfield Gospels, the Book of Kells and the Mac Regol Gospels. These sigla, and all other sigla related to gospel texts, are listed, and their manuscripts described, in *Nouum Testamentum*, ed. Wordsworth and White. Sigla relating to Vetus Latina Bible-texts (other than gospels) are taken from Fischer's edition.

[21] It may be worth noting that a similar type of Bible-text is found for I Tim. VI.7, quoted in a dubious early Glastonbury charter (Birch, *Cartularium Saxonicum*, no. 25 = Sawyer, no. 227, discussed above, p. 29) attributed to Coenwalh in 671. It is discussed by Robinson, *Somerset Historical Essays*, p. 51.

sight seemed so unusual. Theodore of Mopsuestia's Commentary on Ephesians opens by collating the evidence of Acts, the traditions about John and the history of the imperial reigns of Nero and Trajan before moving on to an exegesis of its contents.[22] So the *Laterculus* should almost certainly be redefined, not as a chronicle-text, but as an exegesis of the life of Christ according to Antiochene, and particularly Theodoran, principles. Theodore of Mopsuestia insisted on a rigorously historical understanding of the Bible, including the Old Testament. But although he excluded allegorizing as the imposition of a set of alien, a-historical judgements on the biblical material, he did not exclude typology, which was subtly and rigorously defined: 'the comparison of two poles against a historical, eschatological background, with the belief that a real relationship between the two exists and that the second is a fulfilment of the first and with the conviction that each pole has its own reality'.[23] Thus, Theodore of Mopsuestia's historical sense did not deny an inner meaning to Old Testament history, but treated typology as a *theoria*, 'insight', available to Christians in the light of their new knowledge, though not apparent in Old Testament times.[24]

The only Greek writer actually cited as a source-text in the *Laterculus* is Epiphanius of Cyprus (*c.* 315–403 AD), a learned bishop familiar with Greek, Syriac, Hebrew, Coptic and some Latin.[25] The defence of iconoclasm and the study and analysis of heresy are two salient themes of his work. His great book, the *Panarion*, or *Medicine-Chest Against Eighty Heresies*, is a mine of information on heterodox religion in the eastern empire. The author of the *Laterculus*'s discussion of the episode of the Breaking of the Statues, which is found in a number of apocryphal infancy gospels, is described 'quod et beatus Epyfanius Cyprius episcopus commemorat'. This is treated at length in the Commentary below (n. 63). The author seems also to have drawn on Epiphanius in his discussion of the age of Joseph (n. 68). It is therefore significant that Epiphanius is used in the *Biblical Commentaries*, and that several of his minor works are known to have been at Canterbury, notably his treatises on weights and measures (Περὶ μέτρων καὶ σταθμῶν, in effect a prolegomenon to a dictionary of the

---

[22] Greer, *Theodore of Mopsuestia*, pp. 104–5; *Theodori in Epistolas Commentarii*, ed. Swete I, 112–96, at 112–18.

[23] Greer, *Theodore of Mopsuestia*, pp. 108–9; see also Wallace-Hadrill, *Christian Antioch*, pp. 33–5.

[24] Wallace-Hadrill, *Christian Antioch*, p. 35.   [25] Quasten, *Patrology* III, 384–96.

Bible), and on the Twelve Stones (Περὶ τῶν δώδεκα λίθων). Another Greek writer who seems to have been used on more than one occasion is the sixth-century Procopius of Gaza.[26] Again, Procopius of Gaza is a source for the *Biblical Commentaries*.[27] Another possible source for the *Laterculus* is Hesychius of Jerusalem (*fl. c.* 412), whose exegesis of Isaiah XIX.1 seems to have been taken up in our text (see n. 62).[28] The probably second-century *Epistle of Barnabas* may also have been known to the author of the *Laterculus*. This work enjoyed a very high status in the early church – the fourth-century Greek gospel-book *Codex Siniaticus* ranks it as a canonical epistle – and contains the *locus classicus* for the thesis that the world is to last 6,000 years. Its high status means that ideas from the *Epistle* could have been known to the author of the *Laterculus* without the *Epistle* itself having been known directly. However, the identification of the 'thousand years' and the seven days of creation is not the only point of correspondence. The *Epistle* is also notable for its interest in numerology, something which is also found in the *Laterculus*, and for its development of the idea of the *ogdoad*, which is treated at some length in ch. 22 of the *Laterculus*.[29]

SYRIAC SOURCES AND ANALOGUES

Byzantine Syria in the sixth and early seventh centuries was a culturally complex region. Syria as a linguistic and cultural concept was split down the middle by the Byzantine/Persian border which, while politically significant to the two empires, was in no sense an impermeable boundary at a village level. The language of Syria was closely related to the Aramaic spoken in Palestine at the time of Christ and its Christian tradition was one of considerable antiquity, though the legend that Abgar of Edessa was a contemporary of Christ himself and had accepted the new religion from him directly is of course no more than a legend. By the end of the sixth century, it boasted three mutually unacceptable theological traditions, the

---

[26] See below, Commentary, pp. 170 and 173, nn. 20 and 28, on the creation of the angels, and Phalech/Peleg.

[27] See Lapidge, in *Biblical Commentaries*, ed. Bischoff and Lapidge, pp. 227–9.

[28] Quasten, *Patrology* III, 488–96.

[29] *Epistle* XV.8: 'Not the Sabbaths of the present era are acceptable to me, but that which I have appointed to mark the end of the world and to usher in the eighth day, that is the beginning of the other world. Wherefore we joyfully celebrate the eighth day on which Jesus rose from the dead.'

monophysites, who refused to accept the ruling of the Council of Chalcedon on the two natures of Christ, the orthodox, or pro-Chalcedonians, and the Nestorians, who believed in two natures of Christ, but considered them to be completely separate. The Nestorians were anathematized and persecuted within the empire, and consequently moved away from Byzantine territory into Persian Syria, with their principal school at the trading-town of Nisibis. Connections between Christian communities of one persuasion or another, and links between traders left Byzantine Syria open to a wide variety of influences from Persia and beyond. All the centres of Syriac culture, notably Antioch, Edessa and Nisibis, also had considerable Jewish communities, and Syrian theologians such as Ephrem are clearly influenced by Jewish intellectual traditions.[30] Antioch, the home of John Malalas, was the Mediterranean terminus of the 'Silk Road' which wound from oasis to oasis through Persian territory, Central Asia and Mongolia before terminating at its eastern end in Beijing. The liveliness of Antioch's Hellenistic cultural traditions is suggested by the fact that in the fourth century it was the home of a famous Greek rhetor and educator, Libanius, as well as of Ammianus Marcellinus, the last great Classical Latin historian. It was also the possessor of a distinctive theological school from the fourth century onwards. Edessa and Nisibis had much less well developed traditions of Greco-Roman culture, but drew on rich and complex Semitic traditions which developed simultaneously into Rabbinic Jewish techniques of study and exegesis of the Talmud, and into the related Syriac Christian school of exegesis.[31] Drijvers has commented on the Syrian region (focussing particularly on Edessa) as follows:

The border area fostered a continuous exchange of goods and ideas and stood open to influences from all directions. That means that the question of language is not decisive: almost all writings that originate in that area and date back to the first three centuries AD are handed down in a Syriac *and* a Greek version ...

---

[30] W. A. Meeks and R. L. Wilken, *Jews and Christians in Antioch in the First Four Centuries of the Common Era* (Missoula, MN, 1978), p. 21: 'exegesis depending ultimately on Jewish models becomes a hallmark of the Antiochene school'.

[31] Beggiani, *Early Syriac Theology*, pp. 5–6 : 'even before the time of Narsai, the school of Edessa had adopted the work of Theodore [of Mopsuestia] in Syriac translation as the main source of instruction in biblical exegesis'. See also J-M. Vosté, 'De versione syriaca operum Theodori Mopsuesteni', *Orientalia Christiana Periodica* 8 (1942), 477–81.

whoever was literate in that particular time and area usually knew both languages.[32]

The sixth-century Antiochene John Malalas bore a Syriac name, but wrote in Greek, not unusual in this region.

The most influential theologian of the Syrian Church, St Ephrem, significantly influenced the author of the *Laterculus*. Whether Ephrem's works were read in the original Syriac or through the many Greek translations is a question which a Latin text will hardly permit us to answer.[33] Apart from this generic resemblance between the *Laterculus* and the Antiochene school, there are also a number of specific points where the thought of the *Laterculus* can be shown to derive from the theological tradition of the schools of Antioch, Edessa and Nisibis. The conspicuous typological stratum in the *Laterculus*, discussed above (pp. 43–5), can frequently be paralleled in the Christian Semitic tradition of Ephrem, Narsai and other Syrian exegetes.

The actual citation of Ephrem in the *Laterculus* is as the author of a version of the *ordines Christi*, a minor genre of early medieval literature which is widely attested across the Greek and Roman worlds.[34] Such texts assert that Christ, the fountainhead of sacerdotal authority, can be demonstrated to have performed the functions of each of the grades of the clericate, from a lowly doorkeeper to a bishop, during the course of his life, thus providing a pattern for all of them. No version of the *ordines Christi* can be securely attributed to Ephrem, and to this extent the author of the *Laterculus* is apparently in error. But even though the attribution does not hold good in itself, it suggests that the author of the *Laterculus* considered Ephrem to be an authority. This is borne out in other chapters of his work, since we see interesting reflections of Ephrem's thought in the *Laterculus*.

---

[32] Drijvers, *East of Antioch*, pp. 1–27, at 3. See further Haddad, *Aspects of Social Life in Antioch*, pp. 72–121.

[33] On the translation of Ephrem into Greek, see Brock, 'Greek into Syriac and Syriac into Greek', p. 13, where he notes that Jerome knew of several translations of Ephrem into Greek, only twenty years after Ephrem's death in 373. Brock stresses the enormous influence of Ephrem on Greek writing, particularly on the development of Greek religious poetry.

[34] The ordinals of Christ have attracted an extensive bibliography, and it is one of the main areas of the *Laterculus* to have received scholarly attention. In addition to Reynolds, *The*

The opening of ch. 12, with its comparison between virgin earth and the Virgin, summarizes a favourite theme of Ephrem.[35] Another Ephraimic theme is the representation of Christ as a physician (ch. 14). More specifically, Ephrem's exegesis of Jacob's dream, and the understanding of the significance of the two walls, are apparently the source for the treatment of this theme in the *Laterculus*, ch. 14.[36] Furthermore, Ephrem, more than any other Greek or Syriac writer, insisted on the full competence, mental and physical, of Adam at the time of the Fall, an issue which the *Laterculus* treats at some length in ch. 17.[37]

Another Syriac writer, Narsai (*ob.* 502, one of the leading theologians of Edessa), seems to have been the source for the assertion that Adam and Eve were in paradise for less than a single day, which is also found in the Canterbury *Biblical Commentaries* (PentI 44).[38] The passages quoted from Syriac writers, Ephrem in particular, give some hint of the densely-layered typology which is characteristic of these writers. This is also a salient feature of the *Laterculus*, in which the writer displayed an Antiochene concern with solid facts – for example in the passage on the building of the temple he puzzled himself as to which temple this could be[39] – but at the same time, devoted a great deal of his discussion to typology.

LATIN SOURCES

The Latin echoes in the *Laterculus* form a curious and interesting group, which suggests that the pattern of the author's reading in Latin literature was most unusual. By far the most significant is Caelius Sedulius, an important and influential Christian Latin poet of the early fifth century, whose principal work, the *Carmen Paschale*, recounts Old Testament miracles prefiguring Christ, the miracles of Christ himself, the Resurrection and the Ascension. Thus the structure is to some extent typological,

---

Ordinals of Christ, see also Crehan, 'The Seven Orders of Christ', and Wilmart, 'Les ordres du Christ'.

[35] Commentary, n. 102.   [36] Commentary, n. 130.

[37] Commentary, n. 153.

[38] Commentary, n. 33.

[39] A problem which is not soluble if one assumes the gospels to be perfectly accurate. None of the three temples of Jerusalem, according to the testimony of the Old Testament, Josephus and Eusebius, took as long as forty-six years to build. But it is interesting that this writer is concerned to ask the question.

since it parallels the Old and New Testaments, which may be a particular reason why this writer considered it important.[40] The phraseology of the *Laterculus* is manifestly based on that of Caelius Sedulius in at least ten different places. The other Latin poet whose work he seems to have known well is Faltonia Betitia Proba, a fourth-century Roman lady of good family who composed a 694-hexameter poem, the *Cento Vergilianus, c.* 360, which retells biblical episodes from the Creation to the Resurrection of Christ almost entirely in hexameters taken from Vergil and skilfully spliced together to create a Christian narrative.[41] There are two points of considerable interest here. First, both these poets were Christian. There is nothing to suggest that the author of the *Laterculus* was familiar with pagan Latin poetry, not even the *Aeneid*. Secondly, both appear to have been studied in seventh-century Southumbria. The relationship between Caelius Sedulius's *Carmen Paschale* and the *Laterculus* is beyond doubt. The ten examples of parallel phrasing are noted and discussed in full in the Commentary; it thus seems appropriate to give only a few examples here. For instance, the phrase 'decimi mensis limitem' in ch. 12 clearly recalls

> Iamque nouem lapsis, *decimi de limine mensis*
> Fulgebat sacrata dies . . .[42]

especially since Huemer observes that *limite* occurs as a variant in the manuscript-tradition. Another clear case is in ch. 16, where the phrase 'pondera dura tulit' is taken unaltered from Caelius Sedulius's hymn *Cantemus Socii*, lines 51–2.[43]

The case of Proba is not quite so clear-cut. *A priori*, since the *Cento* is a reworking of lines from the *Aeneid*, there will normally be very little to show whether it is Virgil or Proba that a given writer is familiar with. But there is also one really significant parallel with Proba in the *Laterculus*, in ch. 17, much closer than any parallels with Virgil that I have been able to find. In the passage in question, Proba conflated two widely separated passages of the *Aeneid*, and the *Laterculus* uses phrases from these consecu-

---

[40] F.J.E. Raby, *A History of Christian Latin Poetry From the Beginnings to the Close of the Middle Ages*, 2nd ed. (Oxford, 1953), pp. 108–10.

[41] *Prosopography of the Later Roman Empire*, ed. A.H.M. Jones *et al.*, 2 vols. (Cambridge, 1971–80) I, 732.

[42] *Carmen Paschale* II.41–2 (ed. Huemer, p. 47).

[43] The hymn is in couplets, with the last quarter of the distich repeating the first; thus the phrase occurs twice (ed. Huemer, p. 158).

tive lines of the *Cento*. Furthermore, one of these phrases, *pectore uirgo*, is grammatically anomalous in the *Laterculus* though correct, of course, in Proba's poem. Since the writer is familiar with two important Christian Latin poets, it might have seemed logical that he would also be familiar with others: Juvencus, the fourth-century author of a Christian epic on the gospel, the *Euangelica historia*, is an obvious case in point.[44] In fact, there is no indication in the *Laterculus* that the author had read Juvencus's epic, or any other major works of Christian Latin. Nor can he be shown to have been familiar with any Latin hymns beside those of Caelius Sedulius.

When one considers possible dependence on prose writers, one finds very little unambiguous indication that this author had read any Latin prose writers at all, with the sole exception of Augustine. Most curiously, the main body of Augustine's exegesis does not seem to have been drawn on at all in this work, but he is used as an authority on embryology.[45] The author of the *Laterculus* shows some knowledge of Roman law in ch. 20 which may draw on Justinian, but there is no clear verbal echo. Moreover, the passage in question might very well be based on Caelius Sedulius's *Carmen Paschale*, already identified as a source. The only other point where there seems to be a clear verbal echo of a Latin prose writer is in ch. 6, where the phrase 'mittens manum militarem' resembles a phrase in Gildas's *De excidio*, 'legatos Romam...mittit, *militarem manum* ... poscens ...'[46] There is thus a possible connection with the work of a British Latin writer known to have been taught at Canterbury, which is strengthened by the use in the *Laterculus* of a phrase from the prophet Amos in a Latin version which has been preserved only in Gildas's work.

The absence of any direct evidence for the author's acquaintance with standard, pagan curriculum authors is perhaps explicable if the *Laterculus* is located in the seventh century, and not a product of eighth-century Insular Latin writers' omnivorous enthusiasm for any Latin literature whatsoever. The *Epistola ad Donidium* of the fifth-century Gallo-Roman Bishop Sidonius Apollinaris makes it clear that it was normal in his day for

---

[44] The only point of contact with Juvencus's *Euangelica historia*, the phrase *regeque cruento* in ch. 15 – Juvencus's epic opens, 'rex fuit Herodes Iudaea in gente cruentus' – is more probably to be associated with Caelius Sedulius' *Carmen Paschale* II.119, 'furor est in rege cruento'.

[45] *De diuersis questionibus lxxiii* (PL 40, 11–100, at 39). This is discussed in detail above, pp. 54–5, and again in the Commentary.

[46] Ch. XV.1 (ed. Mommsen, p. 33).

Christian and pagan works to be segregated in a properly organized library. Devotional works were thoughtfully placed near the ladies' seats, while works 'distinguished by the grandeur of Latin eloquence' were in the men's section. In the context of this letter, Sidonius comments with pleasure that unusually, in a library he has recently visited, the best Christian authors, Augustine and Prudentius, have been shelved with Varro and Horace, and are not, thus, implicitly labelled as beneath the interest of an intelligent man.[47] If this implies a somewhat Podsnappian sense that works of pagan literature were unsuitable for the perusal of nicely brought-up girls (rather than simply that they were reckoned to be too stylistically difficult for womens' comprehension), it would not be surprising to find that some monks, at least, rejected pagan literature as unsuitable for their own reading. It may be relevant here to note that the texts excerpted in the Leiden Glossary, which has its origin in Theodore's Canterbury,[48] include no pagan poets whatsoever. Clearly, the demands of effective education ensured that the school of Canterbury taught the Latin classics, and indeed, taught them well. That does not require, however, that Theodore himself had been brought up on Vergil. It is also noticeable in Aldhelm's letter to Wihtfrith that his approach to the moral implications of Classical mythology is extremely austere: this might very reasonably be a product of an education which extracted *sententiae* from Vergil, but treated pagan literature with considerable severity.[49]

---

[47] Sidonius Apollinaris, *Epistolae* II.ix.4 (*Poems and Letters*, ed. and trans. W.B. Anderson, 2 vols. (London and Cambridge, MA, 1936) I, 452–5).

[48] See Lapidge, 'The School of Theodore and Hadrian'.

[49] *Epistola ad Wihtfridum* (*Aldhelmi Opera*, ed. Ehwald, pp. 479–80).

6

The Latinity of the *Laterculus*

The Leiden manuscript is entirely dependent on the Vatican one, as I will seek to demonstrate in ch. 8. Its more correct Latin, therefore, is not in any sense independent, but is an attempt by the Carolingian scribe to tidy up the more obvious errors in his exemplar. Accordingly, the entire discussion of the author's Latinity relates to the text as presented by Pal. lat. 277.

ORTHOGRAPHY

The orthography of the Vatican text of the *Laterculus* is on the whole fairly correct. There are no vulgarisms like syncope or prosthetic vowels. The scribe, writing in an Italian hand in the early eighth century, presumably Italian himself, may well have contributed an additional level of error. The other texts copied in this codex are also carelessly written in this sense, and Lowe[1] noted the presence of Late Latin spellings such as *storia* for *historia*, *Spania* for *Hispania*, consistent confusion of *e* and *i*, *o* and *u* and *b* and *v*, and irregular aspiration in the manuscript as a whole. The Latinity of another work in Pal. lat. 277, the Irish *Questiones sancti Isidori*, came under the scrutiny of Robert McNally.[2] He found that both consonantal and vocalic orthography wandered from the Classical norm in very much the same way as the *Laterculus*, and does not seem to have found the orthographic 'Irish symptoms', such as the conspicuous misuse of single and geminate consonants.[3] All this goes to suggest that the scribe of Pal. lat. 277, probably

---

[1] *CLA* I, no. 91.   [2] *Scriptores Hiberniae minores I*, p. 193.

[3] Irish orthography has been discussed by B. Löfstedt, *Der Hibernolateinische Grammatiker Malsachanus*, Studia Latina Upsaliensia 3 (Uppsala, 1965), 86–107 (on gemination, see

an Italian flourishing around the beginning of the eighth century, is unlikely to have concerned himself with correcting the spelling of his exemplar, but may, on the other hand, have made it worse.

The chief peculiarities of his consonantal orthography are confusion of *v* and *b*,[4] producing *octabam* and *octauam* a few lines apart, *iubenis* for *iuuenis*, *pleui* for *plebi*[5] and *fauricia* for *fabricia*, that is *fabrica*, as well as *gereuat* and *nuuibus*. P for *b* occurs only once, in *rempuplicam*. Words including an *x* are sometimes overdetermined, producing *fincxit* and *coniuncxit*.[6] G is used for *c* in three separate words, *Gregus*, *pernegauit*, and *Magrinus*; the reverse, *c* for *g*, occurs in *coaculatur*. G is also used for consonantal *i* in the word *magestas*. Insular writers in general often have trouble with single and double consonants, and also with *t* and *d*; in the *Laterculus*, we only find *asumptus* with one *s*, *repperiatur* with two *p*s and *trittici* with two *t*s in the first class, and a few confusions in the second, *illut* for *illud*, *capud* for *caput*, *aput* for *apud*, with the more unusual *deliquid* for *deliquit*. Note that all these cases of *t/d* confusion are of the final letter.

There are not many other instances of non-Classical spelling of consonants. Most of these errors relate to the spelling of sounds which had fallen together by the seventh century in speech. Isidore, for example, noted that

Ad, cum est praepositio, *d* litteram; cum est coniunctio, *t* litteram accipit. *Haud*, quando aduerbium est negandi, *d* littera terminatur et aspiratur in capite; quando autem coniunctio disiunctiua est, per *t* litteram sine aspiratione scribitur.[7]

pp. 102–3), and 'Some Linguistic Remarks on Hiberno-Latin', *Studia Hibernica* 19 (1979), 161–9.

[4] Corbett attempted to draw a tentative map of Vulgar Latin spellings as a guide to dating and localization: 'Local variations', pp. 191–3. Confusions of *c:g, p:b, t:d* are universal and are among the earliest to occur, being found in fourth- and fifth-century Italian manuscripts. But he particularly linked the *u:b* confusion with Italy, stating that it was found earliest in southern Italy, and was always commonest there.

[5] Noted as incorrect by the *Appendix Probi* (ed. Foerster, p. 300): '*plebes* non *pleuis*'.

[6] By the seventh century, *x* was not always pronounced, as we can see from Isidore, *Differentiae*, nos. 178 and 182 (PL 83, 9–97, 28–9): 'inter *externum* et *hesternum*. *Hesternum* dicimus pridianum, *externum* autem extraneum, hoc est, alienum' (suggesting a pronunciation /esternum/ for both); and 'inter *exosum* et *odiosum*. *Exosus* dicitur qui aliquam odit, *odiosus*, qui oditur' (suggesting /ezosus/?)

[7] '*ad*, when it is a preposition, has a letter *d*, and when it is a conjunction it has a letter *t*. *Haud*, when it is an adverb of negation, finishes in *d* and has an *h* at the start; when it is the disjunctive conjunction, it is written with a letter *t* and without an *h*' (*Etymologiae* I.xxvii.12).

This explanation makes it quite clear that to Isidore, final *t* and *d* were not phonemically distinct, and that an initial *h* had no particular effect on the spoken sound either. *V* and *b* also fell together in the post-Classical period. The substitution of initial *b* for initial *v*, which we find here in *Bitellius* and *Berus*, is more characteristic of Greek than of Latin writers.[8] The reverse, *v* for *b*, is very rare, and is not found in the *Laterculus*. Intervocalic *b* and *v* are a different matter, and are confused in both directions by many seventh-century writers, for example Isidore: 'inter *uiuit* et *bibit*. *Viuit* de uita, *bibit* de potione.'[9] In England, Aldhelm could be equally confused by *bernaculus* for *vernaculus*. *C* and *g* are also confused in Italian manuscripts of the fourth and fifth centuries, and the confusion is widespread in subsequent centuries.[10]

The writer also has difficulty with vowels. *H* is sometimes supplied when it is not wanted, and absent when it is. *I* and *y* (for Gk. upsilon), *e* and *i*, and *a* and *e* are liable to confusion (e.g., *menime*), but the most common vowel-error is *o* and *u*, giving forms like *nomero*, *Octubrio*, *orbis* (meaning *urbis*), and *pluratus*. In general, though, the writer's spelling is educated in appearance.

This impression of an educated orthography is confirmed on the whole by the low level of aphairesis, prosthetic vowels and syncope.[11]

---

[8] Gratwick, 'Latinitas Britannica', pp. 26–8. The alternative to initial *b* is *ou*, since Greek lacks a consonantal *u* of its own, as in Οὐΐνδικίου (Malalas X.iv, pp. 230–1) for *Vindicii* (*recte* Vinicius, consul in AD 2).

[9] *Differentiae* no. 602 (PL 83, 69).

[10] Corbett, 'Local Variations', pp. 191–3. See also Wright, *Late Latin*, p. 76, who notes that /t/, /k/, /f/, /p/, traditionally spelt *t*, *c*/*qu*, *f*/*ph*, *p*, became in *speech* their voiced counterparts; /t/ > /d/, /k/ > /g/, /f/ > /v/ [p] > [b] by the seventh century. Since the spelling did *not* change, this produced uncertainty and hypercorrection in both directions, e.g. *eglesiae* for *ecclesiae*, against *cloriae* for *gloriae* and *cliscenti* for *gliscenti*, *psalmograve* for *psalmografe*, *nebbotum* for *nepotum*.

[11] Traces of syncope are found in the Insular colloquy *De raris fabulis*: *soldus* for *solidus* (supported by Welsh ⟨swllt⟩ 'shilling', from *[sol'tum] for [sol'dum]: Gratwick, 'Latinitas Britannica', p. 34). On the prosthetic vowel, see Grandgent, *An Introduction to Vulgar Latin*, p. 98, who notes: 'the earliest Latin example is probably *iscolasticus*, written in Barcelona in the second century, it is found repeatedly, though not frequently, in the third century; in the fourth and fifth it is very common: *espiritum*, *ischola*, *iscripta*, *isperabi*' [etc.]. The *Appendix Probi* has 'coruscus non scoriscus', line 161 (ed. Foerster, p. 307). Grammarians took no note of it until the time of Isidore of Seville, in the seventh century. Prosthetic vowels are also found in the Ravenna charters, for example Tjäder, no. XVI (p. 340), line 21: δε σοπρα ισκριπτα (*de suprascripta*). These charters also show a considerable degree of epenthesis, in forms like καρετουλε (*chartule*) and ομενιβως (*omnibus*).

Gaeng[12] noted that aphairesis (*storia* for *historia*) is particularly characteristic of Italian Late Latin: it does appear in this manuscript[13] though not in
the *Laterculus*. Syncope (the disappearance of unstressed syllables, common
in Late and Vulgar Latin) and prosthetic vowels (*i* or *e* added before *sp-* or
sm-) are not found in this manuscript. We find the correct forms *dominus*,
not *domnus*, *populus*, not *poplus*, *spiritus*, not *espiritus*.[14]

The study of the vernacular Latin of seventh-century Italy is made
considerably easier by the survival of a reasonable bulk of non-literary,
bureaucratic Latin, in particular, original charters on papyrus, which have
the extremely valuable feature of preserving a contemporary orthography
uncontaminated by the revisions of medieval copyists. There are nine
private deeds of gift, seven from Ravenna and two from Rome, roughly
contemporary with Archbishop Theodore. They are dated between 600
and 675.[15] These are ordinary business documents with no pretensions to
literary style.[16] Written language is a poor guide to the development of
spoken language since, as Roger Wright reminds us, 'no one is taught to
write without also being taught how to spell. Phonemic (or phonetic)
script does not come automatically to people',[17] and 'it is easier to write
using a system that one has learned than it is to write in a system that one
has not learned, even if the latter is closer to one's vernacular habits'.[18] All
kinds of changes in pronunciation and accidence can be disguised by a
fixed orthography. But there is one small subsection of written evidence
which may provide useful information about speech habits, and that is
writing by people who are using a language other than their own. We are,
as Wright says, taught how to spell. But an inexpert foreigner will tend to

---

[12] *An Inquiry*, pp. 266–7.   [13] See above, n.1.

[14] The *Appendix Probi*, probably a seventh-century text on correct spelling, gives, for
example, 'baculus non uaclus' (ed. Foerster, line 9, p. 294), 'uapulo non baplo' (*ibid.*,
line 215, p. 311). This confirms that the type of mis-spellings avoided by the scribe of
the *Laterculus* were common errors in the seventh century. See C.A. Robson, 'L'Appendix Probi et la philologie latine', *Le moyen âge* 69 (1963), 37–54, who describes it as: 'a
compilation made by a *Scotus* working at Bobbio aimed at written errors common in his
own time ... [whose] standard of correctness was not Classical but contemporary
Visigothic and African Christian Latin' (Gratwick, 'Latinitas Britannica', p. 22).

[15] Tjäder I, nos. XVI–XXIV.

[16] Since the late Roman private deed is the formal ancestor of the Anglo-Saxon charter, the
earliest surviving examples of which emanate from Kent in the age of Theodore, we can
reasonably assume that Theodore was familiar with this class of document.

[17] *Late Latin*, p. 50.   [18] *Ibid.*, p. 129.

manipulate an alien language phonetically, within the terms of the orthographic conventions of his own tongue.[19] An English speaker with a smattering of German who was required to copy a German text from *dictation* would produce a result (possibly all but incomprehensible to a native German) which was highly revealing both of his English phonesis, and the speaker's pronunciation.

The practice in these deeds of gift was for witnesses to make a formal testimony of who they were and what they were witnessing. Thus, the same forty- to fifty-word block of text gets repeated several times in the same document, betraying the spelling-habits of each individual witness.[20] Four of these seventh-century Italian deeds of gift include passages of Latin written in Greek characters, which are revealing in just the sense I described. One such passage was written by a Syrian merchant called Johannes, in Ravenna, *c.* 600.[21] It is a private deed of gift; Sisivera, a Gothic freedwoman, gives a part of the *Fundus Balonianus* to the church of Ravenna.

Ιαννης, σουρος ναγουζατρο, ουεικι καρετουλε δωναζι[..]νε πορεζονε ειν ιντεγρω φονδι σς. βαλονιανι κον ωμενιβως αδ σε γενεραλιτερ περτινεντιβους, σικοδ σουπεριος λεγετορ, φακτε εν σανκτα εκκ. Ραβινατε α σστα Σισιβερα h. φ. δωνατρικι, κουαε με πρεσεντε σιγνουμ σανκτε χουκεσ φικετ, εδ κοραμ νοβις ει ρελικτα εστ, τηστης σουσκριπση, εδ δε κονσερβανδις ομνιβος σστισ αδ ευανγελια χορποραλιτερ πρεβουητ σακραμεντα, ετ ανκ δωναζιονεμ α σστα Σισιβερα Παλομβο β. β. διακονον βικεδωμενον τραδε[. . .] βιδι.[22]

---

[19] For example, Kenneth Jackson recalled acting as a censor for troops' mail during the last war. One letter which went from hand to hand as composed in an unidentifiable language proved, as he suddenly realized, to have been written phonetically in English by an Italian, literate in Italian, but not in English. He gave as an example of this man's orthography the spelling *ciorcio* for *church*. K. H. Jackson, 'Some Questions in Dispute About Early Welsh Literature and Language', *Studia Celtica* 8/9 (1973–4), 1–32, at 22.

[20] See for example *ChLA* IV, no. 240 (Manchester, John Rylands Library Lat. 1; Tjäder, no. XVI) and XXII, no. 718 (Vatican, Pap. Lat. 16; Tjäder, no. XVIII/XIX) which clearly show the different hands.

[21] Tjäder, no. XX, lines 83–9 (p. 350).

[22] The text may be transliterated as follows: 'Ioannes, Syrus negotiator, huic chartule donationis portionis in integro fundi suprascripti Baloniani cum omnibus ad se generaliter pertinentibus, sicut superius legitur, facte in sancta ecclesia Rauennate a suprascripta Sisiuera honesta femina donatrice, que me presente signum sancte crucis fecit, et coram nobis ei relicta est, testis suscripsi, et de conseruandis omnibus suprascriptis ad euangelia corporaliter praebuit sacramenta, et hanc donationem a suprascripta Sisiuera Palumbo uir uenerabilis diacono uicedomeno, traditam uidi.'

One example of a variation from Latin orthographic norms which probably has to do with the difference between Greek and Latin phonemes, is that Latin *ti*, /tsi/, is represented by Greek ζ, perhaps /dz/, in ναγουζατρο in the passage above, and Γαυζιοζο (*Gaudioso*) in Tjäder's XXIV, line 13. But some of the errors made in these Ravenna deeds seem highly significant for the Latinity of the *Laterculus*. Note, in the deposition of Johannes the Syrian, that β is used for both *b* and *v* (this is also found in the parallel Latin depositions). *T* and *d* are easily confused in final position (σικοδ: *sicut*), even in verbs (XXIV, line 16, σουσκριψιδ: *suscripsit*). *C* and *g* are sometimes, though not often, confused (XXIV, line 11, νεγ: *nec*; XVI, line 41, σιγκουμ: *sicut*). Another particularly interesting spelling is in XVI, line 31, μαιεστρο μιλιτουμ for *magistro militum*, which looks like the opposite resolution of a falling-together of *g* and consonantal *i* to the *Laterculus*'s *magestas* for *maiestas*. As far as the vowels are concerned, the Greek confirms the hint given by the Latin of the Ravenna deeds, that *o* and *u*, both long and short, were not distinguished from each other aurally, and that *i* and *e* were equally subject to confusion.

MORPHOLOGY AND SYNTAX

There is also much of interest in the syntax and morphology of the *Laterculus*. Mai's comments in his introduction to the *editio prima* were severe:

quamuis codex littera Romana quadrata scriptus, ad saeculum circiter octauum referendus sit, nihilominus Latinitas ualde squalet, imo, ut certe nunc in codice legitur, soloecismis innumeris et incredibili mendositate laborat.[23]

The language of the Ravenna deeds mentioned in the previous section has been exhaustively analysed by C.M. Carlton, and his conclusions are relevant to the morphology of the *Laterculus*.[24] He notes a number of characteristic features of their Latin; for example, confusion of *o*, long and short, with *u*, long and short, *b* and *v*, uncertainty about the positioning of *h*, the use of *f* for *ph*, especially in words of Greek origin, an extremely

---

[23] A. Mai, repr. in PL 94, 1161. 'Although this is a book written in square Roman script, and should be dated around the eighth century, for all that the Latinity is very bad, it is burdened with incredible falsities and innumerable solecisms, as certainly is read now in the book.'

[24] Carlton, *A Linguistic Analysis*.

frequent loss of final *m*, which he describes as 'probably the single most characteristic phonological feature of popular Latin'.[25] Other phonological features noted by Carlton include the erratic and haphazard *addition* of unnecessary final *m*, particularly in late sixth- and seventh-century texts;[26] voicing of /c/ to /g/ before liquids (as with the *Laterculus*, 'Magrinus') and weakness of final *t* and *d* (though the correct usage of *t* and *d* is conservative in other positions) are other symptoms of popular Latin.[27] He also notes a tendency to the loss of final *s*, which we see dramatically in the deposition of Joannes the Syrian (πορεζονε, etc.), the simplification of geminate consonants and the gemination of simples, most commonly in intervocalic position (pp. 175–8). All these features of the Ravenna legal documents are characteristic to some extent of the *Laterculus*. All of them, in their various ways, represent a movement away from the orthographic norms of Classical Latin into a more relaxed orthography influenced by spoken Latin. But Carlton goes on to focus on an aspect of his texts which shows the opposite tendency, etymological recomposition: *adfines, adlegare, inplore, conlocante, conpraehensam*.[28] He comments, 'the preoccupation with etymology, which often yields forms which resemble those of pre-Classical Latin, is one of the earmarks [*sic*] of Vulgar Latin texts'.[29] This tendency towards recomposition is also highly characteristic of the *Laterculus*.[30] Carlton's evidence led him to suggest that 'there once existed a kind of uniform written Vulgar Latin, paralleling and in many respects similar to Classical Latin',[31] adding that it seemed to be a less rigidly consistent phenomenon than Classical Latin, but was nonetheless, as he says, 'subject to a finite number of possible variations.' The practice of recomposition in particular smacks of an artificial and conventional orthographic code. *Laterculus Malalianus* seems to have been written in something very like the humble, workaday lawyer's Latin described by Carlton, and obeys the same rules.

[25] *Ibid*, p. 137, and see J. Pirson, *La langue des inscriptions latines de la Gaule* (Paris, 1901), p. 100. Cf. also the frequently incorrect treatment of final *m* in the Bobbio Missal (ed. Lowe III, 93).

[26] *Ibid*., pp. 139 and 144.

[27] Also true of the *Laterculus*, for example *inquid*, ch. 4.

[28] Carlton, *Linguistic Analysis*, pp. 183–5.   [29] *Ibid.*, p. 184.

[30] It is also surprisingly common in the Bobbio Missal: see *Bobbio Missal*, ed. Lowe *et al.* III, 93: 'in a manuscript full of corrupt spellings, it is curious to encounter so many unassimilated forms of the verb'.

[31] Carlton, *Linguistic Analysis*, p. 241.

There are three aspects of the morphology of the *Laterculus* which shed light on the nature of its Latinity: the treatment of prepositions, non-Classical sentence-structures and the rules of concord. I will begin by looking at the use of prepositions in the *Laterculus*, and possible contexts for it. The author's practice is not internally consistent. As a statistical average of all prepositions, he is wrong, according to the Classical rules of usage, about one time in five. Of the commonest prepositions, *in* is used correctly 111 times, wrongly twenty-five times, *a* or *ab* is used rightly fifty-six times, wrongly six times. On the whole, his prepositions are apparently distributed promiscuously between accusative and ablative, but, on a single occasion in each case, *secundum* and *de* take a genitive, and *secundum*, *per*, *sub* and *cum* take a nominative. In six of the twenty-seven times it appears, *per* is used with the ablative, and *de* takes an accusative four out of the twenty-one times it is used. We twice find *in* + abl. meaning 'into', in a near-quotation from the Bible, which itself uses *in* + acc. in all versions (ch. 1). He three times uses *de* + acc., *de puerum* (ch. 6), *de fructum* (ch. 14) and *de diem* (ch. 24). The last example is particularly heinous, since he is quoting Matth. XIV.35 and produces *de diem autem illa*, not even *de diem ... illam*. When we ask *why* our learned author is perpetrating these howlers, one answer which comes to my mind is that he was more or less indifferent to correct usage. In this context, it may be useful to quote a familiar remark by a sixth-century Roman writer, Gregory the Great:

nam sicut huius quoque epistolae tenor enuntiat, non metacismi collisionem fugio, non barbarismi confusionem deuito, *situs modosque et praepositionum casus seruare contemno*, quia indignum uehementer existimo, ut uerba caelestis oraculi restringam sub regulis Donati.[32]

The context of Gregory's remarks is a discussion of the irregularities of the Latin Bible, but his words seem to suggest that the proper deployment of prepositions had become something that no longer came naturally, but had to be learned by educated people. Another sixth-century writer, Cassiodorus, remarked helpfully:

---

[32] *Registrum Epistolarum* I.v.53 (MGH, *Epistolae* I, ed P. Ewald and L.M. Hartmann (Berlin, 1887–99), 357): 'For just as the tone of this letter makes clear, I do not avoid collisions of motacism, or confusion of barbarisms, *and I despise the observance of the position, force, or government of prepositions*. For I account it very unseemly to submit the words of the Divine Oracle to the rules of Donatus.'

In uerbis quae accusatiuis et ablatiuis praepositionibus seruiunt, situm motumque diligenter obserua, quoniam librarii grammaticae artis experte ibi maxime probantur errare. Nam si *m* litteram inconuenienter addas aut demas, dictio tota confusa est.[33]

Cassiodorus seems to be speaking in terms of a *visual* rule of adding or omitting an *m*, rather than a difference that is heard or otherwise perceived. The evidence of the Visigothic liturgy, created in the seventh century (which of course is more relevant to the development of Spanish than that of Italian), is that prepositions which used to take the ablative have come to take the accusative.[34] Further support to the idea that the correct use of prepositions was becoming confused in the seventh century is given by Carlotta Dionisotti, commenting on Bede's grammatical activities,[35] who tells us that Bede excerpted from his grammatical sources mainly sections listing anomalies:

the one exception only reinforces the point, substantial excerpts from a chapter on prepositions;[36] notoriously an area of Latin that had changed greatly by Bede's day, in which even the basic rules were now matters worthy of note.

Prepositions aside, the whole text of the *Laterculus* is distinguished by a non-Classical attitude towards Latin grammar. There are several sentences in which both the obvious subject and some other word or words are in the nominative, for example a long sentence in ch. 1, in which the subject of the verb appears to be *dies* (which, by the way, is masculine here, and feminine elsewhere in the text), but *lux uera* also appears in the nominative. The rules of concord are sometimes flouted, as for example in ch. 17, where we find 'pectore *uirgo, decora* in omni membro, iamque *maturam*', as a string of qualifiers for *coniugem*. Similarly, 'coram Deo et homines' is

---

[33] *Institutiones* XV.9 (PL 70, 1105–50, at 1128): 'In cases where words can be either in the accusative or the ablative case after prepositions, look carefully to see if it is place or motion, because copyists who do not know their grammar are particularly liable to get this wrong. For if you put on or take off a letter *m* inappropriately, the whole phrase gets muddled.'

[34] Wright, *Late Latin*, p. 75: 'We know that Spanish nouns normally derive from the accusative form of the original etymon; that the accusative was probably the only surviving form even as early as this [s. vii] can be seen by the way that prepositions which once required other cases take accusatives in the liturgy: e.g. *de insidias* (*Ord.* 240.1) rather than *de insidiis*.'

[35] 'On Bede, Grammars and Greek', p. 117.

[36] *De orthographia*, lines 67–78, 543–9, 813–20 and 998–1018, sourced by K. Barwick, *Remmius Palaemon und die römische 'Ars Grammatica'* (Leipzig, 1922), pp. 30–1.

evidently intended as a unit, and so is 'ascenderunt Ioseph et Mariam'. Rather spectacularly, we have the clause 'dum Deus pater in *uoce*, filius in *hominem*, spiritus sanctus in *columbe speciae*' (ch. 18), in which *in* appears to take a different case on each of its three appearances, despite the triadic structure.[37] Singular and plural subjects are an occasional source of confusion, and we also find nominative absolute constructions.[38]

There are other features of the author's usage which are common to the less formal Latin writers of the sixth and seventh centuries. Vulgar Latin tends to replace the future with the present,[39] which we find in the *Laterculus* in the phrase 'quando non latet quod nunc latet'.[40] In informal Latin, the use of *quia* is considerably extended. The accusative and infinitive construction is replaced by noun clauses introduced by *quia*, as in 'dixi quia mustella comedit': 'I said the cat had eaten it', found as early as Petronius, and in the *Laterculus*.[41] *Quia* is also used for *quod* in Late Latin,[42] and this is an occasional feature of the *Laterculus*, as, for example, 'Dixerunt quia: "quae optulimus munera..."', etc. (ch. 6). Another Late Latin characteristic is the use of *dum* for *cum*, used in the *Laterculus*'s 'reparante auctore Deo *dum* generat' (ch. 16), and paralleled in the translation of Theodore of Mopsuestia's exegesis of the Pauline Epistles; for example, '*dum* Herodes legisperitos interrogaret, respondent ei...',[43] and elsewhere. McNally's researches into one of the Hiberno-Latin texts in Pal.

---

[37] It may, on the other hand, take only two, since *-ae* and *-e* are interchangeable.

[38] F. Stolz, *Lateinische Grammatik: Laut- und Formenlehre: Syntax und Stilistik*, 5th ed. (Munich, 1928), p. 450, noted that nominative absolutes are used by such early Christian writers as Lucifer of Cagliari and Egeria. P. Taylor, *The Latinity of the Liber Historiae Francorum* (New York, 1934), p. 98, found eighteen nominative absolute clauses in the *Historia Francorum*.

[39] Grandgent, *Vulgar Latin*, p. 56, and see also J.N. Adams, *The Vulgar Latin of Claudius Terentianus* (Manchester, 1977), p. 49, where he notes that this is often found in the context of quotation of direct speech, and occurs in the colloquial Latin of *Peregrinatio Egeriae*.

[40] This development is also found in sixth- and seventh-century Greek, for example in the *Pratum Spirituale* of John Moschus, described by Browning as 'an example of the actual state of the language'. See R. Browning, *Medieval and Modern Greek*, 2nd ed. (Cambridge, 1983), p. 35: 'the usual expression of futurity is the present indicative'.

[41] In ch. 2, 'Superius enim ait quia ... conceptus est dominus in utero uirginum.' See Palmer, *The Latin Language*, p. 152, where he quotes this usage from *Cena Trimalchionis*.

[42] Grandgent, *Vulgar Latin*, p. 73 (§ 168).

[43] *In Epistola ad Galatos* III.24 (ed. Swete I, 54); cf. also Ps. LXXV.10, '*dum* resurget'.

lat. 277 have already been mentioned in the context of orthography. With respect to morphology, he found that 'in the use of prepositions there is a pronounced disregard for the grammatical case of its object', and that adjectival agreement, and correct case usage, were also frequently disregarded.

The author of the *Laterculus* was sufficiently in control of written Latin to enjoy Latin poetry, as his fondness for Caelius Sedulius bears witness, and it seems probable that he was a fluent speaker of Latin as it was spoken in seventh-century Rome. His orthographic errors, which I described in some detail, suggest to me a person for whom a number of Classical distinctions, orthographic and syntactic, have never become relevant, though other interpretations are doubtless possible. But although he can express himself quite clearly, and at times forcibly, he is not accurate in his manipulation of the Latin case-system. The reason may lie in the nature of seventh-century spoken Latin. Grandgent, in his *Vulgar Latin*, says:

By the end of the Vulgar Latin period, there probably remained in really popular use (aside from pronouns and a number of set formulas) in Dacia only three cases, in the rest of the empire only two – a nominative and an accusative-ablative. Clerics, however, naturally tried to write in accordance with their idea of correct Latin.[44]

Grandgent, of course, was writing about the turn of the century. More recent writers on this murky issue do not seem inclined to commit themselves with such magisterial confidence. It is obvious to anyone that Latin words, in their transformation into French, Spanish and Italian, must at some point have lost their case-endings, but it is far from clear exactly when this happened, or how long it took. Roger Wright has some comments on this, in connection with the non-literary language of the law:

Sabatini's analysis of legal documents compiled in Early Romance Europe has shown that outside the formulaic sections of those documents the case system tends to break down, with the cases being used as they were in the local vernacular. That is, Italian scribes use the original nominative form, scribes in Spain use the original accusative form, scribes in France usually use only the nominative and their 'oblique' case, whatever the syntax. For more literary genres, more 'correct' morphology was required, and apparently taught. The practical question in writing the old morphology may well have involved such matters as

[44] Grandgent, *Vulgar Latin*, p. 48 (§ 100).

when to insert a silent 'bu' into plural nouns such as MENSIBUS (i.e. into Spanish vernacular *meses* ⟨MENSES⟩)[45] comparable to the problem of whether or not to insert a silent *n* into the same word.[46]

The Politzers' book on Romance trends in seventh- and eighth-century north Italian comments on the disappearance of final /m/.[47] In the first declension, for example, the *-am* ending is often replaced by *-a*, since the *m* no longer carried any phonological or morphological significance.[48] This produces clauses like 'contra hanc pagina' where *pagina* is functioning as an accusative. There are many examples in Tjäder, for instance, αυκ [καρτυ]λαμ ποσιτα σουπερ σανκτα ευανγελια . . .; *rogatus a suprascripta Gaudiosum* . . .[49] Loss of final *m* in this way would go a long way towards explaining the apparent breaks of concord in the *Laterculus*; for instance, the apparently incorrect use of prepositions. The fact that in the singular, the difference between the two is frequently the presence or absence of an *m*, may shed light on some of these errors. The author of the *Laterculus*, as we would hope, can make a rather better shot at a Latin sentence than a seventh-century notary, but I suggest that he has essentially the same problem, as Roger Wright diagnosed it, which is that the Latin orthography he learned to write was markedly different from the pronunciation of the Latin he spoke.

STYLE

The style of the *Laterculus* can briefly be characterized as homiletic and informal. With the exception of the preface, where the author launches boldly, and on the whole disastrously, into Aldhelmian *garrulosa uerbositas*, the sentences are mostly short, there is a tendency towards a paratactic

---

[45] He means that the once-significant distinctions of Latin syntax had become purely orthographic, like English *hole/whole*, or *jam/jamb*, or (a more direct parallel) French *chante*, *chantes*, *chantent*, which are all pronounced the same.

[46] Wright, *Late Latin*, p. 42.

[47] This is also found, for example, in the Bobbio Missal, on which see Lowe, *The Bobbio Missal* III, 111.

[48] F.N. and R.L. Politzer, *Romance Trends in Seventh and Eighth-Century Latin Documents* (Chapel Hill, NC, 1953), p. 16. Note also *Appendix Probi*, ed. Foerster, p. 311, 'numquam non numqua' (line 219), 'pridem non pride' (line 223), 'olim non oli' (line 224).

[49] Tjäder, no. XXIV, lines 17–18 and 26 (p. 374): Ravenna, *c.* 650. Private deed of gift, Gaudiosus, a *defensor* of the Ravenna church, gives it a garden in the city.

construction with long chains of *et . . . et . . .*, an avoidance of elaborate adjectives, flowery phrases, simile and metaphor (other than the strictly biblical), and in general, a pronounced air of *sermo humilis*. The lengthy and intricate sentence with which he opens his work is immediately reminiscent of the style of Aldhelm, with its combination of interlace and an elaborate metaphor on light versus darkness. There is an occasional tendency towards *variatio*, but the style is essentially didactic. First and second person plural are used for emphasis on occasion, to intensify the sense of relevance.

The elements of conscious stylistic ornamentation in the *Laterculus* include the occasional use of grecisms, such as *baselica*, *pelagus* (ch. 21) and *parasceue* (ch. 10), and a more or less self-consciously poetic element. His turn of phrase is occasionally influenced by Latin poetry: Mommsen noted eight phrases reminiscent either of Vergil or, more probably, of Faltonia Proba. The author of the *Laterculus* also has a taste for alliteration, as in *ut sanctorum omnium sepultura sanciret* . . . which is visible throughout his text. He makes an occasional somewhat poetic use of interlace, for example *capitulum rationis protulerunt testimonium ueritatis* (ch. 12), though this is not frequent.

Paradoxically, it is the unpolished character and generally crude Latinity of the *Laterculus* which suggest that it was written by Theodore rather than his pupils. It is the work of a man who is immensely learned and has a considerable gift for communication, but who is indifferent to the rules. These are more comprehensible characteristics for Theodore himself than for Canterbury students, especially since the demonstrable connexion of the author's Latinity with sub-literary Late Latin suggests firmly that his Latin was learned as a living language and not as a 'dead' one.

The *Laterculus* offers the curious spectacle of a writer who can almost always convey without much difficulty what he wants to say (except in the Preface, where the attempt at magniloquence combined with minimal content produces an almost meaningless result), except that one must, as it were, translate the sense rather than the words. It is both pithy and learned, marked throughout with the stamp of a strong and individual intelligence, and yet impatient of certain kinds of detail apparently of little significance to the writer – these not only include Latin syntax, but also scientific chronography. One might take this as a sign of haste in the composition, or of the writer's complete unconcern.

7

Translational technique of the *Laterculus*

Another major aspect of the Latinity of the *Laterculus* which has not yet been discussed is the author's aims and methods in translation from Greek. His work must be set against a background of the concepts of translation and paraphrase relevant to the early medieval west, and in particular, illuminated by the use of Greek in the monastic and papal circles of Rome.[1]

The first impression which one gets from the Malalas translation in the *Laterculus* is that it is appallingly literal. Insofar as the *Laterculus* is based on Malalas's *Chronographia*, it sticks close to its source, though the author felt free to interpolate additional material. His translation technique is not consistent. Some sentences are recast into a Latinate form, within the limitations of his grasp of the language. Others translate whole clauses word by word, keeping the original cases, and producing a result which is effectively a compromise between the two languages. Features of Greek syntax, such as genitive absolute clauses, are taken over completely unchanged from the *Chronographia* to the *Laterculus*. Several curious phrases in the Malalian sections of the *Laterculus* can be explained by looking at the Greek. The un-Latin phrase *ex consolibus* for *exconsule*, an ex-consul, is a Latin calque on Greek ἀπὸ ὑπάτων, and the phrase 'ut Moyses . . . exposuit in suis monumentis' (ch. 3) becomes explicable when we see that Malalas's phrase is ἐν τοῖς ὑπομνήμασιν, and that the meaning of ὑπόμνημα is basically 'memorial, memorandum', though it also embraces the meanings 'treatise' and 'commentary'. This seems to be a small slip by a Greek-speaker who has not quite realized the area of meaning covered by his chosen Latin word. In ch. 6, the phrase 'per aliam

[1] Classical and late antique translations are discussed by Brock, 'Aspects of Translation Technique in Antiquity'.

uiam limitis regressi sunt' is considerably clarified by the Greek δι' ἄλλης ὁδοῦ τῆς τοῦ λιμίτου, that is, 'by another road, by the border'. The Latin genitive *limitis* is explained by the Greek genitive. We also occasionally find Greek genitive absolute phrases translated by Latin genitive absolutes, such as 'sanctorum apostolorum uidentium' and 'sanctorum angelorum dicentium' (ch. 11), translating τῶν ἁγίων ἀπόστολων ὁρώντων and καὶ τῶν ἁγίων ἀγγέλων λεγόντων. But this is not invariable. Later in the same section, a nominative absolute phrase, 'agens in presidatum in Iudaea idem Pontius Pilatus', translates a Greek genitive absolute (ἡγεμονεύοντος τῆς Ἰουδαίας τοῦ αὐτοῦ Ποντίου Πιλάτου). The following three passages are further examples of word by word translation in the first half of the *Laterculus*.

ch. 3: ἀπὸ Ἀδὰμ ἕως τοῦ Φαλὲκ, υἱοῦ Ἑβερ. . .
ab Adam usque a Phalech, fili Eber. . .

ch. 3: καὶ ὑπέπεσε τῇ ἁμαρτίᾳ ὁ ἄνθρωπος
et cecidit sub peccato homo

ch. 4: κατὰ τὸν ἀριθμὸν τῶν ἕξ ἡμερῶν τῆς πλάσεως τοῦ Ἀδαμ
secundum numerum sex dierum plasmationis Adae.

However, it must be noted that this absolutely literal translation is not followed through the Malalian sections of the *Laterculus* as a consistent principle; some sentences are more Latinate than others, though it is fair to say that the translation is always close.

The translation techniques used in the *Laterculus* must be viewed in their appropriate context. There were many Greek monks in Rome and, furthermore, there was a fair amount of translation going on. The *acta*, or minutes, of the Lateran Council of 649, for example, were produced simultaneously in Greek and Latin. But the most important centre for the purposes of this discussion is not the Vatican secretariat, but the monastery of Tre Fontane, or St Anastasius *ad aquas Saluias*, one of the three important Greek monasteries in seventh-century Rome.[2] There are a number of reasons for suggesting that the work of this community may be relevant to the *Laterculus*. It housed a community of Cilicians under their abbot, George, who put their weight behind the pope and against the emperor in the politico-theological battle known as the monothelete controversy. Theodore was, of course, from Tarsus in Cilicia, and it is not

---

[2] Discussed by Ferrari, *Early Roman Monasteries*, pp. 33–48.

only possible, but probable, that Tre Fontane was his monastery.[3] The monks of Tre Fontane brought with them to Rome the head of their patron saint, Anastasius, who was martyred by the Persians in 628, and they quite quickly set about the delicate business of transferring the cult of this saint to Rome, a city which of course was absolutely crammed with home-grown saints of its own. An immediate result of this was, naturally enough, a flurry of literary activity. These Greek monks produced a translation of the *passio* of Anastasius,[4] originally composed (in Greek) in 630. This is how it is described by Paul Meyvaert:

> The Latin follows the Greek word order, line after line. The translation is replete with shortcomings: choice of the wrong word to render the Greek meaning,[5] and an almost total neglect of Latin grammar, syntax and idiom, resulting here and there in statements that remain unintelligible to anyone who is unable to refer back to the original Greek.[6]

Meyvaert further noted that this version of the *passio* was in Northumbria by the beginning of the eighth century, because it was rewritten into more correct Latin by Bede, who described it trenchantly as 'librum uitae et passionis sancti Anastasii, male de greco translatum et peius a quodam inperito emendatum'.[7] What this original version of the *passio* demonstrates is that it was possible for a seventh-century Greek-speaker active in Rome to be satisfied with producing 'translations' from Greek to Latin which made only the most minimal concessions to the characteristics of the latter language. The cult of Anastasius, supported by an important relic (his head), was successfully established in Rome, and there are several later texts which refer to the monastery. Meyvaert says, 'the veneration of this relic by pilgrims coming from all over the west must have prompted the desire to provide a Latin version which would tell the story of the Persian monk's conversion and death.'[8] It seems to me interesting that the obviously inadequate Latin text of the *passio*, for all the shudders it evoked

---

[3] See Lapidge, in *Biblical Commentaries*, ed Bischoff and Lapidge, pp. 68–9.

[4] *Passio S. Anastasii*, *BHG*, no. 84 and *BHL*, no. 410b. The latter is preserved in Turin, Biblioteca nazionale, F. III. 16, fols. 14–23, a former Bobbio manuscript of the tenth century.

[5] Examples are μεγαλοδορεὰν, 'magnale donum', ἐπίνοιαν, 'concinnationem'. Cf. the *Laterculus* (ch. 3), ὑπομνήμασιν, 'monumentis'.

[6] Meyvaert and Franklin, 'Bede's Version', p. 380.

[7] Bede, *Historia ecclesiastica* V.24 (ed. Colgrave and Mynors, pp. 568–70).

[8] 'Bede's Version', pp. 383–4.

in Bede's sophisticated mind, seems to have been thoroughly successful in its avowed intention of putting St Anastasius and his monastery firmly on the pilgrim's map of important holy sites in Rome, since the monastery is mentioned in *De locis sanctis martyrum quae sunt foris ciuitatis Romae*, probably written between 635 and 645.[9]

The Latin translation of the *Passio S. Anastasii* on which Bede based his version may be directly compared with the *Laterculus*.[10] Its method of completely literal translation is immediately reminiscent of the Malalian sections of the *Laterculus*:[11]

καὶ ὁ ἅγιος ἀπεκρινατο·	Et sanctus martyr respondit
Ὅτι μὲν ἐσταυρώθη	quam quidem crucifixus est
ἑκούσιος ὑπὸ Ἰουδαίων	sponte a Iudeis
ἀληθῶς λέγεις·	uerum dicis
αὐτὸς δὲ ἐστὶν	Ipse autem est
ὁ ποιήσας τὸν οὐρανὸν καὶ	qui fecit caelum et
τὴν γῆν καὶ πάντα τὰ ἐν αὐτοῖς	terram mare et omnia quae in eis sunt
καὶ εὐδόκησεν κατελθεῖν	et noluit descendere
ἐπὶ τῆς γῆς	super terram
καὶ ἐνανθρωπῆται καὶ	et humanari et crucifigi
σταυρωθῆναι	
ἵνα ἐλευθερώσῃ τὸ τῶν	ut liberaret genus humanum
ἀνθρώπων γένος	

Meyvaert noted that the author of this translation betrays a close acquaintance with the churches of seventh-century Rome. It does not seem to me impossible that this translation might also be Theodore's work, but the supposition is not necessary. What it does demonstrate quite clearly is that in the Greek circles of seventh-century Rome, Latinity was not always cultivated to a high standard even by those who were seeking to interact with the Latin-speaking community. It makes Theodore's indifference to the case governed by Latin prepositions look more comprehensible and less scandalous.

I have suggested that the monastery of St Anastasius in Rome must be at the least very close to the milieu in which Theodore of Tarsus lived and worked before he came to Canterbury. Meyvaert's discussion of the *passio* shows that a contemporary monk at St Anastasius took the same approach

---

[9] *Itineraria*, ed. Geyer, p. 316, n. 6.   [10] Meyvaert and Franklin, 'Bede's Version'.
[11] *Ibid.*, p. 380.

to the translation of Greek that we find in the *Laterculus*. We can add to this a further insight into the culture of St Anastasius, a text called *Miraculum S. Anastasii*, also written by a monk of St Anastasius,[12] in 712, but an original composition in Latin. Its Latinity has the same un-Classical characteristics as the *Laterculus* (though the style is considerably more flowery), with *dum* used for *cum* (ch. 2), nominative absolutes (ch. 2) and occasional errors of syntax,[13] as well as a similar tendency to use markedly anomalous versions of Latin Bible-texts.[14] The *Miraculum S. Anastasii* is also comparable with the *Laterculus* in other respects. It dates the events of the text by using the year of the emperor and the year of the pope, and uses a number of grecisms (such as *mansio*, meaning 'church', *cynophagus* and *thimiama*).[15] The cases following prepositions show the same indifferent attitude to ablative and accusative that we find in the *Laterculus*, and it is also carelessly composed, though quite comprehensible. We are used, thinking about translation, to accepting the dictum of Jerome, so often quoted, that one ought to translate sense by sense, not word by word;[16] and of course many late antique and early medieval texts, from Jerome's Vulgate itself and Rufinus's translation of Eusebius's *Historia ecclesiastica*, do just that. But there is an alternative trend in early medieval translation, though we tend not to think of it as such, which is glossing; that is, writing word-by-word equivalents over the words of the original texts, as a tenth-century Northumbrian called Aldred did, for instance, in the Lindisfarne gospels (*c.* 960).[17] This approach to the text probably has its origins in the techniques evolved for translating the Bible. It is a method which seems more closely related to the translation technique used in the *passio* and, though less extremely, in the *Laterculus*. It is an indirect but

---

[12] 'Miraculum S. Anastasii'.

[13] For example 'et assumens filiam suam *habens* spiritum immundum'.

[14] For example, 'quaerite et inuenietis, petite *et accipietis*' (Luke IX.3, cited in ch. 7) for 'petite et dabitur uobis, quaerite et inuenietis'; and '*non periet capillus* de capite uestro' (Luke XXI.18, cited in ch. 9) for 'et capillus de capite uestro non peribit'. This writer, like the author of the *Laterculus*, uses Psalms 'iuxta LXX'.

[15] Note the phrase in ch. 11, 'O pastor bonus, quem parua echo (*var.* econ) laudemus'.

[16] PL 22, 568–79, at 571: 'non uerbum e uerbo, sed sensum exprimere de sensu'.

[17] A.S.C. Ross, 'A Connection Between Bede and the Anglo-Saxon Gloss to the Lindis-farne Gospels?', *JTS* ns 20 (1969), 482–94, at 493, says 'surely then what Bede was doing when he was translating was making a word-for-word gloss'. He notes also that the 'translation' was achieved, as the *Epistola* tells us, by dictating to a second party, who wrote down Bede's words.

powerful statement of the primacy of the original text over the independence of the version. The monastery of St Anastasius was by no means
unique in taking this approach to the translation of Greek. For instance,
the original Latin translation of the *uita* of Pelagia the Harlot (or: Penitent)
follows the Greek word by word.[18] In short, the evidence that I have seen
so far suggests that the translation from Malalas in the *Laterculus* appears to
be of a standard acceptable to the majority of the writer's contemporaries,
however much it might wound the sensibilities of an accomplished
Latinist, whether in the seventh century or the twentieth.

Brock has pointed out that the distinction between mere translation and
literary translation is known to both Cicero and Horace. Cicero in his *De
optimo genere oratorum*, ch. 14, notes: 'nec conuerti ut interpres, sed ut
orator' ('do not translate like an interpreter, but as an orator').[19] In the
fourth century, Jerome similarly distinguishes between an *interpres* who
merely translates words, and an *expositor* who translates ideas.[20] Gregory of
Tours describes a two-stage process of translation rather fully, using the
word *interpretatio* in the meaning already established for it by these earlier
writers. In his *De gloria martyrum*, he informs us that he was assisted by a
Syrian called John in translating the Passion of the Seven Sleepers of
Ephesus (whether from Greek or Syriac, he does not say): 'quod passio
eorum, quam Siro quodam interpretante in Latino transtulimus, plenius
prodit.'[21] We have here a dual activity. First *interpretatio* – which probably
means that John the Syrian turned the original text word-by-word into
Latin, without bothering about the literary qualities of this 'crib', then
translatio, performed by Gregory on this rough version, in which, having
grasped the sense, he turned it into intelligible Latin.[22] It is clear from the
context of Greek activity at Rome, notably the *Passio S. Anastasii*, that
interpretatio, or word-by-word translation, could and sometimes did stand

---

[18] *Pélagie la Pénitente: métamorphoses d'une légende*, I. *Les Textes et leur histoire*, ed. P. Petit-
mengin *et al.* (Paris, 1981). The original Latin translation is edited by François
Dolbeau, pp. 161–249, and is a word-for-word rendering of the original. Dolbeau
thinks it was made in the pre-Carolingian period, though he does not commit himself
to any particular century.

[19] Cicero, *Rhetorica*, ed. A.S. Wilkins, 2 vols. (Oxford, 1902–3), *De optimo genere oratorum*
(no page-numbers) 5.14; Brock, 'Aspects of Translation', p. 69.

[20] Jerome, *Epistola* lvii (PL 22, 568–79, at 571).

[21] Gregory of Tours, *De gloria martyrum*, ch. 94 (ed. Arndt and Krusch, pp. 484–561, at
550–2).

[22] See Le Bordellès, *L'Aratus Latinus*, p. 125.

on its own. But there is also the possibility, in such cases, that the *interpretatio* was *intended* to provide the basis for reworking by an accomplished Latinist such as this text ultimately received at the hands of Bede. All I would argue for in the case of the *Laterculus* is that there is reason to suggest that, in a classroom context, *interpretatio* might be held to be sufficient by a fundamentally Hellenophone scholar, forming as it did an adequate basis for analysis and discussion of the meaning of the text. Brock comments on literal translation in general,

The choice of the literal approach for school texts requires no comment. The bilingual Virgil papyri served the same purpose as schoolboy cribs and the more sophisticated, highly literal Latin translations employed today by some Orientalists.[23]

What this suggests about the *Laterculus* is that its translational technique is appropriate, especially if it was actually used for teaching Greek as well as Christian Roman history.

[23] Brock, 'Aspects of Translation Technique in Antiquity', p. 73.

8

Manuscripts

The *Laterculus* is preserved in two manuscripts, one in the Vatican, the other in Leiden. Since the Vatican manuscript is the most important, I begin with it.

VATICAN CITY, BIBLIOTECA APOSTOLICA VATICANA,
PAL. LAT. 277

The Vatican manuscript is apparently composite, consisting of two parts: Part I (fols. 1–93), written in uncial script, and II (fols. 94–115), written in minuscule.[1] It is Part I which includes *Laterculus Malalianus*. The size of the manuscript is 222 x 154 mm. There are thirteen quires in Part I, the first eleven having eight folios, and the last two having only four. Part II consists of four quires, the first two of eight folios, the last two of four folios. There are no quire signatures in the manuscript. The codicological distinction between Part I and Part II is revealed by the different methods used for preparing the parchment. In Part I, the ruling is guided by slits, vertical in some quires (e.g. Quire IX) and horizontal in others (e.g. Quire IV). These sheets were ruled on the hair side, two or three sheets at a time. In Part II, on the other hand, the ruling is guided by pinpricks, and the sheets ruled four at a time – that is to say, quire by quire. The precise quiring of Part I may be set out as follows:

I^8 (fols. 1–8), II^8 (fols. 9–16), III^8 (fols. 17–24), IV^8 (fols. 25–32), V^8 (fols.

---

[1] Vat. Pal. lat. 277 is illustrated in *CLA* I, no. 91. I owe the description and collation of Pal. lat. 277 to Michael Lapidge.

33–40), VI⁸ (fols. 41–7),[2] VII⁸ (fols. 48–55), VIII⁸ (fols. 56–63), IX⁸ (fols. 64–71), X⁸ (fols. 72–9), XI⁸ (fols. 80–7), XII⁴ (fols. 88–9),[3] XIII⁴ (fols. 90–3)[4]

Contents[5]

The contents of Part I may be listed as follows:

1 Isidore, *Liber premiorum siue praefationum ueteris nouique testamenti*: 1r–22r. *inc.* 'Plenitudo noui et ueteris testamenti quam in canon catholica recepit ecclesia . . .'

2 Isidore, *De ortu et obitu sanctorum patrum [sic]*: 22v–23r [*capitula*], 23v–55r [text]. 83 chs., beginning with Adam, ending with Titus.
   Last three lines of 55r, blank; 55v all blank.

3 ⟨Laterculus Malalianus⟩: *incipit auctoritas operis presentis Christe faue uotis bonis*: 56r–81v. Ends with table of emperors (up to Justinianus and Justinus (reg. anni viiii) [= 575?])

4 Isidore, *Questiones tam de nouo quam de uetere testamento*: 82r–89r. *inc.* 'dic mihi quid est inter nouum et uetus testamentum'. *expl.* 'natique sunt et eis filii illi fuerunt gigantes et multa mala fecerunt in terra et non placuit Deo propterea deliuit eos dominus per aquas diluuii'.

5 *Epistula de suppotatione dierum*: 89r–90r. *inc.* 'Anni cum mensibus anni uel bissextis. annus habet dies .ccclxv., mensis .xii., tempora .iiii.' *expl.* 'Ita et bissextus cum uenerit post annum .iiii. dies que uenerit in ordine ducere annum illum ut putit .iii. ferię demittendus est et .iiii. feria computandus sique transit per malorum traditionum bissextum.'

6 *Item computus*: 90v–92r. *inc.* 'Cum omnes apostoli de hac luce migrassent error erat in populo. alii ieiunabant .xx. diebus alii uero. . .' *expl.* 'nos uero a .xvi. usque ad .xxii. in has .vii. lunationes in quo uenerit dies dominicus. infra .xxx. dies sanctificati sunt ad pasca celebrandum.

7 *Sententia papae Leonis [d] apocrifae scripturae*: 92r–93v. *inc.* 'Curandum ergo est et sacerdotali diligentia maxime prouidendum ut falsi codices et ad sencera

---

[2] The folio following fol. 43 was mistakenly passed over when the manuscript was foliated, which accounts for the erroneous impression that this quire consists of only seven folios, and means that the complete manuscript actually contains one more folio than the numeration indicates.

[3] Fols. 3 and 4 of this quire have been cancelled.

[4] 93v is abraded, suggesting perhaps that Pt I circulated for some time on its own before being bound together with Pt II. The last text of this section, *sententia papae Leonis de apocryphis scripturis*, comes to an end partway down 93v, and no new text is started.

[5] The titles used here are not taken from the manuscript.

ueritatem discordis in nulla usu lectiones habeantur apocrifae scripturae...'
expl. 'tractatus uero scī hieronimi ambrosi ceterorum patrum prout ordo poscit
leguntur...'
Remainder of 93v blank.

Part I has a tiny number of small corrections made in Caroline script
(fifteen between fols. 7 and 54), all in the first two works of Isidore (none
are in the *Laterculus*). The scribe was clearly collating from another Isidore
exemplar.

The script of the corrections is Caroline, but it would appear from the
number of ligatures with E, the club-shaped ascenders and the tapering of
the minim strokes, that the correcting was done in a centre in Germany
with Insular scriptorial traditions, perhaps Lorsch.[6] The bulk of Lorsch
manuscripts migrated in 1623 from Heidelberg to the Vatican, so the
present location of the manuscript tend to support this attribution.[7] The
date of these additions is s. ix[1], which suggests that the latest that the
manuscript could have migrated to Germany was the early ninth century.
Part II was probably subjoined to Part I in the ninth century, and bound
together with it at the centre in Germany where the corrections were
added, since a century of independent life would account for the abrasion
to the last folio of Part I. There are two tenth-century catalogues surviving
from Lorsch. It is not possible securely to identify our manuscript with any
of the books listed in it, but there is some possibility that it is the book
referred to in a list of books by Isidore described as 'sententiae et chronica
in quaternionibus'[8] since much of the contents consists of minor works by
Isidore, and there is a chronicle. But it is equally possible that no. 337 was
a quite different book containing the work we ourselves call Isidore's
Sententiae, and Isidore's own chronicle.[9] The corrector of Part I is *not*
identical with the scribe of Part II.

Lorsch was evidently a centre with access to material from the British
Isles, and indeed, from Canterbury. Other Insular items listed in Lorsch
catalogues include Aldhelm's poem *De uirginitate*, his *Enigmata*, Bede's

---

[6] This suggestion was first made by Traube, *Vorlesungen und Abhandlungen* I, 234.

[7] *CLA* IX, p. ix.

[8] Becker, *Catalogi bibliothecarum antiqui*, p. 107 (no. 337).

[9] B. Bischoff, *Lorsch im Spiegel seiner Handschriften* (Munich, 1974), mentions Pt I of Pal.
lat. 277 (p. 48), but has nothing to add about the context of its arrival at Lorsch. Pt II,
which was probably written at that monastery, and extends the Isidorean character of
Pt I (it contains Isidore's *Allegoriae ueteris et noui testamenti*), is described on p. 42.

poem on St Cuthbert, much of Bede's exegesis, and his *De metrica ratione*.[10] These books demonstrate the existence of connexions between Carolingian Lorsch and centres producing copies of works by Insular authors, whether in the British Isles or on the Continent. That one such chain of connexion stretched back to seventh-century Canterbury is strongly suggested by another Lorsch manuscript, now lost, but described in an early-ninth-century Lorsch catalogue: 'liber de abusiuis. interrogationes sancti August-ini de questionibus fidei. exemplar fidei sancti Hieronymi presbyteri *et symbolum quod composuit Theodorus archiepiscopus Britanniae insulae* et liber Gregorii Nazianzeni, in uno codice.'[11] As Michael Lapidge has pointed out, the *orationes* of Gregory of Nazianzus were known to Theodore, possibly suggesting that more than one work in the collection had travelled from Canterbury to Lorsch,[12] and another item in this list also points to the British Isles, the 'liber de abusiuis', which may well be the 'De duodecim abusiuis saeculi' written in Ireland in the mid-seventh century.[13]

Superficially, Pal. lat. 277 appears simply to be a manuscript of Isidore's writings. It was, it seems, so regarded at Lorsch, whether or not it can be identified with their catalogue entry no. 337, since Part II contains Isidore's *Allegoriae*. In fact, there are two texts besides the *Laterculus* itself which suggest an Insular point of origin. Nos. 1 and 2, *Liber praefationum* and *De ortu et obitu patrum*, are genuine works of Isidore.[14] No. 3 is the *Laterculus* itself. But no. 4, *Questiones tam de nouo quam de uetere testamento*, is probably Irish in origin.[15] Pal. lat. 277 is the unique copy of this text. It consists of a series of fifty-five brief questions and answers, each of which is introduced with 'dic mihi. . .', while the answer begins with 'respondit', a catechetical style of writing which is not characteristic of Isidore, but common in early Irish exegesis.[16] McNally associated the composition of this work with the circle of Irish scholars and

---

[10] Becker, *Catalogi bibliothecarum antiqui*, pp. 82–125 (tenth-century Lorsch catalogue), nos. 268–81, 409, 417, 419 and 454.

[11] Becker, *Catalogi bibliothecarum antiqui*, pp. 85–6.

[12] Lapidge, 'The School of Theodore and Hadrian', pp. 50-1.

[13] *BCL*, pp. 96–7 (no. 339)   [14] PL 83, 155–80, and 129–56.

[15] *Scriptores Hiberniae minores I*, ed. McNally (*BCL*, no. 779), discussed *ibid.*, pp. 189–95, and R. E. McNally, 'The Pseudo-Isidorean *De uetere et nouo testamento quaestiones*', *Traditio* 19 (1963), 37–50, and in Reynolds, *The Ordinals of Christ*, pp. 58–61.

[16] See, for example, *The Old Irish Treatise on the Psalter*, ed. K. Meyer, *Hibernica Minora*, Anecdota Oxoniensia, Medieval and Modern Series 8 (Oxford, 1894), 1–104.

exegetes active in southern Germany in the mid-eighth century who were responsible for the composition of the *Liber de numeris*.[17] While it is certainly true to say that there are many points of similarity between our *Quaestiones* and the *Liber de numeris*, the apparent early-eighth-century date of the script of Pal. lat. 277 renders a date as late as the third quarter of the eighth century (suggested by McNally for the composition of the *Liber de numeris*) somewhat problematic. This difficulty can be bypassed by suggesting that our *Quaestiones* are associable with the source(s) of the *Liber de numeris*, rather than cognate with it; and therefore need not derive from precisely the same milieu. A further interesting characteristic of these pseudo-Isidorean *Quaestiones* is that they contain yet another version of the 'Ordinals of Christ'.[18] Wilmart called this the 'B' version, and argued that it belongs to the ABCD recension, of which 'D' is found in the *Collectio Canonum Hibernensis*, and which, in his view, was popularized by the Irish.[19] It is quite different from the version in the *Laterculus*, which I have discussed elsewhere, and certainly strengthens the likelihood that the *Quaestiones* are of Irish origin, though it leaves open the question of whether it was originally written in Ireland, or somewhere on the Continent.

The fifth item in Pal. lat. 277 remains unidentified. It is extremely short, and related to the calculation of time. The seventh item, *sententia papae Leonis*, is a genuine work of Leo the Great.[20] But the sixth is, again, most probably Insular. It is a version of the *Acta [suppositi] concilii Caesareae* (recension B), probably composed in Ireland in the mid-sixth century.[21]

Thus, of the seven items in Pal. lat. 277, Part I, two are Isidorean, two are Irish, one (Leo's *sententia*) is Roman, one is unidentified, and the last is the *Laterculus* itself. Jocelyn Hillgarth and others have long stressed the interest of early Insular scholars in Isidore, and the rapid transmission of Isidorean works to our islands.[22] It is also clear from early English sources

---

[17] *Scriptores Hiberniae minores I*, pp. 194–5.

[18] *Quaestiones*, nos. 41–7, ed. McNally, *ibid.*, pp. 202–3.

[19] Wilmart, 'Les ordres du Christ', pp. 307–9 and 311–13, and F. W. Wasserschleben, *Die irische Kanonensammlung* (Leipzig, 1885), p. 26.

[20] PL 54, 1239–42.

[21] PL 90, 607–10, see B. Krusch, *Studien zur christlich-mittelalterlichen Chronologie: die 84–jährige Ostercyclus und seine Quellen* (Leipzig, 1880), pp. 306–10, and *BCL*, no. 318. I thank Dr Dáibhí Ó Cróinín for his helpful letter on the two computistical texts.

[22] J. Hillgarth, 'Ireland and Spain in the Seventh Century', *Peritia* 3 (1984), 1–16. A caveat has recently been issued by M. Smyth, 'Isidore of Seville and Early Irish

that there was a considerable interchange of scholars, and so probably texts, between Southumbria and Ireland in the sixth and seventh centuries, from the sixth-century Fursa, who settled at Burgh Castle (Norfolk) among pagan Anglo-Saxons, and who was pursued even there by his dedicated Irish followers,[23] to Aldhelm's students Wihtfrith and Heahfrith who made the reverse journey in the seventh century, to the great disgust of their old mentor.[24] The contents of this manuscript therefore support the thesis that the collection was first put together in an Insular milieu, conceivably in the circle of an English missionary on the Continent (several important English missionaries, on the testimony of Bede, were educated in Ireland),[25] though probably not at Canterbury, given the horror with which the Canterbury-educated Aldhelm regarded eighty-four–year Easter cycles. Equally, the Hibernophobic sentiments of the *Laterculus* make it the less likely that the compilation was made by an Irishman, though not, of course, impossible. Many Insular scholars of the seventh century, whatever their racial and linguistic background, were nourished by more than one educational tradition during the course of their development. The gradual, but rapidly increasing, tendency of Anglo-Saxons to make the long journey to Rome offers a possible context for this mixed bag of exegetical and computistical texts falling into the hands of an Italian scribe in the early eighth century.

Script

Part I is written throughout (by one scribe) in uncial. The uncial script has several noteworthy features. The *A* always has a teardrop-shaped lobe. Lowe commented that it was 'written in a small, very neat uncial, the second upright of *N* is often comma-shaped and intersects the cross-stroke; the bow of *R* is low and open.'[26] *E* is closed, and letters like *F* and *L* have a

Cosmography', *CMCS* 14 (1987), 69–102, but it should be noted that her comments on the reception of Isidore in Ireland relate entirely to his cosmological and encyclopaedic works, and do not touch on his biblical exegesis, which was both popular and influential in Ireland from the mid-seventh century.

[23] Bede, *Historia ecclesiastica* III.19 (ed. Colgrave and Mynors, pp. 274–6).

[24] *Aldhelmi Opera*, ed. Ehwald, pp. 479–80 and 488–94.

[25] Bede, *Historia ecclesiastica* III.4, III.27 and V.10 (ed. Colgrave and Mynors, pp. 224, 312–14 and 480). See also D. Ó Cróinín, 'Rath Melsigi, Willibrord, and the Earliest Echternach Manuscripts', *Peritia* 3 (1984), 17–42, at 21–3.

[26] In *CLA* I, no. 91.

small straight line to begin the downstroke, and a wedge-shaped serif on the horizontal strokes. The script's affinities are with Rome itself, and with central and north Italian uncial hands. Lowe dated the manuscript to s. viii[med]; but it may in fact be somewhat earlier, s. vii/viii, or viii[in]. It belongs to a continuum of Italian uncial hands which are hard to date with great precision.

There is a large number of sixth- and seventh-century Italian uncial manuscripts, some of which are directly associable with Rome. One of the key manuscripts is Troyes, Bibliothèque municipale 504, a text of Gregory the Great's *Regula pastoralis* closely linked with Gregory himself,[27] which dates it to the early sixth century.[28] I will attempt a brief description of the script of Troyes 504, as a basis for subsequent remarks on the later developments of Italian uncial. The script is rounded and very regular, with only *L* and *H* rising above the line, and both ascenders and descenders rarely more than half again the height of the line of writing. The space between each line of script is approximately equal to the height of the letters. The *E* is open, and the *A* has a tear-shaped loop. The tail of *G* hangs almost vertically, while the ascender of *D* is very slender, and leaves the bowl of the letter at rather an acute angle. The short descenders taper to a point, enhancing the general impression that all the letters are the same height. This Roman uncial script developed through time. The script of the *Laterculus* manuscript is not identical with the uncial of the sixth century, but is very similar to the uncial of the late seventh and eighth centuries. Two hands closely similar to the script of Pal. lat. 277 are Treviso, Archivio notarile, s.n.[29] and Vat. lat. 1342.[30] The Treviso manuscript is assigned by Lowe to north Italy, s. viii[in], and the Vatican manuscript to Italy, and possibly Rome, s. viii. In both cases, the proportion and spacing of the lines seems very similar to Pal. lat. 277 – that is to say, the lines are spaced a little further apart than is usual with earlier scripts.[31] The ascenders and descenders in all three are rather long, tending towards twice the height of an ordinary letter, and thus giving a more dramatically four-line appearance than sixth- and seventh-century

---

[27] *CLA* VI, no. 838.

[28] Discussed in Petrucci, 'L'onciale romana', pp. 71–80, with a full-page photograph (pl. 1).

[29] *CLA* sup., no. 1763.   [30] *CLA* I, no. 9.

[31] In modern printer's terms, approximately fifteen points on twenty, or, half as much again.

Italian uncial hands, which tend not only to shorten descenders, but to turn the pen sideways and taper them, or draw them entirely as hairlines. All three of these manuscripts have the tear-shaped lobe to the *A*. Vat. lat. 1342 draws double *L* with a single foot,[32] and one of the several hands of the manuscript has the comma-shaped second upright to *N* which is particularly characteristic of Pal. lat. 277. *T* is drawn with small pendent downstrokes on the crossbar, which is often found in Pal. lat. 277, descenders are straight, not tapering, just as in Pal. lat. 277, and *R* has a very low bowl. In spite of the ugly, swift and casual appearance of this very utilitarian manuscript, which boasts a dubious traditional association with the Lateran library, and may therefore be Roman in origin, there are many points of similarity in letter-form with the neat, competent script of the *Laterculus*. Vat. lat. 3835,[33] written in Rome, though it is a more consciously calligraphic script than Pal. lat. 277, with larger, more open letters, is another rather similar script. *A* has a tearshaped lobe, and double *L* is treated in the same way, *S* is a little topheavy, and *R* has a low, open bowl. *T* and *N* have wedge-shaped serifs. But descenders trail to a graceful point, rather than remaining the same thickness all the way down. The script of the rather later Roman manuscript, Rome, Biblioteca Vallicelliana B 25², also has some interesting points of comparison.[34] This script is less even than that of the Troyes *Regula pastoralis*, more like that of Pal. lat. 277. An immediate point of similarity with the *Laterculus* manuscript is that *L* is rather tall, rising to almost twice the height of the main line of script, and double *L*s are drawn together, with a single foot. The *D* resembles that of Pal. lat. 277 in the thickness and angle of its ascender. Points of dissimilarity include pointed rather than tear-shaped lobes to the letter *A*, and (like the Troyes manuscript) vertical descenders to the letter *G*, and forked serifs on some capital letters, a Roman feature which is not found in the *Laterculus* manuscript.

Another manuscript which has features similar to Pal. lat. 277 is the Reculver charter, the only original charter to survive from Kent in the

---

[32] This feature is found in a number of Italian manuscripts, some of which are Roman; for example, Vat. lat. 3835 (*CLA* I, no. 18a) and Cambridge, Corpus Christi College 286 (*CLA* II, no. 127).

[33] *CLA* I, no. 18a; Petrucci, 'L'onciale romana', pl. 17.

[34] See Petrucci, 'L'onciale romana', pp. 120-1, with pl. 19, and *CLA* IV, no. 430. Lowe described it as s. viii/ix: 'late and somewhat artificial uncial'.

lifetime of Theodore.[35] The proportion and spacing of the lines is very similar, the *A* is the same shape, with a tear-shaped lobe, the descender of *G* is angled to the left, the *L* is tall, and the letters have wedge-shaped serifs. The significance of this charter is that it was almost certainly drawn up at Canterbury, which is to say that its scribe was either a member of the entourage which had come to England with Theodore nine years before, or had been trained at Canterbury by Theodore and Hadrian. In either case, the script must be based on seventh-century Roman uncial.[36] Two other early Anglo-Saxon charters, *ChLA* nos. 183 (dated 736) and 187 (dated 690/3, but a late eighth century copy) are in uncial hands – Marichal comments reasonably that the copy would hardly have been made in uncial unless the original was in that script. The Reculver charter makes a remarkable contrast with a Merovingian charter written within a month of it, on 30 June 679 (Paris, Archives nationales K2, no. 13).[37] Merovingian scribes, remote heirs of a continued Gallo-Roman tradition of secular writing, wrote diplomata in an elaborate, cursive chancery-hand.[38] The uncial script of this first surviving Anglo-Saxon charter is an eloquent witness to the imported and ecclesiastical nature of Anglo-Saxon diplomatic. Another pointer connecting this Kentish charter with Rome is its format: as Lowe says, 'late antique and early medieval Italian papyrus records and also papal records of the same and later dates, are characterized by a preference for the tall rectangular format which makes them what are known as *chartae transuersae*.' This format is preferred in the early Anglo-Saxon charters, in which they differ from Merovingian diplomata which normally use the wide rectangular format.[39]

To sum up, the affinities of the script of Pal. lat. 277 are with Italian manuscripts; the closest parallels being either Roman or north Italian. The script is unlikely to be as early as the seventh century, but could reasonably

---

[35] London, British Library, Cotton Augustus II. 2; see *ChLA* III, no. 182 (Birch, *Cartularium Saxonicum*, no. 45 = Sawyer no. 8).

[36] Lowe, *ChLA* IV, p. xvii, pointed out that this charter was written by someone trained to write books rather than legal documents: 'hand, material and ruling are all thoroughly bookish . . . I know of no *continental* early medieval original written in uncial throughout.'

[37] *ChLA* XIII, no. 567.

[38] D. Ganz, 'Bureaucratic Shorthand and Merovingian Learning', in *Ideal and Reality in Frankish and Anglo-Saxon Society*, ed. P. Wormald *et al.* (Oxford, 1983), pp. 58–75.

[39] *ChLA* IV, p. xv.

be placed a little earlier than Lowe's date, near the beginning of the eighth century.

Decoration

Decoratively laid-out letters are found in some of the earliest surviving western books. In Italy, Spain and Francia alike, the first signs of what were to become highly distinctive local traditions of decoration appear in the sixth century. The design repertoire of the sixth century is essentially very simple. Simplified, calligraphic fishes and birds are common motifs, forming parts of initial letters. 'Geometrical patterns, the 8– or rope-motif, leaves and palmettes fill out the bodies of the initials.'[40] Leaves and shoots are sometimes drawn round the bodies of the letters: human forms and interlace are both extremely rare before the mid-eighth century. As we shall see, the decorative scheme in the Vatican manuscript draws on this most common, basic, international repertoire of design in the western manuscript tradition.

The decoration consists of a number of capital letters, up to six times the normal text height, drawn by the scribe, and sometimes decorated with coloured inks. There are no animal or interlace features in these ornamental capitals, which rely to a great extent on simple spirals and curves as decorative motifs. A curious feature of the enlarged initials in the *Laterculus* is that, for the most part, they bear absolutely no relation to any kind of natural breaking or paragraphing in the text itself. They appear at the beginnings of manuscript lines, apparently at random, appearing more than once a page in some sections, every few pages in others, as often as not in the middle of a sentence (though not ever in the middle of a word).

All the decoration is obviously done by the scribe. It is drawn freehand, without the use of a ruler, except that some curves are drawn with the aid of a compass, for instance the bowl of the *Q* on 58v, which clearly shows the little central dots made by the fixed point of the compass as it drew two intersecting arcs.[41] The effect is swift, rough, and casual. The distribution of the decorated capitals seems remarkably capricious. The very large initials of six or more lines' depth are to be found at the beginning and end of the text, but medium initials, between four and two lines deep, seem to

---

[40] Bischoff, *Latin Palaeography*, p. 197.

[41] Bischoff, *ibid.*, notes that the use of a compass is common in sixth- and seventh-century continental manuscripts.

have been scattered at random. For instance, there are no initials, big or small, on the pages between 67v and 68r; then four two-line, coloured initials on 68v. There is no obvious textual justification for this elaborate treatment of 68v.

The vocabulary of ornamentation is extremely simple. Within the outline of the letter (which itself may be majuscule or minuscule in form, especially in the case of Q/q)[42] the ornamentation is built up of double s-chains (which give the impression of a loop of rope twisted into a tight spiral), especially in the long interior rectangle of a letter I, or the descenders of q and p, collars for the ends of interior sections, and such simple geometric figures as chevrons. In the case of one initial I, the long rectangle is subdivided by two horizontal lines into three smaller ones, each of which is further subdivided by a diagonal line. Another character-istic feature of the ornamentation within the border of the letter is the treatment of tapering or triangular forms such as the finial of an I or the two points of a C. Such a triangular field (unless it is too tiny for this to be practicable) always has a pin shape, a line with a little loop at the top, bisecting the acute angle of the triangle, which quite often has the appearance of a schematized fish-head with the mouthline extending up to join the eye.

Outside the boundary of the letter proper, there are four common types of terminal decoration. The most elaborate is a roughly scribbled version of an acanthus leaf seen in profile, but we also find smaller heart- and spoon-shaped leaf terminals, often with a dependent tendril, trifid leaf-ornament (particularly on the terminal points of letters E and C), and also simple triangular or wedge-shaped terminals, with or without curled serifs. Some lines, the top of an I, the wide serif on the tail of a Q, the curl of a tendril, are further decorated, if that is the word, by a scribbled ornament in a roughly scalloped form.

There are two letter forms which are particularly interesting. One is the scribe's only approach to a zoomorphic form: a letter E on 62v in which the central arm combines the familiar little vocabulary of a triangle bisected by a pin, a band, and further pin ornamentation, all enclosed within an oval pointed at both ends and terminated by a trifid leaf-form, to create what seems definitely intended for a fish. We may compare the otherwise very similar E on 61r, which has a simple bar for its central arm, to see how the

---

[42] On 75v, both forms of capital Q appear on the same page.

scribe has rearranged his ornamental elements. The other letter form which may be significant is a treatment of majuscule *A* which appears twice. This *A* has a flat serif, its right arm is formed from two parallel lines with an extended serif at the bottom, and its left arm is composed of one line, flaring out into a wedge shape at the foot. The most interesting feature is that the cross-bar is extended diagonally out to the left beyond the boundary of the letter, with a curl at the end. In the larger of the two examples, the cross-bar within the letter forms a downward-pointing chevron. In the smaller, the cross-bar is completely diagonal, starting near the bottom of the right arm, and crossing the left two-thirds of the way up.

These ornamental features of Pal. lat. 277 can now be compared with those of other manuscripts to see what clues they can offer for the localization of this scribe. It is interesting to observe that its decorative characteristics can be placed in a continuum of developing ornamentation in early Italian manuscripts which goes back to late antiquity. The beautiful Vergil manuscript known as Codex Augusteus, written in square capitals, probably in Italy, in the second half of the fifth century,[43] contains a number of decorative letters, based on a square capital form. The 'thick' strokes – a letter *I*, or the right arm of an *A*, have a double outline, forming a narrow boundary for the letter, and are decorated internally with horizontal and diagonal lines, filled in with colour to form simple triangles. In particular, a ruler-drawn letter *A* on 2v has a thick right arm, decorated internally with triangles, a thin left arm made from two parallel strokes, with little wedge-shaped serifs added at the bottom, a flat top, and the crossbar formed by a downwards-pointing chevron.[44] I will return a little later to the further evolution of this style of capital *A*.

The next design element under consideration is the 'rope' pattern which I have mentioned as particularly characteristic of Pal. lat. 277. In this case, there is a quite visible process of evolution. The uncial gospel book known as the Codex Foro-Julensis, written in north Italy (possibly Aquileia) near the beginning of the sixth century,[45] includes a capital *I* drawn as a narrow rectangle, with spiral flourishes off the two top corners, and filled with a pattern of reversed s-curves, the upper curl of each 's'

[43] Berlin, Deutsche Staatsbibliothek lat. fol. 416 (*CLA* VIII, no. **13). Bischoff prefers the later date of AD 500 (*Latin Palaeography*, p. 189).

[44] Nordenfalk, *Spätantike Zierbuchstaben* II, pl. 21.

[45] Cividale, R. Museo Archaeologico, s.n. (*CLA* III, no. 285).

hooked into the lower curve of the one above to form a delicate chain.[46] The next stage of development is witnessed by another Italian uncial manuscript, of Augustine's *De Genesi ad litteram*,[47] dated to the second half of the sixth century. An initial *I* on 83r is ornamented with a double s-curve, which gives the impression of a double helix, and the same double helix form is found in the early sixth-century Roman uncial manuscript of Gregory the Great's *Regula Pastoralis*.[48] The further development of the double helix into the twisted rope pattern appears in another sixth-century Italian uncial manuscript containing Pelagian works.[49]

The next motif to be traced is the use of a formalized fish as a design element. This appears remarkably early, in contexts otherwise dominated by triangles and s-curves. The Augustine manuscript already mentioned has a rounded, uncial-style capital *E* which forms the upper and lower curves out of two fish, nose-to-nose, and has a straight form resembling a lotus-head sprouting out between them as the central arm.[50] Even more significantly for Pal. lat. 277, which has an *E* with the main curve decorated by abstract pattern, and a fish as the central arm, there is a sixth-century half-uncial manuscript, probably north Italian, with just such an *E*.[51]

---

46 Nordenfalk, *Spätantike Zierbuchstaben* II, pl. 41. The field enclosed by the hooking-together of the *s*'s is distinguished by a blob of colour, making the pattern more definite.

47 Rome, Biblioteca Nazionale Vittorio Emanuele, Sessoriano 13 (2094) (*CLA* IV, no. 418).

48 Troyes, Bibliothèque municipale 504 (*CLA* VI, no. 838). A letter *P* on 4r has the double s-curve in its stem, a compass-drawn almost circular bowl in the same propor-tions as the bowl of the *q* on Pal. lat. 277, 58r, and decoration in the thickness of the bowl of two schematized fish, facing each other. See Nordenfalk, *Spätantike Zierbuch-staben* II, colour plate VII (also illustrated in *CLA*).

49 St Petersburg, Public Library, Q. v. I. 6 + 7 + 8 + 9 + 10 (*CLA* XI, no. 1614). Lowe remarks that, '[the] initials, striking for the sixth century, are delicately drawn and make use of fish, rope, leaf and spiral motifs'.

50 Nordenfalk, *Spätantike Zierbuchstaben* II, plate 60. Compare also an initial *E* in the St Petersburg manuscript mentioned above, 62r, Nordenfalk, *ibid.*, pl. 76, where the design is more abstract, but the overall resemblance to two fish is still noticeable.

51 Milan, Biblioteca Ambrosiana, H. 78 sup. (*CLA* III, no. 347); Nordenfalk, *Spätantike Zierbuchstaben* II, pl. 71. The combination of a schematized fish with otherwise abstract design elements appears again and again in Nordenfalk's collection of early initials. The commonest form is that of an uncial *A*, with a diagonal bar, and a fish hanging half-way down it instead of the lobe of the *A*. There is no need to quote the many examples, since this form does not appear in Pal. lat. 277, but it is found, for

Lastly, there is the 'pin' decoration, used to form schematized fish-heads and also as a diagonal ornament within a rectangle on the initial *I* in 56r. The 'pin' is by no means common. The plethora of schematized fish found all over early decorated manuscripts normally have a little slit for the mouth which is not extended up to meet the eye in the middle of the triangle. But just this form is found in an uncial manuscript of the late seventh or early eighth century probably written in north Italy.[52] As well as forming a fish-head with joined eye and mouth, the 'pin' is found in the same initial marching in a diagonal row down a long rectangle.

This brief survey should have made it clear that all the design elements of Pal. lat. 277 have a clear line of development from the decoration of sixth-century Italian uncial manuscripts: the geometric shapes, the use of a compass, the twisted rope pattern, the fish and the pin. Outside the boundary of the letter proper, the curved finials, spirals and leaf-shaped terminals are also found in sixth-century Italian uncial manuscripts, especially in the St Petersburg manuscript of Pelagian authors. The quality of decoration in the *Laterculus* manuscript is such as to make it extremely unlikely that the scribe did any more than to draw on a small, familiar repertoire of decorative motif, so in this respect, the ornamentation confirms the impression given by the script, that the scribe was trained in central or north Italy.

I observed above that there were two letter-forms in Pal. lat. 277 which were particularly interesting; the *E* with a fish for its central element, for which I hope I have just provided an adequate context, and the non-uncial, square-capital-style capital *A* with a flat top, wide right arm, narrow, wedge-shaped left arm, and cross-bar flourished to the left. Here again, the sixth-century uncials provide a clear line of development, with the *A* of the square-capital Codex Augusteus, described above, as the beginning-point of this development. An uncial manuscript of *Agrimensores*, written

---

example, in the Troyes manuscript of Gregory, written in Rome, on 55v (illustrated by Nordenfalk, *ibid.*, colour pl. VII, and in *CLA* VI, no. 838). Bischoff, *Latin Palaeography*, p. 197, notes that leaves, palmettes, the '8' or 'rope' motif, and geometrical patterning predominate in early manuscripts, and also offers the very early Ravenna Orosius as perhaps the earliest manuscript to show actual initials with various patterns: one, which he shows, is a capital *A* with a fish as its left arm (p. 189).

[52] New Haven, CT, Yale University Library, s.n. (*CLA* II, no. 142). This is the only example of the 'pin' motif illustrated in *CLA*.

at the beginning of the sixth century,[53] has an *A* on 79r with a square top, a thick right arm (decorated internally with a simple *s*-curve), spiral flourishes at top and bottom, and the cross-piece flourished to the left.[54] A sixth-century half-uncial manuscript, also probably Italian, of Augustine's *De ciuitate Dei*,[55] includes a flat-topped *A* with a thick right arm, a thin left arm, and a diagonal cross-bar, flourished upwards on the left.[56] Finally, the St Petersburg manuscript mentioned above has a very elaborate and sophisticated *A* (132r) with a flat top, a thick right arm decorated with a double s-rope, curls and flourishes in leaf-shapes and spirals depending off every available corner, with its crossbar flourished up in a diagonal curve to the left.[57] The decoration of this manuscript is calligraphic, elaborate, and carefully drawn, and uses the full repertoire of fish, rope, leaf and spirals.

The point I wish to make out of this elaborate discussion of manuscript decoration is that there is nothing in the illumination of Pal. lat. 277 which requires the scribe to have been trained outside Italy. We find a similar deployment of the same basic design vocabulary in, for example, an uncial manuscript of Isidore's *De officiis* written at Bobbio at the beginning of the eighth century – which is to say, probably contemporary with the writing of Pal. lat. 277.[58] Flat-topped, square-capital *As* with the cross-bar flourished to the left are to be found in a variety of German and Frankish manuscripts of the eighth and ninth centuries.[59] Not one of these is earlier than the examples in Pal. lat. 277, and they are differently formed and decorated. None of them is as close in shape as the sixth-century *A* from *De ciuitate Dei*, or as close in design and ornamentation as the *A* from the St Petersburg manuscript. An *A* with a chevron-shaped cross-bar is common in Lombard and Frankish inscriptions and manuscripts. But in the context of inscriptions, the *A* with the cross-bar flourished to the left has been identified as a Visigothic feature in the mid-

---

53 The 'Codex Arcerianus', now Wolfenbüttel, Herzog August Bibliothek, Aug. 2°. 36. 23 (*CLA* IX, no. 1374b). This, yet again, is an Italian manuscript.

54 Nordenfalk, *Spätantike Zierbuchstaben* II, pl. 37.

55 Paris, Bibliothèque nationale 12214 (*CLA* V, no. 635).

56 Nordenfalk, *Spätantike Zierbuchstaben* II, pl. 56.

57 *Ibid.*, pl. 75.

58 Vatican City, Biblioteca Apostolica Vaticana, Vat. lat. 5765 (*CLA* I, no. 43).

59 *CLA* V, no. 640; V, no. 687; VII; no. **614; VII; no. 935; IX, no. 1340; IX, no. 1532; and X, no. 1571.

seventh century.[60] Its appearance in manuscripts, on the other hand, appears to be principally an Italian feature. The so-called Bobbio Missal (Paris, BN lat. 13246), fortunately published in a complete facsimile, is closely similar to Pal. lat. 277 in a number of ways.[61] The Bobbio Missal is, at best, carelessly written, and its worst pages are scrawled onto badly-prepared parchment which has caused the ink to blot. It is a small, thick manuscript (300 folios) of a grimly utilitarian nature. Nonetheless, the importance of finding one's way quickly in a liturgical text has ensured the presence of a small number of ornamented capitals. The vocabulary of ornament used in these capitals is very close to that used in Pal. lat. 277. We find the double s-curve 'rope' pattern (e.g. 48r or 219r), squiggly, scribbled finials depending from the top corner (48r), rough leaf-shaped finials (e.g. 39r, 41v), collars subdividing a part of a letter (e.g. 48r), and simple geometric patterns picked out by colours (e.g. 75v). There is one, anomalous example of an uncial-style capital *A* with a pointed lobe which is decorated, Insular-style, with a border of dots (103r), just as there is one capital *Q* ornamented with dots in the *Laterculus* (60v).[62] All the other decoration, within the limits of its extremely incompetent execution, is within the continuum of decoration of the *Laterculus* manuscript. In particular, I find it extremely interesting that the capital *A*s on 26v, 196v and 303v have a flat serif on the top, a right arm composed of two parallel lines with a serif at the bottom, a left arm composed of a single line with a flaring wedge at the base, and possess a diagonal cross bar, flourishing to the left beyond the confines of the letter, and ending in a tight curl. The lone fish of Pal. lat. 277 is curiously paralleled by a single zoomorphic initial in the Bobbio Missal, a capital *I* on 11v decorated with a twisted rope pattern, and finished off at the bottom with a fringe of roughly-drawn scallops, which has a bulbous and eccentric bird squatting on its flat top.[63] The Bobbio Missal, Lowe says, 'could have been written either in northern Italy or in France'. His judgement came down, finally, in favour of France,

---

[60] N. Gray, *A History of Lettering* (Oxford, 1986), p. 44.

[61] *The Bobbio Missal*, ed. Lowe, vol. I.

[62] To outline letters with dots is not purely an Insular habit. It is found, for instance, in the magnificent manuscript of Dioscorides prepared at Constantinople for Julia Anicia in 512 (Vienna, Nationalbibliothek med. gr. 1, 9v), illustrated in Nordenfalk, *Spät-antiken Zierbuchstaben* II, pl. 26–8.

[63] The sixth-century Italian manuscript initials reproduced by Nordenfalk contain birds as well as fish, though not so many.

but he was emphatic that the evidence for this kind of unprofessional and unbeautiful manuscript in the early Middle Ages is insufficient for the drawing of firm conclusions or elaborate theories.[64] He had almost nothing to say about the ornamentation, apart from remarking that it was 'simple in design and crude in execution', and that he perceived some affinity with Frankish style.[65]

Abbreviations

Although there are no traces of influence from Insular script styles on the Italian uncial hand of this manuscript, there is one small indication that an Insular exemplar lay behind it; a confusion of *s* and *r* (*suminantur* for *ruminantur* in ch. 4), impossible in uncial hands, but all too easy with Insular minuscules. The presence of this error makes it clear that it was Insular minuscule which was used for the exemplar of Pal. lat. 277. There may have been two scripts in use in seventh-century Canterbury. There is no manuscript which can be attributed with certainty to Canterbury in the age of Theodore, but this clue in the *Laterculus* suggests the use of Insular minuscule, a script which is also used in the Epinal glossary, a text which derives from Theodore's school, though it was not necessarily written at Canterbury.[66] On the other hand, the Reculver charter, witnessed by Theodore, and written in an uncial hand closely resembling that of Pal. lat. 277, suggests that Theodore brought a tradition of uncial script in the Italian style to Kent.[67] There is no sign of any difficulties caused to the scribe by characteristic Insular abbreviations such as the hooked *h* for *autem*. Pal. lat. 277 is a clearly-written uncial manuscript containing few abbreviations aside from the usual *nomina sacra*. Those abbreviations that there are, are mainly at the ends of lines. The writer uses a stroke above the last letter for *m*, almost always at the end of a line and once for an *n* (*clemētia*). *Ihl* with a stroke above is once used for *Israhel*,[68] *qnm* for *quoniam* appears twice (and is one of the abbreviations

---

[64] *The Bobbio Missal*, ed. Lowe III, 105.   [65] *Ibid.*, p. 96.

[66] Epinal, Bibliothèque municipale 72 (2), fols. 94–107; see *The Epinal, Erfurt, Werden and Corpus Glossaries*, ed. B. Bischoff *et al.*, EEMF 22 (Copenhagen, 1988), esp. 15–17.

[67] London, British Library, Cotton Augustus II. 2 (*ChLA* III, no. 182).

[68] Lindsay, *Notae Latinae*, p. 408, commented that 'Italian scribes favour *ihl* 'Israel' (although they also use *isrl*)'.

attested for this word in early manuscripts from north Italy),[69] as does the rather unusual *prdtum* for *praedictum*. *P̄d* is once used for *praedixit*.[70] Another special abbreviation is *Augſ* for *Augustus*, who happens to be mentioned quite frequently in this text.[71] *Nt* at the end of a line is often a single letter, the bar of the *t* added to the third stroke of the *n*. *E-caudata* is used throughout for *ae*, though *ae* does occasionally appear written in full. The 'tail' is once used to signify an *a* on its own, but that is probably a correction: *diƀulo* for *diabulo*.

LEIDEN, BIBLIOTHEEK DER RIJKSUNIVERSITEIT, VOSS. MISC.11

The second copy of *Laterculus Malalianus* is preserved in a manuscript now at Leiden, part of the collection brought there by Isaac Vossius in the seventeenth century.[72] Voss. misc. 11 consists of four parts, three Greek, one Latin, unrelated to each other in date or content. It is Pt III, written in early Caroline minuscule, which includes the *Laterculus*. The size of the manuscript is 252 x 170 mm. Pt III consists of seven folios, with no visible quire signatures. The leaves were ruled before folding, a quire at a time, thirty-eight lines to a page, with the direct impression on the outside bifolium. There are double boundary lines, and the rulings are guided by pricking in the outer margins. Incipits are in red capital or uncial; the first line of the text is in black uncial. The ink is brown and the vellum prepared in the Insular manner. The contents of the manuscript are as follows:

---

[69] Lindsay, *ibid.*, pp. 263 and 268. The abbreviations *qn̄m̄*, *qm̄* and *qūō* are all found in early northern Italian manuscripts.

[70] Lindsay, *ibid.*, p. 301, noted that *p̄d* and *prdtūs* (both standing for *praedictus*) appear in Lucca, Biblioteca capitolare 490, written probably at Lucca *c.* 800 (*CLA* III, no. 303). This manuscript contains both uncial and minuscule hands of various types. He observes of these abbreviations for *praedictus*, 'these are clearly mere capricious curtailment of a repeated word'.

[71] Lindsay, *ibid.*, p. 420, records a wide variety of capricious abbreviations for *augustus* (whether as emperor, title, or month), which do not in fact include *Augſ*.

[72] K.A. de Meyier, *Codices Vossiani Graeci et Miscellanei*, Bibliotheca Uniuersitatis Leidensis Codices Manuscripti VI (Leiden, 1955), 245–6.

Contents

Pt I, fols. 1–6: Greek, paper, s. xvii. Choricius of Gaza, *Declamatio de tyrannicida*.

Pt II, fols. 7–20: Greek, paper, s. xvii. *Excerpta grammaticalia*.

Pt III, fols. 21–8: Latin, parchment, s. ix, or *c.* 800, 252 x 170mm; fols. 21–6: *Laterculus Malalianus*; fols. 26–7, *De computatione dierum feriarum epactarum* (*inc.* 'Era inuenta est a Iulio caesare', *des.* 'ita sine errore initium quadragesimae inuenies. Deo gracias'); fol. 27: *Fragmenta ex dialogo de sapientia* (*inc.* 'nonne uetus prouerbium est?'); 28r: *Vitae Simeonis Stylitae fragmentum*;[73] 28v *Vitae Genouefae Parisiensis fragmentum*.

Pt IV, Greek, paper, s. xiii. *Galeni fragmenta*.

Pt III was written by five scribes, of whom the first wrote 21–3v, the second fols. 24–6, the third fols. 26–7, the fourth 27v, and the fifth fol. 28. The first three write an early type of Caroline minuscule seen in several manuscripts from Weissenburg. The fourth, who wrote the *Dialogus de sapientia* on an unused page, is a slightly later hand, s. ix[in]. The fifth scribe may be the Adallandus who wrote various charters for the monastery of Weissenburg between 782 and 790. The *Vitae sanctorum* distributed in the bindings of several manuscripts coming from Weissenburg (including this one) are in a hand which very closely resembles that of the charters.[74] Our fol. 28 is part of this early Caroline minuscule book of *vitae* which was dismembered for binding, probably at Weissenburg itself.[75]

Voss. misc. 11 helps to confirm the eighth-century date of Pal. lat. 277, since it was written around 800, as Bernhard Bischoff suggested to de Meyier, or at the very beginning of the ninth century. It may shed further light on when the latter manuscript arrived at Lorsch. The text of the Leiden manuscript is taken directly from that of the Vatican one. There are some very superficial editorial corrections: nouns are often (though not always) put into the correct cases after prepositions where Pal. lat. 277 errs, and the spelling of some words is standardized to a more Classical form. On the other hand, some of the main puzzles in the Vatican text are

---

[73] Fol. 28 is used as a binding: the script is vertical, not horizontal.

[74] H. Butzmann, *Der Weissenburger Handschriften neu beschreiben*, Katalog der Herzog-August Bibliothek Wolfenbüttel X (Frankfurt-am-Main, 1964), 24–5 and 127 (descriptions of Weissenburg binding fragments).

[75] Lowe, *CLA* IX, p. ix (and see also *CLA* VIII, no. 1051).

simply reproduced: for example, *momentis*, apparently for *monumentis*, in ch. 3, *suminantur* for *ruminantur* in ch. 4, *terraarchia* for *tetrarchia* in ch. 7 and the string of genitive absolutes in ch. 11. The correction is on an entirely superficial level.

Another aspect of the Leiden text which shows its dependence on the Vatican text is its decoration. The disposition of decorated initials in Pal. lat. 277 appears to be entirely capricious, not related to sense in any obvious way. Only the first scribe of the Leiden manuscript attempts decorative initials; and in every case, his large initial occurs exactly where one appears in the Vatican manuscript. The shape of the initials is also closely modelled on those of Pal. lat. 277. Even the word-division in the Leiden manuscript proclaims dependence: in ch. 1, for example, the phrases 'ut omnem a nobis amaritudinem tollat aliene doctrine, ut antra caliginis obnuuilante mendacio sua...' appear in Pal. lat. 277 as 'ut omnem anobis. amaritudinem tollat. alie/ne. doctrine. ut antra caliginis/ ob nuuilante mendacio. sua...'. In Voss. misc. 11, we find, as with all Caroline manuscripts, clearer word-division, and less heavy and capricious punctuation points: 'ut omnem *anobis* amaritudinem tollat alienae doctrinae ut antra caliginis *ob nubi lante* mendacio sua...'. The smaller number of punctuation-points in Voss. misc. 11 occur in the same places as points in Pal. lat. 277. The layout of the second *incipit*, after the preface, at the end of ch. 1, which is displayed as a separate paragraph with an unusually large, coloured initial in Pal. lat. 277, is paralleled in Voss. misc. 11 by being laid out as a separate paragraph in red uncial, similar in its proportions to that of the Vatican manuscript. In this way, the details of the layout of the Leiden manuscript confirm the impression given by the actual quality of the text, that this is simply a copy, not a collation of the Vatican text with another, unknown witness.

9

Conclusion

The *Laterculus* has been easily available in both Migne's Patrologia Latina and Mommsen's edition in Monumenta Germaniae Historica for a century without attracting attention: it has always appeared to be a brief and unprepossessing text of which Angelo Mai could say, not unjustifiably, 'Latinitas ualde squalet'. In a context of chronicle texts, it has seemed to earlier commentators to be poor stuff, naive and ill-informed.

This study has sought to demonstrate that it was written in Canterbury by Archbishop Theodore at some point between 669 and 690. Its contents, background, manuscript-context, sources and Latinity are compatible with such a conclusion. No other possible explanation for the text can be proffered which does not create more problems than it solves.

Having exhaustively considered the reasons for assigning it to the school at Canterbury, the second focus of this study has been to demonstrate that, far from being naive and primitive, it is the product of genuine and extensive scholarship, and thus no discredit to one of the outstanding figures of Anglo-Saxon literary culture. The Theodore revealed by the *Laterculus* is a very remarkable man indeed. One salient aspect of the text is its practicality as a teaching document: parts of Malalas's *Chronographia* have been reshaped into a concise text which offers a simple and effective guide to the kind and quantity of world history which an un-Romanized people would need in order to set the central mystery of Christ's life on earth in context. Beneath this simple text, written in crudely vigorous demotic Latin (which still, here and there, suggests a rhetorical training) lies vast resources of scholarship. It demonstrates a mind encyclopaedically well read in Christian Greek and Syriac, and extends the already considerable evidence for Theodore's sophisticated interest in medicine. A further conclusion which can be drawn from the *Laterculus* is that Theodore was the possessor of a mind so vigorous and active that he was both able and willing to defy the proverbial inability of old dogs to learn new tricks, and to start exploring the resources of Latin when he was in his sixties and later. The *Laterculus*, it will be remembered, suggests a great fondness for the works of Caelius Sedulius, whom he could, of course, have begun reading in Rome. But it also seems to imply that he read the *De excidio* of Gildas, known to be a Canterbury school-text, which he was most unlikely to have encountered before his arrival in Kent. Since the *De excidio* is a work of flamboyant style and considerable difficulty, one must conclude that his ability to read and appreciate Latin literature must have far outrun his ability to write it, not an uncommon phenomenon with late-learned languages. The *Laterculus* shows no knowledge of pagan Latin literature. By contrast, Aldhelm, who is generally agreed to have drawn on the Canterbury library, was as well grounded in Classical authors as anyone active in the seventh century anywhere in the western empire. Perhaps teaching in non-Christian curriculum authors was left to Hadrian and other coadjutors. It also seems possible that the *Laterculus* is witness to the early years of Theodore's episcopate, and that in addition to a complete reorganization of the English church, he buckled down to the study of Vergil and the Latin grammarians in his late sixties. The willingness to discard old answers and to respond creatively to the demands of an alien milieu which this would imply is witnessed again and again in the Theodoran penitentials, and an openness to new information is further represented in his use of Anglo-Saxon weights and measures in the *Biblical Commentaries*. The disjunction between the knowledge implied in the *Laterculus* and the knowledge implied by Ehwald's listing of Aldhelm's sources may be in itself evidence for a trajectory of intellectual development over the twenty-two years of Theodore's archiepiscopate.

In any case, it is impressive testimony to the depth and extent of Greek studies in seventh-century Canterbury. Whether Theodore brought many eastern texts with him when he arrived is unguessable: some, such as the minor works of Epiphanius, are virtually certain to have come with him, but much of the exegesis which underlies the *Laterculus* is likely to have been brought in the form of a scholar's well-trained memory rather than as actual manuscripts.

Setting the *Laterculus* beside the *Biblical Commentaries* with which it accords so well reveals an entirely new picture of the Southumbrian scholarship which was so highly regarded in its own time. We will probably never be in a position to trace the influence of this school on men such as Tobias of Rochester and Albinus, who Bede tells us studied Greek there, since we cannot produce any texts provably written by them. However, the possible influence of Greek thought on vernacular Old English prose and verse, mediated through the lost works of these Canterbury alumni, is uncharted territory. It may no longer be wise to assume that a poet such as Cynewulf could draw only on the Latin tradition, or that there is no possible connexion between the *Odyssey* and *Beowulf*.

Text and translation

Editorial Principles

The first edition of the *Laterculus*, that of Cardinal Mai, conformed to the standard practice of his time in emending the text drastically to make it conform to standards of Classical Latinity. The edition of Mommsen, on the other hand, accurately reproduces the spelling of the single manuscript witness known to him. My own edition follows Mommsen's practice in this matter. In the case of the *Laterculus*, the scribe of the Vatican manuscript is separated by perhaps one generation from Theodore himself. Since the orthography and morphology of the *Laterculus* are similar to the characteristics of seventh-century Italian Latin as they are revealed in sub-literary texts, the 'vulgar errors' of the *Laterculus* must be treated as valuable evidence for Late Latin usage rather than the depredations made on a Classically correct original text by an illiterate scribe. Accordingly, my text is printed very much as it appears in the manuscript, with syntactic emendations confined to the *apparatus criticus*. The passages printed in italic in the translation are the sections of the text which are take over directly from Malalas's *Chronographia*.

One respect in which I have made no attempt to reproduce the evidence of the manuscript is in punctuation. My first transcription reproduced the capitalization and punctuation of the manuscript exactly. In the course of making this transcription, it became quite clear that both these aspects of the text were completely capricious. The impression given by the punctuation is that the scribe, during the process of copying, tended to keep perhaps five to seven words in his mind at a time, and having written them, ended his block of words with a point. Since he was well-trained and conscientious, as his swift, even, skilful script also shows, he left no examples of haplography or dittography to confirm this guess at his *modus operandi*. The capitalization, though it occurs at the beginnings of clauses, quite often fails to conform with the division of sentences required by sense and consequently retards rather than expedites comprehension of the text.

119

LATERCULUS MALALIANUS

[V 56r/L 21r] Incipit auctoritas operis presentis: Christe, faue uotis bonis.ᵃ¹

1 Iam tempus est, ut se ueritas luculentis rationis optutibus omnibus semetipsam perlustret in faciem. Iam prudentiori conatu tamquam per obstrusis cauernarum riuulisᵇ nouam et integram se ueritas prodat ex utero. Iam ne nos fallant multoloquio suo Scottorum scolaces,² ipsa se nobis ueritas liquidissimis ᶜ labiorum promat nectareis,³ ut omnem a nobis amaritudinem tollat aliene doctrine, ut antra caliginis obnuuilanteᵈ mendacio sua nos ueritas luce tamquam solisᵉ iubar⁴ inlustret ab alto, ut mendacium fugientes ueritas amplectetur, exutiᶠ caliginemᵍ tenebrose noctis obstante lux ueraʰ causarum   [V 56v] clariscatⁱ omnibus letissimus dies in uultu. Nunc igitur – si placet, ut certum sit – ipsa mundi consilia perquiramus: quo tempore, qua aetate mundi adfuerit Christus saluator in carne, cuius etiam consolatu adque imperio mundo in hoc agebatur,ʲ in terris dum e caelo Dei filius in utero uirginisᵏ uelut rex insederit thalamo.¹⁵ Explicit.ᵐ

Incipit namque historiaⁿ chronica quodᵒ etiam pari modo explanauerunt⁶ Clemens uel Theophilus et Timotheus⁷ dilectissimi Dei episcopi chronographi, et dilectus autem Dei chronographus Eusebius⁸ Pamphiliensis.

2 Anno autem .xlii. Octauiani⁹ Augusti Caesaris natus est Dominus et saluator noster Iesus Christus. Superius¹⁰   [V 57r] enimᵃ ait quia postquam¹¹ transiuit .xl. et primo anno mense sextoᵇ¹² regni eiusdem Caesaris in mense Distro,¹³ id est secundum Latinos Martium,ᶜ .xxv. die mensis hoc est .viii. kal. Apriles,ᵈ qui secundum Gregusᵉ Xanthicus appellatur, hora diurnamᶠ secunda initiante tertia dieᵍ dominica, missus est archangelus¹⁴

L: Leiden, Universiteitsbibliotheek, Voss. misc. 11. V: Vatican, Pal. lat. 277.

1 a bonis uotis L   b rivolis (*for* obstrusos . . . riuulos) L   c loquidissimis VL
d obnnuuilante, *with first n erased* V, obnubilante L   e solis *inserted above the line* V
f *for* et uti   g caligine L   h *for* luci uerae   i clarescat L   j agebatur, *with a*
over erasure V   k uiʳginis L   l thalomo L   m L *omits*   n *for* historica
o *for* quae   2 a L *omits*   b *for* primus annus mensis sextus   c *for* Martio
d Aprelis, *for* Aprilis L   e Grecos L   f diurna L   g dⁱe L

120

TRANSLATION

Here begins the authority of the present work: Christ, look kindly on our good prayers[1]

1 It is now time that truth should survey herself in her own aspect with every brilliant scrutiny of wisdom. Now by more prudent effort, inasmuch as through the teeming streams of caves, let truth reveal herself fresh and unsullied from the womb. Now, lest the twisty reasoners/whelps[2] of the Irish deceive us with their verbiage, let truth disclose herself to us with the most liquid nectar[3] of the lips, so that she may take away from us all the bitterness of strange teaching, so that although falsehood obscures the caves of darkness, truth may illuminate us from on high like a sunbeam[4] with its light, so that truth will embrace those who flee mendacity, and so that although the darkness of black night hinders it, the true light of reasons may grow clear for everyone, like the most joyous day in appearance. Now, therefore – if it pleases you that it should be made certain – let us seek that knowledge of the world: in what time, in which age of the world Christ the Saviour came in the flesh; and also in whose consulship and reign he existed in this world, when the Son of God came from heaven to earth into the womb of a virgin like a king entering a bridal chamber.[5] End.

Here begin the historical chronicles, *which* in equal measure *Clemens or Theophilus and Timothy*[6] set out,[7] *the chronographers*, bishops most beloved of God, *and also the chronographer dear to God, Eusebius Pamphilus.*[8]

2 *Our Lord and Saviour Jesus Christ was born in the year 42 of Octavian*[9] *Augustus Caesar.* It says above[10] that *since, after*[11] *forty years had gone by, in the sixth month*[12] *of the forty-first year of that Caesar, in the month of Dystrus*[13] (that is, according to the Latins, March), *on the twenty-fifth day of the month* (which is the eighth of the kalends of April, which is called Xanthicus according to the Greeks), *on the second hour of the day,* at the beginning of

Gabrihel euangelizare beata Mariah in ciuitatei Galileae cui nomen
Nazareth, in consolatuj Cyrinii et Longini,k[15] cum esset disponsatal uiro
cui nomen erat Ioseph, procurante quidem Syriae Vitellio[16] qui tunc
agebat iubenis sub eodem Augustum Caesaremm .viii. ergo kal. Aprilis,n
id est aequinoctium uernalem,o[17] conceptus est Dominus in utero uirginis. Nam et eadem diemp patibulum crucis ascendit et postea in sepulchro
est positus. [V 57v] Et alia magnalia Domini in ea die gesta sunt, id est,
initium hic mundus[18] ipsa die sumpsit a Deo, et tunc transierunt[19] filii
Israhel per Mare Rubrum tamquam per aridam terram, et tunc expugna-
tus[20] est diabulus et de caelo proiectus est cum angelis suis, et tunc ipsa
die sanctus Iacobus[21] fraterq Domini de pinna templi[22] deorsum proiecer-
unt Iudaei.r Conceptus est igitur Dominus in uterum uirginiss .viii. kal.
Aprilis,t id est .v. [L 21v] et .xx. die mensis Martii, quodu est .xli.
annorumv imperii Augusti Caesaris. Et natus est in anno .xlii. regni[23]
eiusdem Caesaris .viii. kal.w Ianuariarum mense Apilleon,x qui est Decem-
brio, in die .xxv. mensis, hora diei .vii., in ciuitate Iudeae[24] cui nomen est
Bethleem quae est iuxta Hierusalem, sub preside Syriae Cyrino ex consolibus,y consolatuz ueroaa eiusdem [V 58r] Octauiani Augustibb et Siluani.[25]
Toparcha autem Iudeae Herodes ille maior, filiuscc Archelai,dd sicut euangelista testatur.[26]

3 Colligitura[27] ergo ab Adam usque ab Phalech[28] filic Eber annorum tria
milia, et a Phalech usque ad .xl. et .ii. annod regni Augustie Caesaris anni
.ii̅.dcccc.lxvii. Et ita colligiturf ab Adam primi hominisg usque ad incar-
nationemh Domini nostri Iesu Christi et .xlii. annii regni Augusti Caesaris,
annos .v̅dcccclxvii.j Et inde conuersatus cum hominibus super terram
Dominus noster et saluator Iesus Christus circa quod perk annos .xxxiii. non

h beatae Mariae, *for* beatam Mariam L   i *for* ciuitatem   j consulatu L   k *omits* et
Longini   l desoibsata L   m Augusto Caesare L   n Aprelis L   o equinoctium,
for aequinoctio uernali L   p die L   q *for* sanctum Iacobum fratrem   r proiectus est
a Iudeis L   s utero virginis L   t Aprelis L   u *for* qui   v *for* annus
w kalendarium L   x Apellion L   y exconsulibus, *for* exconsule L   z consulatu L
aa L *omits*   bb Augī V   cc *for* Herode ille maiore, filio   dd Archalai L
3 a *for* colliguntur   b *for* ad   c *for* filium (*see note*, pp. 172–3)   d *for* annum
e *for* Augī V   f *for* colliguntur   g *for* primo homine   h V incarnem, *with superscript*
correction   i *for* annum   j *for* anni .v̅dcccclxvii.   k *for* circiter; L *omits* per

the third, *on Sunday, the Archangel Gabriel*[14] *was sent to bear witness to blessed Mary in the city* of Galilee *which is called Nazareth,* she was betrothed to a man named Joseph, *during the consulate of Cyrinus and Longinus,*[15] *while Vitellius,*[16] *who was then a young man under that same Augustus Caesar, was procurator of Syria.* Therefore, on the eighth of the kalends of April, which is the vernal equinox,[17] the Lord was conceived in the womb of a virgin. And on that same day he ascended the gibbet of the Cross and afterwards was placed in the tomb. And other wonderful things were done by the Lord on that day. The world took its beginning[18] from God on the same day, and [it was] then that the children of Israel[19] passed through the Red Sea as if on dry land; and it was then the devil was conquered[20] and cast out of heaven with his angels; and on that same day, the Jews threw down St James[21] the brother of the Lord from the pinnacle of the temple.[22] The Lord, then, was conceived in the womb of a virgin on the eighth of the kalends of April, which is the twenty-fifth day of March, which was in the forty-first year of the rule of Augustus Caesar. *And he was born in the forty-second year of the reign of that same Caesar,*[23] *the eighth of the kalends of January,* in the month Apilleon *(which is December), on the twenty-fifth day of the month, at the seventh hour of the day, in the city of Judaea*[24] *which is called Bethlehem, which is near Jerusalem, when Cyrinus was governor of Syria, the consuls being the same Octavian Augustus and Silvanus,*[25] *and the toparch of Judaea was Herod* the Great, son of Archelaeus, as the evangelist bears witness.[26]

3 3,000 years *are reckoned*[27] *from Adam to Phalech*[28] *son of Eber; and from Phalech to the forty-second year of the reign of Augustus Caesar, 2,967 years. And thus 5,967 years are reckoned from Adam the first of mankind to the Incarnation of our Lord Jesus Christ and the forty-second year of the reign of Augustus Caesar. And from that time on our Lord and Saviour Jesus Christ dwelt among men on the earth for some thirty-three years,* which is hardly complete enough, *as there*

plenos parum quid, ut fiant ab Adam usque ad Domini nostri Iesu Christi, secundum carnem natiuitatem et passionem crucis et adsumptionis[l] eius in caelis[m] ad patrem, annos .vi. plenos.[n][29] Phalech etenim, secundum propheticam uocem Mosy, in dimidium dicitur temporis futurae incarnationis Christi interuenisse aduentum. [V 58v] Sicut enim hominem sexta die de terra plasmauit Deus, ut Moyses magnus scriptor temporum[30] exposuit in suis monumentis,[o][31] ita hoc definiuit: 'et erit', inquid,[p] 'una dies Domini sicut mille[q] anni.'[32] Sexta igitur die fincxit[r] hominem Deus, et cecidit sub peccato[s][33] homo, ut hoc quoque clarius appareat, qui sicut sexta die homo in paradyso[t] plasmatus corruit in peccato[u] ita sexta die milarii[v] mundus in aetate Christus super terram manifestatus est, et saluauit hominem per crucis signaculum ligni et resurrectionis ex mortuis reformando.

4 Quod etiam[34] pari modo Clemens uel Theophilus et Timotheus dilectissimi Dei et episcopi chronographi explanauerunt inuicem hi[a] consonantes. Dilectus autem Dei   [V 59r] chrono/graphus Eusebius Pamphiliensis sextum quidem milarium[b] annorum et ipse dicit apparere saluatorem Christum, secundum numerum sex[c] dierum plasmationis Adae.[35] Prius tamen quam suppleti[d] fuissent sex milia annorum dixit, quia apparuit Dominus Deus Iesus Christus saluator noster ad eripiendum[e] genus humanum. Et natus, inquid,[f] ex uirgine, humanatus est in quinto milario,[g] et quingentisimo et .ii. annorum[h] passus est uiro[i] et resurrexit Dominus noster Iesus Christus et adsumptus est in caelis[j] annorum nomerum[k] saeculi aetatis ab Adam .v̄. milia .dxxxiiii.

In sex milia autem[l] annorum concordant omnes[36] apparuisse Dominum; quamuis Scotti[m] concordare nolunt,[37] qui sapientia[n] se existimant habere, et scientiam perdederunt.[o] Vel si etiam unus plus, alius minus dixerunt, in sexto milario[p] annorum, secundum [V 59v] propheticam uocem elocutionis,[q] uniuersi[r] consentiunt etiam quamuis repigritent[s] qui exposuerunt[t] de nomero[u] annorum. In nouissimis tamen[v] temporibus appar-

l *for* adsumptionem   m *for* caelos   n *for* anni .vi. pleni   o momentis VL
p inquit L   q melle L   r finxit L   s peccato VL, V *with a over erasure, for* peccatum
t paradiso L   u *for* peccatum   v miliarii L   4 a hii L   b *for* sexto. . .miliario
c *for* sextam   d *for* suppleta   e eri[p][i]endum L   f inquit L   g miliario L
h *for* anno   i uero L   j *for* caelos   k numerum L   l L *inserts above line*
m Sco[t]ti L   n sapientiam L   o perdiderunt L   p miliario L   q o *over erasure* V;
elocutionis L   r uniuersis L   s repigritent V, nt *over erasure*   t exposuerunt V,
x *over correction*   u numero L   v L *omits*

should be a full 6,000 years[29] *from Adam to the nativity of our Lord Jesus Christ, according to the flesh, and the Passion of the Cross,* and his assumption into heaven to the Father. *For Phalech, according to the prophetic voice of Moses, is said to come half-way between [Adam and] the advent of the future incarnation of Christ. For just as God shaped man on the sixth day from earth, as Moses* the great chronographer[30] *explained in his writings,*[31] *it is defined thus: 'one day of the Lord',* he says, *'is like a thousand years.'*[32] *So on the sixth day God created man and man fell into sin,*[33] *so that this also appears more plainly: just as on the sixth day man in paradise fell into sin, so on the sixth day of thousands [of years]* in the age of the world, *Christ was manifested on earth and saved mankind through* the sign of the wood *of the Cross, and through his Resurrection* transformed from death.

4 *Concerning whatever*[34] *Clemens or Theophilus and Timothy,* bishops and beloved of God, *the chronographers, explain, they are mutually in agreement. However the chronographer beloved of God, Eusebius Pamphilus, also says that the Saviour Christ appears in the sixth set of a thousand years, following the number of the six days of Adam's shaping.*[35] *First, however, he said that 6,000 years were completed since our Lord Jesus Christ our Saviour first appeared to free the race of man, and born, he says, of a virgin; was made human in the 5,052nd year, suffered as a man, and our Lord Jesus Christ was truly resurrected and assumed into heaven in the number of the years* of secular time from Adam, 5,534.

However, all agree[36] *that the Lord appeared in 6,000 years* – though the Irish do not wish to concur,[37] who judge themselves to have wisdom, and [so] lose knowledge. *But whether one [person] has said more, or another less, everyone agrees to 6,000 years, following the prophetic voice of eloquence (though also all who set out the number of the years retard it).* Nevertheless, all bear witness *that the Saviour is to appear in the last days, as divine scripture testifies.* For also in the holy gospels you find this fact, that while one says Christ was crucified at the third hour [i.e., Mark],[38] the others declare that he

uisse saluatorem, sicut diuina [L 22r] scriptura significat, omnes testati sunt. Nam et in sanctis euangeliis repperies hoc factum: dum unus tertiam horam[w][38] Christum dicit esse crucifixum, id est Marcus, alii uero in sextam[x] eum asserunt ligno crucifixum, quod aput[y] inperitos contraria sibi haec uidebuntur. Sed non sunt contraria in uera ratio,[z][39] ubi se[aa] sic puriter conplectitur diuina scriptura, dum tamen diligentius ruminantur[bb] et bene tractantur ab his qui non de sua, sed de Dei, presumunt sapientia.

[V 60r] 5 Igitur cum natus esset[40] Dominus Iesus in Bethleem, in .xl. et .ii. anno regni Augusti Caesaris, sub Herode rege Iudeorum, et sub preside Cyrino Syriae prouinciae, in duobus annis[41] agens sub ubera uirginis inter homines Dei filius, uenerunt a Persida[a][42] magi, docatum[b] illis prebens[c] stella. Tunc didicit Herodes rex siue toparcha Iudaeorum quod expeculatores uenissent a partibus Persarum, et introissent in Hierusolymam ciuitatem. Et iubens eos adduci, coepit eos interrogare. Venerant enim cognoscentes, quia mistica[d] quedam inbuti, et quae eis apparuerat stella in oriente de humanitatem[e] saluatoris nostri Iesu Christi, deferentesque ei munera tamquam uere regi magno et triumphatori secundum quod eis sidus de caelo nuntiauerat. [V 60v] Qui etiam ab orientalibus aduentantes interrogabant dicentes, 'ubi est qui natus est Iudaeorum rex?' Et conturbati sunt[43] Iudaei. Qui etiam magi cogniti[44] conpraehensi sunt, et introducti sunt ad Herodem regem. Et interrogauit eos quapropter in Iudaeam regionem aduenerint exploratores. Et suggerentes magi miraculum stellae, et quia magnus rex natus est in hoc mundo et quia dona ei[f] cum[g] adduxerint; aduenissent sicut regi magno munera offerturi, dixerunt quia:[h] 'quae optulimus[i] munera ut Deo proferimus. Vidimus enim stellam eius in orientem,[j] et uenimus ut eum adoremus.' Herodes autem, audiens haec, stupens remansit, cogitans quoniam post Augustum Caesarem qualis est uirtus qui natus est regis huius.

[V 61r] 6 Venerunt ergo[45] magi in Hierusolymis[a] sub consolatu[b] Vindicii et Varii anno imperii[46] Augusti[c] Caesaris .xliiii., quia secundo et .xl.

x *for* sexta   y apud L   z *for* uera ratione   aa L *omits*   bb suminantur VL
5 a *for* Perside   b ducatum L   c *for* prebente   d mystica L   e *for* humanitate
f ei *is superscript correction* V   g L *omits*   h q^{u}ia V   i obtulimus L   j *for* oriente
6 a *for* Hierosolymam   b consulatu L   c Aug$\bar{\imath}$ V

was fastened to the wood in the sixth hour; which among the unlearned will seem contradictory to itself. But they are not contradictory[39] in true understanding, where thus divine scripture chastely embraces itself, whilst they are diligently ruminated and well pondered, by those who understand not from their own [wisdom], but from the wisdom of God.

5 Therefore when our Lord Jesus had been born[40] in Bethlehem, in the forty-second year of the rule of Augustus Caesar, under Herod the king of the Jews, and under the governorship of the province of Syria of Cyrinus, and the Son of God had been among men for two years[41] under the breasts of a virgin, *Magi came from Persia,*[42] *with a star giving guidance to them. Then Herod, the king, or toparch, of Jerusalem, learned that seekers had come from the regions of the Persians and entered into the city of Jerusalem. And ordering them to be fetched, he began to question them. For the wise men had come, since they possessed mystic knowledge, and a certain star had appeared to them in the east concerning the humanity of our Saviour Jesus Christ, and they were bringing gifts to him, truly as though to a great king and conqueror,* according to what the star had announced to them from the heavens. *These men who had come from the East began to ask [the Jews], saying: 'where is he who is born king of the Jews?' And the Jews were disquieted.*[43] *And these Magi, once recognized,*[44] *were seized and taken to King Herod. And he questioned them as to why they had come as spies into the land of Judaea. The Magi told of the miracle of the star, and how a great king was born in this world, and that they had brought gifts for him with them, and they came in order to offer gifts to the great king.* And they said: *'the gifts we have offered, we give as to a God. For we have seen his star in the east and came so that we could adore him.'* Herod, however, hearing this, remained astonished, wondering what the nature of this king could be who was born after Augustus Caesar.

6 *The Magi came*[45] *into Jerusalem in the consulate of Vindicius and Varius* in the year[46] of the rule of Augustus Caesar 44, since it was in the forty-

anno eiusdem Augusti[d] Caesaris saluator natus est, et in .ii. anno natiuitatis eius magi uenerunt in Hierusolyma.[e] Exquisiuit[47] igitur ab eis Herodes tempus sideris, et cum didicisset, dixit eis quia: 'ite et scrutamini[48] diligenter de puerum hunc,[f] et cum inueneretis,[g] redientes renuntiate mihi ut ego ueniens adorem eum.' Et abierunt magi, stella quae[h] paululum ab eis abscesserat, prebens[i] iterum[j] illis (sicut prius) ducatum quam in orientem[k] uiderant. Et inuenerunt Iesum[49] et matrem eius Mariam in domo, et cadentes in pauimento terrae, adorauerunt saluatorem Christum, et optulerunt[l] ei munera quae detulerant[m] secum   [V 61v] in suis thensauris[n][50] tamquam Deo et regi[51] aurum, thus[o] et myrra.[p] Et responso accepto[52]   [L 22v] ab angelo[q] per somnio,[r] per aliam uiam limitis[53] regressi sunt in suam regionem in partibus Persarum, contemnentes[s] Herodem regem.

Cumque se inlusum uidisset a magis, Herodes rex iratus est uehementer,[54] et[t] sciscitatus a principibus sacerdotum Iudaeorum ubi Christus nasceretur, didicit ab eis quod in Bethleem Iudeae[u] ciuitatem[v] Dauid nasceretur, secundum quod propheta praedixit.[w][55] Et mittens manum militarem,[56] occidit omnes pueros in Bethleem ciuitatem[v] Iudeae[x] et circa finibus[y] eius a bimatu et infra, secundum tempus quod exquesierat[z] a magis, sicut diuina inquid[aa] scriptura. Et continuo Herodes dum perficisset scelus, scatens uermibus,[57] a Deo percussus[bb] animam   [V 62r] reddidit.

7 Et factus est[a] toparcha[b][58] in terrrchia[c][59] Iudaeorum siue rex Archelaus, filius ipsius Herodis, per annis[d] .viiii., sub consolatu[e] Lamii et Seruiliani;[60] sub quo et saluator et uirgo mater eius Maria cum Ioseph introiit[f] in Egyptum, secundum imperium Dei per angelum[61] apparentis[g] Ioseph, sicut scriptum est:[62] 'ecce Dominus sedet super nubem leuem, ueniet in Aegyptum et comminuet omnia simulacra et sculptilia Aegyptiorum.' Ad aduentum enim saluatoris, sedentis super gremium uirginis matris, dum ingrederentur[63] in Aegypto,[h] erat illic templum

d Augī V   e *for* Hierosolymam   f puero hoc L   g inueneritis L   h *for*
stellaque   i *for* prebente   j *for* itinerem   k *for* oriente   l obtulerunt L
m detulerunt L   n thensauris L *with* n *scratched out*   o tus L   p myrram L
q angelio L   r *for* somnium   s contempnentes L   t L *omits*   u Bethleem
Iudae L   v *for* ciuitate   w p̄d V   v *for* ciuitate   x Iudae L   y *for* fines
z exquaesierat L   aa inquit L   bb percussos L *corrected to* percussus   7 a est *is*
superscript addition V   b thoparcha L   c *for* tetrarchia   d *for* annos
e consulatu L   f *for* introierunt   g *for* apparentem   h *for* Aegyptum

second year of the same Augustus Caesar that the Saviour was born, and the Magi came into Jerusalem two years from his birth. *Therefore Herod enquired*[47] *from them the time of the star*, and when he learned it, *he said to them*: 'Go and enquire[48] carefully about this child, *and when you find him, inform me on your return, so that I may go and adore him.' And the Magi departed, with the star which they had seen in the east* retreating a little from them, again *showing the way to them* as before. *They found Jesus*[49] and Mary *his mother* in a house, *and falling on the floor of earth they adored the Saviour Christ, and offered to him the gifts which they had brought* with them in their treasuries[50] *as if to a God* and king,[51] gold, frankincense and myrrh. *And having*[52] *received a warning* from an angel in a dream, *they returned by another way, by the border,*[53] into their own region *in the lands of the Persians, flouting king Herod.*

When Herod saw that he had been deceived by the Magi, he was very angry,[54] *and having enquired of the leaders of the priests of the Jews where Christ had been born, he learned* from them that he was born in Bethlehem of Judaea, the city of David, following what the prophet predicted.[55] *Sending forth his war-band,*[56] *he killed all the boys in Bethlehem the city of Judaea* and its environs who were two years old or less, according to the time he had established from the Magi, *as holy scripture says. And immediately Herod* had committed this crime, *he was struck by God, and, swarming with worms,*[57] *gave up the ghost.*

7 *And Archelaeus son of that same Herod was made toparch,*[58] *or king, in the tetrarchy*[59] *of the Jews for nine years, under the consulate of Lamius and Servilius,*[60] under him both the Saviour and the virgin Mary his mother, with Joseph, entered into Egypt, following the command of God [expressed] by an angel[61] appearing to Joseph, as it is written:[62] 'Behold, the Lord sits on a light cloud; he will go into Egypt and cast down all the idols and statues of the Egyptians.' At the coming of the Saviour seated on his virgin mother's lap, when they were entering[63] into Egypt, there was

idolorum qui,[i] in presentia Christi, omnia simulacra, de suis locis adque[j] sedilia[k] exsilientes,[l] confracta sunt, in puluerem sunt redacta, quod[m] et beatus Epyfanius Cyprius episcopus conmemorat. [V 62v] Et cum ei expleti essent .iiii. anni[64] in Aegypto, iterum angelus[65] apparens ad Ioseph iubet ut regrediatur in Iudeam terram cum puerum et matrem eius.[n] Et propter metum Archelai[66] filii Herodis habitauit in Nazareth ciuitatem[o] Galileae quasi subocculte. Omnia autem[p] secundum quod ante fuerat praedictum[q] a prophetis sanctis, sicut et in euangelium[r] testimonia proferuntur de propheticis libris.

8 Cum iam autem fuisset puer Iesus annorum .xii., ascenderunt Ioseph et Mariam[a] cum puerum Iesum[b] in templum Domini in Hierusalem, ut Lucas euangelista narrat,[67] et dehinc non amplius infert memoriam de Ioseph, quia scilicet, cum esset senex et plenus dierum, iustus uir in omnibus, requieuit in pacem[c] cum patribus suis. Vsque ad .xii. annos aetatis saluatoris [V 63r] uixit, et deinceps quieuit, sicut nobis paterna conmendat auctoritas.[68]

Augustus[d][69] uero Caesar, .lvi. anno regni sui mense Octubrio, qui et Perbereteo[70] secundum Athineos[e] dicitur, habiit in Capitolium, quod est in medium orbis[f][71] Romae, ut per diuinationem addisceret quis regnaturus fuisset post ipsum in Romanam rempuplicam.[g] Et dictum est ei a pythoniam[h] quod infans hebreus, iubens Deus e caelo beatorum, discutiens hunc[i] domicilium, cetero[j] genitus sine macula, statim iam[k] uenienti,[l] alienusque ab aris nostris. Qui exiens inde Augustus[m] Caesar a diuinationem[n] et ueniens in Capitolium, aedificauit ibi aram magnam in sublimiori loco, in qua et scripsit latinis litteris dicens: haec aram[o] filii Dei est. Vnde factum est post tot annis[p] domicilium adque baselicam[q] [V 63v] beatae et semper [L 23r] uirginis Mariae usque in presentem diem, sicut et Timotheus chronografus commemorat.[r] Post hoc autem ipse Augustus[s] morte sua defunctus est senex, cum esset annorum .lxxv..

i q^{u}i V; quae L   j adque *is superscript addition* V   k *for* sedilibus   l exilientes L
m quo L   n puero et matre L   o ciuitate L   p L *omits*   q prēdtum V
r euangelio L   8 a Maria L   b puero Iesu L   c pace L   d Augs̄ V
e *for* Athinienses   f medio urbis L   g Romana republica L   h *for* pythonia
i hoc L   j *for* ceterum   k L *omits*   l *for* ueniet   m Augs̄ V   n diuinatione L
o ara L   p annos L   q basilicam L   r conmemorat L   s Augs̄ VL

there a temple of idols, in which at the presence of Christ, all the idols starting from their places and thrones were broken and reduced to dust, as the blessed Epiphanius, bishop of Cyprus, records. And when four years were completed for him[64] in Egypt, the angel appearing[65] again to Joseph ordered that he should return into the land of Judaea with the child and his mother. And for fear of Archelaeus[66] the son of Herod, he lived rather clandestinely in Nazareth, a city of Galilee. All this was according to what had previously been predicted by the holy prophets, as the testimony of the gospels sets out from the prophetic books.

8 When the boy Jesus had already reached the age of twelve, Joseph and Mary went up with the boy Jesus to the temple of the Lord in Jerusalem, as the evangelist Luke relates;[67] and he makes no further mention of Joseph, who doubtless, since he was 'an old man and full of days', a just man in all things, rested in peace with his fathers. He lived up to the twelfth year of age of the Saviour, and then died, as patristic authority tells us.[68]

Augustus Caesar,[69] *being in the fifty-sixth year of his reign, in the month of October, which is called Hyperbereteus*[70] according to the Athenians, *went to* the Capitol, which is in the centre of the city[71] of Rome, *so that he could learn by divination, who was to reign after him in the Roman republic. It was said to him by the pythoness that, 'a Jewish baby, a God commanding from the heaven of the blessed,* born without stain *and breaking up this abode for another, is imminently arriving, and is hostile to our altars.' Augustus Caesar, following on from this prophecy, and going to the Capitol, built there a great altar in a higher place, on which he wrote in Latin letters, saying 'This is the altar of the Son of God.'* Whence was made after many years the home and basilica of the blessed and ever-virgin Mary *up to the present day, as Timothy the chronographer notes. After this Augustus died his death, an old man, when he was seventy-five.*

9 Post regnum uero Augusti Caesaris,[72] sub consolatu Sexti et Sexticiani,[73] regnauit Tiberius[a] Caesar, cum esset Dominus Iesus Christus
inter homines habens aetatis annos .xv.. In anno autem .xv. regni[74]
eiusdem Tiberii[b] Caesaris, sub consolatu Siluani et Neri,[75] coepit sanctus
Iohannes precursor predicare baptismum penitentiae,[c] et baptizabatur
omnes Iudea[d] secundum propheticam uocem.

Tunc uenit[76] ad eum Dominus Iesus Christus a Galilea in Iordanne[e]
incipiens annorum .xxx., id est dies .xii. super annos .xx. et .viiii., qui[f]
octaua kal. Ianuarias natus est de uirgine, et .viii. idus Ianuarias baptizatus ex aqua est, ex quo   [V 64r] et mirabilia facere inchoauit. Et baptizatus est in Iordanne[g] flumine Palestine in mense Audineo, qui et Ianuario,
die sexta mensis, .viii. iduum Ianuariarum, in nocte ora[h] decima noctis,
hoc est in diluculo, sub consolatu Ruphi et Rubellionis.[77] Ex quo et
Iohannes baptista declaratus factus est hominibus, quem et decollauit[78]
Herodes in carcerem[i] in Sebastiam urbem[j79] .iiii. kal. Septembris, sub
consolatu[k] Flaconis et Rufini,[80] propter Herodiam[l] uxorem Filippi fratris
sui, eo quod inlicite duxerat eam, sicut scriptum est.

10 Anno igitur[81] .xviii. regni Tiberii[a] Caesaris, mense etiam .vii.
octaui decimi anni regni eius, factus annorum circa[b] .xxxiii. Iesus Christus
Dominus noster traditus est a Iuda Scariotes[c] discipulo suo,   [V 64v]
mense Distro, qui et Martio, .xxiiii. die mensis, id est .viiii. kal. Aprilis,
luna .xiii. habens[d] diem. Erat autem[e] dies .v. feriae, ora[f] nocturna .vi., et
ductus[g] est ad Caipham principem sacerdotum,[h] et inde traditus est
Pontio Pilato[82] presidi prima mane. Et continuo eiusdem Pilati uxor,
nomine Procla,[83] misit ad eum dicens: nihil tibi et iusto illi; multum[i]
enim passa sum hodie per uisum propter eum. Et cognoscentes hoc, Iudaei
seditionem concitauerunt,[84] dicentes: 'tolle, tolle, crucifige eum.'[85]

Erat igitur ora[j] .iii. quando adclamauerunt Iudaei suis uocibus cruci-
figentes filium Dei. Accipiens autem sententia,[k] Dominus noster Iesus

---

9 a Tyberius L   b Tyberii L   c paenitentiae L   d in Iudea L   e Iordanem L
f *for* quia   g Iordane L   h hora L   i carcere L   j Sebastia urbe L
k consulatu L   l Herodiadem L   10 a Tyberii L   b L *omits*   c Scariothis L,
for Scariote   d *for* habente   e L *omits*   f hora L   g deductus L
h sacerdotem L *corrected to* sacerdotum   i *for* multa?   j hora L   k sententiam L

9 *After the reign of Augustus Caesar*[72] *in the consulate of Sextus and Sexticianus,*[73] *Tiberius Caesar reigned,* when the Lord Jesus Christ was among men, being fifteen years of age. *In the fifteenth year*[74] *of the reign of the same Tiberius Caesar, in the consulate of Silvanus and Nerva,*[75] *the Precursor St John [the Baptist] began to preach the baptism of penitence, and all Judaea was baptized according to his prophetic voice.*

Then the Lord Jesus Christ came[76] to him from Galilee *to Jordan, at the beginning of his thirtieth year,* that is, twelve days after his twenty-ninth year. He was born of a virgin on the octave of the kalends of January [25 December], and on the eighth of the ides of January [6 January] he was baptized with water, *after which he began to work miracles. And he was baptized in Jordan, the river of Palestine, in the month Audineus, which is January, on the sixth day of the month,* the eighth of the ides of January, *at night, the tenth hour of the night,* which is the dawn, *in the consulate of Rufus and Rubellio.*[77] *From which John became known to men as the Baptist, whom Herod beheaded*[78] in prison *in the city of Sebaste*[79] on the fourth of the kalends of September [28 August], *in the consulate of Flacco and Rufinus,*[80] *on account of Herodias,* the wife of his brother Philip, *because, as it is written, he had sinfully married her.*

10 *In the eighteenth year*[81] *of the reign of Tiberius Caesar, in the seventh month* of the eighteenth year of his reign, *having lived some thirty-three years, our Lord Jesus Christ was betrayed by Judas Iscariot his disciple in the month of Distrus, which is March, on the twenty-fourth day of the month,* that is on the ninth of the kalends of April, *the thirteenth day of the moon. It was the fifth ferial day [Thursday] and the sixth hour of the night.* He was led to Caiaphas the high priest, and from there was handed over to Pontius Pilate[82] the prefect at dawn. *And immediately, the wife of Pilate, whose name was Procla,*[83] *sent to him saying: 'let there be nothing between you and this just man, for I have suffered much concerning him in a vision.' And getting to know this, the Jews stirred up strife*[84] *against Him, saying 'take Him, take Him and crucify Him.'*[85]

It was then the third hour, when the Jews clamoured with their voices to crucify the Son of God. Accepting their decision, our Lord Jesus Christ

Christus crucifixus est specialiter .viii. kal. Aprilis,[l] mense Martio .xxv. die mensis, luna .xiiii.. Erat autem .vi. feria parasceue[86] ora[m] [V 65r] diei .vi., et obscuratus est sol,[87] et erant tenebrae[88] per uniuersum. mundum. Anno autem .xviii. imperii Tiberii[n] Caesaris haec facta sunt ita, ut fieret defectio solis[89] maximam[o] quam que nota sunt[p] contigisse prius, et fuit nox hora diei .vi., ita ut stellas[q] in caelo apparerent. Saluator uero Iesus Christus tradidit spiritum ora[r] nona. Et statim facta est lux[90] in omnem terram,[s] et terre motus magnus, et patefacta sunt monumenta et petre fissae sunt et mortui resurrexerunt, sicut in diuinis euangeliis efferuntur ueraciter, ita ut dicerent Iudaei:[91] 'uere filius Dei erat iste [L 23v] quem crucifiximus.' Et sepultus est Iesus Christus ora[t] decima in ipsa parasceue die, sub consolatu Sulpicii et Solati,[92] procurante Syriae Casio preside.

11 Surrexit autem[93] Dominus noster et Deus Iesus Christus [V 65v] mense Distro, qui et Martio, uicessima[a] septima die mensis, id est sexta kal. Aprilis ora[b] nocturna .x. circa diluculo,[c][94] lucescente die dominica. In ipso mense Martio, .vii. et .xx. die mensis, luna .xvi. unde et primo quidem apparuit prima mane[95] Mariae Magdalene, et deinde suis discipulis apostolis et aliis sanctis quam plurimis, et commoratus est cum eis per dies .xl. super terram postquam resurrexit a mortuis, et adsumptus est in caelis Dominus noster et Deus Iesus Christus mense Artemisio, qui et Maio, .v. die mensis, id est .iii. nonas Maias die .v. feriae, ora[d] .ii., sanctorum apostolorum uidentium[e][96] et alia turba discipolorum[f] quomodo assumptus est a nuuibus[g], et sanctorum angelorum dicentium[h] illis: 'Quid aspicitis[97] in caelum uiri Galilei? Hic Iesus qui asumptus est a uobis [V 66r] sic iterum ueniet quemadmodum eum uidetis euntem in caelum.'[i]

Discendit autem secundum Domini pollicitationem sanctus et uiuificator spiritus super apostolos mense Artemisio, qui et Maio, .xv. die mensis, die Dominica ora[j] .iii., agens[k] presidatum in Iudaea[l] idem Pontius Pilatus[m][98] qui adsignatus fuerat principari genti Iudaeorum ab ipso Tiberio Caesare, qui dissoluit regnum Iudaeorum et constituens ei[n] principem peresse

---

l Aprelis L   m hora L   o *for* maxima   p *for* quae notae sunt   q *for* stellae
r hora L   s *for* omni terra   t hora L   11 a vicesima L   b hora L
c diluculum L   d hora L   e *for* sanctis apostolis uidentibus   f discipulorum L
g nubibus L   h *for* sanctis angelis dicentibus   i *There is a small cross here*
j hora L   k *for* agente   l Iudea L   m *for* eodem Pontio Pilato   n *for* eis

was crucified specifically *on the eighth of the kalends of April, in the month of March*, on the twenty-fifth day of the month, *the fourteenth day of the moon. It was also* the sixth ferial day [Friday], *the 'day of preparation'*,[86] *at the sixth hour of the day. The sun was hidden*,[87] *and there was darkness*[88] *all over the world. These things happened in the eighteenth year of the reign of Tiberius Caesar, in such a way that, as it is said, there was an eclipse of the sun*[89] *greater than is said to have happened before, and there was night in the sixth hour of the day, so that stars appeared in the sky. The Saviour Jesus Christ gave up his soul at the ninth hour. And immediately it was made* light[90] *over all the earth, and there was a great movement of the earth and the graves were opened and rocks were split and the dead came alive, as is truly reported in the holy gospels, so that the Jews said:*[91] '*This was truly the Son of God whom we crucified.' And Jesus Christ was buried at the tenth hour on that same 'day of preparation' in the consulate of Sulpicius and Solatus*,[92] *with Cassius ruling as governor of Syria.*

11 *Our Lord and God Jesus Christ rose*[93] *in the month Distrus, which is March, on the twenty-seventh day of the month*, that is, the sixth of the kalends of April, *on the tenth hour of the night*, about dawn,[94] *in the first light of Sunday. In the same month of March, the twenty-seventh day of the month, the sixteenth day of the moon*, he first *appeared* in the early morning[95] to Mary Magdalene, and then to his disciples *the apostles, and to as many other holy people as possible, and stayed with them on the earth for forty days after he rose from the dead. And our Lord and God Jesus Christ was taken into the heavens in the month Artemisios, which is May, on the fifth day of the month*, which is the third of the nones of May, *the fifth ferial day, at the second hour, with the holy apostles*[96] *and a crowd of other* disciples *watching how he was taken up from the clouds, with the holy angels saying to them:*[97] '*why do you look at the sky, men of Galilee? This Jesus* who is taken from you will return again in the same way as you see him going up to heaven.'

The holy and life-giving Spirit descended on the apostles by divine command *in the month Artemisios, which is May, on the fifteenth day of the month, on Sunday, at the third hour, when the same Pontius Pilate*[98] *held power in Judaea, who had been assigned to rule over the Jewish people by that same Tiberius Caesar who dissolved the kingdom of the Jews and created for them a leader to be over them*

qualemque[o] uoluisset, sub pontificatus sacerdotio[p] Iudaeorum Annae et Caiphae.[99]

12 Hic[a] namque loco licet inspicere quidquid[b] pertulerit Christus, salus et redimptio[c] nostra. Omnia gesta sunt in hominem plenum[d] cum Deo:[100] nam quod Christus per angelum uirgini nuntiatur ad euacuandum[101] consilium serpentis ad Euam in paradyso; [V 66v] quod autem[102] de uirgine natus est propter protoplaustum Adam[e], quem de uirgine terra et inpolluta ad suam fecit imaginem,[103] qui cum suadente diabulo mortis incorrisset[f] exitium, a solo Domino Christo rerum reparator et conditor[g] eius[h] corporis et animae per inmortalitatis[i] Christi restauraretur[j] domicilium; quod autem decimi mensis limitem[104] tetigisset in uirginis uterum,[k] id est die[l] .vi. super mense nono, perficiens quod nullus ex filiis hominum tangit metrum nascendo per semine, nisi solus Christus uerus filius Dei et hominis sine seminatus[m] ex uirgine, ita ut fiant dies in una collectione constricti .cclxxvi., qui fiunt allegoricae[n] uel tipicam[o] questionem;[105] quod ipse[p] affatus in euangelio ait: 'soluite templum hoc,[106] et ego in tribus [V 67r] diebus suscitabo illud.' Sed Iudaei ignorantes capitulum rationis protulerunt testimonium ueritatis, et ita Domino respondentes aiunt: '.xl. et .vi. annos aedificatum est templum hoc, et tu in tribus diebus suscitabis illud?' Ille autem, inquid[q] euangelista, dicebat de templo corporis sui, cuius dispensationem adpraehendere nequiuerunt Iudaei. Ideoque nomerum[r] annorum aedificationis templi,[107] qui uiri templi formas[s][108] gereuat Domino protulerunt, quem nomerum non sub Salamonem conditorem[t][109] eiusdem templi, sed sub Zorobabil qui et hesdram[u][110] restauratorem[v] contigisse perlegitur, eo quod[w] gentes quae in circuitu erant,[111] opus cottidie praepedibant. Nam Salomon in annis .vii. compleuit opus aedificii templi Domini.

---

o *for* qualemcumque   p *for* pontificatu sacerdotum   12 a *for* hoc
b q[u]idquid V   c redemptio L   d *for* homine pleno   e ad Adam L
f incurrisset L   g *for* reparatore et conditore   h L *omits*   i *for* inmortalitatem
j restauretur L   k *for* utero   l *for* dies   m semine natus L   n alligorice L;
for allegoricam   o typicam L   p L *omits*   q inquit L   r numerum L
s *The missing leaf of L begins here*   t *for* Salomone conditore   u *for* hesdras
v *for* restauratore   w q[u]od V

in whatever way he should wish, in the pontificate of the Jewish priests Annas and Caiaphas.[99]

12 At this point it is appropriate to consider what Christ, our salvation and redemption, accomplished. All things were done in full humanity with God:[100] for Christ was announced to a virgin by an angel, in order to nullify[101] the counsel of the serpent to Eve in paradise; he[102] was born of a virgin, on account of Adam the first man, whom he had made in his own image[103] of virgin and unpolluted earth [but] who, when at the persuasion of the devil he underwent the destruction of death, was restored to his heavenly home by the Lord Christ alone, through the immortality of Christ, restorer of things and creator of his body and soul; he touched the border of the tenth month[104] in the womb of the Virgin, that is, six days over nine months, achieving a measure which no son of man achieved by being born from seed, except Christ alone, the true Son of God and of mankind, born without insemination, from a virgin, so that 276 days were bound together in one unit, which raise a typological or allegorical question,[105] as he himself said in the gospel: 'Cast down this temple,[106] and I will raise it in three days.' But the Jews, not understanding the pillar (or head) of reason, uttered a testimony of truth, and responded thus to the Lord: 'This temple was built in forty-six years, and you will raise it in three days?' But he was saying this, the evangelist tells us, of the temple of his body, the dispensation of which the Jews were not able to grasp. And thus they set out to the Lord the years of the building of the temple,[107] which he gave in the guise of a temple as a man.[108] This should be understood to relate not to the number [of years] under Solomon,[109] the originator of the temple, but to Zorobabil,[110] also called Esdras, the restorer, because the pagans who were around[111] hindered the work daily. For Solomon completed the work of building the temple of the Lord in seven years.

13 Etenim uisus noster pacificus Salomon aedificauit sibi per sapientiam in uirginem[a] sacratissima [V 67v] sui corporis templum per hunc nomerum sanctum,[112] id est per nono[b] menses et dies .vi. quia omnis natiuitas masculi decimi mensis tangit initia,[113] et sic prodit ad huius uitae quatentia.[c][114] Nam hoc ordine, secundum auctoritate[d] maiorum nostrorum adque priorum, dicitur aut legitur: generis humani conceptio quod per .vi. diebus[e][115] lactis similitudinem habens manet[f] semen in uulua.[g] Dehinc conuertetur in sanguinem usque ad dies .viiii..[116] Deinde augetur usque ad .xii., et dehinc adduntur .x. et .viii.: qui mox coaculatur et tendit ad liniamenta membrorum.[117] Ita namque .vi. et .viiii. .xii. et .xviii. fiunt simul .xlv.; addes unum, et fiunt .xlvi.. Et inde ducis per partes,[118] id est sexies quadrageni .ccxl., et iterum idem per sextam sexseni .xxxvi., tries sexis,[h][119] qui in unam[i] summa fiunt .cclxxvi.. Et ideo [V 68r] quod in Domino solo una cadit dies super .xlv., propter singularem eius incarnationem de uirgine sine corruptionem siue gluttinatio[j] seminis. Eo quod secundum typum historiabilis templi .xl. et .vi. annis aedificatum,[k] ita corpus Christi humanitatis suae per hunc gradum restaurans parietem in semetipsos quem in Adam suis fraudulentiis diabulus callidus serpens ruinauerat, illius salutaris[l] aedificium restauraret. Et passus post tertium diem numquam iam moriturus erigeret et sic omnem hominem a[m] subiectione[n] diabuli liberaret.

Nam .xl. et .vi. significat sextam, quam mundus agebat aetatem, dum reparator suae fauriciae[120] adueniret, et perfectam penitentiam per numerum[121] perfectionis quadragensimae ieiunium penitentibus demonstraret. Vnde et ipse saluator temptatus a diabulo[o] uelut homo, uictor exstitit [V 68v] ut Deus ergo per .xl[o]. et sexto numero tertioque duplicato[p] omnem humani generis massa[q] in unam fidei fermentando[122] coagulauit consparsio.[r]

14 Quod autem ex femineo editus uentre, positus in presepio,[123] pannis est obuolutus, propter illum uersiculum quod Dauid iusiurando[a]

---

13 a *for* uirgine   b *for* nouem   c q^u atentia V   d *for* auctoritatem   e *for* dies
f nam et V   g uulba, V *corrected by erasing the ascender of* b   h *for* trecies sexies?
i *for* una   j *for* corruptione siue gluttinatione   k *for* aedificati   l *for* salutare
m ad V, *with* d *scratched out*   n subiectionem V, *with* m *scratched out*   o dibulo V,
with subscript a *added to* b   p *for* xl et sextum numerum tertiumque duplicatum   q *for*
massam   r *for* conspersionem   14 a *for* iureiurando

13 It is seen that our peacemaker Solomon built for himself through wisdom the temple of his body in the most holy Virgin by means of this holy number,[112] that is, by nine months and six days, since all birth of males touches the beginning[113] of the tenth month, and thus it shows forth the [   ][114] of this life. For in this order, according to the authority of our seniors and predecessors, is said, and read, to be the conception of the human race; that for six days[115] the semen remains in the womb, having the appearance of milk. Then it is turned into blood for nine days,[116] then it grows for twelve days, and after that it adds eighteen days: it is soon coagulated, and grows towards the outline of limbs.[117] So six and nine, twelve and eighteen together make forty-five, add one, and make forty-six, and from there you extend through the parts,[118] that is, to six forties, 240. And the same again through the six; six sixes, thirty-six, a three and a six,[119] which in one sum make 276. There is one day over the forty-five in the [case of] the Lord alone, on account of his unique incarnation from a virgin, without sin or the drawing-together of semen. So according to the type [revealed by] the forty-six years of building of the historical temple, thus the body of Christ in his humanity, restoring the wall in Himself through these steps, which the cunning serpent the devil destroyed in Adam with his deceits, restored his healthy building. And having suffered, rose again after the third day never more to die, and thus liberated all mankind from the subjection of the devil.

For forty and six signified the sixth age, which the world was undergoing, when the restorer of its fabric[120] came, and showed forth to the penitent the completed penance through the number[121] of perfection of a forty-day fast. From whence this same Saviour, having been tempted by the devil as if he was a man, was a victor. God therefore, for the fortieth and sixth number, the doubled threes, coagulated the whole lump of humankind into a single faith with scattered leaven.[122]

14 When he had come forth from a female womb, he was placed in a manger,[123] wrapped in swaddling-cloths, according to that verse in which

Deus promiserat dicens: 'de fructum[b] uentris[124] tui ponam super sedem tuam.' Presepium totus mundus adseritur, in quo suis iumentis rationabilibus pabulum subministrat Dominus magestatis. Pannis uero aduoluitur nostras miserias quatiendo, in quibus adibens nobis enplastra nostris uulneribus exibuit medecinam.[125]

Quod autem in Bethleem Iudae[c] ciuitatem[d] Dauid nascere uoluit Christus, propter illut quod ante iam pronuntiatum fuerat Iacob fugienti.[126] [V 69r] Dum suporatus, scalam ibi ad caelum usque conspiceret, et angelos Dei ascendentes et descendentes uidisset, et Deum in summo incubuisset[e] aspiceret.[127] Dixit: 'hic est',[f] et lapidem quem ad caput[g] sibi Iacob posuerat in similitudinem illius lapidis angularis,[128] 'uere domus Dei[129] est et porta caeli,' unde appellatur Bethel; cui iuncti duo[h] parietes[130] e diuerso uenientes condidit, in semetipso copulauit, scilicet populorum conexio[i] Iudaeorum adque gentilium pacem in utrosque perficiens. Quod uero amirauiles pastores uel uigiles[j] inuenitur, siue quod in cunabulis[k] adoratur, typum gerebatur optimorum pastorum, quos Christus paterfamilias constituens super famulos et famulas, ut iuste trittici mensuram distribuant[131] sollicite diligenterque mandauit; [V 69v] uel illius qui ter ait[132] iniungens: 'pasce oues meas,' ne luporum inpetus[l][133] conturbati pascua predant placita mea.

15 Quod autem a magis primo[a] omnium gentium uelut nationum primitias[b][134] adoratur, omnium creatorem et dominatorem significant esse uenturum, et in gentibus crediturum adque in muneribus oblatio[c] Deum et regem. Sed et uictimae sepulturam murram dicitur[135] adtributam,[d] ut per trinae[e] species[136] munerum, id est aurum regi, thus ut Deo, murra ut morituro, tamquam unam deitatem[f] patris et filii ac spiritus sancti sancta et indiuidua trinitas adoraretur in Christo, crederetur in mundo, praedicaretur in gentibus. Quod stella ducatum magis prebuerit, propter illud quod legitur: 'orietur stella',[137] inquid, 'ex Iacob, et ascendit

b *for* fructu   c *for* Iudeae   d *for* ciuitate   e *for* incubuisse   f *For emendation to word-order, see below,* p. 201, n. 127   g *for* capitem (*or* sub capite)   h *for* iunctos duos   i *for* conexionem   j *for* a admirabilibus pastoribus uel uigilibus?   k *for* cunabulo   l *for* inpetu   15 a *for* primis   b *for* primitiis   c *for* munerum oblatione? Or in muneribus offerturum?   d *for* murra. . .adtributa   e *for* trinam   f *for* una deitas

God made a promise to David with an oath, saying: 'I will place the fruit of your belly[124] on the throne.' The whole world is declared the manger, in which the Lord of majesty administers sustenance to his rational draught-animals. He is wrapped in cloths for shaking our miseries, in which, approaching, he showed forth to us medication and plasters for our wounds.[125]

Christ wished to be born in Bethlehem of Judaea the city of David, because of what was previously foretold to the fugitive Jacob.[126] While he was asleep, he saw a ladder reaching up to heaven, and perceived angels of God ascending and descending it, and saw God sitting at the top.[127] He said, 'This is truly the house of God[128] and the gate of heaven,' from which it is called Bethel [House of God]. The stone which Jacob had put under his head is a similitude of the Corner-Stone,[129] from which he made two walls meeting,[130] coming from different directions, and he joined them together, as it were the linking of the Jewish people with the gentiles, creating peace between both. He is found by admirable shepherds and watchmen, like those by whom he was adored in his cradle, and they exist as a type of the good shepherds, whom Christ the paterfamilias commanded sedulously and diligently, setting them over his manservants and maidservants, so that they might justly distribute the measure of wheat;[131] or of him [St Peter], to whom he spoke three times,[132] urging: 'Feed my sheep,' lest disturbed by the attack of wolves[133] they lose my pleasant pastures.

15 Since he was adored by the Magi, the first fruit[134] of all the peoples or nations, they signify that the creator and master of all will return, a God and King, honoured with gifts to believers among the gentiles. For it is said[135] that myrrh was brought for the burial of the victim, so that through the three kinds[136] of gifts, that is, gold to a king, incense to a God, myrrh to one about to die, one Godhead of Father, Son and Holy Spirit in the holy and undivided Trinity might be adored in Christ, believed in the world, and preached among the peoples. This is read on the subject of what the star showed forth in leading the Magi: 'a star arises',[137] it says, 'from Jacob, and a man goes up into Israel and destroys all the

homo in Israhel, et confringet omnes duces   [V 70r] alienige/narum.' Et
illud: 'omnes a Saba[138] uenient ferentes aurum, thus, et murra,g salutare
Domino nuntiantes.'

Quod autem persecutus ab Herode, perfido regeque cruento,[139] ut
adimpleretur scriptura quae dicit: 'uox in excelso',[140] hoc est in Rama,
'audita est; pluratus et luctus magnus, Rachel plurans filios suos, et noluit
consolare, quoniam non sunt.' Inlusus namque a magis, saeuit Herodes
aduersus Christum et quasi posset inter ceteros unum iugulare quem sibi
succedere miser timebat. Milia paruolorum in persona unius infantis
impius et crudelis mactauit; sed ab angelo sancto munitus per uisum,[141]
Ioseph tulit puerum cum matremh eius in Aegyptum. Et Herodes, contra
suum iudicium, sine causa paruorum innocentum crimine, pressum infan-
tum pernegauit[142] exercitum.

[V 70v]   16 Quod autem circumcisionem[143] Christus in carne pertulerit, propter illud quod apostulus ait:[144] 'Christus enim', inquid,a
'ministrum circumcisionis fuisse credendum est.' Et illud de Exodi:b[145]
'cum proficisceretur Moyses imperante Domino ad Aegyptum, et secum
comitaretur coniux cum liberis, occurrit ei angelus interficere illum
uolens. Ad quidc adtonita Sepphora, accipiens lapidem, circumcidit
puerum; et propter sanguinem circumcisionis pueri, pepercit angelus ne
interficeret.' Vnde circumcisiod Christi omnese legis ira cessauit, et
sanguis eius pondera dura tulit,[146] eo quod 'finis legis Christus',[147] 'qui
maledictum[148] uetustatis absoluit', et a seruitutis iugumf nos liberauit.
Quod autem adcreuisse sapientia[149] quoque coram Deo et hominesg
summae adque perfectaeh in hominei plenumj   [V 71r] gessit in aeuo, ita
ut incipiens annorum .xxx.[150] baptismum uoluntarius[151] a Iohanne
peteret in Iordanne, propter illud quod ait apostulus: 'donec omnes',[152]
inquid, 'occurramus in uirum perfectum in mensuram aetatis plenitudinis
Christi.'

17 Nam et primum hominem Deus aetatem perfectum[153] nec non et
intellectum adque rationema praeditum, et suae scilicet uoluntatis

g *for* murram   h *for* matre   16 a inquid V   b *for* Exodo   c *for* Ad quod
d *for* circumcisione   e *for* omnis   f *for* iugo   g *for* hominibus   h *for*
summam ... perfectam   i *for* hominis   j *for* plenitudinem   17 a *for* intellectu
adque ratione

leaders of alien peoples.' And this: 'they all will come from Sheba[138] carrying gold, incense and myrrh, announcing greetings to the Lord.'

Having been persecuted by Herod, the faithless, bloody king,[139] so that the scripture might be fulfilled which said, 'A voice raised up',[140] that is, 'in Rama, was heard weeping and moaning greatly, Rachel weeping for her children, and she would not be consoled, because they were not.' Herod, deceived by the Magi, raged against Christ, as if he was able to kill the one among all the others whom the wretched man feared would supplant him. And the impious and cruel man murdered a thousand babies in the guise of a single infant; but warned by a holy angel in a dream,[141] Joseph took the child with Mary his mother into Egypt, and Herod, in contradiction to his own promise, massacred[142] an oppressed army of babies, without any pretext of crime from the innocent little ones.

16 Christ suffered circumcision[143] in the body, according to what the apostle said:[144] 'It should be believed, I say, that Christ was a minister of the circumcision'. And this is in Exodus:[145] 'When Moses was going to Egypt according to the will of the Lord and took along with him his wife with the children, an angel came to him wishing to kill him. At which the astonished Sepphora, taking a stone, circumcised the child, and on account of the blood of the child's circumcision the angel spared him, and did not kill him.' From this, all the anger of the law ceased at the circumcision of Christ, and his blood bore a heavy weight,[146] because 'Christ is the end of the Law',[147] who dissolved the curse[148] of the Old [Testament] and liberated us from the yoke of slavery. After this, he increased in wisdom[149] before God and men, and he reached the age of full perfection for man, so that at the beginning of his thirtieth year[150] he voluntarily[151] sought baptism from John in the Jordan, according to what the apostle says:[152] 'we will all come to manly perfection; to the measure of the fullness of the age of Christ.'

17 For God made the first man of perfect age[153] endowed made with intelligence and reason; so that he would be the ruler of his will and judge-

143

[L 24r] rector esset arbitrii, de terra fincxit[b]154 incolomem iuuenem, et eius coniugem plenam nubilis[c] annis, pectore uirgo,[d]155 decora[e] in omni membro, iamque maturam, ita pulchrum oculis uisum, eduxit ex latere[156] dormientis. Quia non paruolorum motibus[f] aut teneritate mentium puerorum, in corpore paruo quatentium, adque pedum manuum linguarumue praepeditas[g] sermonum et actuum, [V 71v] sed aetate ratione solidate membrorum adque[h] sapientiae plenos primo Deus ex luto terrae fecisse credendum est;[i] ut ex illorum materiam[j] subolem tamquam ex arborum[k] rami uel fructus primum quidem tenues postea iam paulatim maturi uel firmi uidentur proficere. Ita namque omnis natura firma et solida quidquid protulerit, ostendit reparante auctore deo dum generat.

Et sic quippe credendum est quia homo in primordio factus a Domino aetate legitimus et mente plenus et capacem[l] rationis in qua uictoriam caperet, si mortis superasset auctorem. Et ideo namque pena[m] mortis incurrit, quia non sub paruoli motu et infirmior sensui,[n] sed plenus ratione, homo in paradysu[o] deliquid quia scienti bonum facere et non facien [V 72r] ti peccatum est illi.

Renouatur autem per gratia[p] creatoris qui solum paruolos coronauit, dum natus est uerum aetiam[q] diabulum pescauit cum passus est, donando nobis quod ipse gessit in carne, ut resurrectionis similiter Christi, omnis anima .xxx. surgat[157] annorum aetate, in hac ipsa quam gessit uiuens in corpore carnem,[r] ut recipiat[158] unusquisque iuxta quod egit in corpore siue bonum siue malum.

18 Quod autem baptismum a[a] Iohannem[b] Christus libenter acceperit,[c] ut tu non dedigneris[159] a conseruo suscipere, quod ille non deuitor,[d]160 sed Dominus sine peccato sumere uoluit a seruo, ut inter ipsa fluenta Iordanis super unum mediatorem[161] Dei et hominum sanctae trinitatis declararetur auctoritas, dum Deus pater in uoce,[162] filius in hominem,[e]

b finxit L   c nobilis L; *for* plenis nubilem   d *for* uirginem   e *for* decoram
f metibus L   g *for* praepeditos   h atque L   i *for* credendus   j *for* materia
k *for* arbore   l *for* capax   m *for* penam (*or* penae)   n *for* infirmo sensui
o paradiso L   p *for* gratiam   q etiam L   r *for* carne   18 a L *omits*
b *for* Iohanne   c acciperat L   d debitor L   e *for* homine

ment, he created an unimpaired young man from the earth,[154] and brought forth from his side[155] while he was sleeping his wife of fully mature age, with a virgin breast,[156] graceful in all her limbs and already adult, and thus beautiful to the sight of the eye. Since, not having the movement of babies, or the immaturity of mind of children, stumbling in their little bodies and handicapped in words and in the action of their feet, hands and tongues, but established in the age of control of their members, and full of wisdom: it is thus that God is said to have first made them from mud of the earth, so that from their substance, offspring could be produced, like branches or fruit, which are seen to emerge from trees rather tender at first, then afterwards, little by little, mature and firm. For thus all nature shows firm and solid whatever it has proffered, with God the creator restoring what he creates.

And thus it should be believed that man was made in the beginning by God appropriate in age and capable in mind and full of understanding, with which he could have captured victory, if he had been able to overcome the author of death. And accordingly he incurred the penalty of death, since he was not under the motion of a child and deficient in sense, but a person full of intelligence offending in paradise, since it was in his knowledge [power] to do good and not to do wrong.

Renewed, however, through the creator's grace, who did not only crown babies when he was born, but truly also crushed the devil when he suffered; what he did in the flesh was as a gift for us, so that at the Resurrection all souls will rise[157] like Christ at thirty years old, the age he reached when he was living in the body, so that each one will receive[158] flesh according to what he had in this body, whether good or bad.

18 Christ freely accepted baptism from John the Baptist, which you do not deign[159] to receive from a fellow-slave, but which he did not despise. He, not a transgressor,[160] but the Lord without sin, wished to take it from his servant, and in that flood of Jordan, the authority of the Holy Trinity was declared in one mediator[161] between God and man, when God the Father in his voice,[162] the Son in his manhood, and the Holy Spirit in the form of a dove, showed forth divinity and a single constant and undivided majesty and godhead. When he was cast out from the spirit into the

[V 72v] spiritus sanctus in columbe speciae[f] demonstratur[g] diuinitas, et unam[h] constans indiuisa deitas adque magestas.[i] Quod autem ab spiritu expulsus in deserto,[j][163] id est calefactus[164] homo, quem sumpserat propter ueterem Adam, quem intra delicias[k] paradysi diabulus uicerat, hic in deserto cum inimico comfligere cupiens, et per ieiunii munus de illo uictoriam capiens, omnibus suis fidelibus traderet conculcandum. In qua uictoria ante propheta Zaccharias cecinit[165] dicens: 'uidi', inquid, 'Iesum sacerdotem magnum, et stabat ad[l] dextris eius diabulus,[m] id est ex parte iustitiae, concinnans dolos.[166] Et dixit ad eum: "increpet tibi Dominus, diabule, qui redimit Israhel, et elegit Hierusalem."' Nobis ergo uicit qui solus uictoriam de diabulo capere potuit, [V 73r] quod autem discipolos[n] ex piscatoribus[167] facit, ut non ex sanguine nobilitatis[o][168] plaudentium, sed ex pauperum gregem[p] humiliter sentientium, primos[q] institueret duodicem ecclesiae columnae,[r][169] tamquam ex Iacob .xii.[170] congregationis illius patriarchae.[s] [L 24v] Nam unaquaque tribus Israhel[t] singulos apostolos[u] in nouum testamentum,[v] quasi duodicem lapides uiuos[171] ex Iordanes[w] alueo[172] reddederunt,[x] et sic[y] totum mundum, tanquam menses totius annis, sol[z] in se iustitiae continentes, perlustrauerunt et animas fluctis[aa] exuli uagas, lucida[bb] Dei praecepta[cc] tamquam[dd] in lina manibus ecclesia medio[ee] concluserunt, sic enim ait: 'uenite post me,[173] et faciam uos piscatores fieri hominum'.

19 Quod autem infirmitates[174] adque[a] egrotationes nostras sicut [V 73v] reor praedixerat Esaias libenter portauerit, et sic per omnia currens quemadmodum gigans per uiam,[175] oportit[b] inspicere quomodo in se consecrando ecclesia[c] grados eius per singulos commendauerit, id est, per sex[d][176] grada[e] officii[177] mancipandum, et altario sanciendum;[f] id est: ostiarius, fossarius, lector, subdiaconus, diaconus, presbyter, et episcopus. Hos sex grados impleuit Christus in carne. Nam hostiarius[g] fuit, quando

---

f specie L; *for* columbae specie   g *for* demonstrantur   h *for* una   i atque maiestas L
j diserto L, *for* desertum   k dilicias L   l *for* a   m diabolus L, *corrected from*
diabulus   n discipulos L   o *for* sanguinis nobilitate   p *for* grege   q *for*
primas   r *for* columnas   s *for* patriarchas   t Iħl V   u apostolus L   v *for*
nouo testamento   w *for* Iordanis   x reddiderunt L   y si V, *c added as a correction*
with a thinner pen   z *for* solem   aa *for* fluctibus   bb *for* lucidis   cc *for* praeceptis
dd tamq[u]am V   ee *for* media   19 a atque L   b oportet L   c *for* ecclesiae
d *for* sextem, *or rather*, septem; *see note*, p. 214   e *for* gradus   f sanctiendum L; *for*
sanciuerit   g ostiarius L

desert,[163] that is, the man made warm [?],[164] whom he took on account of old Adam, whom the devil had conquered among the delights of paradise, he [Christ] [was] in the desert, desiring to do battle with the enemy, and by the gift of fasting to capture the victory over him, and he delivered him to be trampled down by all his faithful. The prophet Zachariah[165] sang about that victory beforehand, saying 'I see', he said, 'Jesus the great priest, and the devil standing at his right hand, which is the part away from justice, preparing plots.[166] And he said to him, "the Lord will reprove you, devil, who redeemed Israel, and chose Jerusalem."' Therefore he conquered for us, who alone was able to snatch victory from the devil, when he made disciples out of fishermen[167] and not from those who were honoured with nobility of blood.[168] Instead, it was from the flock of the believing poor that he humbly instituted the twelve pillars of the church,[169] just as from Jacob he chose twelve[170] out of the flock of that patriarch. For each single tribe of Israel, there is one apostle in the New Testament, as if they brought back twelve living stones[171] from the bed of Jordan,[172] and thus they travel through/illuminate the whole world, like the months of a whole year, containing the sun of justice within themselves, and they enclose wandering souls battered by waves with the clear precepts of God in the middle of the church, as if in a fishing-line with their hands. For thus he said:[173] 'follow after me, and I will make you fishers of men.'

19 As I think, Isaiah predicted that he freely carried something of our infirmities[174] and sickness, and running through all things 'like a giant on the road'[175] we ought thus to examine how the church consecrates its grades in itself that it entrusts to individuals that is, through the six [seven][176] grades of office[177] to serve and sanctify the altar, which are doorkeeper, gravedigger, reader, subdeacon, deacon, priest and bishop. Christ fulfilled these six [seven] grades in the flesh. He was a doorkeeper when he opened the door of the ark and closed it again. He was a

147

ostium archae[h] aperuit, et iterum clausit. Fossarius fuit, quando Lazarum[178] de monumento quarto iam fetidum[i] euocauit. Lector fuit,[179]
quando librum Esaiae prophetae in medio synagogae in aures pleui[j]
aperuit, legit, et cum replicuissit,[180] ministro tradidit. Subdiaconus fuit,
quando aqua in pelue[k][181] misit, [V 74r] et humiliter sua sponte pedes
discipolorum lauit. Diacunus[l] fuit, quando calicem benedixit,[182] et apostolis suis ad bibendum porrexit. Presbyter[m] fuit,[183] quando panem benedixit, et eis similiter tradidit. Episcopus fuit, quando in templo populos,
sicut potestatem habens, eos regnum Dei docebat.[184] Et haec quidem
etiam sanctus Ephrem[n][185] commemorat similiter.

20 Nam quod a proprio discipolo[a][186] .xxx. argenteis uenundatur
Iudaeis ante presignatum[187] est in Ioseph, a suis fratribus Ismahelitis
distractus.[b] Quod autem ligatus[188] a ministris hebreorum discribitur, ut
eos qui diabulo compediti[189] tenebantur absolueret, et nexus peccatorum
confringeret. Et quod palmis in faciem uerberatur,[190] nobis ueram libertatem donauit. Et quod colaphis[c] capite caeditur,[d][191] nostrum est sanitate[e]
redditus[f] caput. [V 74v] Et quod inmundi[g] sputaminibus perlinitur,[192]
a[h] nostras facies[i] extersit obprobrium. Et quod dorso flagellis uerberatur,[193] a nobis plagas mortis et diabuli flagella dimouit.[j] Et quod ante
tribunal Pontii Pilati adstatur,[k] a nobis terrorem[l] adque formidinem
iudicum et principum huius mundi abstulit. Et quod multos testes falsos
pertulit, sanctorum suorum contra impios testimonium confirmauit.
Quod autem inter iniquos depotatus est, ut filios adoptiuos[194] per fidem
angelorum participes demonstraret. Quod uero unum susciperit, alterum
reprobauerit, ut quantum inter erit [L 25r] humilitati[m] superbia,[n] et
desperatio ab spe salutis, uel a malitia distet clementia demonstraret. Et
quod clauis configitur, ut acoleum mortis,[195] [V 75r] quod[o] nobis fuerat
permolestum,[p] significaret esset distructum. Quod uero uestes eius in
sorte[196] ceciderit,[q] ut sors sanctorum firmaretur in caelo.[r]

---

h arche L   i fetitum L   j *for* pleuis (plebis)   k *for* peluem   l diaconus L
m presbiter L   n Effrem L   20 a discipulo L   b *for* distracto   c colafis L
d ceditur L   e *for* sanitati   f *for* redditum   g *for* inmundis   h et L   i *for*
a nostris faciebus   j demouit L   k *for* adstat   l terrorum L   m *for* humilitatem
n *for* superbiam   o *for* qui   p *for* permolestus   q *for* ceciderint
r in caelo firmaretur L

gravedigger when he called forth Lazarus[178] already stinking from his tomb on the fourth day. He was a reader[179] when he opened the book of Isaiah in the midst of the synagague to the ears of the people, read and then re-rolled it,[180] and returned it to the priest. He was a subdeacon when he put water in a basin[181] and humbly, of his own will, washed the feet of the disciples. He was a deacon when he blessed the cup[182] and gave it to his apostles to drink. He was a presbyter when he blessed bread[183] and similarly gave it to them. He was a bishop when he taught the people in the temple,[184] as he had the power [to do], about the kingdom of God. And this also is similarly recorded by the holy Ephrem.[185]

20 Because he was sold to the Jews by his own disciple[186] for thirty pieces of silver, as was prefigured in Joseph,[187] handed over to the Ishmaelites by his brothers; and bound[188] by the servants of the Jews, he is [thus] described: that he might loose those fettered persons[189] who are shackled by the devil, and break the bonds of sin. Because he was struck in the face[190] with open hands, he gave true freedom to us. And because he was battered with slaps on the head,[191] he is our true head, returning with health. Because he was streaked with dirty spitting,[192] he cleans shame from our faces. Because he was beaten on the back with whips[193] he removes from us the plagues of death and the whips of the devil. Because he stood before the tribunal of Pontius Pilate, he takes from us the fear and terror of the judges and principals of this world. Because he suffered many false witnesses, he confirms the testimony of his saints against the impious. He was put among the unrighteous in order that he might show his adoptive sons[194] to be companions of the angels through their faith. What one takes up, the other reproves, and he shows as much as lies between pride and desperation without hope of health, and humility, as separates malice from mercy. And because the key is fastened, it signifies that the sting of death,[195] which had been most pernicious to us, had been destroyed. Because his garment fell as a lot,[196] the lot of the saints is confirmed in heaven.

21 Et quod etiam propria potestate morte sua habuit expletione,[a] dicens: 'consumatum est,'[197] et inclinato capite tradidit spiritum, propter illud: 'potestatem habeo[198] ponendi animam meam, et potestatem habeo iterum sumendi eam,' eo quod sacrificium uoluntarie seipsum optulit patri pro nobis. Que[b] unus[c] idemque inter mortuos liber ut nostra mortificatio[199] illius inmortalitate uiuificaretur.[d] Quod autem ceterorum crura confracta, eiusque menime[e] est[f] comminuta, propter illud ante praedictum:[g][200] 'os suum non comminuetis ex eo', ipse namque est[h] agnus pascalis[i][201] populoque mactandus.   [V 75v] Et ab Aegypto[202] suo sancto cruore ad terram promissionis per medium mare proprio sanguine purpuratum patres cum liberisque reducens, postquam Faraonem[j] percusso, et cum suis satellitibus eum inter fluctus altoque pelago[k] demersit.[203]

Quod autem de cruce depunitur,[l] in sepulchris ponitur, ut sanctorum omnium sepultura[m] sanciret,[n] et timorem mortis auferret. Quod uero in inferiora terrae[204] discendit, et a caelestio[o] sede de sinu patris[205] non recessit, ut suos de carceris[p] uinculo educeret, et diabuli potestate[q][206] destrueret, mortisque imperium contereret, et inferni potentia[r] aboleret,[s] et suum regnum non solum iustis, sed etiam latroni[207] donaret. Quod autem a mortuis post triduum resurrexit, mortuis uitam   [V 76r] dedit, et primitias resurrectionis[208] ostendit, et omnium fidelium corda ad reparationem[t] futuram firmauit. Quod autem .xl. dierum spatio[209] cum discipolis[u] suis post suam resurrectionem commoratus est, ut infidelium corda domaret et suae ecclesiae munera legis quadruplo conferret.

22 Quod uero ascendisse ipsoque quadragesimo[a] die perscriuitur[b] in caelum, ut illum cui dictum est post ruinam: 'terra es,[210] et in terram ibis', ipsi post de diabulo capta in Christo uictoria diceretur:[c] 'sede ad dexteram[211] meam donec ponam inimicos tuos scauellum[d] pedum tuorum.' Duxit ergo ascendens Christus[212] captiuam captiuitatem, et sic

---

21 a *for* expletionem   b *for* qui   c unum L   d uiuficaretur V, *the second* i *added with a smaller pen*   e minime L   f *for* sunt   g prdtum V   h L *omits* i paschalis L   j *for* Faraone   k *for* altumque pelagum   l depunitur L, *corrected to* deponitur   m *for* sepulturam   n sanctiret L   o celesti L   p de carcere suos L q *for* potestatem   r *for* potentiam   s *for* aboleret   t reparationem L u discipulis L   22 a *for* quadragesima   b perscribitur L   c deduceretur L, *corrected to* diceretur   d scabillum L

21 By his own power he had fulfilment in his own death; saying: 'it is finished.'[197] and, with his head bowed, he gave up his spirit for this reason: 'I have the power[198] to lay down my life, and I have the power to take it up again', because he offered himself voluntarily to the Father as a sacrifice for us. And one and the same man was free among the dead, and vivified our moribundity[199] with his own immortality. Although the rest had their limbs broken, his were in no way damaged, because it was previously prophesied:[200] 'his bone should not be broken in Him', for he is the Passover lamb[201] slain for the people. And leading back the fathers with their children from Egypt[202] with his holy blood to the Promised Land, through the middle of a sea reddened with his own gore, and, having struck down Pharaoh with his satellites, he drowned him in the waves of the deep sea.[203]

However, having been punished by the Cross, he was placed in the tomb so that he might ratify the tombs of all the saints, and take away the fear of death. He truly descended into the depths of the earth[204] and did not return to the celestial seat in the bosom of the Father,[205] so that he could bring out his followers from the chains of the prison, destroy the power of the devil,[206] crush the rule of death and destroy the power of hell, so that he might give his kingdom not only to the just man, but also to the thief.[207] When he rose from the dead after three days, he gave life to the dead, and showed forth the first-fruits of the Resurrection,[208] and confirmed the hearts of all the faithful towards the future reward. He delayed for the space of forty days[209] with his disciples after his Resurrection, so that he might conquer the hearts of the unbelieving and confer the fourfold gift of the Law [the gospels] on his church.

22 Christ himself was perceived to ascend into the heavens on that same fortieth day. So that to him to whom it was said after the fall: 'you are earth,[210] and to earth you will go'; concerning the devil, when the victory in Christ had been achieved: 'sit at my right hand,[211] and I will place your enemies as a footstool under your feet.' Christ ascending[212] led captivity

secundum suam promissionem^e die pentecosten^f dedit dona[213] hominibus. Ascendit Christus ad patrem, et descendit spiritus sanctus ad plebem. Qui discendit[214] ipse et ascendit   [V 76v] super caelos, ut adimpleret omnia. Qui uero descendit paracletus[215] ad apostolos in ipso confirmantur[216] uniuersa in caelo et in terra, nam spiritu sancto largiuntur dona cunctis fidelibus, et ut ait apostulus^g dicens: 'alii quidem[217] datur sermo sapientiae   [L 25v] secundum eundem spiritum, alii uero sermo scientiae, alii gratia curationum, alii genera linguarum, alii interpretatio linguarum, in eundem spiritum,' et caetera.^h Haec autem omnia dona operatur Deus et Christus in eundemⁱ sanctum spiritum, qui est plenitudo unius deitatis[218] adque^j substantiae, quia tres personas et tres subsistentias^k unam cognuscitur^l esse deitatem adque^m essentiam. Nam quanta largiantur ecclesiae ab uno eodemque Domino Christo, quis digne possit expedire per ordinem? Quidquid igitur in natiuitate,   [V 77r] quid in aetate, quidquid in praedicatione, quidquid in passione, quidquid in resurrectione Christi, quidquid in ascensione Domini, quidquid in diuinis spiritus omnium linguarum elucutione,ⁿ in sacramento uel ministerio sanctae catholicae ecclesiae gesta sunt,^o adque^p in augmento^q filiorum[219] Dei peracta sunt.^r

23 Sed nunc iam ad id unde digressus sum retorquam articulum, ut possim adprobare quod in fine temporum uenerit Christus Dei et hominum mediator in carne. Sicuti superius exposuimus, apostolo predicante postquam ait: 'uenit plenitudo temporis,[220] misit Deus filium suum factum ex muliere', et caetera.^a Et Iohannes euangelista in epistola sua dicit: 'filioli, nouissima ora est.'[221] Sed et beatus Petrus, apostolorum princeps,[222] eadem in epistola^b sua dicit 'non lateat uos,'[223] inquid, 'hoc Dauid,[224] quia mille anni   [V 77v] aput^c Deum sicut dies una et dies una tamquam mille anni.' Sex enim diebus perhibetur hic mundus perficeri^d a Deo, cum omnia^e quae in eo sunt, et in septima requieuisse Deum ab opere suo praedicatur, id est perfecto orbis curriculo requiescit Deus in hominem. Nam post sexti diei operationem non legitur factum hoc aut

e promisionem L   f *for* pentecostes   g apostolus L   h cetera L   i *for* eodem
j atque L   k substantias L   l cognoscitur L   m atque L   n elocutione L
o *for* gestum est   p atque L   q *for* augmentum   r *for* peracta est
23 a cetera L   b epistula L   c apud L   d perficere L; *for* perfectus   e *for* omnibus

captive and thus according to his promise he gave a gift[213] to mankind on the day of Pentecost. Christ ascended to the Father, and the Holy Spirit descended on the people. He who descended was the same as he who ascended,[214] so that he might fulfil everything. He who descended as the Paraclete[215] to the apostles, in him was confirmed[216] all things both in heaven and on earth. For gifts are spread by the Holy Spirit to all the faithful, as the apostle said, saying:[217] 'others are given the speech of wisdom according to that same Spirit, some the speech of knowledge, others the grace of pastoral care [?], others different kinds of language, others the interpretation of languages, by that same Spirit', and so on. In all these gifts God and Christ work through this same Holy Spirit, who is the fulness of a single godhead[218] and one substance, since three persons and three substances are seen to be a single deity and essence. Who is able worthily to narrate in sequence what great bounties are given to the church by one and the same Lord Christ? Whatsoever in his birth, whatsoever in his adult age, whatsoever in his preaching, whatsoever in his Passion, whatsoever in the Resurrection of Christ, whatsoever in the ascension of the Lord, whatsoever in the holy speech through the Spirit in all languages, and in the sacraments and ministry of the holy Catholic church is done and performed for the increase of the sons[219] of God.

23 But now I will turn back again to that point from which I digressed, so that I may demonstrate that Christ will come at the end of time as mediator in the flesh between God and mankind, as we have discussed above, and the apostle prophesying said afterwards: 'he will come in the fullness of time;[220] God will send his Son, born from a woman', and so on. And John the evangelist said in his letter:[221] 'O my dear sons, this is the very last hour.' And blessed Peter also, the prince of the apostles,[222] said in his own letter:[223] 'it is not hidden from you', he said,[224] 'this David, that a thousand years to God is like a single day, and one day like a thousand years.' For this world is understood to have been completed by God in six days, with all that is in it, and on the seventh day God rested from his work, and it is prophesied: 'it is with the completion of the circuit of the world God rests in men.' For after the work of the sixth day it is not

illut^f, sed requieuit inquid Deus in die septimo ab omnibus operibus suis. Ergo requiescit omnes^g homo ab opere suo, uel hic mundus ab studia sua,^{h} tamquam in die septimo post sextam suam aetatem, sicut Deus ab omni opere suo. Sabbatum igitur nunc est ut nullus repperiatur operatur^i uineae Dei,^{225} donec subito ueniat qui repromisit post finem mundi in suis sanctis omnibus requiescere. Namque prima die^j in qua   [V 78r] principia mundi sunt, ipsa^k nobis octabam per resurrectionem^{226} fecit, in qua Deus sanctis requiem donauit.

24 Igitur expletum est sextum millarium^{227} aetatis huius mundi, aetiam^a quamuis contradicant qui hoc percipere nolunt, et septima agit^b saeculus hic^c diem sollemnitatis suae frequentiam, in qua est ignarus^d hora adque diaei^e finis suae, qui sicut in apocalypsin intimatur in septima tuba^{228} seu in septima fiala^{229} irae Dei conplebuntur sermones Dei. Sed ut ne quis^{230} hoc putet, quod .$\overline{VII}$. miliarum annorum expleturus sit mundus frequentia sua nullusmodo^f [L 26r] repperiet istud ante predictum, eo quod sabbatum diem^g requiem habebit hic orbis, sed oram^h et diem incertam^i ab angelis et hominibus ad nostro perhibetur. Ait enim: 'de diem^j^{231} autem illa et horam^k [V 78v] nemo scit, neque angelis^l in caelo neque filius, nisi pater solus.' Et ne quis carnaliter arbitrans putet aliquid scire patrem quod nesciat filius, et in^m aeresim inuolutus incidat, sed magis hoc significare uoluit Dominus, quia filius in patre manens, cum eo uniuersa cognoscet; quidquid enim operatur pater, unum est cum filio et spiritu sancto, sine quibus non operatur; et quidquid operatur filius, unum est cum patre et spiritu sancto sine quibus non operatur; et quidquid operatur spiritus sanctus, unum est cum patre et filio sine quibus non operatur. Ergo et quidquid scit pater simul et filius et spiritus sanctus cum eo pariter cuncta cognoscunt. Quia scilicet pater et filius et spiritus sanctus una adque^n inseparabilis deitas, in semetipsa ineffabiliter [V 79r] cons/tans omnia nouit et cuncta cognoscit.

Dum uero septima iam dies^o ad requiem properat mundus iste, hoc est elementa ipsa quiescant a seruitutem,^{p}^{232} necesse est ut in suis sanctis Dominus requiescat, et ipsi in eum^q perpetuo ad omni fluc-

---

f illud L   g *for* omnis   h *for* studiis suis (*or* studio suo)   i operator L   j *for* primam diem   k *for* ipse   24 a etiam L   b *for* agitur   c *for* saeculum hoc d *for* ignotam   e diei L; *for* horam adque diem   f nullomodo L   g *for* sabbati die h horam L   i *for* hora et die incerta   j *for* die   k *for* hora   l *for* angeli m in *is superscript correction* V   n atque L   o *for* die   p *for* seruitute   q *for* eo

read that he made this or that, but, he says, 'God rested on the seventh day from all his works.' Therefore every man rests from his work, and this world from its enterprise, as in the seventh day after their sixth age, just as God did from all his work. Therefore this is now the Sabbath so that no workman is found in the vineyard of God,[225] until he suddenly returns who promised to rest after the end of the world in all his saints. For on the first day, in which was the beginning of the world, is made the octave[226] for us through the Resurrection, in which God will give rest to his saints.

24 Therefore the six thousands[227] of the age of this world have been fulfilled, even though people may deny it who do not wish to perceive it, and the seventh age brings this day of his solemnity nearer, in which one is ignorant of the hour and the day of one's end, since, as it is hinted in the Apocalypse, the words of God are to be completed in the seventh trumpet[228] or in the seventh vessel[229] of the wrath of God. But lest anyone think[230] that because 7,000 years have gone by in this world, in no way should they evoke this before the prophecy, that this world will have a sabbath day of rest, but the hour and the day is unknown to angels and men, and it is forbidden by God. For he said:[231] 'no one knows about the hour or the day, neither the angels in heaven nor the Son, but only the Father.' And lest, thinking carnally, someone should conclude the Father to know something which the Son did not know, and tangled up, fall into heresy, this is rather what God wished to signify: that the Son remaining in the Father knows all things together with Him; whatsoever the Father does, he is one with the Son and the Holy Spirit, without whom it is not done. And whatsoever the Son does he is one with the Father and the Holy Spirit, without whom it is not done; and whatsoever the Holy Spirit does, it is one with the Father and the Son, without whom it is not done. Therefore whatever the Father knows, the Son and the Holy Spirit know all of it equally at the same time, since it is understood that Father and Son and Holy Spirit are one and inseparable godhead, standing ineffably united in themselves, and they know all things, and understand everything.

While on the seventh day this world hurries to rest, that is, that the very elements rest from their bondage,[232] so it is necessary that God rest in his saints and they in him in the same fluctuation from all things

tuationem[r] quiescant. Et tunc uere sabbatizabunt iusti cum Domino et diem primam fit octauam[s] in resurrectionem[t] sanctorum, quando area uentilata fuerit[233] et a palea discretum est frumentum, quando non latet[u] quod nunc latet.[234] Nam quid, rogo, cernitur mundus dum uilis apparet? Totus ergo super .$\overline{\text{ui}}$.[v] annorum agit nunc perfectionem suam in numero euangelius,[w] et in eis qui futuri sunt ad salutem in quantum concesserit ipsa diuinitas ipsi soli cognitum quantum nobis expediri queat.[x]

[V 79v] 25 Igitur incipiamus ipsorum Caesarum uel imperatorum annos quos regnauerunt, licet ab aduentu saluatoris in carne exponere, secundum chronicam executionem.

Augustus namque qui et Octauianus Caesar uel imperator regnauit annos .lv. Sed in .xlii. anno regni eius natus est Christus in carne de uirgine.

Tiberius regnauit annos .xxii. et dimidium.[a] Sed in quintodecimo regni eius baptizatus est Dominus Iesus in Iordanne flumine a Iohanne precursore, et in .xviii. anno regni ipsius Tiberii Caesaris passus est idem Dominus noster Iesus Christus, et pandit nobis salutare et pretiosum lignum crucis in quo sibi coniuncxit ecclesiam per sanguinem et aqua ex proprio [f 80r] latere.

Post Tiberio uero Gaius[235] regnauit annos .iiii. menses .vii.

Claudius[236] regnauit annos .xiiii. et menses .viiii.

Nero[237] regnauit annos .xiii. et menses .ii.

Galba[238] regnauit anno[b] .i. et menses .vii.

Lucius[239] regnauit menses .iii.

Bitellius[240] regnauit annos .viiii. et menses .viii. semis.[c]

Vespasianus[241] regnauit annos .viiii. et menses .x.

Titus[242] regnauit annos .ii. Hi expugnauerunt[243] Iudaeam et Hierusalem post passionem Domini, usque ad suppremum eos qui increduli remanserunt fidei saluatoris. Nam fidelis custoditi diuinitus in loco qui uocatur Pellan saluati sunt.

Domitianus[244] regnauit annos .xv. et menses .ii. usque ad hunc adductus est in orbe Roma beatus deiloquus Iohannes apostulus et euangelista et usque nunc in hoc mundo durauit et dimisit eum Domitianus et abiit in

r *for* ab omni fluctuatione   s octabam L; *for* dies prima fiet octaba   t *for* resurrectione   u *for* latebit   v sex milia L   w *for* euangeliorum   x L *concludes here*   25 a dim[s] V   b *for* annum   c $\bar{s}$ V

perpetually. And then the just will truly experience the sabbath with God, and the first day will become the octave in the Resurrection of the saints, when the threshing-floor will be blown on,[233] and the wheat will be separated from the tares, when what is hidden now will not be hidden.[234] For why, I ask, is the world seen, when it appears vile? The whole world on top of the 6,000 years comes now to its perfection in the number of the evangelists, and in those who are to come for salvation, and that same divinity concedes how many in his thought alone, as many as can be brought forth for us.

25 Therefore let us begin to set out the years in which the Caesars or emperors reigned, just from the advent of the Saviour in the flesh according to chronological investigation.

Augustus, who was also Octavianus Caesar or emperor, reigned for fifty-five years, but in the forty-second year of his reign Christ was born in the flesh from a virgin.

Tiberius reigned for twenty-two years and a half. In the fifteenth year of his reign the Lord Jesus was baptized in the river Jordan by John the precursor. And in the eighteenth year of the reign of the same Tiberius Caesar our same Lord Jesus Christ suffered, and offered us salvation, and the precious wood of the Cross, in which he joined the church to himself through the blood and water from his own side [the eucharist].

After Tiberius *Gaius*[235] *reigned for four years, seven months.*

Claudius[236] *reigned for fourteen years and nine months.*

Nero[237] *reigned for thirteen years and two months.*

Galba[238] reigned for one year and seven months.

Lucius[239] *reigned for three months.*

Vitellius[240] *reigned for nine years, eight months and a half.*

Vespasian[241] *reigned for nine years and ten months.*

Titus[242] *reigned for two years.* They [Titus and Vespasian] fought against[243] Judaea and Jerusalem after the passion of the Lord, to the destruction of those who remained unbelieving in the faith of the Saviour. For the faithful were found divinely guarded, and were saved in a place called Pellan.

Domitian[244] *ruled for fifteen years and two months. It was at this time that the blessed and divinely inspired John the apostle and evangelist was brought to the city of Rome, and up to this time he still lived in this world. Domitian dismissed him, and he went to Ephesus.*

157

Ephesum. Post Domitianum [V 80v] Neruas[245] regnauit anno .i. et mense[d] .i.

Traianus[246] regnauit annos .xviiii. menses .vi.

Adrianus[247] regnauit annos .xxii.

Antoninus Pius[248] regnauit annos .xxiii.

Marcus[249] regnauit annos .xviii. menses .viiii.

Antoninus Berus[250] regnauit anno[e] .i.

Commodus[251] regnauit annos .xxii. menses .viii.

Pertinax[252] regnauit anno[f] .i. menses .ii. dies .xviii.

Didius Iulianus[253] qui et Siluius regnauit menses .vii.

Seuerus Septimius Afrus[254] regnauit annos .xvii., et menses .viiii. semis.[g]

Antoninus Gestas[255] regnauit anno[h] .i.

Antoninus Caracallus[256] filius Seueri regnauit annos .vi. et dies .xxii.

Valerianus[257] regnauit annos .vi.

Magrinus Gallus regnauit annum .i. menses .vii.

Ilius[i] Antoninus regnauit annos .iiii. et menses .ii.

Alexandrus Mameas regnauit annos .viii menses .iiii.

Maximus regnauit annos .iii. menses .x.

Balbinus regnauit anno[j] .i. menses .iii.

Pulpius regnauit menses .iii. semis.[k]

Gordianus regnauit dies .xxii.

[V 81r] Alius Gordianus regnauit annos .xx.

Tertius Gordianus regnauit annos .vi.

Marcus regnauit annos .vi.

Filippus regnauit annos .vi. et semis.

Valerianus regnauit annos .ii. et dimidium.[l]

Gallus paruissimus regnauit menses .v.

Decius regnauit anno[m] .i. et menses .viii.

Emilianus regnauit menses .iiii.

Valerianus regnauit annos .vi.

Gallienus[258] qui et Licinius regnauit annos .xiiii.

Claudius[259] qui et Pullianus regnauit annos .viiii.

Cytallianus[260] regnauit dies .x. et .vii.

Aurelianus[261] regnauit annos .vi.

Tacitus[262] regnauit menses .vii.

---

d *for* annum mensem   e *for* annum   f *for* annum   g s̄ V   h *for* annum
i *for* Alius   j *for* annum   k s̄ V   l dim̄ V   m *for* annum

After Domitian, *Nerva*[245] *ruled for one year and one month.*

Trajan[246] *ruled for nineteen years and six months.*

Hadrian[247] ruled for twenty-two years.

Antoninus Pius[248] *ruled for twenty-three years.*

Marcus [Aurelius][249] *ruled for eighteen years and nine months.*

Antoninus Verus[250] ruled for one year.

Commodus[251] *ruled for twenty-two years and eight months.*

Pertinax[252] ruled for one year, two months and eighteen days.

Didius Iulianus,[253] *also called Silvius, ruled for seven months.*

Severus Septimus Afrus[254] ruled for seventeen years and nine-and-a-half months.

Antonius Geta[255] ruled for one year.

Antonius Caracalla,[256] son of Severus, ruled for six years and twenty-two days.

Valerianus[257] *ruled for six years.*

Magrinus Gallus ruled for one year and seven months.

Another Antoninus ruled for four years and two months.

Alexander Mameas ruled for eight years and four months.

Maximus ruled for three years and ten months.

Balbinus ruled for one year and three months.

Pulpius ruled for three-and-a-half months.

Gordianus ruled for twenty-two days.

Another Gordianus ruled for twenty years.

A third Gordianus ruled for six years.

Marcus ruled for six years.

Philip ruled for six-and-a-half years.

Valerianus ruled for two years and a half.

The least of the Galli ruled for five months.

Decius ruled for one year and eight months.

Emelianus ruled for four months.

Valerianus ruled for six years.

Gallienus,[258] *also called Licinus, ruled for fourteen years.*

Claudius,[259] *also called Pullianus, ruled for nine years.*

Cytallianus[260] *ruled for seventeen days.*

Aurelianus[261] *ruled for six years.*

Tacitus[262] *ruled for seven months.*

Florianus[263] regnauit menses .ii.

Hilius[264] Probus regnauit annos .iii. et menses .iii.

Carus[265] regnauit annos .ii.

Numerianus[266] regnauit annos .ii.

Carinus[267] regnauit annos .ii.

Licinnianus[268] regnauit annos .vii.

Dioclitianus et Maximianus[269] regnauerunt annos .xviiii.

[V 81v] Constantinus maior[270] regnauit annos .xxxii.

Constantius[271] regnauit anno[n] .i.

Iulianus[272] transgressor regnauit annos .vii.

Iobianus[273] regnauit menses .vii. et semis.

Valentinianus[274] regnauit annos .xvii.

Valens[275] regnauit annos .xiii.

Gratianus[276] regnauit annos .vii. et menses .x.

Theodosius maior[277] regnauit annos .xvii.

Arcadius[278] regnauit annos .xxiii.

Honorius[279] regnauit annos .xxxi.

Theodosius minor[280] regnauit annos .xlviii.

Marcianus[281] regnauit annos .vi. et menses .v.

Leo maior[282] regnauit annos .xvi. et menses .xi.

Leo iunior[283] regnauit anno[o] .i. et dies .xxii.

Zeno[284] regnauit annos .xv. et menses .ii.

Anastasius[285] regnauit annos .xxvii. et menses .viiii. et dies .viiii.

Iustinus[286] regnauit annos .viiii. et dies .xxii.

Iustinianus[287] regnauit annos .xxxviiii. et dimidium.[p]

Iustinus[288] regnauit annos .viiii.

Explicit chronica Deo gratias; amen.

n *for* annum o *for* annum p dim[s] V

160

Florianus[263] *ruled for two months.*

Elius Probus[264] *ruled for three years and three months.*

Carus[265] *ruled for two years.*

Numerianus[266] *ruled for two years.*

Carinus[267] *ruled for two years.*

Licinnianus[268] *ruled for seven years.*

Diocletian and Maximianus[269] ruled for nineteen years.

Constantine the Great[270] *ruled for thirty-two years.*

Constantius[271] ruled for one year.

Julian the Sinner [Apostate][272] *ruled for seven years.*

Jovianus[273] *ruled for seven months* and a half.

Valentinian[274] ruled for seventeen years.

Valens[275] *ruled for thirteen years.*

Gratian[276] ruled for seven years and ten months.

Theodosius the Greater[277] *ruled for seventeen years.*

Arcadius[278] *ruled for twenty-three years.*

Honorius[279] *ruled for thirty-one years.*

Theodosius the Lesser[280] ruled for forty-eight years.

Marcian[281] *ruled for six years and five months.*

Leo the Greater[282] *ruled for sixteen years and eleven months.*

Leo the Lesser[283] *ruled for one year* and twenty-two days.

Zeno[284] *ruled for fifteen years* and two months.

Anastasius[285] *ruled for twenty-seven years,* nine months and nine days.

Justinus[286] *ruled for nine years and twenty-two days.*

Justinianus[287] ruled for thirty-nine years and a half.

Justinus[288] ruled for nine years.

Here ends the Chronicle, thanks be to God; amen.

Commentary

I should perhaps describe my practice in quoting from primary sources. Where the original is in Latin or Greek, I quote the original (with translation). Where the source-text was written (or survives) in Syriac, Armenian, Irish or another language, I quote only the translation. In a case where, for example, the original Greek of Theodore of Mopsuestia survives only in Syriac, and is translated by its editor into French, I quote the French translation rather than risk further distortion, since I am regrettably unable to judge whether the French accurately represents the Syriac. In some cases, a Syriac original is represented by a modern Latin translation. When the Latin translation is itself early medieval, I will endeavour to make this clear. Page-references to Malalas's *Chronographia* throughout are to Dindorf's edition, since this has been taken as a standard by von Stauffenberg, the PG text and the Jeffreys translation, all of which print Dindorf's pagination in the margin.

1 *Christe, faue uotis bonis.* This opening invocation is possibly a significant feature of the *Laterculus*. The *Christe faue* formula is not all that common. Victor, the bishop of Capua, entered *XF* in the *Codex Fuldensis* (*CLA* VIII, no. 1196, a sixth-century uncial gospelbook, which may just possibly have been in England, since it was used by Boniface). Donatus, a priest who read and annotated the copy of Ambrosiaster's commentary on the Pauline epistles preserved in Monte Cassino, Archivio della Badia 150, in Naples in the year 570, placed *XF* in the margin opposite the initial line (*CLA* III, no. 374a). The gospelbook Oxford, Bodl. Auct. D. II. 14 (*CLA* II, no. 230, uncial, s. vii), has *XPE F* at the beginning of each gospel. The Codex Amiatinus, written at Jarrow in the seventh century (*CLA* III, no. 299), has *XPE FAUE* at the opening of Matthew. And, finally, the Martyrology of St Willibrord (Paris, BN, lat. 10837), written in England in the early eighth century, has *XPE FAUE UOTIS* in the top margin of 2r (see *CLA* II, xix, and the facsimile volume, *The Calendar of St Willibrord, from MS Paris Lat. 10837*, ed. H.A. Wilson, HBS 55 (London, 1918), fol. 2). So this form of words is first used in Italy in the sixth century, whence it is picked

162

up by English writers. The phrase was used from the mid-sixth century onwards in Italy to head formal (biblical or conciliar) texts, and came to the British Isles by the second half of the seventh century (see M. Huglo, 'Christe faue uotis', *Scriptorium* 8 (1954), 108–11, and D.A. Bullough, 'Christe faue uotis', *Scriptorium* 14 (1960), 346–8). It is noteworthy that the most developed form outside that used in the *Laterculus* itself, that used by St Willibrord, is by a nearly contemporary Northumbrian writer. Its appearance in the Codex Amiatinus may be derived from the Italian exemplar of that codex, but its appearance in Southumbria may be a contribution from Hadrian, who lived for a long time near Naples before coming to England according to Poole, 'Monasterium Niridanum'. If it is not simply to be taken as a contribution from the north Italian scribe of Pal. lat. 277, its presence at the beginning of the *Laterculus* may be held to strengthen the Southumbrian connexions of this text. It may also be relevant to mention that the *Carmen Paschale* of Caelius Sedulius includes the line '*Christe, faue uotis*, qui mundum in morte iacentem' (I.351, ed. Huemer, p. 41), since this is not the only echo of Sedulius in the *Laterculus*.

CH. I

2 *scolaces*. This may be a piece of wordplay at the expense of the Irish, a punning combination of *scholares*, the appropriate word, and *scolax*, 'twisted', which devalues their scholarship. Alternatively (or additionally) the wordplay may be on σκύλαξ, pl. σκύλακες, 'puppy, whelp', especially when we remember that *o* and *u* are frequently confused in this text, calling up the image of yapping (ironically, 'eloquent') little dogs. Interestingly, Aldhelm also envisages confrontation between Theodore and the Irish in terms of dogs – though he thinks of the Irish as Molossian hounds, rather than puppies (*Aldhelmi Opera*, ed. Ehwald, p. 493). Theodore's image may be related to the Greek rhetorical figure χλευσασμοί, which is described in the *Biblical Commentaries* (EvII 86): as Lapidge says, 'it refers to the mockery or derision used by an orator in the attempt to provoke scornful laughter' (*Biblical Commentaries*, p. 524). It is also possible that, in addition to being a pun between Latin and Greek, this carefully chosen word might also be a pun in Irish; for a *Scot scelach* is a 'prattling Irishman'. A Middle Irish poem quoted by James Carney in his 'A Maccucáin, sruith in Tíag', *Celtica* 15 (1983), 25–41, at 40, which begins 'Cindus atá do t(h)indremh' (Brussels, Bibliothèque royale, 20979, 57v) includes the line, 'Foimhne narab Scot scélach': 'take care that you be not a prattling Irishman'. It is clear from other writings of Archbishop Theodore that he had a good memory for languages: it is not beyond possibility that he had a few words of Irish at his command.

3 *liquidissimis labiorum ... nectareis*. *Nectareum* (or *nectareus*) is a very rare word, but it is also found in the preface to Caelius Sedulius's prose *Opus paschale*, in the

phrase 'gemmatis flauescunt nectareis' (ed. Huemer, p. 176). It is interesting that it is used in the preface in both cases.

4 *tamquam solis iubar*. Vergil, *Aeneid* IV.130: 'it pontis iubare exorto'; *Aeneid* I.160, I.297: 'ab alto'. The phrase *iubare exorto* is discussed by the Vergil scholiasts in several places. Servius's comment is, 'alii iubar solem, alii splendorem siderum dicunt' (see also Isidore, *Etymologiae* III.lxxi.18). The phrase 'iubar solis exortum' appears in Suetonius, *De uita caesarum libri*, *Augustus* XCIV.4 (ed. M. Ihm (Leipzig and Berlin, 1923), p. 101). S.J. Tibbetts, in *Texts and Transmission*, ed. Reynolds, p. 400, notes that there are possible uses of Suetonius by both Aldhelm and Bede, though most likely through intermediate sources. It is thus on the whole unlikely that Suetonius's work was available in Canterbury, but not entirely impossible.

5 *uelut rex insederit thalamo*. Ps. XVIII.6 (LXX): 'et ipse tamquam sponsus procedens de *thalamo* suo'. Cf. Theodore of Mopsuestia's exegesis of this clause, in his *Expositiones in Psalmos* (ed. de Coninck, pp. 100–1): 'sponso comparatus sol propter splendorem nimium uel decorem' with 'tamquam solis iubar inlustret ab alto', above. Caelius Sedulius uses the passage in relation to the incarnation in his *Opus paschale* II.4 (ed. Huemer, p. 200): 'cum Christus splendore sidereo uelut sponsus procedens de thalamo suo, Mariae processit ex utero'. There seems to be no obvious explanation of why the *Laterculus* has the king entering rather than leaving his bridal chamber.

6 *quod ... explanauerunt*. Presumably taken from Malalas, *Chronographia* X.2 (p. 228), though if so the quotation is repeated in ch. 4.

7 *Clemens uel Theophilus et Timotheus*. These earlier Greek chronographers were primary sources for Malalas, who quite often cited them as a group. The reference here is taken over directly from the *Chronographia*. Clemens is probably Clement of Alexandria, the exegete (though no history has come down to us from him). Theophilus may possibly be identified with the Theophilus who was bishop of Antioch in AD 169, or alternatively, a fourth-century bishop of Alexandria. Timotheus (not an uncommon name) is unidentifiable (see Croke, 'Early Byzantine Chronicles', in *Studies*, p. 36, and Jeffreys, 'Malalas' Sources', in *Studies*, pp. 194–5). In one of the more confusing notes in the *Biblical Commentaries* (PentI 24) Gregory of Nazianzus and an unidentified Theophilus are cited, apparently as experts on chronography. This may also be a reference to the unknown Theophilus who is a source for Malalas.

8 *Eusebius*. Malalas, like all other Christian historians, owed an enormous debt to the *Historia ecclesiastica* of Eusebius. Much of Malalas's comparative biblical and

historical data can be traced directly to this source, and he also copied Eusebius's way of dating events, as this example will show (*HE* VIII.ii.3; ed. Schwarz II, 742): ἔτος τοῦτο ἦν ἐννεακαιδέκατον τῆς Διοκλετιανοῦ βασιλείας, Δύστρος μήν, λέγοιτο δ᾿ ἂν οὗτος Μάρτιος κατὰ Ῥωμαίους, ἐν ᾧ τῆς τοῦ σωτηρίου πάθους ἑορτῆς . . . ('It was the nineteenth year of Diocletian's reign and the month Dystrus, called March by the Romans and the festival of the Saviour's passion was approaching . . .').

A curious aspect of the *Laterculus* is the name *Eusebius Pamphiliensis*. Eusebius took the cognomen Παμφίλου in honour of his revered and martyred mentor, Pamphilus, and it is accordingly normally Latinized as *Pamphili*. The *Laterculus* gives the impression of having mistaken it for a place-name, 'Eusebius of Pamphile'. I do not know of a parallel example of the *-ensis* ending used for a patronymic or similar formation.

CH. 2

9 Malalas, *Chronographia* X.1 (p. 227). Octavian Augustus's regnal date was established by Eusebius, and arrived at by reckoning from the death of Julius (*HE* I.v.2; ed. Schwarz I, 44, and see Finegan, *Handbook*, pp. 150–2). Malalas followed Eusebius, whom he acknowledged as a primary authority, as does the *Laterculus*.

10 *Superius*. Mai put forward the suggestion that *superius* should be emended to *Eusebius*. This is an attractive reading because Eusebius was responsible for the date, and the use of the *Historia ecclesiastica* in ch. 25 proves that the author of the *Laterculus* had independent acquaintance with it. But it is also true that the *Laterculus*'s main business was with bk X of Malalas's *Chronicle* and that it harks back here to the end of bk IX, so *superius* also makes contextual sense. It may be worth noting that phrases like 'superius legitur' are part of Late Latin legal phraseology, since Roman law was one of the subjects taught in Theodore's school, on the evidence of Aldhelm's letter to Leuthere (ed. Ehwald, p. 476). See also R.M. Thomson, 'Supplementary List of Authors and Works Known to William of Malmesbury', *Revue Bénédictine* 86 (1976), 328–35, at 329, on the provenance of the copy of the law-book *Breviarium Alaricum* known to both Aldhelm and William.

11 Malalas, *Chronographia* IX.25, p. 226.

12 *mense sexto*. Luke I.26: 'in mense autem sexto'.

13 The month-names given by Malalas are those of the Macedonian calendar as it

165

was used in the near east. The months correlate with Jewish and Julian months as follows (Finegan, *Handbook*, p. 73).

1	Ξανθικός	Nisan	March/April
2	Ἀρτεμίσιος	Iyyar	April/May
3	Δαίσιος	Sivan	May/June
4	Πάνεμος	Tammuz	June/July
5	Λῷος	Ab	July/August
6	Γορπιαῖος	Elul	August/September
7	Ὑπερβερεταῖος	Tishri	September/October
8	Δῖος	Marheshvan	October/November
9	Ἀπελλαῖος	Kislev	November/December
10	Ἀδυναῖος	Tebeth	December/January
11	Περίτιος	Shebat	January/February
12	Δύστρος	Adar	February/March

14 *missus est archangelus*. Luke I.26: 'missus est angelus Gabrihel a Deo in ciuitatem Galileae cui nomen Nazareth ad uirginem desponsatam uiro cui nomen erat Ioseph de domo Dauid et nomen uirginis Maria.' Sunday, 25 Dystrus is the regular Byzantine date for the Annunciation (Jeffreys, 'Chronological Structures', in *Studies*, p. 120).

15 *in consolatu Cyrinii et Longini*. Cyrinus and Longinus are not to be found in the *fasti consulares*, which give L. Cornelius Lentulus and M. Valerius Messalinus as the consuls for 3 BC – that is, the year before the consulate of Octavian and Silvanus, in which, according to Malalas, Christ's birth took place (these and subsequent consular dates are taken from Bickermann, *Chronology*, p. 182: Jeffreys, 'Chronological Structures', gives the consuls for 3 BC as P. Cornelius [Lentulus] Scipio and T. Quinctius Crispus Valerianus). The text of Malalas as printed by Dindorf (based on the Codex Baroccianus) gives the name of these consuls as Κουρινίου καὶ Λογγίνου; but refers to Κυρηνίου τοῦ ἀπὸ ὑπάτων on the same page, just as the *Laterculus* names the first Cyrinius and the second Cyrinus, though it is highly probable that the same person is referred to in both places.

16 *Vitellio*. The *Laterculus* here follows the account by Malalas in the *Chronographia*, who gives Cyrinus, with Longinus, as consul for that year and Vitellius as the governor of Syria. There is no evidence that this was the case. The accepted sequence of governors of Syria has P. Quinctilius Varus in office 6–4 BC, and P. Sulpicius Quirinus 3–2 BC (Finegan, *Handbook*, p. 235). The phrase 'qui tunc agebat iubenis' results from a mistranslation of Malalas's προαχθέντος νεωστὶ ὑπὸ τοῦ Αὐγούστου Καίσαρος (p. 226: 'Recently appointed by Augustus Caesar'), in which νεωστί ('lately, recently'), the adverb of νέος, has been taken either as a

form of the adjective (which can be used to mean 'young man') or perhaps as a variant on νεότης, 'youth'. This is hard to explain. The confusion and misunderstanding of the Sybil's prophecy in ch. 8 suggest that the text of Malalas available to the writer was either corrupt or hard to interpret, and the present misunderstanding may also result from translating from a faulty exemplar. There are no signs elsewhere in the text that the writer had any difficulty in comprehending Greek. On the contrary, the translation of ἐν τοῖς ὑπομνήμασιν as *in suis monumentis* (ch. 3, below) suggests that he is more at ease with Greek than with Latin.

17 *aequinoctium uernalem*. The vernal equinox was a matter of some importance since from the third century onwards it was added to the other variables of the stage of the moon and the day of the week in the calculation of Easter. Ch. 2 says simply '.viii. ergo kal. Apriles, id est aequinoctium uernalem'. 25 March was accepted as the equinox in the western empire down to the time of Isidore, proving that Rome 'had nothing more than an inherited astronomy' (*BOT*, p. 22, and see R. R. Newton, *Medieval Chronicles and the Rotation of the Earth* (Baltimore and London, 1972), pp. 22–7). The Alexandrians, who unlike the Romans were actually capable of original astronomical calculation, set the date of the vernal equinox at 21 March and this date was accepted, from the point of view of calculating Easter, by the Council of Nicaea and tacitly accepted by Rome, which continued officially to cling to the old date. According to Jones, 'from the fourth century on, the Roman church tried, not very diligently, to reconcile the two dates without having to discard one of them' (*BOT*, p. 345). Note also that, since Bangor believed in the 25 March equinox, this tacit acceptance of Easter celebrations from the 21st on is the subject of one of Columbanus's most vehement attacks in his letter to Gregory the Great (*Epistola I*, ed. Walker, pp. 2–12, at 2–4). Bede noted that the Equinox was established 'iuxta sententiam omnium Orientalium et maxime Aegyptiorum' at 21 March (*BOT*, pp. 126–7), and claims to have tested this by inspection – though since the vagaries of the Julian calendar had caused the equinox to slip back to 17 March by Bede's time, his techniques of measurement cannot have been at all accurate. Nonetheless, it is a tribute to his scientific genius that he even *thought* of attempting to corroborate this datum.

To return to the *Laterculus*, the simple acceptance of the 25 March dating suggests that here, as elsewhere, the writer is anxious to be seen supporting a straightforward Roman line without going off into potentially confusing subtleties. This might be held to prove that he was old-fashioned or unscientific: it might also represent the reasonable desire of a teacher not to make his pupils run before they can walk. Leaving the uniquely-gifted Bede to one side, we have the heartfelt testimony of Aldhelm that the confusion and conflicting theories in computistics, together with its sheer technical difficulty, made it an area of study that only the strongest intellects could attempt (*Epistola ad Leutherum*, ed.

Ehwald, pp. 477–8). The focus on 25 March as a date for new beginnings may also have had a personal significance for Theodore. Bede tells us that his consecration was on Sunday, 26 March, the nearest Sunday to our day (*Historia ecclesiastica* IV.1, ed. Colgrave and Mynors, p. 330). Since Theodore's preparation for his new life was leisurely, the choice of day may be of some significance.

18 *initium hic mundus*. The Hieronymian group of martyrologies lists the Annunciation, the Crucifixion and the death of James on 25 March. The *Martyrology of Tallaght* adds the Creation to this list, but the *Laterculus* goes considerably further by adding the crossing of the Red Sea and the creation and fall of the angels as well. The Jewish exegetical tradition, represented by the first-century (AD) Palestinian Targum, quoted by G. Vermes, *Scripture and Tradition*, p. 216, treats Nisan as a month of redemption: 'the night of Passover is the memorial of the Creation, of the Covenant with Abraham, of the birth of Isaac, of his Akedah (sacrifice), of the delivery of the Israelites from Egypt, and finally of the coming of messianic salvation'.

The curious list of disparate events in the *Laterculus* is interestingly comparable with the Jewish traditions noted above: the point of contact, if there was one, would most probably have been through the schools of Syria, which owed a great deal to Jewish scholarship. Elsewhere in the Insular world, we find some similarities between the list of events occurring on 25 March in the *Laterculus*, and the list of events taking place at midnight in the vernacular Irish apocryphal text, *The Ever-New Tongue*, believed to have been based on a lost gospel of Philip: 'At midnight: the Lord arose, *the world was created, the devil was banished*, man made, Cain committed fratricide, Sodom destroyed, the Flood began, Passover happened, *the hosts went through the Red Sea*, Babylon was overcome, *Christ was born and crucified*, harrowed hell', etc. (chs. 140–50, ed. Stokes, pp. 138–41). Another type of list, also found in Celtic sources, the collection which André Wilmart christened *Catechèses celtiques*, lists important events happening on a Sunday (pp. 111–12), which include the Creation and the Crossing of the Red Sea, though not the other items of our list. C. M. Dugmore (*The Influence of the Synagogue upon the Divine Office*, 2nd ed. (Westminster, MD, 1964), p. 26) noted that this motif of events on the Lord's day had an ultimate origin in Rabbinic traditions of events on the sabbath.

Several Jewish authorities of the patristic period were of the opinion that the world was created in the month of Nisan. This can be deduced from a careful correlation of the Jewish apocryphal texts, I Enoch and Jubilees (quoted in the *Biblical Commentaries*, PentI 46) which have compatible calendars. Jubilees does not specifically fix 'the first month'; however, Adam is said to have dwelt in the garden for precisely seven years (Jubilees III.17 (ed. Charles, p. 16): this is not the opinion held in the *Laterculus*: see discussion below on ch. 3), and the reckoning of time was begun from his expulsion, which would seem to imply that the world was created in the spring (Jubilees VI.23, *ibid.*, p. 22). In I Enoch, the first month is the month of the vernal equinox, that is, Nisan (I Enoch LXXII.6, *ibid.*, p. 238). See further Finegan, *Handbook*, pp. 50–3, and Philo Judaeus, *Questions and Answers on Exodus* I.i (surviving only in ancient Armenian), trans. R Marcus (Cambridge, MA and London, 1963), p. 5: 'Now the season in which the world was created, as anyone will ascertain in truth who uses a proper method of enquiry and deliberation, was the season of spring, since it is at this time that all things in common blossom and grow, and the earth produces its perfected fruits.' Later Jewish thought favoured an autumn date for the Creation (Ginzberg, *Legends* V, 98).

Christian writers of the eastern empire seem to have been influenced by the earlier stages of Jewish thought on this matter. Jacob of Sarug stated in his *Hexemeron* that: 'la sixième jour du mois de Nisan, le domaine édifié par le créateur étant achevé' ('L'Hexaméron', ed. and trans. Jansma, p. 37). The creation was linked directly with the equinox by Theodore of Mopsuestia, in his commentary on Genesis: 'Car il est manifeste que [le prophète] nomme le changement d'époque et l'équinoxe *le premier mois*, puisqu'alors la création a commencé tout comme il qualifie également de *premier jour* ce [jour] où la création a commencé' (ed. and trans. Jansma, p. 81).

The concatenation of events here links the *Laterculus* to the Roman computistical tradition. In the western empire, the doctrine of the creation of the world on a vernal equinox set at 25 March went back to the third-century computist Hippolytus, and acquired a status of near-dogma in succeeding centuries. As Jones reminds us: 'his doctrine about Creation appears again in every purely Roman computus and occupies a place in Bede's writings seemingly out of all proportion to its merit' (*BOT*, p. 13, and see also Ó Cróinín, 'The Irish Provenance of Bede's Computus', p. 234). So its appearance here in the *Laterculus* appears to be a further witness, like the 25 March equinox itself, to the Romanizing sympathies of the writer. Greek, Oriental and Jewish writers, as we have seen, are considerably more tentative in their approach to this theory. One of the better parallels to this section of the *Laterculus* is Victorius of Aquitaine's prologue to his *Cursus Paschalis*, chs. 8–9, in which he commented that the world was created on the eighth of the kalends of April (25 March), and that the first Passover and the Last Supper also occurred on that date (*Chronica Minora I*, ed. Mommsen, pp. 682–3). The apocryphal *Acta Pilati* (used by Malalas, as n. 83 demonstrates, and possibly independently known to the author of the *Laterculus*) are one of the earliest documents to date the Crucifixion to 25 March (see *Studien zur christlich-mittelalterliche Chronologie*, ed. Krusch II, 24).

19 The dating of the crossing to the month of Nisan is obvious from the book of Exodus and the timing of Passover. It is additionally spelled out by Josephus,

Antiquitates Iudaicarum I.iii.3 (ed. Niese I, 19): Μωυσῆς δὲ τὸν Νισᾶν, ὅς ἐστι Ξανθικός, μῆνα πρῶτον ἐπὶ ταῖς ἑορταῖς ὥρισε κατὰ τοῦτον ἐξ Αἰγύπτου τοὺς Ἑβραίους προαγαγών ('Moses appointed that Nisan, which is the same as Xanthicus, should be the first month for their festivals, because he brought them out of Egypt in that month'). This fact was known to Bede, who mentioned it in his *De templo* I (ed. Hurst, p. 157).

20 The implication of this addition to the list is firstly that the angels were created right at the beginning (a subject on which Genesis is silent), and that Satan and his legions fell almost immediately, on the same day. Neither of these was a subject of general agreement. Several of the Greek fathers asserted the primacy of the angelic orders; and Procopius of Gaza gave an interesting reason for it, in *Commentarii in Genesin* (PG 87, 21–511, at 48): Μετὰ τοῦ οὐρανοῦ δὲ καὶ τῆς γῆς, καὶ τοὺς ἀγγέλους παραγαγών, εἶτα παιδεῦσαι τούτους βουλόμενος, ὡς καὶ αὐτῶν ἐστι δημιουργός, μή ποτε αὐτομάτως ὑφεστάναι νομίσωσι, τὴν μετὰ ταῦτα πᾶσαν κτίσιν φωνῇ ποιῶν ἐπιδείκνυται ('He created the angels along with the heaven and earth; since he wished to teach them, as their creator. Lest they think they existed of themselves, he conducted all the subsequent creation in their sight, using his voice'). Procopius of Gaza is probably a source for the *Biblical Commentaries*, and his work may have been used elsewhere in the *Laterculus*. See further Theodoret, *Quaestiones in Genesim* (PG 80, 77–226, esp. 79–86), and Gregory of Nazianzus, *Oratio in Theophania* XXXVIII.ix (PG 35, 311–34, at 319–22). The idea dates back to Jubilees II.2, and is also found in Augustine, *De ciuitate Dei* XI.ix (ed. Dombart and Kalb II, 328–9). Augustine further believed that the rebel angels fell on the day of their creation (P. E. Dustoor, 'Legends of Lucifer in early English and in Milton', *Anglia* 54 (1930), 213–68, at 216, and B. J. Bamberger, *Fallen Angels* (Philadelphia, PA, 1952), p. 34), and this elaboration is also found in medieval Ireland, in the prose version of *Saltair na Rann* in the *Leabhar Breac Codex Palatino-Vaticanus* (ed. and trans. Mac Carthy, p. 47): 'And the writers say that there are a thousand years from the formation of the angel to his transgression. Other writers say it is thirteen hours and a half from formation of the angel to his transgression, as said the poet:

> Half an hour and three hours [and] ten
> It is true and it is not a very great falsehood,
> From formation of the world pleasant
> To the offence of the angel.'

21 *Iacobus.* Compare *Breuiarium apostolorum ex nomine uel locis ubi praedicauerunt orti uel obiti sunt* (*Liber sacramentorum romanae aeclesiae* (*Vat. reg. lat* 316), ed. L.C. Mohlberg (Rome, 1960), p. 261): 'hic dum Hierusalem Christum dei filium praedicaret, de templo a Iudaeis praecipitatus lapidibusque oppremitur ibique

iuxta templum humatur. Eius natalicum et ordinacio eius *VI Kalendas Ianuarias* colitur'. The *Martyrologium Hieronymianum* (pp. 159–60), on the other hand, celebrates James on 25 March: 'Hierosolyma Dominus noster Ihesus Christus crucifixus est. passio Iacobi iusti fratris Domini'. The Annunciation and the Sacrifice of Isaac are also noted for this day. The *Martyrology of Tallaght* gives a fuller version similar to the list in the *Laterculus*: 'Dominus noster Iesus Christus crucifixus est. et conceptus et mundus factus est. passio Iacobi fratris Domini. et conceptio Mariae et immolatio Isaac a patre suo Abraam in monte Morae' (*The Martyrology of Tallaght*, ed. Best and Lawlor, p. 27).

This sentence has been wrongly constructed, with a sort of *nominatiuus pendens*. The subject is *Iudaei*, and James, though he appears in the nominative, must be the object.

22 *de pinna templi*. James was cast down specifically from the pinnacle of the temple according to Hegesippus, who was quoted by Eusebius (*Historia ecclesiastica* II.xxiii.12; ed. Schwarz I, 168; and see *ANT*, pp. 20–1): ἔστησαν οὖν οἱ προειρημένοι γραμματεῖς καὶ Φαρισαῖοι τὸν Ἰάκωβον ἐπὶ τὸ πτερύγιον τοῦ ναοῦ ('so the scribes and pharisees made James stand on the sanctuary parapet'). Hegesippus also supplied the date: εἰς τὴν ἡμέραν τοῦ πάσχα. In this case, it is possible that the phrasing in the *Laterculus* has been influenced by a knowledge of Rufinus's Latin translation, which reads 'statuerunt igitur supra dicti scribae et Pharisaei Iacobum supra *pinnam templi*' (ed. Mommsen, *apud* Schwarz I, 169). See below, n. 243, for the possible significance of this addition to Malalas's account.

23 Malalas, *Chronographia* X.1 (p. 227). According to Quasten, *Patrology* II, 172, Hippolytus of Rome was the first patristic writer to give the dates of Christ's birth and death, in his *Commentarius in libro Danielis* IV.xxiii, where he stated that Christ was born on Wednesday, 25 December, in the forty-second year of the Emperor Augustus and died on 25 March. In the *Laterculus*, however, this information is derived directly from Malalas.

24 *in ciuitate Iudeae*. The *Laterculus* substitutes *in* + abl. for the Vulgate's *in* + acc., though the latter clearly makes better sense.

25 *Octauiani Augusti et Siluani*. 2 BC, Imp. Caesar diui f. Augustus .xiii., and M. Plautius Siluanus. Epiphanius also thought that Christ's birth occurred in this consular year (*Panarion* LI.xxii.3, ed. Holl II, 284).

26 *sicut euangelista testatur*. Curiously, neither Luke nor the other evangelists precisely confirm this set of statements. Cyrinus is indeed named as governor of Syria in Luke II.2, but the phrase 'ex consolibus' is an extra-biblical detail which

follows Malalas's ἀπὸ ὑπάτων (p. 227) literally, rather than using the more natural Latin, *exconsule*. The consular names given here are not found in the gospels; it is Pontius Pilate who is named as governor of Judaea in Luke II.1. Herod is described by Luke as the tetrarch of Galilee. This Herod is not distinguished as *filius Archelai*, or as *Herodes magnus*, in any gospel. Theodore of Mopsuestia gave some guidance on the Herods and their activities (*Fragmenta in Matthaei*, PG 66, 703–16, at 709): [Matth. XIV.1] Ἕτερός ἐστιν Ἡρώδης ὁ βασιλεὺς, καὶ ἕτερος ὁ τετράρχης ὁ υἱὸς αὐτοῦ. Μετὰ γὰρ τὸν τοῦ βασιλέως Ἡρώδου θάνατον εἰς τετραρχίας διεῖλον οἱ Ρωμαῖοι τὴν βασιλείαν αὐτοῦ, ὁ δὲ τούτου υἱὸς ἐν μέρος τῆς τετραρχίας εἶχεν· οὗτος δὲ ην ὁ τὸν Πρόδρομον κατατομήσας ('One Herod is the king, the other, the tetrarch, is his son. For after the death of Herod the king, the Romans divided his kingdom into tetrarchies, and his son, who beheaded the Precursor [John the Baptist], took one of them').

CH. 3

27 Malalas, *Chronographia* X.2 (pp. 227–8).

28 *Phalech*. Genesis X.23 reads 'natique sunt Eber filii duo nomen uni Faleg eo quod in diebus eius diuisa sit terra'. The name Phaleg (variously spelt) was glossed by many writers, all of whom referred the meaning of the name ('division') either to the splitting up of peoples or of languages. For example, Epiphanius has: Ἐβερ γεννᾷ τὸν Φαλὲκ καὶ γίνεται γῆς καὶ γλωσσῶν διαμερισμός ('Heber begat Phalec, in whose time the division of the earth and of languages was made'; *Ancoratus* CXIV.vii, ed. Holl (Leipzig, 1915), p. 162). A Syriac text, *The Book of the Cave of Treasures*, is more specific (ed. Budge, p. 132): 'From Adam until this time they were all of one speech and one language ... in the days of Peleg the Tower which is in Babel was built and there the tongues of men were confounded.' A marginal note in the manuscript adds: 'the division of tongues took place at midnight' – compare the Irish text *The Ever-New Tongue*'s interest in the hour of midnight. Ephrem similarly considers the division to be one of language: 'In the days of Peleg the earth was divided into seventy tongues' (Ephrem, *De natiuitate* I.46, trans. in Kronholm, *Motifs from Genesis*, p. 212). Rabbinic exegesis was more inclined to stress the divisions of peoples, as we find in Josephus (*Antiquitates Iudaicarum* I.vi.4, ed. Niese I, 36): Ἐβερος δὲ Ἰούκταν καὶ Φάλεγον ἐγέννησεν· ἐκλήθη δὲ Φάλεγος, ἐπειδὴ κατὰ τὸν ἀποδασμὸν τῶν οἰκήσεων τίκτεται· φαλὲκ γὰρ τὸν μερισμὸν Ἑβραῖοι καλοῦσιν ('Heber begat Joctan and Phaleg: he was called Phaleg because he was born at the dispersion of the nations to their several countries, for *phaleg*, among the Hebrews, signifies "division"').

The phrasing here, 'ab Adam usque a Phalech *fili* Eber', follows the grammar of the Greek: Ἀπὸ Ἀδὰμ ἕως τοῦ Φαλεκ, υἱοῦ Ἐβερ, which has 'son' in the genitive after ἕως, rather than the Latin construction with the accusative *filium* after *usque ad* (*usque a* is clearly a slip).

John Malalas's use of Phaleg as a *time*-divider is found in only four other texts I know of. One is a Syriac fragment, *Expositio quomodo se habeant generationes*. The body of the text appears to be eighth-century, though it draws on considerably earlier sources. Concerning Phalech, it says: 'Eber uiuit 134 annos et genuit Phaleg. Et eius diebus terra diuisa est. Generationes sunt .v., anni 402 [from the Deluge], et ab Adamo generationes .xv., anni 2642' (*Chronica Minora*, ed. and trans. E. W. Brooks *et al.*, pp. 267–75, at 268). The second writer is an anonymous Latin chronographer (*Anonymi chronologica*, ch. 13, PL 97, 78): 'Ab Adamo itaque ad diluuium anni numerantur .mmcclxii.: a diluuio ad linguarum confusionem obitum Phaleci (cuius nomen Diuisionem sonat) anni .dxxxvi.' Neither of these writers uses Phalech as the sole point of division between Adam and Christ. The total of years given by these writers from Adam to Phalech is, respectively, 2642 and 2,898, which accords reasonably well, though not perfectly, with the *tria milia* of the *Laterculus*. The last two writers have versions of the Phalech story very close to that of Malalas. One is Procopius of Gaza, whose commentary on Genesis was written in the early sixth century (*Commentarii in Genesin*, PG 87, 14–512, at 316) similarly states that not only the earth, but also time, was divided by Phalech's life: Ἀπὸ κτίσεως ἕως τοῦ Φαλεκ συνάγεται ἔτη χ, τὸ ἥμισυ τοῦ σύμπαντος χρόνου τῆς συστάσεως τοῦ κόσμου. οὐ γὰρ μόνον ἡ γῆ, ἀλλὰ καὶ ὁ χρόνος αὐτοῦ ἐμερίσθη ('From the Creation to Phalech may be counted 600 years, the half-way-point of the whole time since the creation of the world. For it was not the earth alone, but also time, which was divided'). It is probable that χ: 600, is a textual corruption for an original .γ: 3,000: a gamma with a downstroke in front of it could very easily be mistaken for a chi. If this were so, then the version here would be very close to that of Malalas. The fourth of these writers, whose version is also close to that of Malalas, is Julius Africanus, a second-century Christian army officer who served most of his time at Emmaus in Palestine and thus had access to Jewish thought. His *Chronicles*, which survive only in fragments and which were published in AD 221, state that the present world is to last for 6,000 years, and that the year 3,000, the halfway point, is marked by Peleg son of Eber, who is thus a 'division' of time as well as of the earth. Christ appeared 2,500 years after Peleg (see M.J. Routh, *Reliquiae Sacrae II* (2nd ed. Oxford, 1846), pp. 244, 245, 306 for the surviving text). It should be added that Malalas's *Chronographia* itself does not give the figure 3,000 at this point, but 2,533, with 2,967 years from Phalech to the forty-second year of Augustus, thus giving 5,500 years from Adam to the Incarnation. The *Laterculus* keeps the first figure, but not the second, so as to give 6,000 years from Adam to the *Passion*, an independent variant with no obvious source. In bk 1, the

Chronographia gives 2,922 years from Adam to the completion of the tower of Babel, normally taken as contemporary with Phalech (as translated in Jeffreys, p. 5: cf. Dindorf's edition, p. 13, which prints an anonymous chronicle in place of the missing first book).

There is a passage parallel to this section of Malalas, attributed to his contemporary Hesychius, Ἡσυχίου ἐκ τοῦ εἰς τὴν Χριστοῦ γέννησιν edited by H. Hody, in Dindorf's *Chronographia*, pp. lii–liii (see K. Krumbacher, *Geschichte der byzantinischen Literatur*, 2 vols. (Munich, 1897) I, 325). This text is of interest here, for it resembles the chronology of the *Laterculus* more than that of the *Chronographia* as we have it. It begins by saying, like the *Laterculus*, ἀπὸ κτίσεως κόσμου ἕως τῆς Χριστοῦ γεννήσεως καὶ σταυρώσεως, ξ ('there are six thousand years from the creation of the world to the birth of Christ and the Crucifixion'). Neither this text nor the *Laterculus* is troubled by the reflection that there must be 6,000 years from Adam either to the Nativity, or the Crucifixion, but not both. Hesychius similarly gives 3,000 years from Adam to Phalech, though he gives 1,067 not 2,967 (which must surely be some kind of curious slip, since the total is 6,000) from Phalech to the forty-second year of Augustus. The significant common denominator is the number 67, since it gives a round number with the addition of 33, the age of Christ at the Crucifixion. It seems to me more likely that the Hesychius fragment is based on Malalas than that it is a source for the *Chronographia*. Its thinking is very little less confused, but it does seem to be extending the argument to some extent. Much of the wording is very close indeed to the *Chronographia*. It is perhaps possible that the version of Malalas's chronicle known to the author of the *Laterculus* had interpolated, or substituted, the Hesychius discussion at this point. The text of Malalas, as the variety of quotations from it scattered among Greek writers indicates (on which see Jeffrey's translation and its introduction), does not seem to have been entirely static; there were certainly two editions, one put together in the 530s, and the other possibly as late as the 570s (Jeffreys, in *Chronographia*, p. xiii), which gives considerable scope for a proliferation of variants.

29 Malalas's discussion of the framework of world history, despite his appeals to the authority of Timothy, Clemens and Eusebius, was unusual to the point of uniqueness, an eclectic combination of elements from different systems. His text – followed by the *Laterculus* – implies a belief in the World Week, giving a round 6,000 years from Adam to the Passion. F.E. Robbins (*The Hexemeral Literature*, p. 27) pointed out that the idea that the world is to exist for 6,000 years followed by a millennium of rest is already found in Jewish apocrypha. The situation in the *Laterculus* is rather different, as 6,000, not 5,000, years are deemed to have passed. Therefore the seventh millennium cannot be a thousand-year rest, by analogy with the seventh day in Genesis when the Lord rested, but is the *dies dominica*, the Christian era, which though differentiated from the 6,000 years that

proceeded it, is evidently not yet all that peaceful. This will be followed by an eternal Day Eight beginning after the Last Judgement, which will be the true sabbath: 'Namque prima dies in qua principia mundi sunt, ipsa nobis octabam per resurrectionem fecit, in qua deus sanctis requiem donauit' (ch. 23). See further Luneau, *L'Histoire du salut*, p. 41, who quoted a similar scheme from the Talmud: 'un millénaire de repos succédera aux six mille ans'. But the author of the *Laterculus* speaks of this in terms of a threefold scheme, giving Phalech as a temporal half-way point, 3,000 years after Adam, bisecting the pre-Christian era. This must surely bear some relationship to the established tripartite division of world history, into the natural law, the law of Moses and Christianity, discussed by Luneau, *ibid.*, p. 47, and Jones, *BOT*, p. 345, in which the division should come, obviously, at Moses. Malalas here produced what appears to be an unique theory (see detailed discussion of Malalas's theory and what may lie behind it, above, pp. 21–2, and Croke, 'Early Development', in *Studies*, p. 27).

It is a point of considerable interest that the learned and sophisticated author of the *Laterculus* made no attempt to correct, emend, or offer alternatives here. It is unlikely to the point of being inconceivable that he knew no other *sex aetates* texts. One can only conclude that history, as Bede would understand the term, interested him hardly at all. And indeed, historical writing is never mentioned as a particular concern of the Canterbury school.

The genitive phrase *primi hominis* follows the Greek τοῦ πρωτοπλάστου.

30 *Moyses magnus scriptor temporum*. This phrase is apparently an addition to the text of Malalas, which reads 'as Moses said . . .'. But the Slavonic version of Malalas reads 'and Moses the Great said . . .' (*Chronicle*, trans. Spinka [and Downey], p. 41), which raises the possibility that the text of the *Chronicle* available to the author of the *Laterculus* may also have qualified the name in some way. The description of Moses as a chronographer rather than a lawgiver is most unusual. Although the Pentateuch of course includes the Creation story in the book of Genesis, his name is more normally linked with the giving of the Law in Exodus and Leviticus. A possible parallel is in Cosmas Indicopleustes, λέγει τοίνυν ὁ θεῖος κοσμογράφος Μωϋσῆς (ed. Wolska-Conus I, 310: 'Moses, the Divine Cosmographer, says. . .').

31 *monumentis*. The manuscript reading here is *momentis*, emended by Mommsen to *commentis*, and by Mai to *monumentis*. The latter suggestion has the advantage of being in close accord with Malalas's Greek, ἐν τοῖς ὑπομνήμασιν, since the primary meaning of ὑπόμνημα is 'memorial, memorandum', though it also embraces the meanings 'treatise' and 'commentary'.

32 II Pet. III.8: 'unus dies apud dominum sicut mille anni'. See also Ps. LXXXIX.4 (LXX): 'quoniam mille anni ante oculos tuos tamquam dies hesterna

quae praeteriit et custodia in nocte' (also quoted in *Biblical Commentaries*, ed. Lapidge, p. 386). The word *inquid* here in the *Laterculus* is something of a puzzle, as the only possible referent is Moses. While it is not impossible that Moses and David, authors of the Pentateuch and the Psalms, could merge together in a speaker's memory, the quotation is quite obviously from the New Testament Epistle. Note also the preference in the *Laterculus* for *dies* as a feminine noun (though this is not consistent: it is masculine in ch. 13), where the Vulgate prefers the masculine. ἡμέρα ('day') is a feminine noun in Greek.

33 Note that this writer believes that Adam and Eve fell on the same day that they were created. There was an enormous amount of theorization about the first six days, and the length of time in which the primal pair managed to remain sinless attracted its fair share. The version followed by the *Laterculus* is also found, pithily expressed, in the Syrian writer Narsai: 'Adam et Eve ne restèrent qu'un jour au paradis, car le jour (même) où ils avaient été constitués, ils mangèrent, péchèrent et s'en allèrent', *Homélies de Narsai*, ed. and trans. Gignoux, p. 452, and Homily IV, line 259 (p. 627); see also A. Levene, *The Early Syrian Fathers on Genesis, from a Syriac MS on the Pentateuch in the Mingana Collection* (London, 1951), p. 78, and comment on p. 154: 'there is a [Rabbinic] tradition ... that the paradisal felicity which Adam enjoyed did not last six hours'. This is also stated in ps.-Athanasius, *Quaestiones ad Antiochum ducem*, a tract which seems to be a source both for the *Laterculus* and for the *Biblical Commentaries* (PG 28, 629–30): Οἱ μὲν γάρ φασιν ἐξαμηνιαῖον χρόνον, οἱ δὲ πλείονα· ἄλλοι δὲ τοσαύτας ὥρας καὶ μόνον, ὅσας ὁ Κύριος ἐν τῷ ξύλῳ τοῦ σταυροῦ πεποίηκεν, ὅπερ οἶμαι ἀληθέστερον εἶναι ('some think he stayed there six months, others longer, and others that he stayed there as many hours (and no more) as the Lord stayed on the Cross, which I think the more plausible'). The paralleling of Adam and Christ is found both here in ps.-Athanasius, and also in Cosmas Indicopleustes (*Topographie Chrétienne* II, 94–5, ed. Wolska-Conus I, 413–15), and is present here in a slightly different form in the *Laterculus*.

The idea reached the British Isles, since it is also found in Ireland, in the prose version of the *Saltair na Rann*, preserved in the *Leabhar Breac* (Mac Carthy, *Codex Palatino-Vaticanus*, p. 47):

> An hour beyond mid-day, without defect,
> I tell plainly, very precisely,
> That [was] the time of Eve in Paradise
> And of Adam, before [they committed] offence.

Note also that the ungrammatical 'cecidit sub peccato' reflects the Greek phrase καὶ ὑπέπεσε τῇ ἁμαρτίᾳ ὁ ἄνθρωπος.

It is interesting to find that the *Biblical Commentaries* (at PentI 44), also attributed to Theodore's school, shows knowledge both of this doctrine and of

Jubilees: 'Iohannes Crisostomus [probably a reference to ps.-Athanasius] dicit Adam factum tertia hora et sexta peccasse et quasi ad horam nonam eiectum de paradiso . . . Alii autem septem annos peregisse in paradiso praeter .xl. dies, ut in Lepti geneseos [Jubilees III.17, ed. Charles, p. 16] dicit.'

CH. 4

34 *Quod etiam.* Malalas, *Chronographia* X.2 (pp. 228–9).

35 This is another case of literal translation. 'Secundum numerum sex dierum plasmationis Adae' parallels κατὰ τὸν ἀριθμὸν ἓξ ἡμερῶν τῆς πλάσεως τοῦ ᾽Αδάμ. It is, however, also curiously reminiscent of a sentence in Julian of Toledo's *De comprobatione sextae aetatis* I.4, ed. Hillgarth, p. 151: 'quamquam etiam et *secundum numerum sex dierum* sex millibus annis secundum istud a quibusdam stare credatur'.

36 The author of the *Laterculus* is right to say that most Greek chronographers gave between 5,000 and 6,000 years from Adam to Christ, though it is also true that all the most influential chronographies give 5,500 years or less, so he is being a little misleading. Both the third-century Julius Africanus and Hippolytus agreed on 5,500 years (Finegan, *Handbook*, pp. 143–4); Eusebius favoured the lower figure of 5,200 years (Mosshammer, *The Chronicle*, p. 78).

37 These parenthetic remarks about the Irish breathe a spirit of animosity and controversialism which may easily be paralleled in a seventh-century context. Cf. the way that Romans X.2, 'aemulationem Dei habebant, sed non secundum scientiae' is used by Bede, *Historia ecclesiastica* V.22 (ed. Colgrave and Mynors, pp. 552–4), to describe the Irish. The paschal controversy in particular evoked reflections on the perversity of the Celts in standing out against the whole of the rest of Christendom, expressed most trenchantly by the Irish 'Romanist' Cummian in his letter to his obdurate fellow-countrymen: 'Quid autem prauius sentiri potest de Ecclesia matre, quam si dicamus, Roma errat, Hierosolyma errat, Alexandria errat, Antiochia errat, totus mundus errat; soli tantum Scoti et Britones rectum sapiunt?' ('What can be more distorted than to say Rome errs, Jerusalem errs, Alexandria errs, Antioch errs, the whole world errs; only the Irish and British know what is right?'). (See PL 87, 969–78, at 974, Lapidge and Sharpe, *BCL*, pp. 78–9 (no. 289), and *BOT*, p. 92.) A degree of Hibernophobia and in particular a sense of the waywardness of the Irish learned tradition is also evident in Aldhelm's letters to Wihtfrith and Heahfrith.

Strong feelings – amounting almost to an accusation of heresy against him – were aroused when Bede, in his early work *De temporibus*, decided that the length of time between Adam and the birth of Christ was 3,852 years rather than approximately 5,000 (*BOT*, pp. 133–4). Bede was subsequently bitter about the political and emotional dimension that this issue (which was to him academic and a matter only for rational debate among specialist chronologists) acquired in the hands of the Wilfredian party, as he shows in his *Epistola ad Pleguuinam* (*BOT*, pp. 307–15).

However, this debate between Bede and the forces of conservatism may prove to bear directly on the *Laterculus*. Jones, speaking primarily of Easter computations (*BOT*, p. 111), noted: 'Bede's works indicate that Northumbrian schools largely depended upon Irish knowledge and methods. We would expect no less. Not only was Northumbria originally evangelised by the Irish, but the stream of communication between the two nations was friendly and constant.' Bede, as the foregoing sentences indicate, appeared to have been a lone voice in assigning 4,000, rather than between 5,000 and 6,000, years to the period before Christ. Yet the *Laterculus*, ch. 4, says: 'In sex milia autem annorum concordant omnes apparuisse dominum, *quamuis Scotti concordare nolunt, qui sapientia se existimant habere et scientiam perdederunt.*' The jeering tone of this remark about Irish chronographers is parallel to the animosity Bede also found himself facing. Did the theory of a rather shorter age of the world originate in some Irish centre such as Bangor, home of the sapient computists, rather than with Bede himself? There is no trace of it now in the surviving early Hiberno-Latin computistical or cosmographic texts, but that proves nothing either way. Bede's dependence on Irish sources, acknowledged or otherwise, is set out by Ó Cróinín, 'The Irish Provenance of Bede's Computus'.

38 *unus tertiam horam.* Mark XV.25: 'erat autem hora tertia et crucifixerunt eum'. Cf. Matth. XXVII.45: 'a sexta autem hora tenebrae factae sunt super uniuersam terram usque ad horam nonam', Luke XXIII.44: 'erat autem fere hora sexta ...', and John XIX.14: 'erat autem parasceue paschae hora quasi sexta'.

39 *non sunt contraria in uera ratio.* Theodore of Mopsuestia's comments on the Passion are closely similar in their approach to some remarks on the Crucifixion in the *Laterculus*: 'the various accounts exhibit a great harmony in the essentials; in the unimportant things and in those things which small men value, their words are by no means in perfect accord ... Therefore even in those things which seem contradictory to calumniators I find, after a careful study, perfect accord ...' (Greer, *Theodore of Mopsuestia*, p. 116, translated from *Commentarius in Euangelium Iohannis Apostoli*, trans. J.-M. Vosté (Louvain, 1940), pp. 244–5). Cf. the *Laterculus*: 'dum unus tertiam horam Christum dicit esse crucifixum, id est Marcus, alii uero in sextam eum asserunt ligno crucifixum: quod aput inperitos contraria sibi haec uidebuntur, sed non contraria in uera ratio, ubi se sic puriter conplectitur diuina scriptura, dum tamen diligentius ruminantur et bene tractantur ab his, qui non de sua, sed de Dei presumunt sapientia.' The writer shows the

same resolute refusal either to allegorize away the discrepancy, or to treat it as a stumbling-block. Finegan, *Handbook*, p. 291, also commented on the significance of these variant hours.

40 *cum natus esset*. Matth. II.1–4: 'cum ergo natus esset Iesus in Bethleem Iudeae in diebus Herodis regis, ecce magi ab oriente uenerunt Hierosolymam dicentes "ubi est qui natus est rex Iudeorum, uidimus enim stellam eius in oriente, et uenimus adorare eum."'

41 *in duobus annis*. There was more than one theory about the relationship between the nativity and the journey of the Magi. It was assumed, practically, that it took the Magi some time to get from the east (Persia, according to Malalas) to Bethlehem. In addition, the fact that Herod ordered the murder of children two years old or less led to the reasonable deduction that Christ might have been about two by this time. Accordingly, the alternatives were that the star appeared some time before the birth, or that it appeared *at* the birth and the Magi arrived some time later. The latter is the opinion which was held by the author of the *Laterculus* and some Greek writers, including Eusebius: οὐκοῦν διετὴς χρόνος ἤδη παρελήλυθει ἀπὸ τῆς Ἰησοῦ γενέσεως καὶ ἐπὶ τὴν ἄφιξιν τῶν εἰρημένων (*Quaestiones ad Stephanum* XVI.ii, PG 21, 933: 'Two years had gone by from the birth of Jesus to the coming of the Magi'); and by the Syrian Fathers, for example Ephrem: 'It was the opinion of Mar Ephrem that the Magi came to Bethlehem two years after the birth of Christ' (*Fragments of the Commentary of Ephrem*, ed. Harris, p. 37). Harris quotes Bar-Hebraeus, *ibid.*, pp. 38–9: 'Eusebius and Epiphanius and Mar Ephrem and Mar Jacob say that after two years, when they brought him up to Jerusalem and when they were at Bethlehem, the magi came.' The Epiphanius reference is to *Panarion* LI.xxii.13 (ed. Holl II, 287). See also Theodore of Mopsuestia, *Fragmenta in Matthaeum*, PG 66, 705–6. This passage dissents from the *Biblical Commentaries*, which otherwise are very closely parallel to the *Laterculus*, in that EvII 3 asserts the less common view that the Magi arrived at the time of Christ's birth.

42 *uenerunt a Persida*. Malalas, *Chronographia* X.4 (pp. 229–30).

43 *Et conturbati sunt*. Matth. II.3: 'audiens autem Herodes rex turbatus est et omnis Hierosolyma cum illo'.

44 The meaning of this word here is clarified by the Greek: οἵτινες μάγοι γνωσθέντες συνεσχέθησαν ('when the Magi were recognized, they were arrested').

CH. 6

45 *Venerunt ergo*. Malalas, *Chronographia* X.4 (pp. 230–1). AD 2, P. Vinicius, P. Alfenus Varus. Codex Baroccianus gives the names as Οὐϊνδικίου καὶ Οὐαλερίου, sharing the mis-spelling of *Vinicius*, but having a defective form of *Varus*.

46 This section begins by recapitulating data already given; we were told in ch. 2 that Christ was born in the forty-second year of Augustus and in ch. 5 that he was two when the Magi came from the east; so therefore they arrived in the forty-fourth year of Augustus. The consular date for this year was contributed by Malalas and is consistent with AD 2.

47 *Exquisiuit*. Matth. II.7: 'Tunc Herodes clam uocatis magis diligenter didicit ab eis tempus stellae quae apparuit eis.' This passage is translated from Malalas and follows his paraphrase of the gospel narrative.

48 *ite et scrutamini*. This phrase is an addition to Malalas and it is therefore interesting that it appears to reflect a non-Vulgate reading. The Vulgate gives 'ite et interrogate'; a sixth-century Vetus Latina text, the Codex Brixianus (*Nouum Testamentum*, ed. Wordsworth and White I, 46), gives 'euntes *requirite* diligenter de puero'. The *Laterculus*'s *scrutamini* appears to be a unique version. *De* + acc. (*de puerum*) is a grammatical error which appears two or three times in this text. The Vulgate's 'qui cum audissent regem *abierunt*' may give 'et *abierunt* magi' in the *Laterculus*. But the wording throughout this passage does not appear to reflect any known Latin Bible-text directly. In addition to the instances already noted, 'stella quae paululum abscesserat' is very different from 'stella . . . antecedebat eos'. Even in paraphrase, the vocabulary of a well-known text tends to come to mind; so this treatment of Matthew may suggest that the writer's primary familiarity is with the Greek Bible and therefore that we have here an independent translation.

49 *inuenerunt Iesum*. Matth. II.11: 'et intrantes domum inuenerunt puerum cum Maria matre eius, et procidentes adorauerunt eum. Et apertis thesauris suis obtulerunt ei munera, aurum, tus et murram.' 'Cadentes in pauimento' in the *Laterculus* is an otherwise unattested version.

50 *thensauris*. This spelling is found in some early gospelbooks; the sixth-century Codex Brixianus, J (s. vi/vii), L (the Lichfield gospels), Z (s. vi/vii).

51 *tamquam Deo et regi*. See commentary on ch. 15 below, p. 203.

52 *Et responso accepto*. Matth. II.12: 'et responso accepto in somnis, ne redirent ad Herodem. Per aliam uiam reuersi sunt in regionem suam.' The *Laterculus* shares

the ablative absolute clause with the Vulgate, but adds *ab angelo*. It substitutes *regressi sunt* for *reuersi sunt*, a variant which is found in some Spanish Bibles (BCT) and in Lichfield (L) and Kells (Q). *In suam regionem* is also found in the Mac Regol Gospels (R).

53 The translation of *limitis* as 'by the border' is based on the Greek: δι' ἄλλης ὁδοῦ (= 'per aliam uiam', 'by another road'), τῆς τοῦ λιμίτου (= 'limitis': note that both the Greek and Latin words are in the genitive).

54 *iratus est uehementer*. Matth. II.16: 'iratus est ualde'. The Vetus Latina Codex Brixianus gives 'iratus est *uehementer*'.

55 *quod propheta praedixit*. Matth. II.6.

56 *Et mittens manum militarem*. Matth. II.16: 'et mittens occidit omnes pueros qui erant in Bethleem et in omnibus finibus eius a bimatu et infra secundum tempus quod exquisierat a magis.' From 'finibus eius' to 'a magis', the *Laterculus* is completely in accord with the Vulgate. *Circa* as a preposition takes the accusative: its attraction into the ablative here ('et circa finibus') may have resulted from the Vulgate's ablative phrase, 'et in omnibus finibus', or it may just be another testimony to the writer's shaky grasp of prepositions. The phrase *manum militarem* is an addition: Malalas has καὶ πέμψας τοὺς στρατιώτας ('and he sent his soldiers'), which is evidently the basis, but the use of a figurative phrase rather than the simple *miles* is not directly paralleled. It is therefore extremely interesting that the phrase is found with the same meaning in Gildas, *De excidio* I.vii, 'non tam militari manu', and I.xv.1, 'legatos Romam ... mittit, *militarem manum* ... poscens...' (note that the verb *mittere* is used here) (ed. Mommsen, p. 33). I am grateful to Neil Wright for pointing this out. Wright, 'Did Gildas read Orosius?', *CMCS* 9 (1985), 31–42, at 39, notes that the phrase in Gildas may itself have conceivably been derived from Orosius, *Historia aduersus paganos* VII.xlii.14, though in the context of the *Historia* it is likely to mean 'the hand of a soldier' rather than, as in *De excidio* and the *Laterculus*, 'a war-band'.

57 *scatens uermibus*. The phraseology here is probably based on Acts XII.23: 'confestim autem percussit eum angelus Domini, eo quod non dedisset honorem Dei, et consumptus a uermibus exspirauit.' The subject of this sentence is Herod Agrippa; but Josephus, followed by many eastern writers, including Eusebius, held that a similar fate had overtaken Herod the Great. Josephus regarded this as the punishment for a long life of strenuous iniquities, whereas Christian writers associated his death specifically with the massacre of the innocents. Eusebius (*Historia ecclesiastica* I.viii.5; ed. Schwarz I, 64; trans. Williamson, p. 58)

described: ὡς δ' ἄμα τῇ κατὰ τοῦ σωτῆρος ἡμῶν καὶ τῶν ἄλλων νηπίων ἐπιβουλῇ θεήλατος αὐτὸν καταλαβοῦσα μάστιξ εἰς θάνατον συνήλασεν ('how, from the moment of the plot against our Saviour and the other helpless infants, a scourge wielded by the hand of God struck Herod and drove him to death . . .'). See also Josephus, *Antiquitates Iudaicarum* XVII.vi.5 (ed. Niese IV, 100). The Syriac *Book of the Cave of Treasures* (ed. Budge, p. 218) gives a version similar to that of Eusebius.

CH. 7

58 *Et factus est toparcha*. Malalas, *Chronographia* X.4 (p. 231).

59 *terraarchia*. This is an extremely odd spelling of *tetrarchia*. It is as though 'the rule of a fourth [part]' has been broken down into 'rule of the land' – which, since *terra* is, of course, Latin and -αρχία Greek, is a particularly egregious blunder which one hesitates to attribute directly to the learned author of the *Laterculus*. The spelling τετρααρχία is attested alongside τετραρχία in Greek, so it is possible either that the scribe of the Vatican manuscript misread *tr* as *rr*, or took too hasty a glance at the whole word and automatically wrote the familiar *terra*.

60 *Lamii et Seruiliani*. Like all consular dates in this text, this is taken straight from Malalas, the Codex Baroccianus forms being Λαμία καὶ Σερελλιανοῦ. L. Aelius Lamia and M. Seruilius were consuls in AD 3.

61 *per angelum*. Matth. II.13: 'ecce angelus Domini apparuit in somnis Ioseph dicens "surge et accipe puerum et matrem eius et fuge in Aegyptum".'

62 *scriptum est*. Isaiah XIX.1: 'ecce dominus ascendet super nubem leuem et ingredietur Aegyptum et mouebuntur simulacra Aegypti a facie eius.' The verbs used by the *Laterculus* are found in the forms *sedet*, *uenit* and *comminuentur* in various Vetus Latina readings attested by Sabatier (*Versiones antiquae* II, 547), but *simulacra* is Vulgate and both *et sculptilia* and *Aegyptiorum* for *Aegypti* are otherwise unattested. The verse is briefly explained by Hesychius (*Interpretatio Isaias*, ed. Faulhaber, p. 56): Ἰδοὺ κύριος κάθηται ἐπὶ νεφέλης κούφης: ὁ Χριστὸς ἐπὶ τῆς παρθένου ('"See, the Lord is seated on a light cloud": Christ on (in the arms of) the Virgin').

63 *dum ingrederentur*. Here we have an apocryphal story of the Holy Family in Egypt, allegedly 'quod et beatus Epyfanius Cyprius episcopus commemorat'. This, on the face of it, is a direct reference to the works of the fourth-century bishop of Cyprus, best known for his *Panarion*, or 'Medicine-chest against eighty

182

heresies', an extremely lengthy mine of information on heterodox religion in the eastern empire, though this particular story cannot, in fact, be found there. The 'breaking of the statues' episode quoted in the *Laterculus* is found in ch. 23 of the gospel of ps.-Matthew (preserved in Latin), in *Euangelia Apocrypha*, ed. C. Tischendorf, 2nd ed. (Leipzig, 1876), pp. 51–112, at 91, and in a similar infancy-gospel preserved in Arabic and probably translated from a Syriac original. The stories associated with the Flight into Egypt, this among them, were also probably based on an older written source, on which see E. Hennecke and W. Schneemelcher, *New Testament Apocrypha*, 2 vols. (London, 1963–5) I, 404 (the episode of breaking the statues is at I, 412–13). Some version of the gospel of ps.-Matthew was certainly in existence by the fourth century, and known to Epiphanius, who quoted it in *Panarion* XXVI.xii (ed. Holl I, 290–2) – unfortunately, the section quoted is not the relevant one.

Epiphanius was noted even in his own day for the vehemence of his iconoclasm. He wrote three separate tracts against image-worship, not one of which has survived except as fragments quoted by other controversialists, Novatian (who disagreed with him) and Jerome (who agreed). The fragments quoted by Novatian are in K. Holl, *Gesammelte Aufsätze zur Kirchengeschichte*, 3 vols. (Tübingen, 1927–8) II, 536–63 (and see also Quasten, *Patrology* II, 391–3). Jerome's translation of excerpts from these commentaries are in his *Epistolae* LI and LVI (and see P. Maas, 'Die ikonoklastische Episode in dem Brief des Epiphanios am Johannes', *BZ* 30 (1929–30), 279–86; and B. Hemmerdinger, 'Saint Epiphane, iconoclaste', *SP* 10 [=TU 108] (1970), 188–20). Although Novatian's excerpts do not quote this story, it is quite probable that this infancy-tale, widely known and accepted in the east, as I shall show, was used by Epiphanius, somewhere in the portions of his iconoclastic work which have not survived, to demonstrate the complete futility of idols and their cult. The story is certainly to be found in other early Greek sources, including Eusebius and Ephrem, both almost certainly known to the author of the *Laterculus*. Eusebius referred to it three times, in *Commentaria in Isaiam*, PG 24, 89–526, at 219–20, *Demonstratio euangelica* VI.xx.11, PG 22, 9–794, at 469–72, and *Eclogae propheticae*, *ibid.* 1017–1262, at 1213. It also appears twice in the collected works of Ephrem Syrus, *Ephraem Syri Opera*, ed. Assemani II, 49–50 and 144–5. The *Biblical Commentaries* contain evidence that books by both Epiphanius and Ephrem were in the library at Canterbury.

Perhaps the most conspicuous place where this story is found is in the extremely well-known sixth-century Greek *Akathistos* hymn on the Virgin (PG 92, 1335–48, at 1341): Λαμψας ἐν τῇ Αἰγύπτῳ φωτισμὸν ἀληθείας, ἐδίωξας τοῦ ψεύδους τὸ σκότος· τὰ γὰρ εἴδωλα ταύτης, Σωτήρ, μὴ ἐνέγκαντά σου τὴν ἰσχὺν πέπτωκεν· οἱ τούτων δὲ ῥυσθέντες ἐβόων πρὸς τὴν Θεοτόκον ('Having shed in Egypt the beams of your truth, you chased the darkness of untruth, for its idols, O

Saviour, unable to meet your strength, fell down, and as many as were freed from them cried out to the God-Bearer'). The closest parallel to the version in the *Laterculus* of all these is the first version of Ephrem, which includes the phrase *'uirginis ulnis* Aegypto inuectus est', equivalent to the passage in ch. 7, 'ad aduentum enim saluatoris sedentis *super gremium uirginis matris'*. However, not one of these texts includes the detail of the statues crumbling into dust.

But Mommsen had tacitly convicted the author of the *Laterculus* of a serious error, for his marginal note refers the reader to 'Epiphanius schol. hist. trip.'. This is to imply that the story is found in the *Historia ecclesiastica tripartita* written by Cassiodorus and Epiphanius Scholasticus, *Historia ecclesiastica tripartita* VI.42 (ed. R. Hanslik, CSEL 71 (Vienna, 1952), 364–5): 'Cum uiderent rerum talium destructorem, nec non et omnibus simulacris Aegyptiorum secundum Esaiae prophetam, fugatoque daemonio pro testimonio Christi arborem uacuam reman-sisse.' Since the *Historia tripartita* was written in Latin in the late fifth century, the author of the *Laterculus* should not have easily confused it with the writings of a fourth-century Greek-speaker. Nor, in fact, is the resemblance to the rather graphic version found in the *Laterculus* particularly close. It would also make it one of the very few significant *Latin* sources for the *Laterculus*.

64 expleti essent .iiii. anni. The chronology of the infancy of Christ was not a matter of general agreement. Epiphanius, who was well known to this writer, gave the duration of the Holy Family's sojourn in Egypt as two years: καὶ ποιήσας ἔτη δύο λαμβάνεται ὑπὸ τοῦ ᾿Ιωσὴφ εἰς Αἴγυπτον ... κάτεισι δὲ εἰς Αἴγυπτον καὶ διατελεῖ ἐκεῖσε ἄλλα δύο ἔτη (*Panarion* LXXVIII.x.1, ed. Holl III, 460): 'then after two years he was taken away into Egypt by Joseph ... so having gone into Egypt, he stayed there two years'; and this is shared by Origen and Eusebius (Finegan, *Handbook*, pp. 233–4). Finegan pointed out that this chronology is distinctive in that it apparently confuses the reign of Herod with that of Augustus. All these writers accept that Herod died immediately after the massacre of the innocents (that is, when Christ was two or less, as I noted above in the context of the timing of the visit of the Magi). Archelaus succeeded his father in the normal fashion, without the two-year interregnum which these writers have tacitly assumed.

The phrasing of the *Laterculus* is not entirely clear, but 'cum ei expleti essent .iiii. anni in Aegypto' could just stretch to meaning not that four years had been spent in Egypt, but that Jesus was four years old when Joseph had his dream, which would fit with Epiphanius and Eusebius. Admittedly, this is not the most natural meaning of the sentence, but it must be obvious by now that the syntax of the *Laterculus* is frequently obscure or strained. Hippolytus, however, gave the length of time as three-and-a-half years, on which see R.E. Witt, 'The Flight into Egypt', *SP* 11 [= *TU* 108] (1972), 92–8, at 94. Particularly interesting in this context is the 'Maronite Chronicle', a fragmentary chronicle in Syriac dating to the seventh century. It gives a version of the infancy of Christ which has a good deal in common with both Malalas's *Chronographia* and with the *Laterculus*, and there seems to be nothing against Malalas being one of its sources. On this point, it says: 'ipsa nocte qua a Magis uisus est, descendit in Aegyptum ubi egit .ii. annos. Tum, nuntio accepto Herodem mortuum esse, ascendit ex Aegypto, cum esset natus .iv. annos' (*Chronicon Maroniticum*, in *Chronica Minora*, ed. and trans. E. W. Brooks *et al.*): 'Cum esset natus ... annos' is an idiom which appears elsewhere in this Syriac text. One wonders whether 'expleti essent .iiii. anni' might also prove to have some non-Latin idiom lurking behind it.

65 *iterum angelus*. Matth. II.19: 'defuncto autem Herode, ecce apparuit angelus Domini in somnis Ioseph in Aegypto dicens "surge et accipe puerum et matrem eius et uade in terram Israhel".' *Cum* + acc. ('cum puerum et matrem') occurs several times in the *Laterculus*, but may be influenced here by the case of these words in the Vulgate passage just quoted.

66 *propter metum Archelai*. Matth. II.22–3: 'audiens autem quod Archelaus regnaret in Iudea pro Herode patre suo timuit illo ire et admonitus in somnis secessit in partes Galileae et ueniens habitauit in ciuitate quae uocatur Nazareth, ut adimpleretur quod dictum est per prophetam.' The message referred to, 'he shall be called a Nazarene' is not in fact to be found in the Old Testament and may have been invented by Matthew.

CH. 8

67 *ut Lucas euangelista narrat*. Luke II.42: 'et cum factus est annorum duodecim ascendentibus illis in Hierosolymam secundum consuetudinem dies festi'.

68 *paterna conmendat auctoritas*. The author's treatment of Joseph is an interesting illustration of his interweaving of biblical and non-biblical detail and his rationalistic approach. Joseph is nowhere stated in the gospels to be an old man, though he is so described in apocrypha such as the Protevangelium of James IX.2 (*ANT*, p. 42) and the Coptic *History of Joseph the Carpenter* (*Apocryphal Gospels, Acts and Revelations*, ed. A. Roberts and J. Donaldson (Edinburgh, 1870), p. 68). But the deduction of the approximate time of Joseph's death from the information in the gospels appears to be unique to the *Laterculus* and an example of the literal, Antiochene cast of mind at work on the sacred text. The section does claim to rely on some patristic authority: 'sicut nobis paterna conmendat auctoritas'. The *auctoritas* here may well be Epiphanius of Cyprus, who made a similar chain of deduction in the *Panarion* LXXVIII.x.5–9 (ed. Holl III, 460–1), noting first

that Joseph was more than eighty-four when the Holy Family returned from Egypt and secondly that he must have died between Christ's twelfth year and that visit of Christ to Galilee when the people said 'ecce mater tua et fratres foris stant' (Mark III.32), not *pater tuus*, as would have been proper were he still alive. The phrase *senex et plenus dierum* referred originally to Isaac, in Gen. XXXV.29.

69 *Augustus*. Malalas, *Chronographia* X.5–6 (pp. 231–2). One of the most interesting western references in this text is an expansion of Malalas's account of the dream of Augustus. Augustus, alarmed by the prophecy, built a great altar on the heights of the Capitol. The author of the *Laterculus* adds, 'unde factum est post tot annis domicilium adque baselicam beatae et semper uirginis Mariae usque in presentem diem'. It would appear that this writer had some knowledge of the *contemporary* topography of Rome. There was indeed a church of the Virgin built on the Capitol in the seventh century: see C. Hülsen, *Le chiese di Roma nel medioevo* (Florence, 1927), pp. 323–4; and also Ferrari, *Early Roman Monasteries*, p. 212. Enthusiasm for the Virgin and her cult became an increasingly significant part of Christian worship in the eastern empire after the Council of 431 and subsequently spread from the east to Rome, particularly in this century (Llewellyn, *Rome in the Dark Ages*, pp. 170–1). Note the use of the Greek word *baselica* for *ecclesia*.

There are two additional points of interest in this section. One is that the phrasing of the *Laterculus*, 'infans hebreus iubens Deus e caelo beatorum discutiens hunc domicilium', suggests a mistranslation of the Malalas original, which speaks of a child *ruling* in the heavens:

> Παῖς Ἑβραῖος κέλεταί με Θεὸς μακάρεσσιν ἀνάσσων
> τόνδε δόμον προλιπεῖν καὶ Ἄϊδος αὖθις ἱκέσθαι
> καὶ λοιπὸν ἄπιθι ἐκ πρόμων ἡμετέρων.

('A Hebrew child ruling as god over the blessed ones bids me abandon this abode and return to Hades. So now depart from our leaders'). The passage as a whole has been badly mistranslated, possibly owing to a faulty exemplar: με is unrepresented in the Latin, which has therefore translated κέλεταί as a participle, since it seemed to have no object, and the next verse was misunderstood because the translator sought to apply it to the 'infans Hebraeus' rather than to the pythoness herself. The *Laterculus* seems to translate as if the first verse of the exemplar read ἀνάξων rather than ἀνάσσων. A further indication that the author of the *Laterculus* had a faulty exemplar to work with is the variant which appears in the third line, represented by *ab aris nostris*. The Suda lexicon, a late tenth-century compilation drawing, *inter alia*, on Malalas's *Chronographia*, quoted the line as λοιπὸν ἄπιθι σιγῶν ἐκ βωμῶν ἡμετέρων, with βωμός, 'altar' rather than πρόμος, 'leader', which clearly must have been the version known to the *Laterculus* (*Suidae Lexicon*, ed. Adler I, 411).

Another point is that the word *discutiens* provides a clue that this text was read and used on the Continent. As Hülsen pointed out ('The Legend of Aracoeli', *Journal of the British and American Archaeological Society of Rome* 4 (1907), 37–48), 'the Dream of Augustus' enjoyed some vogue as a theme for painters in the later Middle Ages and could have come from the various Greek historians who drew on Malalas's *Chronographia*, except that it is iconographically associated with a prophecy of the destruction of the Capitol. This strongly suggests that our Latin text is the source, since none of the Greek versions contains any phrase equivalent to 'discutiens hunc domicilium'.

70 *Perbereteo*. A garbled form of Ὑπερβερεταῖος. *Athineos* must simply be a variant for *Graecos*, since this is a month of the Macedonian calendar, which had come into widespread use after the conquests of Alexander.

71. *orbis Romae*. The scribe's indifference to any distinction between *u* and *o* is most clearly illustrated by this spelling, which evidently stands for *urbis*.

CH. 9

72 Malalas, *Chronographia* X.7 (p. 232).

73 *Sexti et Sexticiani*. AD 14, Sextus Pompeius and Apuleius Sextus. The *Laterculus* agrees with Codex Baroccianus, Σέξτου καὶ Σεκτικιανοῦ (p. 232). The Chronographer of AD 354 gives them as *duobus Sextis* (*Chronica Minora I*, ed. Mommsen, p. 56).

74 *in anno autem .xv. regni*. Malalas, *Chronographia* X.11 (p. 236). The Baptism and the beginning of Christ's ministry is most carefully dated in Luke II.1–2: 'anno autem quindecimo imperii Tiberii Caesaris, procurante Pontio Pilato Iudeam, tetrarcha autem Galileae Herode ... sub principibus sacerdotum Anna et Caipha, factum est uerbum Dei super Iohannem.' Anna and Caiphas and the prefecture of Pontius Pilate will be referred to below in ch. 11, and Herod was referred to above as *toparcha...Iudaeorum* (ch. 7), though never, curiously, as tetrarch of Galilee. 'Toparch' is not a precise title; it simply meant 'ruler'.

75 *Siluani et Neri*. AD 28, C. Appius Iunius Siluanus, P. Silius Nerua. Codex Baroccianus gives the very different version Ἀλουανοῦ (i.e. *Albani*) καὶ Νερούα.

76 *tunc uenit*. Mark I.9: 'et factum est in diebus illis uenit Iesus a Nazareth Galileae et baptizatus est in Iordane ab Iohanne.'

77 *sub consolatu Ruphi et Rubellionis.* AD 29, C. Fufius Geminus, L. Rubellius Geminus. The *Laterculus* is precisely in agreement with Codex Baroccianus, 'Ρούφου καὶ 'Ρουβελλίωνος. Fufius and Rubellius, sometimes called the *gemini consules*, are not normally associated with the date of the baptism of Christ, but with the year of the Passion. The tradition that Christ died in the year of the *gemini consules* goes back as far as the second century, and was held by most authorities, both Greek and Latin, including Epiphanius, and two of the most important figures in the western computistical tradition, Victorius and Prosper of Aquitaine, among many others. (For Victorius, see *Chronica Minora*, ed. Mommsen, p. 686; and for Prosper of Aquitaine, *ibid.*, p. 410, and see also *BOT*, p. 6.) Well supported though the tradition is, it is not necessarily correct.

78 *quem et decollauit.* Matth. XIV. 10: 'misitque [Herodes] et decollauit Iohannem in carcere'; XIV. 4: 'propter Herodiam uxorem fratris sui'.

79 *in Sebastiam urbem.* The place of the Baptist's death is not mentioned in the Bible. The *Laterculus* follows Malalas in giving Sebaste, which was also the place given by the Roman Martyrology (*Martyrologium Hieronymianum*, 28 August (.iv. kal. Sept.), p. 474). Jerome, *Commentarium in Michaeam* I.1 (PL 25, 1156), and *Commentarium in Osee* I.1 (PL 25, 825), noted that Sebaste claimed to preserve the Baptist's body. On the other hand, Josephus gave the place as Macherus (*Antiquitates Iudaicarum* XVIII.v.2 (ed. Niese IV, 161–2)), and the Martyrology of Tallaght gave it as 'Emisma ciuitate Feniciae'.

80 *Flaconis et Rufini.* This consular date is of course from Malalas, *Chronographia*, Φλάκκωνος καὶ 'Ρουφίνου (p. 236), and it is grotesquely wrong. It can only refer to L. Pomponius Flaccus and C. Caelius Rufus, who were consuls in AD 17 – that is, if one is dating the baptism of Christ to AD 29, some thirteen years too early for the death of John the Baptist. It is noteworthy that the author of the *Laterculus* appears to have had no access to any version of the *fasti consulares*, since he accepted many garbled names, and failed to correct this conspicuous error.

CH. 10

81 Malalas, *Chronographia* X.14 (p. 240). Jeffreys, 'Chronological Studies', in *Studies*, p. 121, points out that the 'long' chronology for Christ's mission on earth which is set out here was accepted by Byzantine chroniclers from Eusebius onwards.

82 *traditus est Pontio Pilato.* Matth. XXVII. 2: 'et uinctum adduxerunt eum et tradiderunt Pontio Pilato praesidi'. The addition of 'prima mane' in the *Laterculus* appears to have no scriptural authority.

83 *Procla*. Matth. XXVII. 19: 'misit ad illum uxor eius dicens nihil tibi et iusto illi, multa enim passa sum hodie per uisum propter eum.' The *Laterculus* substitutes *multum* for *multa*; there is no obvious reason for this and it agrees with no version of the gospel-text. The Greek is πολλὰ γὰρ ἔπαθον. Malalas's use of the name Procla for Pilate's wife shows that he is familiar with the apocryphal material on Pilate, perhaps the *Anaphora*, or the 'Letter of Pilate to Herod' (*Anaphora*, in *ANT*, pp. 153–5, at 155, and 'The Letter of Pilate to Herod', *ibid.*, p. 155).

84 *seditionem concitauerunt*. This is a case where the diction of the *Laterculus* appears to be affected by that of the Vulgate, although no direct parallel can be brought. The closest is Acts XXIV. 5: 'et concitantem seditiones omnibus Iudaeis in uniuerso orbe', but see also Num. XXVII. 3.

85 *dicentes: 'tolle, tolle, crucifige eum'*. John XIX. 15: 'illi autem clamabant: tolle tolle crucifige eum'. The *Laterculus*'s *adclamauerunt* is not otherwise attested, but *dicentes* is found in Codex Usserianus Primus (r) and in some Greek texts of John (*Nouum Testamentum*, ed. Wordsworth and White I, 632).

86 *parasceue*. John XIX. 14: 'erat autem parasceue paschae hora quasi sexta'.

87 *et obscuratus est sol*. Luke XXIII. 45: 'et obscuratus est sol'.

88 *et erant tenebrae*. Matth. XXVII.45: 'sexta autem hora tenebrae factae sunt super uniuersam terram usque ad horam nonam'.

89 *defectio solis*. Here the *Laterculus* draws directly on Malalas, who claimed to cite 'the most learned Phlegon of Athens'. In fact, he was almost certainly citing at second hand from the *Chronicon* of Eusebius. Newton pointed out that Eusebius's identification of Phlegon's eclipse with the events reported in the gospels is necessarily absurd, since, 'because of the way Passover is determined, the Crucifixion had to occur within a day or two of the full moon', and a solar eclipse can occur only at new moon (R.R. Newton, *Ancient Astronomical Observations and the Acceleration of the Earth and Moon* (Baltimore and London, 1970), pp. 110–13). The concord of this misinformation, consequently, shows that neither Malalas nor the author of the *Laterculus* was aware of basic astronomical principles.

90 *facta est lux*. This is not quite clear. Mai conjectured *nox* for *lux*: certainly *u* and *o* fall together for this scribe, but *n* and *l* are a different matter. In any case, *lux* is not necessarily inappropriate. The writer is following carefully through Matthew's account of the Crucifixion, using the other gospels for supplementary information. It is generally noteworthy in this text that he regarded Matthew as his

primary source, though of course he wove into the Matthaean account the additional infancy-narration of Luke. Here, we have Matthew's witness that the sun was darkened until the ninth hour (XVII.45). This is *followed* (XVII.51–2) by 'et terra mota est, et petrae scissae sunt, et monumenta aperta sunt, et multa corpora sanctorum qui dormierant surrexerunt', just as it follows on here in the *Laterculus*. It is not unreasonable to read the gospel as implying that darkness fell for three hours, the sixth to the ninth, and that after Christ's death during the ninth, the light immediately (*statim*) returned, and the other alarming phenomena occurred after, not during, the darkness in which Christ suffered. This is how the author of the *Laterculus* appears to have understood it.

91 *ut dicerent Iudaei*. Both Malalas and the *Laterculus* are guilty of a mis-statement here. They refer to Matth. XXVII. 54 'centurio autem et qui cum eo erant custodientes Iesum, uiso terraemotu et his qui fiebant, timuerunt ualde dicentes: uere Dei Filius erat iste.' These guards are presumably Romans: the gospels do not in any version put this all-important admission into the mouths of the Jews.

92 *Sulpicii et Solati*. AD 33, L. Livius Ocella Sulpicius Galba and L. Cornelius Sulla Felix. As I pointed out in relation to the *gemini consules*, Malalas is unusual in setting the birth of Christ at AD 1, the baptism at 29 and the Passion at 33, since AD 29 was widely accepted as the *annus Passionis*, but he is (with the exception of 'Flaco and Rufinus') internally consistent: that is, his consular dates do not contradict the periods of time said by his authorities to have elapsed. This is further discussed by Jeffreys, 'Chronological Structures', *Studies*, pp. 120–3, where she points out that aspects of Malalas's detailed dates conflict: his consular dates are mutually consistent, but not consistent with his dates by the year of Antioch (which the *Laterculus* does not reproduce), and furthermore that the Holy Week data set the Passion at AD 30 and the regnal date of Tiberius at AD 33. The obvious conclusion is that Malalas was bringing together chronographic data from a variety of sources and attempting, not always successfully, to reconcile them.

The main reasons for assuming that Christ was born in 4 BC and died AD 29 are that Herod the Great died in 4 BC and, at the other end, that Christ was widely believed to have lived for thirty-three years. The whole problem has been discussed at length by Finegan, *Handbook*, pp. 215–32. He found a reasonable consensus among early Greek writers on 3–2 BC as the date of the nativity, but concluded (p. 431): 'the date of Herod's death seems . . . firmly established. In the light of this date and of the references in Matth. II. 1 and Luke I. 5, it seems necessary to conclude that the birth of Jesus could not have been later than the spring of 4 BC.' Malalas's statement that the nativity was in AD 1 is obviously incompatible with the facts as set out in Matthew and Luke. Most writers of the fifth century and later, both eastern and western, put the nativity (like Malalas) at

AD 1, which is how the Christian era became established at this point. For some reason, Sulpicius Severus is an exception: he stated that 'Christus natus est Sabino et Rufino consulibus, .viii. kal. Ianuarias' (*Chronica* II.27, ed. C. Halm, CSEL 1, 82), which is to say, 4 BC. However, modern sifting of the astronomical and chronographic data of the gospels suggests that Malalas's dating of the Crucifixion to AD 33 is more likely to be correct than the traditional dating to the *gemini consules* (J. K. Fotheringham, 'The Evidence of Astronomy and Technical Chronology for the Date of the Crucifixion', *JTS* 35 (1934), 146–62, at 161). If one insists on combining this dating of the Crucifixion with the traditional thirty-three years of Christ's life on earth, then this must bring down the date of the nativity. Perhaps the best solution of the conflicting evidence is that Luke underestimated the age at which Christ was baptized.

Here again, the *Laterculus* has accepted a considerably garbled form of a consul's name ('Solatus' for 'Sulla'), which the Codex Baroccianus got right for once, Σουλπικίου καὶ Σῶλα. The Chronographer of 354 gave the pair as Galba and Sulla (*Chronica Minora I*, ed. Mommsen, p. 56).

CH. 11

93 Malalas, *Chronographia* X.14 (p. 241).

94 *circa diluculo*. This detail is found in Mark XVI. 9 and Luke XXIV. 1. The latter reads 'ualde diluculo uenerunt ad monumentum'.

95 *apparuit prima mane*. Mark XVI.9: 'surgens autem mane prima sabbati apparuit primo Mariae Magdalenae'.

96 *sanctorum apostolorum uidentium*. The two sets of genitive absolute phrases in this sentence result from a completely literal translation of the Greek: τῶν ἁγίων ἀπόστολων ὁρώντων, and καὶ τῶν ἁγίων ἀγγέλων λεγόντων (*Chronographia*, p. 241).

97 *Quid aspicitis*. Acts I. 11: 'Viri Galilei quid statis aspicientes in caelum? hic Iesus qui adsumptus est a uobis in caelum sic ueniet quemadmodum uidistis eum euntem in caelum' becomes 'quid aspicitis in caelum, uiri Galilei? hic Iesus qui asumptus est a uobis, sic *iterum* ueniet, quemadmodum eum uidetis euntem in caelum.' The addition of *iterum* appears to be quite unauthorized. This emendation may be explicable in the light of Theodore of Mopsuestia's quasi-Nestorian distinction between the two natures of Christ, the *homo assumptus* and *verbum assumens* (*Commentary on the Nicene Creed*, ed. Mingana, p. 82: 'The one who assumed is God, while the one who was assumed is a man'). In this commentary,

191

Theodore noted the appropriateness of the phrasing in the Nicene Creed: 'he shall come *again* to judge the quick and the dead', where he takes 'he' to refer to the *verbum assumens*, or Christ as second person of the Trinity. But he goes straight on to quote this very passage of Acts and notes the *absence* of 'again': 'To this man [i.e. the *homo assumptus*, or Christ as mortal man], the word *again* is not fitting. Indeed it is not he who came, but it is the Godhead that came down from heaven' (*ibid.*, p. 81). It is as though the author of the *Laterculus* is trying to quash this particular Christological misapprehension; but it would only have occurred to him to do so if he was both familiar with Theodore's thought and anxious to maintain orthodoxy.

98 *Pontius Pilatus*. Malalas was probably drawing on Eusebius, *Historia ecclesiastica* I.ix.2 (ed. Schwarz I, 72; trans. Williamson, p. 60): Ὁ δ᾽ αὐτὸς ἐν ὀκτ- ακαιδεκάτῳ τῆς Ἀρχαιολογίας κατὰ τὸ δωδέκατον ἔτος τῆς Τιβηρίου βασιλείας ... Πόντιον Πιλᾶτον τὴν Ἰουδαίαν ἐπιτραπῆναι δηλοῖ, ἐνταῦθα δὲ ἐφ᾽ ὅλοις ἔτεσιν δέκα σχεδὸν εἰς αὐτὴν παραμεῖναι τὴν Τιβηρίον τελευτήν ('In *Antiquitates Iudaicarum* book XVIII the same writer [Josephus] informs us that in the twelfth year of Tiberius ... Judaea was entrusted to Pontius Pilate and that Pilate remained there ten years, almost till Tiberius' death'). The use of a nominative absolute here in the *Laterculus* is not a reflection of the Greek text, which has a genitive absolute phrase; ἐγεμονεούοντος τῆς Ἰουδαίας τοῦ αὐτοῦ Ποντίου Πιλάτου.

99 *Annae et Caiphae*. Luke III. 2.

CH. 12

100 *plenum cum Deo*. This sentence may be eastern in inspiration. Drijvers drew attention to the late Antiochene and Syrian insistence on the clear distinction between Christ's actions as man and his actions as God implied in this passage (*East of Antioch*, p. 13), which may also be seen as a faint reflection of the Christological controversies which shook the eastern churches in the fifth and sixth centuries, stressing as it does the orthodox definition of Christ's simultaneous humanity and divinity which was thrashed out at Nicaea and Chalcedon (Greer, *Theodore of Mopsuestia*, pp. 33–5).

101 *ad euacuandum*. The opposition of Eve and Mary, Adam and Christ, is of course widely attested, as H. Graef demonstrated in *Mary: A History of Doctrine and Devotion*, 2 vols. (New York and London, 1963) I, 37–45. Kronholm (*Motifs from Genesis*, p. 51) noted: 'The entire biblical story of the Creation (and subsequent fall) of Adam/man is a mysterious *reuelatio* of God's first-born in his creat-

ing and redeeming activity throughout the history of mankind.' Cf. also Caelius Sedulius, 'Cantemus socii', lines 7–8,

> Sola fuit mulier, patuit quae ianua leto
> et qua uita redit, sola fuit mulier (ed. Huemer, p. 155).

102 The opening of the exegetical section of the *Laterculus* (ch. 12) is powerfully reminiscent of Ephrem: 'nam quod Christus per angelum uirgini nuntiatur, ad euacuandum consilium serpentis ad Euam in paradyso. quod autem de uirgine natus est, propter protoplaustum Adam, quem de uirgine terra et inpolluta ad suam fecit imaginem'. The concept of the virgin earth, paralleled with the Virgin, is found several times in Ephrem, for example in *Hymni de natiuitate* I.xvi and II.xii,1–4, ed. and trans. E. Beck, *De natiuitate*, pp. 3 and 14 (both translations quoted here are from Kronholm, *Motifs from Genesis*, p. 55):

> The virginal earth bore that Adam/man, the head of the earth
> The Virgin bore today [the second] Adam, the head of heaven

> Thou, O my Lord, teach me how and why
> it pleased thee to appear from a virginal womb,
> was its *typos* that of the pure/glorious Adam/man, who from the ground
> the virginal, not yet tilled, received his form?

See further R. Murray, 'Mary, the Second Eve in the Early Syriac Fathers', *Eastern Churches Review* 3 (1970/1), 372–84, and Kronholm, *Motifs from Genesis*, pp. 54–5. The basic idea of the virgin earth is Hebraic, witnessed by Josephus, *Antiquitates Iudaicarum* I.i.2 (ed. Niese I, 10): ὁ δ᾽ ἄνθρωπος οὗτος Ἄδαμος ἐκλήθη· σημαίνει δὲ τοῦτο κατὰ γλῶτταν τὴν Ἑβραίων πυρρόν, ἐπειδήπερ ἀπὸ τῆς φυρρᾶς γῆς φυραθείσης ἐγεγόνει, τοιαύτη γάρ ἐστιν ἡ παρθένος γῆ καὶ ἀληθινή τοιαύτη γάρ ἐστὴν ἡ παρθένος γῆ καὶ ἀληθινή ('this man was called Adam, which in the Hebrew tongue signifies one that is red, because he was formed out of red earth, compounded together, for of that kind is virgin and true earth'). Naturally, Josephus makes no parallel with Christ and Mary. Exactly the same motif is found in the writings of John Chrysostom, who spent much of his life in Antioch and was influenced by the Antiochene school of thought (*De mutatione nominum* II. 3, PG 51, 113–56, at 129): Διὰ τοῦτο Ἐδὲμ αὐτὴν ἐκάλεσεν, ὅπερ ἐστὶ παρθένος γῆ. Αὕτη ἡ παρθένος ἐκείνης τῆς Παρθένου τύπος ἦν. Ὥσπερ γὰρ αὕτη ἡ γῆ μὴ δεξαμένη σπέρματα ἐβλάστησεν ἡμῖν τὸν παράδεισον· οὕτω καὶ ἐκείνη μὴ δεξαμένη σπέρμα ἀνδρὸς ἐβλάστησεν ἡμῖν τὸν Χριστόν ('Thus it was called Eden, because it means 'virgin earth'. This virgin [earth] is a type of the Virgin. For that earth generated Paradise for us, having taken in no seed, and thus she generated Christ for us, having received no seed from a man'). This elaboration of the ancient parallelism between Eve and Mary appears to belong both to the Greek and Syriac patristic traditions.

103 *ad suam fecit imaginem*. It is Christ who is here spoken of as the shaper of mankind. The fact that it is Christ who makes man in his own image, not God the Father, is also important to Ephrem: 'As the First-born *imago Dei inuisibilis* and *primogenitus omnis creaturae*, Christ functions as the mediator, voice and hand of the divine Majesty in every aspect of the creation of the world and the living creatures. However, he acts above all as the creating agent of the triune God in forming Adam/man into *imago imaginis dei*' (Kronholm, *Motifs from Genesis*, p. 51). Caelius Sedulius also expresses the close but antithetical relationship between Christ and Adam in 'Cantemus socii', lines 5–6,

> Unius ob meritum cuncti periere minores
> saluantur cuncti unius ob meritum (ed. Huemer, p. 155).

104 *decimi mensis limitem*. This must surely be a reminiscence of Caelius Sedulius, *Carmen paschale* II.41–3:

> Iamque nouem lapsis, *decimi de limine mensis*
> fulgebat sacrata dies, cum uirgine feta
> promissum compleuit opus: uerbum caro factum. (ed. Huemer, p. 47).

Note that *limite* is found in the manuscript-tradition, in Huemer's A, Basle (Basiliensis) O. IV. 17, written in Anglo-Saxon minuscule (s. ix) and E, Montpellier, Ecole de Médécine 362 (s. ix). In both cases, it is an alternative, *-te* is a correction in A, and E has *uel limite* as a gloss.

105 The author here begins an interweaving of themes which he will develop more fully in the next section: the length of time from the conception to the birth of Christ and the allegorical relationship between this and the building of the temple at Jerusalem, a strange mixture of embryology, number-theory, allegory (which, typology aside, is not characteristic of this text) and historical data. The problem he is faced with is the statement in John that the temple took forty-six years to build and that, since it will be rebuilt in three days, this number must be relevant to the body of Christ. Since Jesus traditionally lived for thirty-three rather than forty-six years, the writer takes refuge in embryological theory in order to account for this number.

106 *soluite templum hoc*. John II. 19–20: 'soluite templum hoc et in tribus diebus excitabo illud. Dixerunt ergo Iudaei: quadraginta et sex annis aedificatum est templum hoc, et tu in tribus diebus excitabis illud? Ille autem dicebat de templo corporis sui.' The version of these verses used in the *Laterculus* differs from the Vulgate standard, and runs: 'soluite templum hoc et *ego* in tribus diebus *suscitabo* illud.' Many early writers, such as Irenaeus, Hilary and Ambrose, read *suscitabo*,

and so does the early Latin translation of Theodore of Mopsuestia (*In Epistola ad Philippenses* II. 8, ed. Swete I, 219), but *ego* is found only in Tertullian, '*diruite templum istud, et ego* in triduo *resus*citabo illud' and in Cassiodorus, who has '*destruite fanum istud,* et *ego* in tribus diebus excitabo illud' (*Versiones antiquae*, ed. Sabatier III, 394).

107 Although some patristic authorities, like Theodore of Mopsuestia, followed by the author of the *Laterculus*, applied this to the Second Temple, Finegan suggested that this tradition was mistaken, and that the statement was originally intended to apply to the Third Temple, begun by Herod, which was still standing in the time of Christ (Finegan, *Handbook*, pp. 276–80).

108 Both Aphrahat and Ephrem describe Christ's body as a temple, as the *Laterculus* does in these sections (Murray, *Symbols*, pp. 70 and 74). Aphrahat made use of John II.19 in exactly the same way as the author of the *Laterculus*, enriching the theme further with a typological comparison with the tabernacle raised by Moses. A sentence in Ephrem's *Commentary on the Diatessaron*, 'for the earth is the body of Mary, the temple which received the seed', is a further Syriac parallel to ch. 12 (Beggiani, *Early Syriac Theology*, p. 95; Murray, *Symbols*, pp. 83–4). Kelly comments (*ECD*, p. 284), 'the use of this image was not confined to the Antiochenes,' and notes that it was used by Athanasius (*ibid.*, pp. 284) and Diodore: 'the Word dwelt in the flesh as in a temple' (p. 303).

109 *non sub Salamonem.* III Kings VI.38: 'aedificauit eam anni septem'.

110 Ezra IV-VII. No statement of the period of time for the building of this second temple is given here. The views of the *Laterculus* on the building of the temple are directly paralleled by Theodore of Mopsuestia's exegesis of the same passage (namely John II.19). Theodore of Mopsuestia wrote (*Commentarius in Iohannem*, ed. and trans. Vosté, p. 43): 'Aedificationem templi dicunt per quadraginta sex annos durasse, inde scilicet a reditu Babylonis; per totum illud spatium enim aedificatum est. Non quod tantum tempus pro aedificatione necessarium fuerit, sed *illam impedientes causa fuere ut tamdiu protraheretur eius fabricatio*, prout accurate ex libris historicis sciri potest.' The *Laterculus* gives the same temple and a similar note on the excessive length of time given for building it. Some remarks on the second temple by Methodius are also in concord with both writers (*Ex libro de resurrectione* III.ix.9, ed. G. N. Bonwetsch, GCS 27 (Leipzig, 1917), 403): Εἴργοντο γοῦν ὑπὸ τῶν ἀλλοεθνῶν, πολλάκις οἰκοδομῆσαι θελήσαντες τὸν ναόν. ὅθεν καὶ ἐν τεσσαράκοντα αὐτὸν καὶ ἓξ ἔτεσι μόλις ἐδυνήθησαν δείμασθαι, τοῦ Σολομῶντος ἐν ἑπταετεῖ χρόνῳ ἐκ θεμελίων αὐτὸν συμπληρώσαντος ('when they intended to build the Temple they were prevented

by other nations. Whence, also, they were hardly able to build that in forty-six years which Solomon completed from the foundations in seven years').

111 *gentes . . . erant.* This phrase is common in the Old Testament, the most exact parallel being Ezekiel XXXVI. 7 'ego leuaui manum meum ut gentes quae in circuitu uestro sunt. . .'

CH. 13

112 This section lays out a scheme for the development of the human embryo which is ultimately based on the Greek tradition of theoretical and practical medicine deriving from the writings of Hippocrates, and closely dependent on Augustine. According to the author of the *Laterculus*, semen lies in the womb for seven days, retaining its milky colour. After that time, it appears bloody and begins to grow. At forty-five days, it is solid and beginning to sprout limbs. The total length of time given for human gestation is 276 days – nine twenty-eight day months, and four days. This information is remarkably precise, even authoritative; however, it seems to have been arrived at by Augustine in order to reconcile the figure 46 with the Galenic tradition of embryology.

Augustine's essay *De annis quadraginta sex aedificandi templi* (in *De diuersis quaestionibus lxxiii*, PL 40, 39) is the very closely-followed source. For ease of reference, I italicize clauses which have a direct, close parallel in the *Laterculus*:

Sex, nouem, duodecim, decem et octo, haec in unum fiunt quadraginta quinque. Adde ergo ipsum unum, fiunt quadraginta sex: hoc sexies, fiunt ducenta septuaginta sex. *Dicitur autem conceptio humana* sic procedere et perfici, *ut primis sex diebus quasi lactis habeat similitudinem, sequentibus nouem diebus conuertatur in sanguinem, deinde duodecim diebus solidetur, reliquis decem et octo diebus formetur usque ad perfecta lineamenta omnium membrorum,* et hinc iam reliquo tempore usque ad tempus partus magnitudine augeatur.

Quadraginta ergo quinque diebus addito uno, quod significat summam *quia sex et nouem et duodecim et decem et octo in unum coactis, fiunt quadraginta quinque: addito ergo, ut dictum est, uno, fiunt quadraginta sex.* Qui cum fuerint multiplicati per ipsum senarium numerum, qui huius ordinationis caput tenet, fiunt ducenti septuaginta sex: id est, *nouem menses et sex dies,* qui computantur ab octauo calendas Aprilis, quo die conceptus est Dominus creditur, quia eodem die passus est, usque ad octauam calendas Ianuarias, quo die natus est. Non ergo absurde quadraginta sex annos dicitur fabricatum esse templum, quod corpus eius significabat ut quot anni fuerunt in fabricatione templi, tot dies fuerunt in corporis Domini perfectione.

The arithmetic in the two texts is very slightly variant. The series six, nine, twelve, ten, eight in the Augustine passage is paralleled by the series six, nine, twelve, eight, ten in the *Laterculus*. Both writers then add one, to make forty-six, the number they want, since John's gospel states that the temple took forty-six years to build. Augustine then multiplies forty-six by six to get 276, described by both as nine months and six days, whereas the author of the *Laterculus* multiplies forty by six, and then six by six, and adds the two together. Augustine, followed by the author of the *Laterculus*, is markedly divergent from Classical embryological theory. Galen gives gestation time as 280 days – forty weeks, or ten lunar months – a figure accepted as authoritative by all subsequent writers that I know of (*Opera*, ed. Kühn XVII.A, 449–50). No other writer gives the figure of 276 days, which is quite obviously arrived at by simply counting the number of days from 25 March to 25 December (inclusive), which does, indeed, come out at 276, and is therefore specific to this particular birth rather than derived from any general theory of pregnancy. Note, however, that the author of the *Laterculus* makes an attempt to reconcile his figure with Galen's 'ten months' dictum.

The *corpora* of two encyclopaedic writers, Galen and Oribasius, are of interest here as the context for the information offered by Augustine. Galen, who flourished in the second century, encoded practically the whole of contemporary Greek thought on physiology and medicine. He stands at the head of the entire medical literature of the Middle Ages. Oribasius, a contemporary of Julian the Apostate (fourth century), made a new synthesis of medical thought in his own time, which drew to a great extent on Galen himself as well as on many lesser-known writers.

113 Galen is also concerned to demonstrate the difference between the male foetus and the female, and the greater vigour of the latter; the male is formed earlier and moves earlier (*Opera*, ed. Kühn XVII.A, 444). Hence females come sooner both to maturity and to senescence (*ibid.* XVII.A, 445). However, Galen added in this passage that females were born *later* than males (because babies were held to contribute to their own birth, so the more vigorous the infant, the faster it would break free): ἐν δὲ τῷ σώματι κίνησον παρέχεται μᾶλλον ὡς ἐπὶ τὸ πολὺ τὸ ἄρρεν τοῦ θήλεος καὶ τίκτεται θᾶττον, τὰ δὲ θήλεα βραδώτερον. ('the male agitates in the body more than the female, and with bigger movements, and is born more easily; the female is slower') (*ibid.* XVIIIA, 445).

114 *quatentia*. Obscure. Mai conjectured *patentia*.

115 Galen comments on the character of semen, which is also of course obvious to direct observation: λευκὸν γὰρ καὶ παχὺ καὶ γλίσχρον ἐστὶ τὸ σπέρμα ('semen is white, thick and viscous') (*ibid.* IV, 556). Galen assumed that semen is, literally, a seed and the mother's body no more than a field which provides the right conditions for growth, going so far as to speak of the foetus in its early stages as a plant, not an animal: τὸ μὲν κύημα κατὰ τὸν πρῶτον καὶ δεύτερον χρόνον, ἡνίκα ὑπογραφήν τινα καὶ οἷν σκιαγραφίαν ἔχει πάντων τῶν μορίων, μήπω ζῷον δεῖ καλεῖσθαι, ἀλλ' ὡς φυτὸν ἄπασαν τὴν γένεσιν ἔχει ('the foetus in the first and

197

second months, of which we have a description and account of all parts, is scarcely to be called an animal, rather it has a plant-nature in all its beginning': *ibid*. XV, 402–3). This is the Classical Greek understanding of human conception, attested as early as Aeschylus's *Eumenides* and almost certainly common also to Augustine and the author of the *Laterculus*. The information that the semen remains in its original form for six days appears ultimately to derive from Galen, who perceived a difference in the semen after six days: πρῶτος μὲν, ἐν ᾧ κατὰ τὰς ἀμβλώσεις τε καὶ κατὰ τὰς ἀνατομὰς ἡ τοῦ σπέρματος ἰδέα κρατεῖ. . .ἐπειδὰν δὲ πληρωθῇ μὲν τοῦ αἵματος, ἡ καρδία δὲ καὶ ὁ ἐγκέφαλος καί τὸ ἧπαρ ἀδιάρθρωτα μὲν ἔτι καὶ ἄμορθα ('In the first stage, the form of the semen remained in abortions and dissections. . . After this time (six days) the foetus is formed from blood, though heart, brain and liver are still indistinct and unformed': *ibid*. IV, 542). Here we may turn for further information to Oribasius XXII.9, περὶ διαμορφώσεως: ἡ δὲ πρώτη δια-μόρφωσις τῶν ἐμβρύων διασημαίνει περὶ τὰς τεσσαράκοντα ἡμέρας. ἕως μὲν γὰρ θ' ἡμερῶν οἷον γραμμαί τινες αἱματώδεις ὑποφέρονται. περὶ δὲ τὰς ὀκτωκαίδεκα θρόμβοι σαρκώδεις καὶ ἰνώδη τινὰ διασημαίνεται, καὶ σφυγμὸς ἐν αὐτοῖς εὑρίσκε-ται ὁ τῆς καρδίας. περὶ δὲ τὰς τρεῖς ἐννεάδας, ὥς φησιν ὁ Διοκλῆς, ἐν ὑμένι μυξώδει γίνεται φανερῶς ἀμυδρὸς ὁ τύπος τῆς ῥάχεως, καὶ ὁ τῆς κεφαλῆς. περὶ δὲ τὰς τέσσαρας ἐννεάδας ὁρᾶται πρῶτον διακεκριμένον ὅλον τὸ σῶμα, ἢ τὸ τελευταῖον, μιᾶς προστεθείσης τετράδος, περὶ τὴν τεσσαρακοντάδα. (*Œuvres d'Ori-base*, ed. V.C. Bussemaker and C. Daremberg, 6 vols. (Paris 1851–76) III, 78–9: 'the configuration of the foetus begins to manifest itself around the fortieth day, since, up to the ninth day, it is nothing, so to speak, but a few bloody lines which appear in relief, and around the eighteenth day, it displays fleshly swellings and fibrous bodies within which one can discern the beating of the heart. About the eighteenth day, as Diocles says, it clearly forms faint indications of the spine and the head within a mucous membrane. After the thirty-sixth day or afterwards, four days later, around the fortieth day, one sees the whole body made distinct for the first time.') This passage is far closer to the doctrine found in Augustine and the *Laterculus* than any other in the Greek medical tradition. Note that it identifies the change from a bloody and shapeless mass to the beginnings of bodily form as occurring at the ninth day, and the appearance of a beating heart at the eighteenth, at which time it also shows the first traces of spine and head ('tendit ad liniamenta membrorum'), and that traces of the whole body become apparent on the thirty-sixth. All three of these days are used as time-markers by Augustine, and in the *Laterculus*.

116 From this point on, confusion and difficulty sets in. Although this naturally appears to mean 'up to day nine', the subsequent arithmetic shows that an additional period of nine days is meant, comparable with Augustine's 'sequenti-bus nouem diebus conuertatur in sanguinem'. The information that semen

changes into blood after six days is likely also to be based on Galen, who recorded a famous case written up by Hippocrates (*ibid*. IV, 654–5): a dancer who (he believed) successfully aborted herself by violent exertion after only a few days (six, according to Galen), the conceptus appearing as a rounded, reddish and nearly shapeless mass, somewhat resembling a raw egg (*ibid*. IV, 662–63). According to the *Laterculus*, the conceptus grows (*augetur*, Augustine has *solidetur*) for the next twelve days, then for another eighteen (Augustine uses the phrase 'formetur usque ad perfecta lineamenta omnium membrorum'). The reasons for splitting this thirty-day period into two must be numerological, since the author does not suggest that anything essentially different is happening in the second half from the first. Galen recognized four main stages in the growth of a foetus: a stage of complete shapelessness; the appearance at about the thirtieth day in the male (the fortieth in the female) of the beginnings of the three vital organs, liver, heart and brain; a stage where at least the beginnings of all bodily parts are visible; and the last, where human form is completely distinct (*ibid*. IV, 542–3 and XV, 400). Oribasius gives us nine days, eighteen days and thirty-six days for what are effectively the same three stages, mentioning that heart and head (though he omits consideration of the liver) are visible by the eighteenth day.

117 At this point – we are now forty-five days from conception – the foetus 'mox coaculatur et tendit ad liniamenta membrorum', which sounds like the equivalent of Galen's third stage (*ibid*. IV, 672–3), and Oribasius's precisely-given thirty-six to forty days. That is to say, the conceptus has solidified into a recognizable shape, and its limbs have begun to bud out. The phrase is reminiscent of Galen's: τὸ μὲν θῆλυ τὴν πρώτην πῆξιν ἐν τεσσαράκοντα ἡμέρῃσι καὶ δύο τὸ μακρότατον ('the female [conceptus] acquires its first solidification on the forty-second day at the most': *ibid*. XVIIIA, 446). However, Galen says that the male conceptus is formed by the thirtieth day. Augustine and the author of the *Laterculus* are on the whole compatible with Galen's views, but have forced them into congruency with those of Oribasius, and make no reference to the triad of liver, heart and brain which is so significant to Galen. Galen, as befitted a respectable empirical researcher into human biology, committed himself only in very vague terms to precise lengths of time; certainly not to the very short units favoured by the author of the *Laterculus*. Oribasius seems to have provided a more congenial basis for numerological fantasy. The phrase *liniamenta membrorum* is found in Aldhelm, prose *De uirginitate*, ch. 60 (ed. Ehwald, p. 322), 'pulcherrima *membrorum liniamenta*', as well as in this passage of Augustine.

118 From the forty-sixth day onwards, the foetus, now shaped and fully human (as, in Galen's view, it was *not* until the third stage had been reached) continues to grow until 276 days have passed. We must probably conclude that these sixes,

forty-fives and so forth have an importance in the realm of number-symbolism rather than of embryology, although this of course shifts the problem rather than solving it. The author certainly had a strong interest in the number 6. What matters here is that the forty-six years to build the temple are paralleled by the forty-six days from conception to solidification, that is, the distinction drawn by Galen between mere plant-like growth and entering into the beginnings of the human condition. But that does not explain the twelve and eighteen: certainly, one is twice six, the other three times six and twice three is six, but this is quite liable to be a numerological grace-note of my own, since the writer does not in any way call this to the reader's attention.

119 *tries sexis*. The only way I can make sense of this is to regard it as another way of saying 'thirty-six': 'a three and a six'.

120 *fauriciae*. An example of the falling-together of consonantal *u* and *b*; the word is *fabricia*, for *fabrica*. Augustine uses *fabricatus*, *fabricatio*, of the temple, in the last sentence of the passage quoted above, which may have influenced its use here.

121 *per numerum*. This sentence gives another way of regarding the number 46: composed of six, which is not only a perfect number, but the number of days of the creation, and 40, the period of Christ's fast in the wilderness and thus a number connected with the resurrection of the world. It should perhaps be added that four (and thus, forty) is the 'earthly' number, there being four compass-points, and so forth, whereas the associations of three (and six) are 'heavenly'. Hopper analysed the techniques of medieval numerology, and concluded that 'all large numbers are reduced to their roots for explanation', while adding numbers sums up their significance into a single unit (*Medieval Number Symbolism*, p. 82). Augustine says of the number forty in *De diuersis quaestionibus*, no. lvii, 'quadragenarius ergo numerus, ut dictum est, temporalem ipsam dispensationem non incongrue significare creditur' (PL 40, 40).

122 *in unam fidei fermentando*. The image of the leaven may draw on *Diatessaron* 11.21: 'Again, the leaven in the mass [is] His body in the mass of the family of Adam' (Murray, *Symbols*, p. 73).

CH. 14

123 *positus in presepio*. Luke II. 7: 'et peperit filium suum primogenitum et pannis eum inuoluit, et reclinauit eum in presepio quia non erat locus in diuersorio.'

124 *de fructum uentris*. Ps. CXXXI. 11: 'de fructu uentris tui ponam super sedem tuam'. The *Laterculus* is here making a direct quotation from the Vulgate, apart

from a further example of the scribe's, or writer's, conviction that *de* takes the accusative.

125 *exibuit medecinam*. Ephrem's favourite metaphor for Christ, the Physician (Murray, *Symbols*, p. 200), is implied here and found in the letter of Archbishop Theodore to Æthelred in 686 (*Councils*, ed. Haddan and Stubbs III, 171), and in the preface to the Penitential of Theodore's *discipulus Umbrensium* (ed. Finster-walder, p. 287). Another Syrian writer, Marutha, twice used the metaphor of spiritual bandages and dressings (Murray, *Symbols*, p. 201).

126 *Iacob fugienti*. Gen. XXVIII.12–13: 'uiditque in somnis scalam stantem super terram et cacumen illius tangens caelum, angelos quoque Dei ascendentes et descendentes per eam, et Dominum innixum scalae dicentem sibi: ego sum Dominus Deus Abraham.' The *Laterculus* is evidently paraphrasing this story, since the details of its diction cannot be paralleled in any version of Genesis. The choice of words is slightly closer to the Vetus Latina in one clause: 'dominus autem incumbebat super illam' (*Genesis*, ed. Fischer, p. 302) uses the same verb as the *Laterculus*'s *incubuisse*. The phrasing suggests that elegant variation is of some importance to the writer: 'scalam ibi ad caelum *conspiceret* et angelos. . .*uidisset* et deum. . . *aspiceret*. . .'

127 It seems to me very likely that the next couple of sentences have got into the wrong order. They should probably be read like this, and I have so translated them: '. . .et Deum in summo incubuisset aspiceret. Dixit: "hic uere domus Dei est et porta caeli," unde appellatur Bethel. Et lapidem quem ad caput sibi Iacob posuerat, in similitudinem est illius lapidis angularis, cui iuncti duo parietes e diuerso uenientes condidit. . .' It is obvious that *domus Dei* and *Beth-el* (house of God) were meant to go together, and equally, *cui iuncti* must refer to the corner-stone. *Est* is superfluous after *hic*, and wanted with *similitudinem*.

128 *lapidis angularis*. The 'corner-stone', a concept based on the words of Christ reported in Matth. XXI.42 and Mark XII.10, was a fruitful one in the development of patristic thought, particularly among the Syriac Fathers; see for example Murray, *Symbols*, pp. 206–7. The Hebrew text of Ps. CVIII, which Jesus was quoting in both the gospel passages mentioned, may be translated: 'a stone the builders rejected: it became the head (or, at the head) of the corner'. Exactly what all these writers are referring to is explained by J. D. M. Derrett ('The Stone the Builders Rejected', *Studia Evangelica* 4 [= *TU* 102] (1968) 180–6, at 181): 'The final stone, which serves to complete the corner of the house, binding two walls together and which serves also as an ornament, a shelter on the roof and a part of the parapet which every Jewish house must have, is called the "head of the corner". A house would have no less than four.'

129 *uere domus Dei*. Gen. XXVII. 17 expresses this negatively: 'non est hic aliud nisi domus Dei et porta caeli.' The version given in the *Laterculus* is shared only with Isidore, *Etymologiae* XV.i.22: 'uere hic domus Dei est et porta caeli.'

130 *duo parietes*. This exegesis of Jacob's dream demonstrates that the author of the *Laterculus* was familiar with the real meaning of *lapis angularis* in its original context of Middle eastern architecture, as the quotation from Derrett, above, explained it. A closely-woven texture of symbolism and parallelism is created in this section around the idea of the stone on which Jacob laid his head (Gen. XXVIII.11–19). We have the 'corner-stone' (Ephes. II.15) and the House of God (Beth-El). The writer continues with an image of two walls: 'cui iuncti duo parietes e diuerso uenientes condit in semetipso copulauit, scilicet populorum conexio Iudaeorum adque gentilium pacem in utrosque perficiens.' Ephrem may be the source here also (*Exposition of the Gospel*, ch. 6): 'And David was not the corner, for one wall of the buildings was made in him, only circumcision. Now since Christ preached circumcision and uncircumcision, two walls were made from him and he became the head/chief (the corner-stone?)' (*Saint Ephrem: An Exposition of the Gospel*, trans. G. A. Egan (Louvain, 1968), p. 8). Implicit in the comments of Ephrem is the idea of one wall being the Gentiles (the uncircumcised) and one wall being the Jews (the circumcised). Christ appears, as in the *Laterculus*, to be the corner-stone, with two walls shooting off at angles from him. Irenaeus used the same theme (*Aduersus Haereses* III.v.3, ed. Harvey II, 20): 'Hic in nouissimis temporibus apparens, lapis summus angularis, in unam legit, et uniuit eos qui longe, ut eos qui prope, hoc est, circumcisionem et praeputium' ('He, appearing in the last days, the chief corner-stone, gathered into one and united those who are far off and those who are near, i.e., the circumcision and the uncircumcision'). Note also the interest of the author of the *Laterculus* in the theology of circumcision, further evidenced in ch. 16.

131 *mensuram distribuant*. This is based loosely on Luke XII.42: 'quis putas est fidelis dispensor super familiam suam, ut det illis in tempore tritici mensuram'. The *Laterculus*'s use of the verb *distribuo* may suggest acquaintance with an archaic version of this verse, since the fourth- or fifth-century Codex Palatinus (e) has the reading 'ut distribuat cibaria conseruis suis' (*Nouum Testamentum*, ed. Wordsworth and White I, 401).

132 *ter ait*. John XXI.15–17 repeats the phrase 'pasce *agnos* meos' three times. The reference here to the special status of Peter (to whom Jesus addressed these words), which is also emphasized in ch. 23, might at first suggest a highly Romanist point of view. But reverence for Peter was not confined to the Christians of the west: it was also particularly relevant in Syrian Christianity (*The Tradition of*

Commentary

the Syriac Church of Antioch Concerning the Primacy and the Prerogatives of St Peter and of his Successors the Roman Pontiffs, ed. C.B. Benni (London, 1971); Syriac exegesis of John XXI.15–17 is given on pp. 17–18 and 50–1). Note further that Peter was the rock on which the church was founded (Matth. XVI.18), which is why he has been introduced at the close of this section, which dealt largely with the typological implications of Jacob's stone. Wallace-Hadrill (*Christian Antioch*, p. 39) noted a comparable passage in Aphrahat: '[he] allows "the stone rejected by the builders" to attract to it other passages concerning rocks'. Beggiani (*Early Syriac Theology*, p. 85) noted that Aphrahat and Ephrem applied the figure of 'the rock' both to Christ and to Peter: 'Simon's name *kepha* is once again seen as a functional title shared with Christ'. This helps to account for this somewhat confusing passage in which, if I have understood it rightly, Christ is portrayed as the type of the Good Shepherd, but the author adds somewhat parenthetically that the same typology applies equally to Peter.

133 *luporum inpetus*. This appears to be suggested by the Bible, but is not directly biblical. John X. 12 is probably the closest: 'uidet lupum uenientem et dimittit oues et fugit et lupus rapit et dispersit oues'.

CH. 15

134 *primitias*. This may be very loosely Pauline in inspiration, since St Paul refers several times to the 'first-fruits' taken in a spiritual rather than literal sense.

135 *dicitur*. Matth. XXVI.12: 'mittens enim haec unguentum hoc in corpus meum ad sepeliendum me facit.'

136 *trina species*. The exegesis of the significance of the three gifts of the Magi is found in both Irenaeus and Ephrem, among many other writers: 'myrrham quidem, quod ipse erat, qui pro mortali humano genere moreretur et sepeliretur: aurum uero, quoniam rex, cuius regni finis non est: thus uero quoniam Deus', etc. (*Aduersus Haereses* III.x.1, ed. Harvey II, 32, and Harris, *Fragments of the Commentary of Ephrem*, p. 36, which also gives a translation of Ephrem's version).

137 *orietur stella*. Num. XXIV.17. The version quoted here is quite different from the Vulgate and evidently based either on the Septuagint or the Vetus Latina. The Vetus Latina reads 'orietur stella ex Iacob, et exsurget homo de Israel, et confringet duces Moab, et praedabitur omnes filios Seth' (*Versiones antiquae*, ed. Sabatier I, 308). The closest parallel to the version in the *Laterculus* I know of is that used by Leo the Great: 'orietur stella ex Iacob, et exsurget homo ex Israel, et dominabitur gentium' (*Sermo* XXXIV, PL 34, 137–463, at 245). Both this

quotation from Numbers and the one from Isaiah which follows on are typological expressions of the importance of the Magi in the context of the mission to the Gentiles and as such fit well within the Antiochene system of exegesis.

138 *omnes a Saba*. Isaiah LX. 6: 'omnes a Saba uenient aurum et tus deferentes et laudens Domino adnuntiantes.' The version in the *Laterculus* is so loose, like that of the preceding quotation from Numbers, it is probably from memory and possibly translated from the Septuagint. Although naturally most of the fathers who attempted an exegesis of Isaiah referred this passage typologically to the visit of the Magi, not one of them quotes a similar version and in particular, none of them adds 'myrrh' to the gold and frankincense. Cf. the version of the Septuagint used by Hesychius (*Interpretatio Isaiae*, ed. Faulhaber, p. 186: πάντες ἐκ Σαβὰ: διὰ τῶν μάγων. ἐκεῖθεν γὰρ ὑπάρχουσιν ὡς ʼΑσσύροι. ἥξουσι φέροντες χρυσίον καὶ λίβανον οἴσουσι καὶ λίθον τίμιον... (the gloss quotes Matth. II.2): "'All from Sheba..." Concerning the Magi, from thence as Assyrians from those regions. "...will come carrying gold, and will bring frankincense and a precious stone"'), and the text of the fourth-century Codex Siniaticus, which adds καὶ λίθον τίμιον (... 'and a precious stone').

139 *regeque cruento*. This might be an echo of Juvencus, *Euangelia historia* I.1, 'Rex fuit Herodes Iudaea in gente *cruentus*'. Juvencus's poem was known to Aldhelm (and also to Adomnán), and was thus available in the British Isles in the seventh century. Alternatively, and perhaps more plausibly, the echo is of Caelius Sedulius, *Carmen paschale* II.119, ...'furor est in *rege cruento*' (ed. Huemer, p. 52). The first line of the first book of any poem is naturally particularly memorable, but there is other evidence for Caelius Sedulius as a source for this composition.

140 *uox in excelso*. *Laterculus* conflates the versions of Jerem. XXI.15 and Matth. II.18 in quoting this verse: Jeremiah has: 'uox in excelso', Matthew 'uox in Rama'. But no version of either gives 'pluratus et *luctus* magnus': Jeremiah gives 'fletus et luctus', Matthew 'ploratus et ululatus' and the *Laterculus* combines the two. No known Latin text uses *magnus* rather than *multus*.

141 *munitus per uisum*. Matth. II.13. The *Laterculus* again uses *cum* + acc: *cum matrem*.

142 *pernegauit*. The translation of this passage assumes that *pernecauit* is meant (*necare* with an intensifier). Alternatively the sentence would have to mean that Herod attempted to deny responsibility for the massacre of the innocents. Since nothing is said about this in the gospels, one presumes that it is derived from one of the apocryphal infancy narratives, though in all the familiar apocryphal versions

of the story, Herod's crime is shown as insensate tyranny rather than hypocrisy, and he dies raging to the last. The word-use is a little odd: *iudicium* is not a normal Latin choice for 'promise', but if Herod's promise to the Magi is not what is referred to, then the clause must mean either 'against his own judgement' or 'against the judgement [of history] against him', either of which gives a far more strained meaning.

CH. 16

143 *circumcisionem*. The writer may be best understood as reacting *against* eastern ideas. His insistence on the fleshly circumcision of Christ may be in opposition to a Docetic trend in some Syriac writings, which insist that Christ's body, being perfect, was not mutilated in this way (*The Book of the Cave of Treasures*, ed. Budge, pp. 213–14). See also the discourse on Proverbs of the Antiochene Eustathius, PG 18, 680, which makes a positive point similar to that in the *Laterculus*.

144 *apostulus ait*. Rom. XV. 8: 'dico enim Christum Iesum ministrum fuisse circumcisionis'. This section is noteworthy for the way it weaves together ideas found in various parts of the Pauline Epistles into a single unit of thought.

145 *illud de Exodi*. The *Laterculus* summarizes the story in Ex. IV.21–6 in a way which demonstrates influence from Jewish exegesis of this difficult passage. Verses 24–5 of the Vulgate Exodus read 'occurrit ei Dominus et uolebat occidere eum. Tulit ilico Seffora acutissimam petram et circumcidit praeputium filii sui ... et dimisit eum postquam dixerat sponsus sanguinem ob circumcisionem'. The earliest Jewish exegesis of this passage was written in Palestine before 200 BC and established the following points: the object of the assault is Moses; the assailant is not Jahweh but an angel of the Lord; it is to the angel that Zipporah speaks in IV.25; and Moses's life is saved because of the sacrificial atoning value of the blood that is shed (G. Vermes, 'Baptism and Jewish Exegesis: New Light from Ancient Sources', *NTS* 4 (1957–8), 308–19, at 313). This ancient Jewish reading of the text affected the Septuagint, Vulgate and Peshitta (B. P. Robinson, 'Zipporah to the Rescue: A Contextual Study of Exodus IV.24–6', *Vetus Testamentum* 36 (1986), 447–61, at 456). Ex. IV. 21–6 is also discussed in Greek Christian exegesis, in the works of Theodoretus (*Quaestiones in Exodi*: PG 80, 225–98, at 241–4) and Procopius of Gaza (*Commentarii in Exodi*: PG 87, 511–690, at 537–40). These two versions are rather similar, and appear not to be relevant to the *Laterculus*. They do not emphasize the sacrificial aspect, and they add explanations of why the child had remained uncircumcised up to this time. The Persian exegete Aphrahat used the story quite differently, as part of a misogynist diatribe (*Demonstrationes* VI.3, ed. and trans. D. J. Parisot, Patrologia

Syriaca 1 (Paris, 1894), 256), and I am not aware of other Syriac treatments of the episode.

The *Laterculus* is very much in the Jewish exegetical tradition, as the writer gives the non-biblical *angelus* rather than *Dominus*, it is Moses whom the angel attempts to kill and the sacramental, redemptive power of the blood shed in circumcision is stressed, with its obvious typological value as a prefiguration both of the blood shed in the circumcision of Christ and the blood shed on the cross. Cf. the very similar glossing of this passage in *Biblical Commentaries* (PentI 231–3): '"occurrit ei Dominus": uult angelum intellegi; "tetigit pedes eius": .i. angeli pedes; "sponsus sanguinum": .i. adsignatur sanguine.' This is evidently following the same set of ideas.

It should also be noted that the LXX reading, which is unsupported by any known Hebrew text, refers, like the *Laterculus*, to the *angel* of the Lord rather than the Lord himself: Ἐγένετο δὲ ἐν τῇ ὁδῷ ἐν τῷ καταλύματι συνήντησεν αὐτῷ ἄγγελος Κυρίου καὶ ἐζήτει αὐτὸν ἀποκτεῖναι ('It happened that on the way, in a resting-place, an angel of the Lord met with him and tried to kill him', *The Old Testament in Greek*, ed. Brooke and Maclean I, 166–7). This suggests quite strongly that the writer is thinking in terms of the Septuagint. The Vetus Latina reads 'et factum est in uia, ad refectionem obuiant ei angelus, et quaerebat eum occidere' (*Versiones antiquae*, ed. Sabatier II, 97–8). Although this was clearly translated from the Septuagint, the vocabulary is so different from the *Laterculus* – note *occidere* rather than *interficere*, *obuiare* not *occurrere*, and that Zipporah seizes a *calculus* rather than a *lapis* – that it seems very unlikely that the *Laterculus* drew on the Vetus Latina.

146 *pondera dura tulit*. The phrase is drawn from Caelius Sedulius, 'Cantemus socii', lines 51–2,

> *Pondera dura tulit mandatum legis et iram*
> *gratia mandati pondera dura tulit.* (ed. Huemer, p. 158).

The second occurrence of the phrase, though it does not mention blood, uses the expression in exactly the same context of redemptive grace. Note further that *omnes legis ira cessauit* occurs in the previous clause of this poem.

147 *finis legis Christus*. Rom. X.4: 'finis enim legis Christus.'

148 *qui maledictum*. Galat. III.13 'Christus nos redemit de maledictione legis'.

149 *adcreuisse sapientia*. Luke II.52: 'et Iesus proficiebat sapientia aetate et gratia apud Deum et homines.' Note that the ungrammatical 'coram Deo et homines' may be influenced by the Vulgate's *apud*, after which the accusative *homines* is, of course, correct.

150 *incipiens annorum .xxx.*. Luke III.23: 'et ipse Iesus erat incipiens quasi annorum triginta'.

151 *uoluntarius*. Here and elsewhere in the *Laterculus*, there is a certain stressing of the free will of Christ. In ch. 18, we find 'quod autem baptismum a Iohannem Christus libenter acceperit' and in ch. 19, 'quod autem infirmitates adque egrotationes nostras ... libenter portauerit'. This stress is obviously in the interests of doctrinal orthodoxy.

152 *donec omnes*. Eph. IV.13: 'donec occurramus omnes in unitatem fidei et agnitionis filii Dei, in uirum perfectum, in mensuram aetatis plenitudinis Christi'. The *Laterculus*, whether by a slip of the memory or design, has left out two whole clauses, somewhat altering the meaning of the sentence.

CH. 17

153 *aetatem perfectum*. This section makes a firm statement that Adam and Eve were both created with full adult vigour and capabilities in both body and mind: 'homo in primordio factus et a Domino, aetate legitimus et mente plenus et capacem rationis, in qua uictoriam caperet, si mortis superasset auctorem.' This is intelligible in the light of teachings like these: τῇ δὲ οὔσῃ ἡλικίᾳ ὅδε ᾽Αδὰμ ἔτη νήπιος ἦν. διὸ οὕτω ἠδύνατο τὴν γνῶσιν κατ᾽ ἀξίαν χωρεῖν ('In his actual age Adam was as old as an infant, therefore he was not yet able to acquire knowledge properly': Theophilus of Antioch, *Ad Autolycam* II.xxv, ed. and trans. Robert M. Grant (Oxford, 1970), p. 66); and οὕτως καὶ ὁ Θεὸς αὐτὸς μὲν οἷός τε ἦν παρασχεῖν ἀπ᾽ ἀρχῆς τῷ ἀνθρώπῳ τὸ τέλειον, ὁ δὲ ἄνθρωπος ἀδύνατος λαβεῖν αὐτό; νήπιος γὰρ ἦν ('so God also was indeed able himself to bestow on man perfection from the beginning, but man was incapable of receiving it, for he was a child': Irenaeus, *Aduersus haereses* IV.lxii.1, ed. Harvey II, 292–3). Syriac writers, on the other hand, were influenced by the Jewish midrashic tradition which made Adam fullgrown, either twenty or forty (Ginzberg, *Legends* I, 59: 'like all creatures formed on the six days of creation, Adam came from the hands of the Creator fully and completely developed. He was not like a child, but like a man twenty years of age': see further V, 98 (n. 21), and V, 106 (n. 97)). Even so, Narsai appeared to endorse the idea of Adam as mentally undeveloped ('Homélie sur la création', ch. 61): 'Adam fut splendidement formé, aussi bien dans son corps que dans son âme; mais son discernement resta caché jusqu'à la transgression du commandement' ('Homélie de Narsaï sur la création', ed. Gignoux, p. 316).

Ephrem, however, was unaffected by this Greek tradition and concerned himself with the original kingly authority of Adam and its relationship to his free will (*Commentarius in Genesim*, ed. and trans. R.-M. Tonneau, p. 24): 'si enim paruuli fuissent, sicut dicunt profani, non diceretur illos nudos non erubuisse;

nec etiam diceretur Adam et uxor eius, nisi quia adulescentes. Sufficiunt autem nomina ab Adam imposita ad persuadendum de sapientia eius; et quod dicitur: ut operaretur et custodiret illum (sufficit) ad significandum robur eius; et lex ei inposita testis est de adulta aetate eorum.' Jacob of Sarug in his *Hexemeron* (ed. and trans. Jansma, p. 37) shares the same tradition of thought about Adam: 'nouveau-né, petit garçon, adolescent, adulte, tout cela dans le même instant'. It may readily be seen that Adam's nature at the time of the Fall (and hence his culpability) was a focus of controversy in the very areas which the author of the *Laterculus* draws on for other themes and ideas. Hence, perhaps, the somewhat polemic tone of this section.

The 'perfect age' understood in this text appears to be thirty, since this was the age at which Christ was baptized, and, at the end of this section, it is said that we are all to be resurrected aged thirty. The creation of Adam as a man of thirty is asserted in later English texts, notably the prose *Solomon and Saturn*, in *The Prose Solomon and Saturn and Adrian and Ritheus*, ed. J. E. Cross and T.D. Hill (Toronto, 1982), p. 26 (question 10): 'Saga me on hwilcere ylde wæs adam ða he geseapen wæs. Ic me secge, he wæs on .xxx. wontra yldo.' The *Rituale ecclesiae Dunelmensis* (ed. U. Lindelöf, Surtees Society 140 (Durham and London, 1927), 197), gives Eve's age, also, as thirty. Cross and Hill (*ibid.* p. 71) add that a twelfth-century note on BL Cotton Claudius B. iv attributes this idea to Methodius, an early fourth-century Greek exegete who wrote a treatise on the resurrection: 'Methodius cwað. adam wæs gesceopa man on wlite of ðritig wintra.' It is not to be found in the surviving parts of Methodius's treatise, which, however, is very lacunose.

154 *de terra fincxit*. This version of Gen. II.7 is closer to the Vetus Latina (*Genesis*, ed. Fischer, p. 38) than to the Vulgate: 'et tunc finxit Deus hominem de limo terrae'.

155 *pectore uirgo*. Proba, *Cento*, lines 131–2 'insignis facie et pulchra pectore uirgo / iam matura uiro, iam plenis nubilis annis' (references to Faltonia Proba are by line to *Cento*, ed. Schenkl; cf. Vergil, *Aeneid* III.426, and VII.53: 'iam matura uiro, iam plenis nubilis annis'). It is this passage which is the real indicator that this writer was familiar with Proba: it is especially significant that *pectore uirgo* makes no grammatical sense in the context, since it must be dependent on *coniugem*.

156 *eduxit ex latere*. Paraphrased from Gen. II.21–2.

157 *omnis anima .xxx. surgat*. The source here appears to be ps.-Athanasius, *Quaestiones ad Antiochum ducem* (PG 28, 612): καὶ πῶς λοιπὸν ἐπιγνώσεται, εἶπέ μοι, πατὴρ τὸ ἴδιον τέκνον νήπιον τελευτῆσαν, καὶ τριακονταετῆ τέλειον ἄνθρωπον

ἀνιστάμενον, καθὼς καὶ ὁ Χριστὸς τριακονταετὴς ἐβαπτίσθη; ('And how will it be possible for a father to recognize his own child who had died in infancy, resurrected as a person thirty years old, the age Christ was baptized?'). Interestingly, the *Laterculus* is slightly at variance. The age of thirty is given in the *Laterculus* as 'hac ipsa quam gessit uiuens in corpore'; but elsewhere (ch. 3) He is said to have lived to thirty-three and to have been baptized at thirty (ch. 9), so this must be a slip. The *Biblical Commentaries* are completely in accord with the *Laterculus* on this point. *Gn-Ex-Evla* 22 states: 'Iohannes Crisostomus ait omnes homines resurrecturos quasi .xxx. annos habentes.'

According to Stokes, this statement is to be found in the Koran, which of course drew widely on the traditional lore of the middle east, including Jewish and Christian apocrypha. It also occurs in a middle-Irish tract, *Scela na esergi* ('Tidings of the Resurrection') (in W. Stokes [ed. and trans.], 'Tidings of the Resurrection', *Revue Celtique* 25 (1904), 232–59, ch. 8, at 238–9): 'It is then asked, since all human beings will arise out of death, in what age or form will their resurrection be? And the apostle deals with that question when he says "all men", quoth the apostle, "will arise out of death in the likeness of the age and form of Christ" . . . it is therefore that all men will arise at the same age, to wit, at the age of thirty.' It is interesting to observe that this Irish tract syncopates Eph. IV.13 in exactly the same way as the *Laterculus* does in ch. 16 (above, n. 152), and to make the same point. In the Latin tradition, Augustine, under the topic *paruulorum resurrectio qualis* (*Sermo* ccxlii.3), commented 'credibilius tamen accipitur et probabilius et rationabilius, plenas aetates resurrecturas, ut reddatur munere, quod accessurum erat tempora.' But he did not extend the statement by committing himself to the precise figure of thirty years.

158 *carnem, ut recipiat.* II Cor. V.10: 'ut referat unusquisque propria corporis prout gessit siue bonum siue malum'. The *Laterculus* here contradicts ps.-Athanasius, the principal source (see the beginning of n. 157). Ps.-Athanasius *quaestio* as a whole states that people will not recognize each other in the new bodies they will receive at the Resurrection, since not only age, but shape, colour and even gender are merely mortal details, and irrelevant to the new, eternal bodies which will be (like Adam's before the fall) the image of God. The *Laterculus* specifically opposes this view, preferring that expressed by St Paul.

CH. 18

159 *ut tu non dedigneris.* This parenthetic aside to the listener is a rhetorical touch. I do not know of a specific historical context to which it is relevant: does it imply that certain persons haughtily refused to be baptized at all, or does 'a conseruo suscipere' suggest that the character of the person officiating was believed to be

relevant to the quality of the sacrament received? Two stories of Bede's may be apposite. In the first, the king and his immediate retinue received baptism from the bishop, the *plebes* from his priests: 'Itaque episcopus concedente immo multum gaudente rege primos prouinciae duces ac milites sacrosancto fonte abluebat; uerum presbyteri Eappa et Padda et Burghelm et Oiddi ceteram plebem uel tunc uel tempore sequente baptizabant' (*Historia ecclesiastica* IV.13, ed. Colgrave and Mynors, p. 372). In the second, Bede reported that Cædwalla, king of the west Saxons, appeared to have entertained the naive belief that one got a better class of baptism at Rome, and therefore deferred the ceremony until he was able to make the pilgrimage, receiving baptism only ten days before his death (*ibid.* V.7, p. 470): 'hoc sibi gloriae singularis desiderans adipisci ut ad limina beatorum apostolorum fonte baptismatis ablueretur'. Cædwalla died the year before Theodore, in 689. The remarks in the *Laterculus* seem calculated to counteract this attitude to baptism and its efficacy, which may not have been unique to Cædwalla.

160 *ille non deuitor*. The supreme and extraordinary humility of Christ was stressed by many patristic writers, including Theodore of Mopsuestia: 'And what did [man] do that he humbled himself to such an extent for him as to become like him and to take upon him the form of a servant and to be a man for our salvation and to make himself manifest to all and to assume upon himself all that which belonged to the nature of that man and to be exercised in all [human] faculties?' (*Commentary on the Nicene Creed*, ed. Mingana, p. 53). There are similar comments in Cyril of Alexandria, PG 74, 963. Sahdona contrasted the humility of Christ with the pride of Satan in his *Liber perfectionis* II.x.23–9 (ed. and trans. A. de Halleux, CSCO 252–3 [Script. Syr. 110–11] (Louvain, 1965), 55–7). See also Wallace-Hadrill, *Christian Antioch*, pp. 152–3 and 157.

161 *unum mediatorem*. I Tim. II.5: 'unus enim deus unus est mediator dei et hominum homo Christus Iesus'.

162 *pater in uoce*. Luke III.24 (and see also Matth. III.16–17).

163 *in deserto*. Matth. IV.1: 'tunc Iesus ductus est in desertum ab spiritu et temptaretur a diabolo' (see also Luke IV.1–2).

164 *calefactus*. A mysterious epithet, for which I can suggest no explanation. Mai emended to *caro factus*. It has no biblical basis. The complete phrase 'calefactus homo *quem sumpserat*' suggests that the author's thinking has been affected by Theodore of Mopsuestia's *homo assumptus/verbum assumens* distinction, as humanity is here 'taken on' by the Son as if the human body of Jesus was a sort of garment for

Commentary

divinity (Theodore of Mopsuestia, *In Psalmo* XLIV.9, ed Devreesse, p. 11). But
we also find 'tu ad liberandum suscepturus hominem' in the *Te Deum*, which has
never been considered heretical in its tendencies, so we may absolve the author of
the *Laterculus* from Nestorian sympathies. There is a comparable phrase in
Hippolytus, Ἀπόδειξις περὶ Χριστοῦ καὶ ἀντιχρίστου, ch. 4 (PG 10, 725–88,
732), ἐνεδύσατο τὴν ἁγίαν σάρκα ἐκ τῆς ἁγίας Παρθένου, ὡς νυμφίος ἱμάτιον
ἐξυφάνας ἑαυτῷ ἐν τῷ σταυρικῷ πάθει: 'he put on holy flesh from the holy Virgin,
like a bridegroom weaving a garment for himself with the suffering on the cross'.

165 *propheta Zaccharias cecinit.* The writer's treatment of Zach. III.1–2 appears to
be an example of free paraphrase. Sabatier's Vetus Latina text runs: 'Et ostendit
mihi Dominus Iesum sacerdotem magnum stantem ante faciem angeli Domini, et
diabolus stabat a dextris eis ut aduersaretur ei. Et dixit Dominus ad diabolum:
increpet Dominus in te diabole: et increpet in te Dominus, qui elegit Ierusalem'
(*Versiones antiquae*, ed. Sabatier II, 988). Cf. the text of the *Laterculus*, ch. 18:
'*Vidi*', inquid, 'Iesum sacerdotem magnum et stabat *ad* dextris eius diabulus, *id
est ex parte iustitiae, concinnans dolos*. Et dixit *ad eum*: increpet *tibi* dominus, *diabule*,
qui *redimit Israhel et* elegit Hierusalem.' The *Laterculus* has missed out one phrase,
replaced two, added a gloss, changed the grammar of the second verse and
attributed a speech of the Lord to Jesus the High Priest. And yet this passage is
emphatically presented as a quotation: 'propheta Zacharias cecinit dicens: "uidi",
inquid...', etc.

166 *concinnans dolos.* Cf. Ps. XLIX. 19 (LXX): 'os tuum dimisisti ad malitiam et
lingua tua concinnauit dolos.' This verse is the only instance of the phrase in the
Vulgate.

167 *ex piscatoribus.* Cf. Sulpicius Severus, *Vita S. Martini*, praef. (ed. Fontaine I,
248): '...quia regnum Dei non in eloquentia, set in fide constat. Meminerit
etiam salutem saeculo non ab oratoribus ... sed a piscatoribus praedictum.' See
further H. Hagendahl, '*Piscatorie et non Aristotelice*: zu einem Schlagwort bei den
Kirchenvätern', in *Septentrionalia et Orientalia. Studia B. Karlgren dedicata*
(Stockholm, 1959), pp. 184–93. The phrase 'discipuli ex piscatoribus' is also
reminiscent of Caelius Sedulius, *Opus paschale* II.xiv (ed. Huemer, p. 219): 'exin
discipulos ex piscatoribus quosdam sibimet sociauit accitos'.

168 *ex sanguine nobilitatis.* This, like the direct address at the beginning of this
section, appears to be a hit against some rather aristocratic concept of Christianity
in which family pride and social position had been allowed too great a scope. In
early Anglo-Saxon England, Christianity was an aristocratic rather than a popular
religion. It was necessary to secure the conversion of the ruling classes before it

211

was possible to bring any kind of ministry to the peasantry; but the curious little anecdote Bede tells of St Cuthbert and the local rustics suggests that in some parts of the country Christian kings had interdicted pagan worship without managing to create a psychologically satisfactory replacement (Bede, *Vita S. Cuthberti*, in *Two Lives of St Cuthbert*, ed. B. Colgrave (Cambridge, 1940), p. 162: 'quasi merito tali paterentur, qui communia mortalium iura spernentes, noua et ignota darent statuta uiuendi'; see R. Hill, 'Bede and the Boors', in *Famulus Christi*, ed. G. Bonner (London, 1976), pp. 93–105). Most – though not quite all – Anglo-Saxon saints were of noble birth; there were several royal saints, such as Oswald, Æthelflæd, Hild, noblemen like Wilfrid, Guthlac and probably Aldhelm. Cuthbert may have been an exception. The point is that most of these people would preach the word of God backed by the authority of secure social position as well as personal conviction; and perhaps rather in the spirit that someone who was brought up with the authority to tell peasants to fight and die could equally well tell them to pray and live. The disadvantages of this are as obvious as the advantages.

Things were rather different in the middle east. Of course, bishops like Chrysostom were drawn from the higher echelons of Greco-Roman society. But there was a great deal of fervent grassroots piety; and illiterate peasant monks could, and did on occasion, exert a great deal of influence not only with the populace at large but even with the course of official policy. W.H.C. Frend commented that 'the emperors, whatever their failings by modern western standards, had the good sense to consult the monastic leaders and use them as channels of public opinion' ('Paulinus of Nola and the Last Century of the Western Empire', *Journal of Roman Studies* 59 (1969), 1–11, at 9–10). See also P. Brown, 'The Rise and Function of the Holy Man in Late Antiquity', in his *Society and the Holy in Late Antiquity* (London, 1982), pp. 103–52, at 139–41, and D. Attwater, *St John Chrysostom, Pastor and Preacher* (London, 1959), pp. 14–15 and 49–50. Lip-service, and occasionally a genuine regard, was paid to the idea that Christ came primarily to the poor, and chose to live among them. We may see here Theodore, with his Asiatic background, pitting himself against a potentially disquieting trend in Anglo-Saxon Christianity.

169 *ecclesiae columnae*. This phrase conceals a concatenation of themes. First is Rev. XXI. 14: 'et murus ciuitatis habens fundamenta duodecim, et in ipsis duodecim nomina duodecim apostolorum agni'. But the word here is decidedly 'foundation-stone' (θεμελίος). The pillars of the church appear widely in patristic writings and derive primarily from I Tim. IV.15: 'quae est ecclesia Dei uiui columna et firmamentum ueritatis'. Peter and Paul are referred to as 'pillars of the church' in I Clement V (*Patrum Apostolicorum Opera*, ed. A. R. M. Dressel (Leipzig, 1857), pp. 50–1). Athanasius made a similar linking of themes in his comment on Ps. LXXIV.4 (*Expositio in Psalmos*, PG 27, 339): Ἐγὼ ἐστερέωσα

τοὺς στύλους αὐτῆς. Στῦλοι τῆς Ἰερουσαλὴμ οἱ ἅγιοι ἀπόστολοι, κατὰ τὸ ἐρημέ-νον. Στῦλος καὶ ἑδραίωμα τῆς ἀληθείας ('I have established its pillars. The pillars of Jerusalem are the holy apostles, according to that which was said: a pillar and foundation of the truth' (I Tim. IV.15)).

170 *ex Iacob .xii.* The identification of the number of apostles with the number of tribes was made by Narsai: 'Twelve priests he [Christ] chose him first, according to the number of the tribes and instead of the People he called all peoples to be his' (*The Liturgical Homilies of Narsai*, XXXII: 'On the Church and Priesthood', trans. R.H. Connolly (Cambridge, 1909), p. 63).

171 *lapides uiuos.* 1 Pet. II.5: 'et ipsi tamquam lapides uiui superaedificamini domus spiritalis sacerdotium sanctum'. The Vetus Latina version is 'et uos ergo tamquam lapides uiui aedificamini in domum spiritalem' (*Versiones antiquae*, ed. Sabatier III, 948).

172 *ex Iordanes alueo.* Joshua IV.2–3: 'elige duodecim uiros singulos per singulas tribus, et praecipe eis ut tollant de medio Iordanis alueo ubi steterunt sacerdotum pedes duodecim durissimos lapides.' There are clear eastern antecedents to this section. It gives a series of justifications for twelve as the chosen number of apostles, including the sentence: 'nam unaquaque tribus Israhel singulos apostolos in nouum testamentum quasi duodecim lapides uiuos ex Iordanes alueo reddederunt.' Cf. the thirteenth homily of Narsai (Murray, *Symbols*, p. 210): 'He fixed the number twelve, like the twelve hours of the day for which the world was lit up and like the twelve stones which Joshua took out of the Jordan (Josh. IV.3, 8, etc.). . . and like the twelve springs which Moses found at Elim . . . these were types prefiguring the apostles themselves.' The *duodecim lapides* merit further discussion. Note that they are *lapides uiui*. I Peter II. 4–8 is of obvious relevance to this concept but Murray (*Symbols*, p. 208) pointed out that this epistle was not known to the Syrian fathers. It may, however, have been known to the author of the *Laterculus*. The imagery of rocks – Christ as a rock, Peter, of course, as the rock on which the church was built and also the apostles generally as foundation-stones, is pervasive and important in Syriac writings (Murray, *Symbols*, pp. 205–38 and his 'The Rock and the House on the Rock'). In addition, Syriac texts often parallel Joshua and Jesus; for example, Jesus is buried in a tomb originally made for Joshua (*The Book of the Cave of Treasures*, ed. Budge, p. 236). It was at the crossing of the Jordan when the twelve stones were taken up that the Jews entered the promised land and the typological implications of this were brought out in an Ethiopic text: 'as Joshua brought them into the Land of Promise, so shall the Saviour bring you into the Garden of Delight'. (*The Queen of Sheba and her only son Menyelek, being the History of the Departure of God and his Ark of the Covenant from Jerusalem to Ethiopia, and the Establishment of the Religion of the Hebrews and the*

Solomonic Line of Kings in that Country, ed. E.A.W. Budge (London, 1922), p. 110). This brief section on the twelve apostles thus appears to be a concatenation of Syriac themes.

173 *uenite post me*. Matth. IV.19: 'uenite post me et faciam uos fieri piscatores hominum.'

CH. 19

174 *infirmitates*. Matth. VIII.17: 'ut adimpleretur quod dictum est per Esaiam prophetam dicentem: ipse infirmitates nostras accepit et aegrotationes portauit.' Isaiah LIII. 4: 'uere languores nostros ipse tulit et dolores nostros ipse portauit'. The *Laterculus* is evidently quoting Matthew quoting Isaiah, rather than using the Old Testament directly.

175 *quemadmodum gigans per uiam*. Ps. XVIII.6 (LXX): 'exsultauit ut gigans ad currendam uiam suam'; Vetus Latina 'exsultauit ut gigas ad decurrendam uiam' (*Versiones antiquae*, ed. Sabatier II, 38).

176 An odd feature of this passage is that, although the word *sex* appears twice, seven grades are actually listed. Perhaps this slip is connected with the author's evident enthusiasm for the number 6.

177 *per sex grada officii*. Reynolds notes of the ordinals in the *Laterculus* that some of their features suggest an eastern, late patristic background. The grades and their sequence are exactly those found in the Ethiopic version of *Didascalia Apostolorum* and in the interpolated *Didascalia* in the *Constitutiones Apostolorum* (which are of Syrian origin; on which see Reynolds, *Ordinals of Christ*, p. 12) with the exception of the *fossarius* and the absorption of the cantor by the lector. The *fossarius* is an archaic member of the ecclesiastical hierarchy, mentioned in ps.-Jerome, *De vii ordinibus ecclesiae* (PL 30, 148–62), a tract which may have been written either in fifth-century Gaul or in seventh-century Spain. The unusual dominical sanction for the grade of lector seems also to be eastern and also dependent on the interpolated *Didascalia* (*ibid.*, p. 44). So the author of the *Laterculus*, noting a presumably late patristic eastern ordinal known to him under the name of Ephrem as 'similar' to the one he actually quotes, is corroborated by the most recent study of the ordinals as a genre. The ordinals of Christ have been frequently discussed. Apart from Reynolds's recent survey, the studies which particularly contribute to the understanding of this aspect of the *Laterculus* include Traube's revised version of his article on the *Laterculus*, 'Chronicon Palatinum', in his *Vorlesungen und Abhandlungen* III, 201–4, which adds further references to manuscripts containing versions of the ordinals. See also A. Wilmart, 'Les ordres du Christ', and J. Crehan, 'The Seven Orders of Christ'.

214

178 *Lazarum*. John XI.19: 'ait Iesus: tollite lapidem. Dicit ei Martha soror eius qui mortuus fuerat: Domine iam fetet, quadriduanus enim est.' Caelius Sedulius's well-known alphabetic hymn, 'A solis ortus cardine' has as the first line of stanza Q, 'Quarta die iam fetidus' (ed. Huemer, p. 166), which is interestingly close to the version in the *Laterculus*, certainly much closer than the Vulgate.

179 *Lector fuit*. Luke IV.16–17: 'et intrauit secundum consuetudinem suam die sabbati in synagogam, et surrexit legere. Et traditus est illi liber prophetae Esaiae.'

180 *cum replicuisset*. Luke IV. 20: 'et cum plicuisset librum, reddidit ministro et sedit.' *Replicuisset* and *tradidit* are not listed among the known variants for this verse (*Nouum Testamentum*, ed. Wordsworth and White I, 331).

181 *aqua in pelue*. John XIII.5: 'deinde mittit aquam in peluem et coepit lauare pedes discipulorum.'

182 *calicem benedixit*. Luke XXII.17: 'et accepto calice gratias egit et dixit: accipite et diuidite inter uos.'

183 *panem benedixit*. Luke XXII.19: 'et accepto pane gratias egit et fregit et dedit eis.'

184 *eos regnum Dei docebat*. Luke IV.20–1: 'coepit autem dicere ad illos quia hodie impleta est haec scriptura in auribus uestris.'

185 *sanctus Ephrem*. The reference in the *Laterculus* to an Ephremic version of the *ordines Christi* cannot be traced to a genuine surviving work of Ephrem. But Ephrem, who was both prolific and extremely distinguished, rapidly acquired a large body of *dubia et spuria* in both Syriac and Greek and, furthermore, some of his genuine works have been lost. No aspersions need be cast on the good faith of the author of the *Laterculus*, since there are indeed several Syriac witnesses for the ordinals of Christ, any of which could have come to him bearing an attribution to Ephrem (Reynolds, *Ordinals of Christ*, pp. 11–13). There is a sermon attributed to Ephrem, preserved in a Latin translation, which divides the clericate into five grades, *episcopi*, *diaconi*, *subdiaconi*, *cantores* and *lectores*, the same grading which is found in the fourth-century *ordines Christi* passage of the *Constitutiones apostolorum*, but it is not itself a witness to the *ordines Christi*, so is unlikely to be the work the author of the *Laterculus* had in mind (Ephrem, *Sermo paraeneticus de secundo aduentu domini et de paenitentia*, *Opera omnia quotquot in insignioribus Italiae bibliothecis*, ed. G. Vossius (Antwerp, 1619), p. 380, and see discussion in Reynolds, *Ordinals of Christ*, pp. 12–14).

CH. 20

186 *a proprio discipolo.* Matth. XXVI.14: 'Tunc abiit unum de duodecim qui dicitur Iudas Scarioth ad principes sacerdotum et ait illis: quid uultis mihi dare et ego uobis eum tradam? At illi constituerunt ei triginta argenteos.'

187 *ante presignatum.* Gen. XXXVII.28: 'uendiderunt Ismahelitis uiginti argenteis.'

188 *Quod autem ligatus.* Matth. XXVII.2: 'et uinctum adduxerunt eum et tradiderunt Pontio Pilato praesidi.'

This is another place in the *Laterculus* where Ephrem's thought seems particularly relevant, with its series of paradoxes on the Jews' mercilessness to Christ and Christ's mercy to mankind. The theme is found in Ephrem's hymns, one of which has the line: 'he who gives drink to all entered and experienced thirst' (S. Brock, 'The Poet as Theologian', *Sobornost* 7 (1977), 243–50, at 244). Even more appositely, another reads: 'Christ came as a slave to liberate freedom, he even suffered being stricken on the face by servants so that "he broke the yoke that was on the free"' (Beggiani, *Early Syriac Theology*, p. 66). Cf. the *Laterculus*: 'quod autem ligatus a ministris Hebraeorum discribitur, ut eos qui diabulo compediti tenebantur absolueret et nexus peccatorum confringeret. et quod palmis in faciem uerberatur, nobis ueram libertatem donauit.' The long series of paradoxical statements, as well as the precise context in the life of Christ, are exactly paralleled in the morning office of the Maronite prayers for Good Friday, which begin: 'On this day...you were brought to trial scornfully before Pilate, you who are seated in glory at the right of your Father. You remain silent before your judges, but by it, you speak all things.' The prayer continues in this vein for some sixteen lines (Beggiani, *Early Syriac Theology*, pp. 30–1). Similar antitypical expositions are also found in Ephrem (Kronholm, *Motifs*, p. 102), and the concept is found in the west in Caelius Sedulius's *Carmen paschale*, V.97–104 (ed. Heumer, p. 121).

189 *compediti.* Ps. LXXVIII.11: 'introeat in conspectu tuo gemitus compeditorum.'

190 *palmis in faciem uerberatur.* Matth. XXVI.67 'alii autem palmas in faciem ei dederunt'. The use made of this verse in the *Laterculus* only makes sense if one assumes a knowledge in the writer and his audience of the Roman ritual of *manumissio*, which Isidore explained in the following way: 'Manumissus dicitur quasi manu emissus. Apud ueteres enim quotiens manu mittebant, alapa percussos circumgerebant, et liberos confirmabant; unde et manumissi dicti, eo quod manu mitterentur' (*Etymologiae* IX.iv.48). This is confirmed by the *Nouellae Iustiniani*: 'si emancipationis actio...facta cum iniuriis et alapis liberabit eos

[filios] huiusmodi uinculis' and also by the *Codex Iustinianus* (*Nouellae Iustiniani* LXXXI.praef., ed. R. Schöll and W. Kroll, in *Corpus Iuris Ciuilis*, ed. T. Mommsen *et al.*, 3 vols. (Berlin, 1908–12) III, 397 and *Codex Iustinianus* VII.xlviii.6, ed. P. Krüger, *ibid.* II, 318). The same paradox was also drawn by Caelius Sedulius, *Carmen paschale* V.103: 'his [Christi] alapis nobis libertas maxima plausit' (ed. Huemer, p. 121). The source of this motif in the *Laterculus* is thus a moot point. Ephrem appears to be extremely important to the writer, but there are also several places in the *Laterculus* which appear to draw on the dual *Opus paschale* of Caelius Sedulius. Caelius Sedulius was certainly very well known to Aldhelm, and so probably at Canterbury. Roman law, on the witness of Aldhelm's letter to Leuthere, was one of the studies at Theodore and Hadrian's school (*Aldhelmi Opera*, ed. Ehwald, p. 476). Specifically, Theodore drew in his *Iudicia* on the *Codex Iustinianus* and the *Nouellae* (Lapidge, 'The School of Theodore', p. 53).

191 *colaphis capite caeditur.* The primary source for this is the same verse, Matth. XXVI.67: 'et colaphis eum ceciderunt'. But the phrase is also closely reminiscent of a version of Amos II.7: 'et colaphis caedebant capita pauperum' whose only other witness is the sixth-century British writer, Gildas (*De excidio* II.liii.1, ed. Mommsen, p. 57). It has long been recognized that Gildas used a version of the Minor Prophets which was based very closely on the LXX (*Councils*, ed. Haddan and Stubbs I, 184–5 and 188–92): so, this passage suggests, did the author of the *Laterculus*, whose preference for Latin versions based on the Septuagint must now be clear. Caelius Sedulius's *Carmen Paschale* V.97: 'uel *colaphis* pulsare *caput*, uel *caedere* palmis. . .' (ed. Huemer, p. 121) may also be relevant.

192 *inmundi sputaminibus.* Matth XXVI.67 'tunc expuerunt in faciem eius.'

193 *flagellis uerberatur.* John XIX.6: 'tunc ergo adprehendit Pilatus Iesum et flagellauit.'

194 *filios adoptiuos.* This is a particularly Pauline concept: see in particular Galat. IV.5 'ut eos qui sub lege erant redimeret ut adoptionem filiorum reciperemus', but also Romans VIII.15 and 23. A possible additional source is Caelius Sedulius, *Carmen paschale* II.242–3:

> . . .cui nos duce Christo
> *fecit adoptiuos coelestis* gratia natos.

See also Hebr. I–II, III.1, and III.14. The idea is developed by a number of patristic writers, notably Gregory of Nyssa (*Contra Eunomium* III, PG 45, 243–1122, at 609) and Cyril of Alexandria (*In Rom.* I.3). See further Kelly, *ECD*, pp. 431–2.

195 *acoleum mortis.* I Cor. XV.55–6: 'ubi est mors stimulus tuus? stimulus autem mortis peccatum est.' Many patristic writers, notably Augustine, use *aculeus* rather than *stimulus*; so do the Spanish Bibles C θ T and the Book of Armagh (D) (*Nouum Testamentum,* ed. Wordsworth and White II, 274; see also *Versiones antiquae,* ed. Sabatier III, 722).

196 *uestes eius in sorte.* Matth. XXVII.35: 'postquam autem crucifixerunt eum diuiserunt uestimenta eius sortem mittentes'. See also John XIX.24.

CH. 21

197 *consummatum est.* John XIX.30: 'cum ergo accepisset Iesus acetum dixit consummatum est, et inclinato capite tradidit spiritum.'

198 *potestatem habeo.* John X.18: 'nemo tollit eam a me, sed ego pono eam a me ipso. Potestatem habeo ponendi eam, et potestatem habeo iterum sumendi eam.' The *Laterculus*'s addition of *animam meam* is found in G and T (Saint-Germain and Toledo) and in the Canterbury Codex Aureus (aur.) (*Nouum Testamentum,* ed. Wordsworth and White I, 579).

199 *nostra mortificatio.* I Cor. XV.22: 'et sicut in Adam omnes moriuntur, ita et in Christo omnes uiuificabuntur' and also I Cor. XV.53: 'oportet enim corruptibile hoc induere incorruptelam et mortale hoc induere inmortalitatem'.

200 *illud ante praedictum.* John XIX.35: 'facta sunt enim haec ut scriptura impleatur: os non comminuetis ex eo', drawing on Ex. XII.46 'nec os illius confringetur'. The *Laterculus*' 'os suum' is shared with a Spanish Bible, Cauensis (C) (*Nouum Testamentum,* ed. Wordsworth and White I, 636).

201 *agnus pascalis.* This phrase is more problematic than it looks. According to *TLL, mactare* was not taken over by the Christians for their ecclesiastical vocabulary, but continued to bear connotations of pagan sacrifice. The use of this word here is therefore poetic, in that it is striking and unexpected. It may therefore be significant that the verb *mactare* is used by Caelius Sedulius in a context which deliberately evokes the Lamb of God by typology, the offering ('*Akedah*) of Isaac:

> *mactandum*que Deo pater obtulit, at sacer ipsam
> pro pueri iugulis aries *mactatur* ad aram...
> amplexus praecepta Dei, typicique cruoris
> auxilio uentura docet, quod sanguine Christi
> *humana pro gente pius occumberet agnus.*

(*Carmen paschale* I, 114–15, 117–20, ed. Huemer, p. 24). The last line quoted parallels the meaning, though not the vocabulary, very closely. G. Vermes (*Scripture and Tradition*, pp. 243–5) noted that the Christian concept of the *Agnus Dei* draws on a concatenation of Hebrew themes: the lamb of sin-offering, the Passover lamb, the lamb of Isaiah LIII, the ram which is the leader of the flock in Enoch LXXXIX.46 (which stands for the Royal Messiah), the lamb of perpetual sacrifice and, most importantly, the ram which is substituted for Isaac. See further I. Levi, 'Le sacrifice d'Isaac et la mort de Jésus', *Revue des études juifs* 64 (1912), 161–84, and H. J. Shoeps, 'The Sacrifice of Isaac in Paul's Theology', *Journal of Biblical Literature* 65 (1946), 385–92. I have not been able to parallel this phrase more precisely than in the Caelius Sedulius passage quoted above, but the concept of Christ as the Paschal lamb is, of course, familiar to Christian writers, for example Gregory of Nyssa: Ἐτύθη γὰρ ὡς ἀληθῶς ὑπὲρ τὸ Πάσχα Χριστός (PG 46, 264: 'For Christ the Paschal offering is truly sacrificed for us'); and Cyril of Alexandria: νυνὶ δὲ ὁ πάλαι δι' αἰνιγματων ζωγραφούμενος ὁ ἀληθινὸς Ἀμνός, τὸ ἄμωμον ἱερεῖον ὑπερ πάντων ἄγεται πρὸς σφαγήν, ἵνα τοῦ κόσμου τὴν ἀμαρτίαν ἐλάσῃ (*In Ioannis euangelium libri II*, II, praef., PG 73, 192: 'For now that Lamb, which was symbolically prefigured of old, that immaculate sacrifice on behalf of all, is brought to the slaughter, so that he may release the sins of the world').

The liturgical resonance of the phrase does not in fact correspond with anything in Latin liturgy. However, it may be relevant to note that the Greek 'Liturgy of John Chrysostom' lays particular emphasis on the sacrifice of the Lamb. The bread used for the eucharist is stamped with a rectangular impression enclosing the letters ΙΣ ΧΣ ΝΙ ΚΑ. This is ceremonially detached from the loaf with an instrument called a 'spear', while the celebrant (in the modern version) recites Isaiah's prophecy referring to Christ as the sacrificial lamb (Is. LIII.7–8), 'he is brought as a lamb to the slaughter' (Brightman, *Liturgies Eastern and Western*, p. 356). This piece of bread is then referred to as 'the Lamb'. The earliest surviving manuscript to contain the three Byzantine liturgies is Vatican City, BAV, Barberini Gr. 336 (s. viii/ix). G. Galavaris, *Bread and the Liturgy: The Symbolism of Early Christian and Byzantine Bread Stamps* (Madison, WI, 1970), p. 75, has argued that this ritual was already in place in the Byzantine Church in the seventh century, on the evidence of the stamps used to mark 'the Lamb' on eucharistic loaves, though direct literary evidence is lacking. The invocation over the square of bread given in the Barberini manuscript is ἀμνὸν ἄμωμον ὑπὲρ τῆς τοῦ κόσμου ζωῆς 'a blameless lamb [sacrificed] on behalf of the life of Creation' (Brightman, *Liturgies Eastern and Western*, p. 309). This phrase in the *Laterculus*, then, suggests that the author was familiar with the principal liturgy of the Byzantine church, and that when he tried to render the solemn phrase of the *prothesis* in Latin, he chose a word known to him from Caelius Sedulius's poem (a work which he clearly regarded highly) but which would probably never have been chosen in this context by a native Latin speaker because its nuance was pagan.

The emotional significance of the 'Lamb of God' for the seventh-century Greek church is also witnessed by Theodore's contemporary, Pope Sergius (687–701), a Syrian whose family was from the region of Antioch, according to the *Liber pontificalis*, who introduced the singing of 'Agnus Dei, qui tollit peccata mundi' at the time of the Fraction into the Roman church (*Liber pontificalis*, ed. Duchesne I, 372).

202 *ab Aegypto*. Ex. XIV.27–31. There is no direct correspondence of vocabulary between the *Laterculus* and the biblical account of the Crossing of the Red Sea.

203 *altoque pelago demersit*. Cf. perhaps Vergil, *Aeneid* IX.81: 'pelagi petere alta parabat'.

204 *in inferiora terrae*. Ephes. IV. 9: 'et descendit primum in inferiores partes terrae'.

205 *de sinu patris*. John I.18: 'unigenitus filius qui est in sinu patris ipse enarrauit'.

206 *diabuli potestate destrueret*. Heb. II.14: 'quia ergo pueri communicauerunt et carni et ipse similiter participauit hisdem, ut per mortem destrueret eum qui habebat mortis imperium'.

207 *sed etiam latroni*. Luke XXIII. 24–5: 'et dicebat ad Iesum: Domine memento mei cum ueneris in regnum tuum. Et dixit illi Iesus: amen dico tibi hodie mecum eris in paradiso.'

208 *primitias resurrectionis*. Probably a reference to the waking of the dead at the Crucifixion (Matth. XXVII. 52). See also I Cor. XV.20: 'nunc autem Christus resurrexit a mortuis primitiae dormientium'. See also Theodore of Mopsuestia, *In epistolam ad Galatos* I.2, in *In epistolas Pauli*, ed. Swete I, 4; 'qui suscitauit eum ex mortuis: nouitatem enim designare cupit futurae uitae, cuius *primitiae* dominica extitit resurrectio.'

209 *.xl. dierum spatio*. Acts I.3: 'per dies quadraginta apparens eis et loquens de regno Dei'.

CH. 22

210 *terra es*. The *Laterculus* is quoting the Vetus Latina version, Gen. III.17: 'quoniam terra es et in terra(m) ibis' (*Genesis*, ed. Fischer, p. 74), rather than the

Vulgate, which uses *puluis*. The Greek word used in the Septuagint is γῆ ('earth'). The paralleling of Adam with Christ, emphasized in ch. 12, is repeated here.

211 *sede ad dexteram*. Acts II.34–5: 'dixit dominus deus meo sede a dextris meis donec ponam inimicos tuos scabillum pedum tuorum', quoting the identical version in Ps. CIX.1. The *Laterculus'* 'sede *ad dexteram'* is shared by Irenaeus and other church fathers and is found in the Codex Bezae (d) (*Nouum Testamentum*, ed. Wordsworth and White III, 48).

212 *ascendens Christus*. Eph. IV.8: 'ascendens in altum captiuam duxit captiuitatem'. This section, like ch. 21, is a tissue of references to the Pauline Epistles, interwoven with other biblical material.

213 *dedit dona*. Eph. IV.8: 'dedit dona hominibus'.

214 *Qui discendit*. Eph. IV.9–10: 'quod autem ascendit quid est nisi quia et descendit primum in inferiores partes terrae. Qui descendit ipse est et qui ascendit super omnes caelos ut impleret omnia.' The *Laterculus's adimpleret* is found in several texts, including the Book of Armagh (CDH θ TU^cW^c; *Nouum Testamentum*, ed. Wordsworth and White II, 435).

215 *paracletus*. Acts II.2: 'tamquam aduenientis spiritus uehementis et repleuit totam domum ubi erant sedentes'.

216 *confirmantur*. Coloss. I.17: 'et ipse est ante omnes, et omnia in ipso constant.' See also Eph. III.15: 'ex quo omnis paternitas in caelis et in terra nominatur'.

217 *alii quidem*. This is a somewhat abbreviated version of I Cor. XII.8–11: 'alii quidem per spiritum datur sermo sapientia, alii autem sermo scientiae secundum eundem spiritum, alteri fides in eodem spiritu, alii gratia sanitatum in uno spiritu, alii operatio uirtutum, alii prophetatio, alii discretio spirituum, alii genera linguarum, alii interpretatio sermonum. Haec autem omnia operatur unus atque idem spiritus.' *Curationum* for *sanitatum* is found in Hilary, Ambrose, the Book of Armagh (D) and fc (*Nouum Testamentum*, ed. Wordsworth and White II, 241).

218 *plenitudo unius deitatis*. Coloss. II.9: 'quia in ipso inhabitat omnis plenitudo diuinitatis corporaliter'. *Deitatis* is a variant attested in Origen (*Nouum Testamentum*, ed. Wordsworth and White II, 508).

219 *augmento filiorum*. This phrase may be seen as a reflection of the adoptionist ideas of Theodore of Mopsuestia. See, for example, 'the baptism of Christ was in

fact symbolically drawn to the pattern of ours ... in this he showed the grace of the adoption of children for which baptism takes place' (*Catechetical Commentary*, ed. Mingana, p. 66, and see Greer, *Theodore*, pp. 72 and 80). See also the Syriac writer, Philoxenus of Mabbug (*The Matthew-Luke Commentary*, ed. and trans. Fox, p. 153): 'He is considered the natural Father of Him and of us who have been baptised in grace, because we have become brothers of the (divinely) natural Son by baptism, and from henceforth we are called the Son's brothers, and the Father's children.'

CH. 23

220 *uenit plenitudo temporis*. Galat. IV.4 'at ubi uenit plenitudo temporis, misit Deus filium suum factum ex muliere factum sub lege.' The concept of a 'mediator between God and man' may be illuminated by Nemesius of Emesa (an Antiochene theologian, quoted by Greer, *Theodore of Mopsuestia*, p. 22); 'man's being is on the boundary between the intelligible order and the phenomenal order ... it would seem that the Creator linked up each several order of creation with the next, so as to make the whole universe one and akin.'

221 *noussima ora est*. I John II.18: 'filioli nouissima ora est'

222 *apostolorum princeps*. The singularity of Peter goes back to the gospels, where he is named as the rock on which the church will be built. The ascendancy of Peter over the other apostles was recognized by Fathers of both the eastern and western churches. Clement of Alexandria, in the second century, called him ὁ πρῶτος τῶν μαθητῶν (C. F. B. Allnatt, *Cathedra Petri, or, the Titles and Prerogatives of St Peter and of his See and Successors as Described by the Early Fathers, Ecclesiastical Writers and Councils of the Church*, 3rd ed. (London, 1883), p. 40), and Jerome was among the earliest writers to use *princeps apostolorum* (*ibid.* p. 45).

223 *non lateat uos*. II Peter III.8: 'unum uero hoc non lateat uos carissimi quia unus dies apud Dominum sicut mille anni et mille anni sicut dies unus.'

224 *hoc Dauid*. This is an interpolation into the text of Peter and refers back to Ps. XC.4.

225 *uineae Dei*. Matth. XX. 1–16, the Parable of the Vineyard.

226 *octabam per resurrectionem*. The source here is probably the *Epistle of Barnabas*, written probably in the second century, which enjoyed a very high status in the early church (the *Codex Sinaiticus* puts it among the canonical epistles): 'Cernite,

quomodo loquatur: non mihi accepta sunt praesentia sabbata, sed illud quod ego feci; quando scilicet, uniuersis finem imponens, octaui diei faciam initium, hoc est, initium alterius mundi. Idcirco et diem octauum in laetitia agimus, quo et Iesus resurrexit a mortuis' (*Epistola*, ed. Dressell, pp. 36–7). This concept may also be paralleled in Ambrose, *Epistola* xliv (PL 16, 1135–41), ch. 4: 'hebdomas ueteris testamenti est octaua noui, quando Christus resurrexit, et dies omnibus nouae salutis illuxit' (1137), and ch. 12, 'ergo Hippolytus et Solon uel septem aetates, uel hebdomas aetatum norunt. In illis se hebdomas aetatum praeferat: octaua autem unam et perpetuam aetatem inuehit, qua excrescimus in uirum perfectum' (1140).

CH. 24

227 *sextum milarium*. See discussion of the age of the world in chs. 3–4.

228 *septima tuba*. Rev. XI.15: 'et septimus angelus tuba cecinit'.

229 *septima fiala*. Rev. XVI.17: 'et septimus effudit fialam suam in aerem'.

230 *Sed ut ne quis*. The writer evidently became anxious lest the six thousand years he gave as the time from Adam to the Passion mislead the reader into believing that there would be a thousand years from Christ to the Second Coming. Some of the earlier Christian writers believed that the world would exist for 6,000 years only, a thesis which is found in the second-century Epistle of Barnabas, ch. 15 (in *Patres Apostolici*, ed. Dressell, pp. 34–5): 'Fecitque Deus in sex diebus opera manuum suarum, et desiit die septima, et ea requieuit, et sanctificauit eam. Aduertite filii, quid dicat: consummauit in sex diebus. Id ait: omnia consummabit Dominus in sex millibus annorum; nam apud illum dies aequiparatur mille annis...Itaque, filii, in sex diebus, hoc est, in sex annorum millibus consummabuntur uniuersa'; and also in Irenaeus, *Aduersus haereses* V.xxviii.3 (ed. Harvey II, 402–3). It was discarded by fourth-century theologians like Augustine, for example in *Enarrationes in Psalmos* VI (PL 36, 90); see further *Catholic Encyclopedia*, X.308–9, s.v. 'Millennium'. Isidore also said (*Chronicon*, in *Chronica Minora II*, ed. Mommsen, p. 481): 'residuum saeculi tempus humanae inuestigationis incertum est'.

231 *de diem*. Matth. XXIV.36. In the current Vulgate, this is 'de die autem illa et hora nemo scit nisi pater solus'. This is another instance of the text of the *Laterculus* giving the accusative after *de*. The addition in the *Laterculus* of *neque filius* seems at first sight perverse, since it exacerbates the writer's difficulties with its implications for the proper understanding of the Trinity. But one of the

fourth-century Greek Bibles, the *Codex Vaticanus*, has οὐδὲ ὁ υἱός and Jerome testified that this reading was not unknown to him in Latin (*Commentarium in Euangelium Matthaei ad Eusebium libri quatuor*: PL 26, 15–218, at 181): 'In quibusdam Latinis codicibus additum est, *neque filius*: cum in graecis, et maxime Adamantii et Pierii exemplaribus, hoc non habeatur ascriptum: sed quia in nonnullis legitur, disserendum uidetur. Gaudent Arius et Eunomius, quasi ignorantia magistri, gloria discipulorum sit, et dicunt: Non potest aequalis esse non nouit, et qui ignorat. Contra quos breuiter ista dicenda sunt: cum omnia tempora fecerit Iesus, hoc est, Verbum Dei: omnia enim per ipsum facta sunt'. ('In certain Latin copies, there is added "nor the Son", which is not written in Greek exemplars, particularly not in those of Adamantius and Pierius, but since it is the reading in a good few copies, it should be discussed. Arius and Eunomius [the heretics] rejoice, as though the ignorance of the master ought to be the glory of his disciples, and they say: "He cannot be equal, who does not know, and who is ignorant." This should briefly be stated against these men: Since Jesus, that is, the word of God, made all times, everything was made through him.'). The fragmentary Arian tract *Aduersus orthodoxos et macedonianos* preserved in a Bobbio palimpsest put together in the seventh century (Vatican City, BAV, lat. 5750 and Milan, Biblioteca Ambrosiana E.147 sup.; *CLA* I, 31) confirms that this text was indeed used by Arian writers: 'filius qui negauit se scire diem illam, et pater qui in sua posuit potestate, qui iudicaturus est filius et qui neminem indicat pater, sed omnem iudicium dedit filio' ('the son who denies that he knows that day, and the father who has put it in his power, the son who is to judge and the father who will in no way reveal it, but who gives the whole judgement to the son'); *Scripta Ariana Latina* I, ed. R. Gryson, CCSL 87 (Turnhout, 1982), 229–65, at 255. The authenticity of the *neque filius* clause was upheld by V. Taylor, *The Names of Jesus* (London, 1953), pp. 64–5. It should therefore be noted that this *neque filius* reading occurs in both the early gospel books associated with Canterbury, CCCC 286 and Bodley Auct. D. II. 14, as well as in the eighth-century gospels written at Canterbury, the Codex Aureus. It also appears in the Irish Codex Usserianus Primus. This version of the verse contributes to the impression that the writer's Bible is based on earlier types of text than the revised version of the near-contemporary Codex Amiatinus. Some remarks by F. Conybeare ('Three Early Doctrinal Modifications of the Text of the Gospels', *Hibbert Journal* 1 (1903), 98–113, at 112) may be relevant: 'it is quite erroneous to assert, as Westcott and Hort asserted, that the text of the gospels bear no trace of having been altered anywhere for doctrinal or dogmatic reasons … And, what is more, the interpolated texts have been regularly appealed to for centuries in defence of the very doctrines in behalf of which they were inserted' – or in this case, deleted.

232 *quiescant a seruitutem*. Rom. VIII.21: 'quia et ipsa creatura liberabitur a

seruitute corruptionis in libertatem gloriae filiorum Dei'. Cf. Jacob of Sarug (*Hexemeron*, ed. and trans. Jansma, p. 38): 'au septième millénaire, la création se reposera, comme elle fait de son travail, le septième jour'.

233 *quando area uentilata fuerit.* Matth. III.12: 'cuius uentilabrum in manu sua et permundauit aream suam, et congregabit triticum suum in horreum paleas autem conburet igni inextinguibili'.

234 *non latet quod nunc latet.* Mark VII.24: 'neminem uoluit scire, et non potuit latere' and see also Sap. X.8 'ut in his, quae peccauerunt, nec latere potuissent'. Note the use of the present tense for the future, characteristic of Late Latin.

CH. 25

235 *Gaius.* Malalas, *Chronographia* X.17 (p. 243). It should be noted that the *Laterculus*'s use of Malalas is highly selective. Unlike Malalas, the writer does not make clear that many of these reigns overlapped to a substantial extent as a result of the appointment of co-emperors. In the latter half of the *Laterculus*'s list, the writer chose to record only the emperors of the east (a further indication, despite the language of the text, of the priority which the author gives to the east), and passed over Malalas's record of the emperors at Rome. See also discussion by Jeffreys, 'Chronological Structures: Roman Imperial Reigns', *Studies*, pp. 138–43.

236 *Claudius.* Malalas, *Chronographia* X.22 (p. 246).

237 *Nero.* Malalas, *Chronographia* X.29 (p. 250).

238 *Galba.* Malalas, *Chronographia* X.41 (p. 258): μετὰ δὲ τὴν βασιλείαν Νέρωνος ἐβασίλευσεν Γαλβᾶς Αὔγουστος μῆνας ζ ('after the reign of Nero, Galba Augustus reigned for seven months').

239 *Lucius.* Malalas, *Chronographia* X.42 (p. 258).

240 *Bitellius.* Malalas, *Chronographia* X.43 (p. 259). The text of Malalas does not include 'and a half'.

241 *Vespasianus.* Malalas, *Chronographia* X.44 (p. 260).

242 *Titus.* Malalas, *Chronographia* X.47 (p. 262).

243 *Hi expugnauerunt*. The account of the Roman war under Titus against the Jews in this section is based on Eusebius, conceivably via the Latin translation of Rufinus. But nothing in the phrasing of the *Laterculus*'s précis bears any direct resemblance to the phrasing of Rufinus and there is a small pointer in the direction of the Greek, in that the place-name is given as *Pellan*, following the Greek accusative Πελλάν rather than the Latin *Pellam* given by Rufinus (Eusebius, *Historia ecclesiastica* III.v.1–4, ed. Schwarz, pp. 196–7). It is interesting to note that this chapter of the *Historia ecclesiastica* was sufficiently important to the author of the *Laterculus* to provide two of his additions to Malalas (this comment, and his account of the martyrdom of James in ch. 3), in the light of Aldhelm's detailed paraphrase of the same chapter in the seventh of his *Carmina ecclesiastica* (ed. Ehwald, pp. 26–7), suggesting that this episode, with its vivid juxtaposition of a guiltless death and awful retribution, may have been memorably taught in the school at Canterbury.

244 *Domitianus*. Malalas, *Chronographia* X.48 (p. 262): 'et usque nunc in hoc mundo durauit' is an addition to Malalas's text.

245 *Neruas*. Malalas, *Chronographia* X.53 (p. 267).

246 *Traianus*. Malalas, *Chronographia* XI.1 (p. 269).

247 *Adrianus*. Malalas, *Chronographia* XI.13 (p. 277). Malalas gave twenty-two years, five months.

248 *Antoninus Pius*. Malalas, *Chronographia* XI.21 (p. 280).

249 *Marcus*. Malalas, *Chronographia* XI.28 (p. 281).

250 *Antoninus Berus*. Malalas, *Chronographia* XI.32 (p. 282), gave eight years, not one.

251 *Commodus*. Malalas, *Chronographia* XII.1 (p. 283).

252 *Pertinax*. Malalas, *Chronographia* XII.14 (p. 290), gave two months, eighteen days.

253 *Didius Iulianus*. Malalas, *Chronographia* XII.15 (p. 290).

254 *Seuerus Septimus Afrus*. Malalas, *Chronographia* XII.18 (p. 291), gave seventeen years, nine months.

Commentary

255 *Antoninus Gestas.* Malalas, *Chronographia* XII.23 (p. 295), gave the name as Geta rather than Gestas. One wonders whether the change in the *Laterculus* may result from contamination from the Greek exegetical tradition of names for the Good and Bad Thieves (Gestas and Dysmas), on which see B.M. Metzger, 'Names for the Nameless in the New Testament. A Study in the Growth of Christian Tradition', *Kyriakon. Festschrift Johannes Quasten*, ed. P. Granfield and J.A. Jungmann, 2 vols. (Münster, 1970) I, 78–99, at 90–1. Gestas may have been the more familiar name either to the scribe of the copy of Malalas's *Chronographia* used by the author of the *Laterculus*, or to that author, than the name of this minor emperor.

256 *Antoninus Caracallus.* Malalas, *Chronographia* XII.24 (p. 295).

257 *Valerianus.* Malalas, *Chronographia* XII.26 (p. 295). The text of Malalas's *Chronographia* makes it clear that Valerian is intended to follow Caracalla: μετὰ δὲ τὴν βασιλείαν ᾿Αντονίνου Καρακάλλου ἐβασίλευσε Βαλεριανὸς ἔτη ζ, 'after the reign of Antoninus Caracalla, Valerian reigned for seven years'. But the *codex unicus* of the Chronicle is lacunose at this point, missing out some forty years' worth of imperial reigns. The author of the *Laterculus* may very well have had a more complete version of the chronicle to work from, but something certainly seems to have been wrong with it at this point, for he makes a doublet of Valerian, bracketing the additional emperors.

258 *Gallienus.* Malalas, *Chronographia* XII.27 (p. 298).

259 *Claudius.* Malalas, *Chronographia* XII.28 (p. 298), gave the name as Claudius Apollianus.

260 *Cytallinus.* Malalas, *Chronographia* XII.29 (p. 299), gave the name as Quintilianus.

261 *Aurelianus.* Malalas, *Chronographia* XII.30 (p. 299).

262 *Tacitus.* Malalas, *Chronographia* XII.31 (p. 301).

263 *Florianus.* Malalas, *Chronographia* XII.32 (p. 301).

264 *Hilius Probus.* Malalas, *Chronographia* XII.33 (p. 302).

265 *Carus.* Malalas, *Chronographia* XII.34 (p. 302).

266 *Numerianus.* Malalas, *Chronographia* XII.35 (p. 303).

227

267 *Carinus.* Malalas, *Chronographia* XII.36 (p. 304).

268 *Licinnianus.* Malalas, *Chronographia* XII.49 (p. 314). The *Laterculus* here divagates substantially from Malalas's text as we have it, which gives Diocletian as the successor to Carinus, reigning for twenty years nine months, and adds that he appointed his son Maximianus as Caesar after he had ruled for three years (Malalas, *Chronographia* XII.38 (p. 306)). Maximianus took over from Diocletian and ruled for nineteen years (Malalas, *Chronographia* XII.15 (p. 311)), followed by Maxentius for three years (*ibid.* XII.47, p. 312) and Constantius Chlorus for thirteen years (*ibid.* XII.48, p. 313). Only then do we have Maximus Licinianus.

269 *Dioclitianus et Maximianus.* The *Laterculus* gave the reign of Maximianus alone (Malalas, *Chronographia* XII.45 (p. 311).

270 *Constantius maior.* Malalas, *Chronographia* XIII.1 (p. 316). Malalas, *Chronographia*, gave Constantius Junior as Constantine's successor (XIII.15, p. 315), reigning for twelve years, then Constans for sixteen years (XIII.xvii (p. 325)).

271 *Constantius.* Malalas, *Chronographia* XIII.17 (p. 325), gave Constantius a reign of thirty years, in Constantinople.

272 *Iulianus.* Malalas, *Chronographia* XIII.18 (p. 326).

273 *Iobianus.* Malalas, *Chronographia* XIII.26 (p. 336).

274 *Valentinianus.* Malalas, *Chronographia* XIII.28 (p. 337), gave sixteen years.

275 *Valens.* Malalas, *Chronographia* XIII.34 (p. 342).

276 *Gratianus.* Malalas, *Chronographia* XIII.36 (p. 343), gave a reign of seventeen years, but added that Theodosius was proclaimed emperor by Gratian in the sixth year of his reign.

277 *Theodosius maior.* Malalas, *Chronographia* XIII.37 (p. 344).

278 *Arcadius.* Malalas, *Chronographia* XIII.37 (p. 344): ὁ δὲ αὐτὸς βασιλεὺς ἔστεψε τοὺς δύο αὐτοῦ υἱούς, οὓς ἔσχεν ἀπὸ τῆς προτέρας αὐτοῦ γυναικὸς Γάλλης, καὶ τὸν μὲν ᾿Αρκάδιον ἐποίησε βασιλέα ἐν Κωνσταντινουπόλει, τὸν δὲ ᾿Ονώριον ἐν ῾Ρώμῃ ('the emperor crowned his two sons whom he had by his first wife Galla and made Arcadius emperor in Constantinople and Honorius in

Rome'). Malalas, *Chronographia* XIII.46 (pp. 348–9), said that Arcadius reigned for twenty-three years in all.

279 *Honorius*. Malalas, *Chronographia* XIII.68 (p. 349).

280 *Theodosius minor*. Malalas, *Chronographia* XIV.1 (p. 351), gave fifty years, seven months. The Slavonic text of the chronicle shares the *Laterculus*'s forty-eight years.

281 *Marcianus*. Malalas, *Chronographia* XIV.28 (p. 367).

282 *Leo maior*. Malalas, *Chronographia* XIV.35 (p. 369).

283 *Leo iunior*. Malalas, *Chronographia* XIV.47 (p. 376), gave one year, twenty-*three* days.

284 *Zeno*. Malalas, *Chronographia* XV.1 (p. 377), gave fifteen years only.

285 *Anastasius*. Malalas, *Chronographia* XVI.1 (p. 392).

286 *Iustinus*. Malalas, *Chronographia* XVII.1 (p. 410).

287 *Iustinianus*. Malalas, *Chronographia* XVIII.1 (p. 425), gave thirty-eight years, seven months, thirteen days.

288 *Iustinus*. Malalas's chronicle as we have it ended with Justinian. But it is possible that the version from which the author of the *Laterculus* worked went on to the ninth year of Justin's thirteen-year reign. Another possibility is that a doublet of the first Justin was accidentally included in the list. A third possibility suggested by Jeffreys, 'Chronological Structures', *Studies*, p. 143, is that 'there was a note in the copy used by the compiler of the *Laterculus* that that particular manuscript was copied or revised in the ninth year of Justin II, a process which need not have involved the entry of additional material in the chronicle after the end of Justinian's reign.' This is a major issue in the dating of Malalas's *Chronographia* since the *Laterculus* is by far the earliest witness to it, and there is a fragment of uncertain size missing from the end of the Codex Baroccianus. If the end of the *Chronicle* can be dated, by using this line in the *Laterculus* to the ninth year of the reign of Justin II (575) it would give us a very precise date of composition. But it is far from clear that the *Laterculus*, which is notably imprecise and casual about historical niceties, can bear such a burden of proof.

Appendix

Variant and anomalous Biblical texts

In this section, the Vulgate text is cited first, then the version in the *Laterculus*, then other relevant *varia*.[1]

Gen. II.7: 'formauit igitur dominus deus hominem de limo terrae'
Lat ch. 17: '*de terra fincxit* incolomem iuuenem'
　　VL (Fischer) L: 'et tunc *finxit* deus hominem de limo terrae'[2]

Gen. III.19: 'quia puluis es et in puluerem reuerteris'
Lat ch. 22: '*terra* es et in *terram ibis*'
　　VL (Fischer) L: 'quoniam *terra es et in terra(m) ibis*'.[3]

Gen. XVIII.17: 'non est hic aliud nisi domus Dei et porta caeli'
Lat ch. 14: 'hic est . . . *uere domus Dei est* et porta caeli'
　　Isidore, *Etymologiae* XV.i.22: '*uere hic domus dei est* et porta caeli'[4]

---

[1] The Vulgate text of the New Testament taken as standard here is the edition of Wordsworth and White. Manuscripts of the Latin Bible are identified by the sigils used in this edition. For the Old Testament I have been using Quentin together with Sabatier's edition of the Vetus Latina, and for Genesis, the new critical edition by Fischer, with his identifying sigla. In referring to the Septuagint, I take Rahlf's Göttingen edition as standard (using Brooke and Maclean where Rahlfs is incomplete), and with additional reference to Vaticanus and Siniaticus.

[2] *Genesis*, ed. Fischer, p. 38.　　[3] *Ibid.*, p. 74.

[4] *Ibid.*, p. 305. See also, with respect to the same passage, E. Le Blant, *Inscriptions chrétiennes de la Gaule antérieures au viiie siècle*, 2 vols (Paris, 1856) I, p. 239 (no. 177), a sixth-century inscription from the first basilica of St Martin at Tours, which gives the version 'quam metuendus est locus iste, uere templum dei est et porta caeli'.

Num. XXIV.17: 'Orietur stella ex Iacob et consurget uirga de Israhel; et percutiet duces Moab uastabitque omnes filios Seth'
Lat ch. 15: 'orietur stella . . . ex Iacob et *ascendit homo* in Israhel et *confringet omnes duces alienigenarum*'

>VL (Sabatier): 'orietur stella ex Iacob, et exsurget *homo* de Israel, et *confringet duces* Moab, et praedabitur omnes filios Seth'[5]
>Leo the Great, *Sermones* XXXIV: 'orietur stella ex Iacob, et exsurget *homo* ex Israel, et *dominabitur gentium*'[6]

Ps. XVIII.6 (LXX): 'et ipse tamquam sponsus procedens de thalamo suo'
Lat ch. 1: '*uelut rex insederit* thalamo'

Ps. XVIII.6 (LXX): 'exsultauit ut gigans ad currendam uiam suam'
Lat ch. 19: '*quemadmodum* gigans per uiam'

Is. XIX.1: 'ecce Dominus ascendet super nubem leuem et ingredietur Aegyptum et mouebuntur simulacra Aegypti a facie eius'
Lat ch. 7: 'ecce dominus *sedet* super nubem leuem *ueniet* in Aegyptum et *comminuet* omnia simulacra *et sculptilia Aegyptiorum*'

>Ambrose *In Ps. CXVIII*: 'ecce dominus *sedet* super nubem leuem, et *ueniet* in Aegyptum'[7]

Is. LX.6: 'omnes de Saba uenient aurum et tus deferentes et laudens Domino adnuntiantes'
Lat ch. 15: 'omnes a Saba uenient *ferentes* aurum, thus *et murra, salutare* Domino *nuntiantes*

>edit. Rom.: '*ferentes* aurum'[8]
>LXX Siniat., Hesychius *In Isaiam*: + καὶ λίθον τίμιον

Amos II.7: 'quae calcant super puluerem terrae, et pugno percutiebat capita pauperum'[9]
Lat ch. 20: 'et quod *colaphis capite caeditur. . .*'
Gildas, *De excidio* II.liii.1 (ed. Mommsen, p. 570): 'quae calcabant super puluerem terrae, et *colaphis caedebant capita* pauperum'

---

[5] *Versiones antiquae*, ed. Sabatier I, 308.   [6] Leo, PL 34, 137–463, at 245.
[7] *Versiones antiquae*, ed. Sabatier II, 547.
[8] *Ibid.* II, 623.   [9] *Ibid.* II, 921

Zach. III.1–4: 'et ostendit mihi Iesum sacerdotem magnum stantem coram angelo domini, et satan stabat a dextris eius ut aduersaretur ei. Et dixit dominus ad satan: increpet dominus in te satan: et increpet dominus in te qui elegit Hierusalem'

Lat ch. 18: 'uidi ... Iesum sacerdotem magnum et *stabat ad dextris eius diabulus, id est ex parte iustitiae, concinnans dolos*. Et dixit ad *eum*: increpet tibi Dominus, *diabule, qui redimit Israhel et* elegit Hierusalem'

VL (Sabatier): 'et ostendit mihi dominus Iesum sacerdotem magnum stantem ante faciem angeli Domini, *et diabolus stabat a dextris eius* ut aduersaretur ei. Et dixit dominus ad diabolum: increpet dominus in te *diabole*: et increpet in te dominus, qui elegit Ierusalem'[10]

Matth. II.8: 'ite et interrogate diligenter de puero'
Lat ch. 6: 'ite et *scrutamini* diligenter de *puerum*'
   f: 'euntes *requirite*'

Matth. II.8: 'et procidentes adorauerunt eum'
Lat ch. 6: 'et *cadentes in pauimento terrae* adorauerunt'

Matth. II.12: 'et responso accepto in somnis ... per aliam uiam reuersi sunt in regionem suam'
Lat ch. 6: 'et reponso accepto *ab angelo per somnio* per aliam uiam ... *regressi* sunt in suam regionem'
   BCT: *regressi* L: *regesi* Q: *regresi*
   R: *in suam regionem*

Matth. II.16: 'iratus est ualde'
Lat ch. 6: 'iratus est *uehementer*'
   f: 'iratus est *uehementer*'

Matth. II.16: 'et mittens occidit omnes pueros qui erant in bethleem et in omnibus finibus eius a bimatu et infra'
Lat ch. 6: 'et mittens *manum militarem* occidit omnes pueros in Bethleem *ciuitatem Iudeae* et *circa* finibus eius a bimatu et infra'

[10] *Ibid.* II, 988.

Matth. II.18: 'uox in Rama audita est ploratus et ululatus multus, Rachel plorans filios suos et noluit consolari quia non sunt' (Jerem. XXXI.15: 'uox in excelso audita est lamentationis fletus et luctus, Rachel plorantis filios suos et nolentis consolari super eis quia non sunt')
Lat ch. 15: 'uox in excelso, *hoc est in Rama*, audita est, pluratus et *luctus magnus*; Rachel plurans filios suos, et noluit consolari *quoniam* non sunt'

Matth. VIII.17: 'ut adimpleretur quod dictum est per Esaiam prophetam dicentem: ipse infirmitates nostras accepit et aegrotationes portauit' (Is. LIII.4: 'uere languores nostros ipse tulit et dolores nostros ipse portauit')
Lat ch. 18: 'infirmitates *adque* egrotationes nostras . . . *libenter* portauit'

Matth. XXIV.36: 'de die autem illa et hora nemo scit neque angeli caelorum nisi pater solus'
Lat ch. 23: 'de diem autem illa et hora nemo scit neque angelis in caelo *neque filius* nisi pater solus'
BJOX, graec. ℵ,BD, and a b c d e f ff.1.2. h l q r aur.: + *neque filius*[11]

Matth. XXIV.46: 'Quis putas est fidelis seruus et prudens quem constituit dominus suus supra familiam suam ut det illis cibum in tempore?'
Lat ch. 14: '[Christus paterfamilias] constituens super famulos et famulas, ut iuste *trittici mensuram distribuant*'
    e: 'ut *distribuant* cibaria conseruis suis'
    f: 'ut det illis in tempore *trittici mensuram*'

Luke II.52: 'et Iesus proficiebat sapientia et gratia apud Deum et homines'
Lat ch. 16: '[quod autem] *adcreuisse* sapientia *quoque coram* Deo et homines'

Luke IV.20: 'et cum plicuisset librum reddidit ministro et sedit'
Lat ch. 19: 'et cum *replicuisset*, ministro *tradidit*'

John X.18: 'potestatem habeo ponendi eam et potestatem habeo iterum sumendi eam'

---

[11] *Nouum Testamentum*, ed. Wordsworth and White I, 144.

Lat ch. 21: 'potestatem habeo ponendi *animam meam* et potestatem habeo iterum sumendi eam'
GT, aur.: + *animam meam*[12]

John XIX.15: 'illi autem clamabant tolle tolle crucifige eum'
Lat ch. 10: '(Iudaei seditionem concitauerunt) *dicentes* tolle tolle crucifige eum'
r: + *dicentes*, cum gr. U min

John XIX.36: 'facta sunt enim haec ut scriptum impleatur: os non comminuetis ex eo'
(Ex. XII.46: 'nec os illius confringetur')
Lat ch. 21: 'os *suum* non comminuetis ex eo ipse'
C: + *suum*[13]

Acts II.34–35: 'dixit dominus domino meo sede a dextris meis, donec ponam inimicos tuos scabillum pedum tuorum' (Ps. CIX.1: 'dixit dominus domino meo sede a dextris meis donec ponam inimicos tuos scabillum pedum tuorum')
Lat ch. 22: 'sede *ad dexteram* meam, donec ponam inimicos tuos scauellum pedum tuorum'
d Iren., Uict., Af.: *ad dexteram*[14]

Rom. X.4: 'finis enim legis Christus'
Lat ch. 16: 'finis legis Christus'.

Galat. III.13: 'Christus nos redemit de maledictio legis'
Lat ch. 16: '*qui maledictum* uetustatis *absoluit*'

I Cor. XII.8–11: 'alii quidem per Spiritum datur sermo sapientiae, alii autem sermo scientiae secundum eundem spiritum, alteri fides in eodem spiritu, alii gratia sanitatum in uno spiritu, alii operatio uirtutum, alii prophetatio, alii discretio spirituum, alii genera linguarum, alii interpretatio sermonum. Haec autem omnia operatur unus atque idem spiritus'
Lat ch. 22: 'alii quidem datur sermo sapientiae secundum eundem spiri-

[12] *Ibid.* I, 579.   [13] *Ibid.* I, 636.   [14] *Ibid.* III, 48.

tum, alii uero sermo scientiae, alii gratia *curationum*, alii genera linguarum, alii interpretatio *linguarum* in eundem spiritum'
   (first clause) Hil. (Ps. LXIV) Ambr. (Inc.) Cassiod. omit *per spiritum*;
   D f Hil. (Ps. LXIV) Ambr (Inc.), etc.: *curationum*[15]

I Cor. XV.55–56: 'ubi est mors stimulus tuus? stimulus autem mortis
peccatum est'
Lat ch. 20: 'ut *acoleum* mortis'
   CD θ TU f g: *aculeus* (also frequently in Augustine)[16]

II Cor. V.10: 'omnes enim nos manifestari oportet ante tribunal Christi,
ut referat unusquisque propria corporis prout gessit siue bonum siue
malum'
Lat ch. 17: '*carnem* ut *recipiat* unusquisque *iuxta quod egit in corpore* siue
bonum siue malum'
   r: *recipiat* (also in Tertullian, Origen, Jerome and frequently in
   Augustine)[17]

Eph. IV.8: 'ascendens in altum captiuam ducit captiuitatem dedit dona
hominibus'
Lat ch. 22: 'duxit *ergo* ascendens *Christus* captiuam captiuitatem ... dedit
dona hominibus'

Eph. IV.9–10: 'qui descendit ipse est et qui ascendit super omnes caelos ut
impleret omnia'
Lat ch. 22: 'qui discendit, ipse et *ascendit* super caelos, ut *adimpleret* omnia'
   CDH θ TUW σ: *adimpleret*[18]

Eph. IV.13: 'donec occurramus omnes in unitatem fidei et agnitionis filii
dei, in uirum perfectum, in mensuram aetatis plenitudinis Christi'
Lat ch. 16: 'donec omnes occurramus in uirum perfectum, in mensuram
aetatis plenitudinis Christi'

Coloss. II.9: 'quia in ipso inhabitat omnis plenitudo diuinitatis corporaliter'
Lat ch. 22: 'qui est plenitudo *unius deitatis adque substantiae*'
   Orig (int. II, 77, IV, 515)[19]

[15] *Ibid.* II, 241   [16] Ibid. II, 274   [17] *Ibid.* II, 314.   [18] *Ibid.* II, 435.

2 Pet. III.8: 'unum uero hoc non lateat uos carissimi, quia unus dies apud dominum sicut mille anni, et mille anni sicut dies unus' (Ps. LXXXIX.4 (LXX): 'quoniam mille anni ante oculos tuos tamquam dies hesterna quae praeteriit et custodia in nocte')

Lat ch. 3: '*una* dies Domini sicut mille anni'

Lat ch. 23: 'non lateat uos hoc Dauid,[20] quia mille anni aput Deum sicut dies una et dies una *tamquam* mille anni'

> U*: *una dies*
>
> t: Caesarius *tamquam*[21]

---

[19] *Ibid.* II, 508.

[20] This refers the verse back to its origin in Ps. LXXXIX.4, rather than to the Petrine version which is in fact quoted.

[21] *Nouum Testamentum*, ed. Wordsworth and White III, 329–30.

Bibliography

Adler, A., ed., *Suidae Lexicon*, 4 vols. (Leipzig, 1928–38)

Anon. ed., 'Miraculum Sancti Anastasii Martyris', *AB* 11 (1892), 233–41

Arndt, W., and B. Krusch, ed., Gregory of Tours, *Opera*, MGH SSRM 1 (Hanover, 1885)

Assemani, G. S., *et al.*, ed and trans., Ephrem, *Ephraem Syri opera omnia*, 6 vols. (3 vols. Syriac-Latin, 3 vols. Greek-Latin) (Rome, 1732–46)

Athanasius, *Expositio in psalmos*, PG 26, 53–546

(pseudo)Athanasius, *Quaestiones ad Antiochum ducem*, PG 28, 597–710

Attwater, D., *St John Chrysostom: Pastor and Preacher* (London, 1959)

Augustine, *De diuersis quaestionibus*, PL 40, 11–100

Beck, E., ed. and trans., Ephrem, *Des heiligen Ephraem des Syrers Hymnen de Natiuitate (Epiphania)*, CSCO 186–7 [Script. Syr. 82–3] (Louvain, 1959)

Beggiani, S. J., *Early Syriac Theology, with Special Reference to the Maronite Tradition* (New York, 1983)

Best, R.I., and H.J. Lawlor, ed., *The Martyrology of Tallaght from the Book of Leinster and MS. 5100–4 in the Royal Library, Brussels*, HBS 68 (London 1931)

Bickermann, E. J., *Chronology of the Ancient World*, rev. ed. (London, 1980)

Bidez, J., 'Sur diverses citations et notamment sur trois passages de Malalas retrouvées dans un texte hagiographique', *BZ* 11 (1902), 388–94

Birch, W. de G., ed., *Cartularium Saxonicum*, 3 vols. and Index (London, 1883–99)

Bischoff, B., 'Wendepunkte in der Geschichte der lateinischen Exegese im Frühmittelalter', *Mittelalterliche Studien. Aufsätze zur Schriftkunde und Literaturgeschichte*, 3 vols. (Stuttgart, 1966–81) I, 205–73 (first ptd *Sacris Erudiri* 6 (1954), 189–279), trans. as 'Turning-points in the History of Latin Exegesis in the Early Middle Ages', in *Biblical Studies: the Medieval Irish Contribution*, ed. M. McNamara (Dublin, 1976), pp. 74–160

Bischoff, B., and M. Lapidge, ed., *Biblical Commentaries from the Canterbury School of Theodore and Hadrian* (Cambridge, 1994)

Bibliography

Le Bourdellès, H., *L'Aratus Latinus: Etude sur la culture et la langue latine dans le Nord de la France au viie siècle* (Lille, 1985)

Brightman, F.E., ed., *Liturgies Eastern and Western: Being the Texts Original or Translated of the Principal Liturgies of the Church: I. Eastern Liturgies* (Oxford, 1896)

Brock, S. P., 'Greek into Syriac and Syriac into Greek', *Journal of the Syriac Academy* 3 (1977), 1–17 [422–35]

'Aspects of Translation Technique in Antiquity', *Greek, Roman and Byzantine Studies* 20 (1979), 69–87

'Syriac and Greek Hymnography: Problems of Origin', *SP* 15 (for 1975) [= *TU* 128] (1984), 77–81

Brooke, A.E., and A. N. McLean, ed., *The Old Testament in Greek, according to the text of Codex Vaticanus, supplemented from other Uncial Manuscripts*, 3 vols. (Cambridge, 1906–40)

Brooks, E.W., *et al.*, ed. and trans., *Chronica Minora*, CSCO 1–6 [Script. Syr. 3.4] (Leipzig, 1933–5)

Brooks, N., *The Early History of the Church of Canterbury. Christ Church from 597 to 1066* (Leicester, 1984)

Budge, E.A. Wallis, ed. and trans., *The Book of the Cave of Treasures. A History of the Patriarchs and the Kings their Successors from the Creation to the Crucifixion of Christ* (London, 1927)

Carlton, C. M., *A Linguistic Analysis of a Collection of Late Latin Documents Composed in Ravenna Between AD 445–700: a Quantitative Approach*, Janua Linguarum, Series Practica 89 (The Hague, 1973)

Colgrave, B., and Mynors, R.A.B., ed., Bede, *Historia ecclesiastica gentis Anglorum* (Oxford, 1969)

de Coninck, L., ed., Theodore of Mopsuestia, *Theodori Mopsuesteni Expositiones in Psalmos Iuliano Aeclanensi interprete in latinum uersae quae supersunt*, CCSL 88A (Turnhout, 1977)

Connolly, R.H., ed. and trans., Narsai, *The Liturgical Homilies of Narsai* (Cambridge, 1909)

Conybeare, F. C., 'The Relation of the Paschal Chronicle to Malalas', *BZ* 11 (1902), 395–405

'Three Early Doctrinal Modifications of the Text of the Gospels', *Hibbert Journal* 1 (1903), 98–113

Corbett, P. B., 'Local Variations of Spelling in Latin MSS', *SP* 1 [= *TU* 63] (1957), 188–93

Crehan, J., 'The Seven Orders of Christ', *Theological Studies* 19 (1958), 81–93

Cummian, *Epistola*, PL 87, 969–78

Dean, R.E., ed., Epiphanius, *Epiphanius's Treatise on Weights and Measures. The Syriac Version* (Chicago, 1935)

Bibliography

Delehaye, H., and H. Quentin, ed., Hieronymus, *Martyrologium Hieronymianum*, *Acta Sanctorum Nouembris II* (Brussels, 1931)

Dindorf, L., ed., John Malalas, *Ioannis Malalae chronographia*, Corpus Scriptorum Historiae Byzantinae 10 (Bonn, 1831)

Dionisotti, A. C., 'On Bede, Grammars and Greek', *RB* 92 (1982), 111–41

Dombart, B., and A. Kalb, ed., Augustine, *De ciuitate Dei*, 2 vols., CCSL 47–8 (Turnhout, 1955)

Downey, G., 'The Calendar Reform at Antioch in the Fifth Century', *Byzantion* 15 (1940/1), 39–48

  A History of Antioch in Syria from Seleucus to the Arab Conquest (Princeton, NJ, 1961)

  'The Perspective of the Early Church Historians', *Greek, Roman and Byzantine Studies* 6 (1965), 57–70

Dressell, R.M., ed., Barnabas, *Epistola*, *Patrum Apostolicorum Opera* (Leipzig, 1857), 1–45

Drijvers, H. J. W., *East of Antioch: Studies in Early Syriac Christianity* (London, 1984)

Duchesne, L., ed., *Liber Pontificalis*, 3 vols. (Paris, 1886–1957)

Edwards, O. C., 'Diatessaron or Diatessara?' *SP* 15 (for 1975) [= *TU* 128] (1984), 88–92

Egan, G.A., ed. and trans., Ephrem, *Saint Ephrem. An Exposition of the Gospel*, CSCO 291 [Script. Armen. 5–6] (Louvain, 1968)

Ehwald, R., ed., *Aldhelmi Opera*, MGH, AA 15 (Berlin, 1919)

El-Khoury, N., 'The Use of Language by Ephraim the Syrian', *SP* 15 (for 1975) [= *TU* 128] (1984), 93–9

Epiphanius, *Liber de mensuris et ponderibus*, PG 43, 257–94

Eusebius, 'Quaestiones euangelicae ad Stephanum', PG 22, 879–935

Faulhaber, M., ed., Hesychius, *Hesychii Hierosolymitani Interpretatio Isaiae Prophetae* (Freiburg i. B., 1900)

Ferrari, G., *Early Roman Monasteries: Notes for the History of the Monasteries and Convents at Rome from the V through the X century* (Vatican City, 1957)

Finegan, J., *Handbook of Biblical Chronology. Principles of Time Reckoning in the Ancient World and Problems of Chronology in the Bible* (Princeton, NJ, 1964)

Finsterwalder, P.W., ed., *Die Canones Theodori Cantuariensis und ihre Überlieferungsformen* (Weimar, 1929)

Fischer, B., ed., *Vetus Latina: Die Reste der altlateinischen Bibel nach Petrus Sabatier: Genesis* (Beuron, 1954)

Foerster, W., ed., 'Die *Appendix Probi*', *Wiener Studien* 14 (1892), 278–322

Fox, D.J., ed. and trans., Philoxenus of Mabbug, *The Matthew-Luke Commentary of Philoxenus* (Missoula, MA, 1975)

Bibliography

Gaeng, P., *An Inquiry Into Local Variation in Vulgar Latin as Reflected in the Vocalisation of Christian Inscriptions* (Chapel Hill, NC, 1968)

Geyer, P., *et al.*, ed., *Itineraria et alia geographica*, CCSL 175 (Turnhout, 1965)

Gignoux, P., ed. and trans., 'Homélie de Narsaï sur la Création d'Adam et d'Eve et sur la transgression du commandement', *L'Orient Syrien* 7 (1966), 307–36 Narsai, *Homélies de Narsai sur la création*, Patrologia Orientalis 24.3–4 (Turnhout, 1968)

Ginzberg, L., *The Legends of the Jews*, 7 vols. (Philadelphia, PA, 1911–38)

Grandgent, C. H., *An Introduction to Vulgar Latin* (Boston, 1907)

Grant, R.M., ed., Theophilus of Antioch, *Ad Autolycum* (Oxford, 1970)

Grattan, J.H.G., and Singer, C., *Anglo-Saxon Magic and Medicine, Illustrated Specifically from the Semi-Pagan Text 'Lacnunga'* (London, 1952)

Gratwick, A. S., 'Latinitas Britannica', in *Latin and the Vernaculars in Early Medieval Britain*, ed. N. Brooks (Leicester, 1982), pp. 1–79

Gray, P. T. R., *The Defence of Chalcedon in the East* (Leiden, 1979)

Greer, R. A., *Theodore of Mopsuestia: Exegete and Theologian* (London, 1961)

Haddad, G., *Aspects of Social Life in Antioch in the Hellenistic-Roman Period* (Chicago, 1947)

Haddan, A. W., and W. Stubbs, ed., *Councils and Ecclesiastical Documents relating to Great Britain and Ireland*, 3 vols. (Oxford, 1869–78)

Hanslik, R., and T. Mommsen, ed., Cassiodorus, *Historia ecclesiastica tripartita*, CSEL 71 (Vienna, 1952)

Harris, J. Rendel, ed. and trans., Ephrem, *Fragments of the Commentary of Ephrem Syrus upon the Diatessaron* (London, 1895)

Harrison, K., 'The Beginning of the Year in England, *c*. 500–900', *ASE* 2 (1973), 51–70
The Framework of Anglo-Saxon History to AD 900 (Cambridge, 1976)
'Easter Cycles and the Equinox in the British Isles', *ASE* 7 (1978), 1–8

Harvey, S.A., 'Remembering Pain: Syriac Historiography and the Separation of the Churches', *Byzantion* 58 (1988), 295–308.

Harvey, W.W., ed., Irenaeus, *Sancti Irenaei episcopi Lugdunensis libros quinque aduersus haereses*, 2 vols. (Cambridge, 1862)

Herrin, J., *The Formation of Christendom* (Oxford, 1987)

Hillgarth, J.N., 'Historiography in Visigothic Spain', *SettSpol* 17 (1970), 261–311

Hillgarth, J.N., *et al.*, ed., Julian of Toledo, *Opera*, CCSL 115 (Turnhout, 1976)

Holl, K., Epiphanius, *Panarion*, 3 vols., GCS 25, 32 and 38 (Leipzig, 1915–33)
Gesammelte Aufsätze zur Kirchengeschichte, 3 vols. (Tübingen, 1927–8)

Hopper, V. F., *Medieval Number Symbolism: its Sources, Meaning and Influence in Thought and Expression* (New York, 1928)

Huemer, J., ed., Caelius Sedulius, *Opera*, CSEL 10 (Vienna, 1885)

Hunter Blair, P., 'The Historical Writings of Bede', *SettSpol* 17 (1970), 197–221

Hurst, D., ed., Bede, *De templo*, in *Bedae Venerabilis Opera Exegetica* IIA, CCSL 119A (Turnhout, 1969)

Jansma, T., trans., Jacob of Sarug, 'L'Hexaméron de Jacques de Sarug', *Orient Syrien* 4 (1959), 3–42, 129–62 and 253–84

    Theodore of Mopsuestia, 'Théodore de Mopsueste. Interpretation du livre de la Genèse, fragments de la version syriaque (BM Add. 17189 f. 17–21)', *Muséon* 75 (1962), 63–92

Jeffreys, E., *et al.*, trans., John Malalas, *The Chronicle of John Malalas: a Translation*, Byzantina Australiensia 4 (Melbourne, 1986)

    'Malalas's Use of the Past', in *Reading the Past in Late Antiquity*, ed. G.W. Clarke *et al.* (Canberra, 1990), pp. 121–46

John Malalas, *Chronographia*, PG 97, 9–806

Jones, C.W., ed., Bede, *De temporum ratione*, *Bedae Opera Didascalia II*, CCSL 123B (Turnhout, 1977)

Kenney, J. F., *The Sources for the Early History of Ireland*, I: *Ecclesiastical* (New York, 1929)

Kronholm, T., *Motifs from Genesis 1–11 in the Genuine Hymns of Ephrem the Syrian, with Particular Reference to the Influence of Jewish Exegetical Tradition* (Uppsala, 1978)

Kühn, K.G., ed., Galen, *Claudii Galeni Opera Omnia*, 22 vols. (Leipzig, 1821–33)

Laistner, M. L. W., 'Some Reflections on Latin Historical Writings in the Fifth Century', in his *The Intellectual Heritage of the Early Middle Ages*, ed. C.G. Starr (Ithaca, NY, 1966), pp. 3–21

    'Antiochene Exegesis in Western Europe during the Middle Ages', *HTR* 40 (1947), 19–32

Landes, R., 'Lest the Millennium be Fulfilled: Apocalyptic Expectations and the Pattern of Western Chronography 100–800 CE', in *The Use and Abuse of Eschatology in the Middle Ages*, ed. W. Verbeke, D. Verhelst and A. Welkenhuysen (Louvain, 1988), pp. 137–211.

Lapidge, M., 'A Seventh-Century Insular Latin Debate Poem on Divorce', *CMCS* 10 (1985), 1–23.

    'The School of Theodore and Hadrian', *ASE* 15 (1986), 45–72

Lapidge, M., ed., *Archbishop Theodore* (Cambridge, 1995)

Laterculus Malalianus, PL 94, 1161–74

Lindsay, W. M., ed., Isidore, *Etymologiae*, 2 vols. (Oxford, 1911)

    Notae Latinae (Cambridge, 1915)

Llewellyn, P. A. B., *Rome in the Dark Ages* (London, 1971)

Lowe, E.A., ed., *The Bobbio Missal: A Gallican Massbook*, 3 vols., HBS 53–61 (1917–24)

Luneau, A., *L'Histoire du salut chez les Pères de l'Eglise: la doctrine des âges du monde* (Paris, 1964)

MacCarthy, B., ed., *The Codex Palatino-Vaticanus, no. 830*, R.I.A. Todd Lecture Series 3 (Dublin, 1892)

McNally, R.E., ed., *Quaestiones tam de nouo quam de uetere testamento, Scriptores Hiberniae Minores I*, CCSL 108B (Turnhout, 1973), 189–205

Macomber, W.F., ed., Theodore of Mopsuestia, 'Newly Discovered Fragments of the Gospel Commentaries of Theodore of Mopsuestia', *Muséon* 81 (1968), 441–7

Mango, C., 'La culture grecque et l'Occident au viiie siècle', *SettSpol* 20 (1972), 683–721

Marcus, R., trans., Philo Judaeus, *Questions and Answers on Exodus, Translated from the Ancient Armenian Version of the Original Greek* (Cambridge, MA, and London, 1963)

Mayr-Harting, H., *The Coming of Christianity to Anglo-Saxon England*, 3rd ed. (London, 1991)

Meyvaert, P., and C. Franklin, 'Has Bede's Version of the *Passio S. Anastasii* Come Down to Us in BHL 408?', *AB* 100 (1982), 373–400

Mingana, A., ed. and trans., Theodore of Mopsuestia, *Commentary of Theodore of Mopsuestia on the Nicene Creed* (Cambridge, 1932)

Mommsen, T., ed., *Chronica Minora saec. .iv., .v., .vi., .vii.*, 3 vols., MGH, AA 9, 11 and 13 (Berlin, 1882–98)

  Isidore, *Chronica Maiora*, *Chronica Minora*, MGH, AA 11 (Berlin, 1894), 391–468

  Gildas, *De excidio Britanniae*, *Chronica Minora*, MGH, AA 13 (Berlin, 1898), III, 1–85

  Laterculus Malalianus, *Chronica Minora*, MGH, AA 13 (Berlin, 1898), III, 424–37

Mosshammer, A. A., *The Chronicle of Eusebius and Greek Chronographic Tradition* (Cranbury, NJ, 1979)

Murray, R., 'The Rock and the House on the Rock. A Chapter in the Ecclesiological Symbolism of Aphraates and Ephrem', *Orientalia Christiana Periodica* 30 (1964), 315–62

  'Mary, the Second Eve in the Early Syriac Fathers', *Eastern Churches Review* 3 (1970/1), 372–84

  Symbols of Church and Kingdom (Cambridge, 1975)

Niese, B., ed., Josephus, *Antiquitates Iudaicarum*, 4 vols. (Berlin, 1887–90)

Nordenfalk, C., *Die spätantike Zierbuchstaben*, 2 vols. (Stockholm, 1970)

Ó Cróinín, D., 'The Irish Provenance of Bede's Computus', *Peritia* 2 (1983), 229–47

Ortiz de Urbina, I., *Patrologia Syriaca* (Rome, 1965)

Bibliography

Palmer, L. R., *The Latin Language* (London, 1954)

Petrucci, A., 'L'onciale romana', *Studi medievali* 3rd ser. 12 (1971), 71–134

Petschenig, M., ed., Cassian, *De Institutis Coenobiorum et de octo principalium uitiorum remediis*, CSEL 17 (Vienna, 1888)

Poole, R. L., 'Monasterium Niridanum', *EHR* 36 (1921), 540–5

    Chronicles and Annals: a Brief Outline of their Origin and Growth (Oxford, 1926)

Procopius of Gaza, *Commentarii in Genesin*, PG 87, 14–512

Quasten, J., and A. di Bernadino, *Patrology*, 3 vols. (Utrecht, 1950–63)

Quentin, H., *et al.*, ed., *Biblia sacra iuxta latinam uulgatam uersionem*, 16 vols. (Rome, 1926–81)

Rahlfs, A., ed., *Septuaginta. Vetus testamentum Graecum*, 19 vols. (Göttingen, 1931–)

    Septuaginta: id est uetus testamentum graece iuxta LXX interpretes, 2 vols. (Stuttgart, 1935)

Ramsay, R.L., 'Theodore of Mopsuestia in England and Ireland', *ZcP* 8 (1910–12), 652–97

Reynolds, L.D., ed., *Texts and Transmission: a Survey of the Latin Classics*, 2nd ed. (Oxford, 1986)

Reynolds, R. E., *The Ordinals of Christ from their Origin to the Twelfth Century* (Berlin, 1978)

Richards, J., *The Popes and the Papacy in the Early Middle Ages, 476–752* (London, 1979)

Riedinger, R., ed., *Concilium Lateranense a. 649 celebratum* (Berlin, 1984)

Robbins, F. E., *The Hexaemeral Literature: a Study of the Greek and Latin Commentaries on Genesis* (Chicago, 1912)

Robinson, J. A., *Somerset Historical Essays* (London, 1921)

Sabatier, P., ed., *Bibliorum sacrorum latinae uersiones antiquae*, 3 vols. (Rheims, 1743)

Sansterre, J.-M., *Les Moines grecs et orientaux à Rome aux époques byzantine et carolingienne*, 2 vols. (Brussels, 1983)

Schenk von Stauffenberg, A., ed., John Malalas, *Die römische Kaisergeschichte bei Malalas: Griechischer Text der Bücher IX-XII und Untersuchungen* (Stuttgart, 1931)

Schenkl, C., ed., Faltonia Proba, *Cento, Poetae christiani minores* I, CSEL 16 (Vienna, 1888), 511–609

Schwarz, E., ed., Eusebius, *Historia ecclesiastica*, with parallel text of Rufinus's Latin translation, ed. T. Mommsen, 2 vols. GCS 9 (Leipzig, 1903–9)

Sellers, R. V., *Two Ancient Christologies: A Study in the Christological Thought of the Schools of Alexandria and Antioch in the Early History of Christian Doctrine* (London, 1940)

Sims-Williams, P., 'Thoughts on Ephrem the Syrian in Anglo-Saxon England', *Learning and Literature in Anglo-Saxon England: Studies Presented to Peter Clemoes on the Occasion of his Sixty-fifth Birthday*, ed. M. Lapidge and H. Gneuss (Cambridge, 1985), pp. 205–26

Spinka, M., and G. Downey, trans., John Malalas, *Chronicle of John Malalas, Bks VIII-XVIII, Translated from Church Slavonic* (Chicago, 1940)

Stokes, W., ed. and trans., 'Scela na esergi, Tidings of the Resurrection', *Revue Celtique* 25 (1904), 232–59

'The Ever-New Tongue', *Ériu* 2 (1905), 98–162

Stratos, A.N., *Byzantium in the Seventh Century*, trans. M. Ogilvie-Grant, 5 vols. (Amsterdam, 1968–80)

Swete, H.B., ed., Theodore of Mopsuestia, *Theodori Episcopi Mopsuesteni in Epistolas B. Pauli Commentarii: The Latin Version with the Greek Fragments*, 2 vols. (Cambridge, 1880)

Temkin, O., 'Byzantine Medicine: Tradition and Empiricism', *Dumbarton Oaks Papers* 18 (1962), 97–116

Theodore of Mopsuestia, 'Fragmenta alia in Genesin', PG 66, 633–46

Tonneau, R.-M., ed. and trans., Ephrem, *Sancti Ephraemi Syri in Genesim et in Exodum commentarii*, CSCO 152–3 [Script. Syr. 71–2] (Louvain, 1955)

Traube, L., *Vorlesungen und Abhandlungen*, ed. F. Boll, 3 vols. (Munich, 1909–20)

Vermes, G., *Scripture and Tradition on Judaism: Haggadic Studies*, 2nd ed. (Leiden, 1973)

Vosté, J.-M., trans., Theodore of Mopsuestia, *Commentarius in euangelium Iohannis apostoli*, CSCO 115–16 [Script. Syr. 4.3] (Louvain, 1940)

Walker, G.S.M., ed., Columbanus, *Sancti Columbani opera* (Dublin, 1957)

Wallace-Hadrill, D. S., *Christian Antioch: a Study of Early Christian Thought in the East* (Cambridge, 1982)

Weber, R., ed., *Biblia sacra iuxta uulgatam uersionem*, 2 vols. (Stuttgart, 1969)

Wilmart, A., 'Les ordres du Christ', *Revue des sciences religieuses* 3 (1923), 305–27

'Catechèses celtiques', in his *Analecta Reginensia: Extraits des manuscrits latins de la reine Christine conservés au Vatican*, Studi e Testi 59 (Vatican City, 1933), 29–112

Wolska-Conus, W., ed., Cosmas Indicopleustes, *Topographie chrétienne*, 3 vols., SChr 141, 159 and 197 (Paris, 1968–73)

Wordsworth, J., H. J. White and H. F. D. Sparks, ed., *Nouum Testamentum domini nostri Iesu Christi latine secundum editionem s. Hieronymi*, 4 vols. (Oxford, 1889–1954)

Wright, R., *Late Latin and Early Romance* (Liverpool, 1982)

Young, F. M., *From Nicaea to Chalcedon* (London, 1983)

Index of biblical sources

I OLD TESTAMENT

Genesis

II.7 (ch. 17)
II.21–2 (ch. 17)
III.19 (ch. 22)
XXVIII.12–13 (ch. 14)
XXVIII.17–19 (ch. 14)
XXXV.29 (ch. 8)

Exodus

IV.21 (ch. 16)
IV.24–5 (ch. 16)
IV.26 (ch. 16)
XIV.27–31 (ch. 21)

Numbers

XXXIV.17 (ch. 15)

III Kings

VI.38 (ch. 12)

Joshua

IV.2–3 (ch. 18)
IV.8 (ch. 18)

Psalms

XVIII.6 (ch. 1)
XVIII.6 (ch. 19)
XLIX.19 (ch. 18)
LXXVIII (ch. 20)
LXXXIX.4 (ch. 3)
CIX (ch. 22)
CXXXI.11 (ch. 14)

Jeremiah

XXXI.15 (ch. 15)

Isaiah

XIX.1 (ch. 7)
XXVIII.10 (ch. 21)
LIII.4 (ch. 19)
LIII.5 (ch. 14)
LX.6 (ch. 15)

Ezra

IV-VII (ch. 12)

Zachariah

III.1–2 (ch. 18)

Amos

II.7 (ch. 20)

Ezekiel

XXXI.15 (ch. 21)
XXXVI.7 (ch. 12)
XLIII.27 (ch. 23)

Sapientiae

X.8 (ch. 24)

2 NEW TESTAMENT

Matthew

II.1–2 (ch. 5)
II.2–3 (ch. 5)
II.7 (ch. 6)
II.9 (ch. 6)
II.11 (ch. 6)
II.12 (ch. 6)
II.13 (ch. 15)
II.13–15 (ch. 7)
II.16 (chs. 6 *and* 15)
II.18 (ch. 15)
II.19 (ch. 7)
II.22–3 (ch. 7)
III.12 (ch. 24)
III.16–17 (ch. 18)
IV.1 (ch. 18)
IV.19 (ch. 18)
VIII.17 (ch. 19)
XIV.2–3 (ch. 9)
XIV.10 (ch. 9)
XV.25 (ch. 4)
XVI.2 (ch. 11)
XVI.9 (ch. 11)
XX.1–16 (ch. 23)
XXIV.36 (ch. 24)
XXIV.45 (ch. 14)
XXVI.12 (ch. 15)
XXVI.14 (ch. 20)
XXVI.67 (ch. 20)
XXVII.2 (chs. 10 *and* 20)
XXVII.19 (ch. 10)
XXVII.35 (ch. 20)
XXVII.45 (chs. 4 *and* 10)
XXVII.51–52 (ch. 10)
XXVII.52 (ch. 21)
XXVII.54 (ch. 10)

Mark

I.9 (ch. 9)
VII.24 (ch. 24)

Luke

I.26–7 (ch. 2)
II.2–3 (ch. 2)
II.7 (ch. 14)
II.8 (ch. 14)
II.16 (ch. 14)
II.42 (ch. 8)
II.46 (ch. 8)
II.52 (ch. 16)
III.1–2 (ch. 9)
III.2 (ch. 11)
III.19–20 (ch. 9)
III.23 (ch. 17)
III.24 (ch. 18)
IV.1–2 (ch. 18)
IV.16–17 (ch. 19)
IV.20–1 (ch. 19)
XII.42 (ch. 14)
XXII.17 (ch. 19)
XXII.19 (ch. 19)
XXIII.24–5 (ch. 21)
XXIII.44 (ch. 4)
XXIII.45 (ch. 10)
XXIV.1 (ch. 11)

John

I.18 (ch. 21)
II.19 (ch. 19)
II.19–20 (ch. 12)
X.12 (ch. 14)
X.18 (ch. 21)
XIII.5 (ch. 19)
XIX.6 (ch. 20)
XIX.14 (chs. 4 *and* 10)
XIX.24 (ch. 20)
XIX.30 (ch. 21)
XIX.36 (ch. 21)
XXI.15–17 (ch. 14)

Acts

I.3 (ch. 21)
I.9 (chs. 11 *and* 22)
I.11 (ch. 11)
II.1–2 (ch. 22)
II.34 (ch. 22)
II.34–5 (ch. 22)
XII.23 (ch. 6)

Pauline Epistles

Romans

VIII.15 (ch. 20)
VIII.21 (ch. 24)
VIII.23 (ch. 20)
X.2 (ch. 4)
X.4 (ch. 16)
XV.8 (ch. 16)

I Corinthians

XII.8–11 (ch. 22)
XV.20 (ch. 15)
XV.22 (ch. 21)
XV.23 (ch. 15)
XV.53 (ch. 21)
XV.55–6 (ch. 20)

II Corinthians

V.10 (ch. 17)

Ephesians

III.15 (ch. 22)
IV.8 (ch. 22)
IV.9–10 (ch. 22)
IV.13 (ch. 16)

Index of biblical sources

Galatians

III.13 (ch. 16)
IV.4 (ch. 23)
IV.5 (ch. 20)

Colossians

1.17 (ch. 22)
II.9 (ch. 22)

I Timothy

II.5 (ch. 18)

Hebrews

II.14–15 (ch. 21)

Catholic Epistles

I Peter

II.5 (ch. 18)

II Peter

III.8 (ch. 23)

I John

II.18 (ch. 23)

Revelation

X.7 (ch. 24)
XI.15 (ch. 24)
XVI.17 (ch. 24)
XXI.14 (ch. 18)

General index

Abgar of Edessa 67
Abraham 46, 168, 171, 201
Adam 5, 7, 24, 45, 70, 88, 95, 122–3,
    124–5, 136–9, 142–5, 172, 176,
    177, 192–3, 207, 209, 218, 221,
    223
Adomnán 204
Aeschylus 198
Æthelbert, king of Kent 29
Æthelred, king of Kent 201
Aetius of Amida 49
Agatho, pope 16, 34–5, 37–8
akathistos, hymn 6, 183–4
Albinus of Canterbury 3, 17, 116
Aldhelm 3, 8, 9, 10, 11, 12, 13, 16, 17,
    18, 20, 27, 43, 76, 86, 96–7, 99,
    115, 163, 164, 165, 167, 199, 204,
    212, 217, 226
Aldred 91
Alexander of Tralles 49, 55
Alexandria 48, 164, 167, 177
Ambrose of Milan 64, 96, 194, 221, 223
Ambrosiaster 162
Ammianus Marcellinus 68
Amphilocius of Iconium 35
Anastasius, St 18, 19, 89–90
Annunciation, the 5, 6, 45, 55, 120–1,
    166, 168
annus mundi 5, 7, 22, 24, 26, 122–3
Anthemius of Tralles 49
Antioch 5, 13, 22, 26, 39, 41, 43, 57,
    58, 68–9, 164, 177, 190, 220

Antiochene exegesis 3–4, 6, 13, 15, 16,
    17, 23, 41, 42, 43–7, 50, 56, 65–6,
    70, 185, 192, 195, 204, 210, 222
Aphrahat 195, 203, 205
appendix Probi 75, 76, 77, 85
apocalypticism 22, 24–6, 124, 125,
    152–5, 223
apocrypha 16, 168, 169, 172, 174, 177,
    182, 185, 189, 227
Arabs *see* Muslims
Aracoeli (S. Maria in Capitolio) 8–9,
    186–7
Arians 223–4
Aristotle 49
Athanasius 195, 212
Augustine of Canterbury 28, 29
Augustine of Hippo 23, 36, 37, 38, 39,
    45, 46, 53, 54–5, 61, 64, 72, 73,
    97, 106, 108, 170, 196–200, 209,
    218, 223
    de ciuitate Dei 23, 46, 108, 170
    de diuersis quaestionibus 46, 54, 196–7
    enarrationes in Psalmos 53, 55, 223
Augustus, emperor 2, 5, 7, 18, 60,
    120–3, 126–31, 156–7, 164, 165,
    166, 180, 184, 186–7

Bangor 178
Bar-Hebraeus 179
Basil of Caesarea 17, 35–6, 50
Bede 2, 3, 4, 9, 11, 13, 14, 15, 16, 17,
    18, 20, 21, 23, 26, 28, 34, 50, 51,

54, 82, 89–90, 93, 96, 99, 116, 164, 167, 168, 169, 170, 175, 177, 178, 210, 212
Benedict Biscop 2–3, 9, 20
Bentley, Richard 59
Beowulf 116
Bethlehem 5, 123, 126–9, 138–41, 179, 201
Boniface, St 9
Book of the Cave of Treasures, the 172, 182
breviarium Alaricum 165

Cædwalla, king of the West Saxons 9, 210
canon law 6, 13, 19, 35–6, 47, 52, 53, 217
Canterbury 2, 3, 8, 11, 12, 13, 14, 15, 17, 19, 20, 21, 26, 29–30, 31, 34, 48, 55, 66, 72, 90, 96–7, 99, 102, 110, 114–15, 164, 175, 183, 217
Cassiodorus 61, 81–2, 184, 195
charters, from Glastonbury 29
 Kentish 12, 29, 77, 101–2, 110
 from Ravenna 76, 77–80, 85
Choricius of Gaza 111
Christ *see* Jesus
chronicles 21, 59, 114, 185
Chronographer of 354, the 191
chronography 2, 6–7, 21–31, 86, 122–5, 164, 173, 175, 177–8, 184–5, 188, 191, 225, 229
church councils 19
 Council of Caesarea 98
 Council of Chalcedon (451), the 31, 36, 40, 41, 67, 192
 Council of Ephesus (431), 40, 41, 186
 Council of Hatfield (680), the 11, 28, 36, 37, 41
 Council of Nicaea (325), 41, 42, 167, 192
 Fifth General Council (553; also known as the Second Council of Constantinople) 32, 40, 41
 First Council of Constantinople (381) 36, 41

Lateran Council of 649 33, 39, 41, 42, 88
Lateran Council of 1215 51
Sixth General Council (680/1) 37
Synod of Milan (680), the 37
Synod of Rome (680), the 37–8
Third Council of Toledo (688) 37
Cicero 92
Clemens 56, 120, 121, 124, 125, 164, 174
Clement of Alexandria 222
Columbanus, St 10, 40, 167
collectio canonum Hibernensis 98
computus 1, 95, 98, 167–9
Constans II, emperor 32–3
Constantine IV, emperor 34
Corpus-Epinal-Erfurt glossaries 12, 14
Constantinople 5, 28, 32, 33, 34, 38, 39, 43, 48, 49, 58
Cosmas Indicopleustes 175, 176
Crucifixion, the 6, 45, 132–5, 168, 171, 189–90, 220
circumcision 7, 142–3, 205–6
constitutiones Apostolorum 215
Cummian, 10, 177
Cuthbert, St 212
Cynewulf 116
Cyril of Alexandria 57, 210, 217, 219

Dadisho' of Quatar 37
dating 6, 22–3, 26, 28, 56, 91, 120, 121, 122, 123, 132, 133, 134, 135, 165–70, 187
de duodecim abusiuis saeculi 97
de vii ordinibus ecclesiae 214
Diatessaron 62, 200
Didascalia 214
Diodore of Tarsus 39, 41, 44, 195
'discipulus Umbrensium', the 11, 35, 42, 201
dogs 11, 163
Donatus 162
Donus, pope 43

Easter, date of 1, 10, 27, 29, 167–9, 177

Edessa 13, 40, 41, 43, 68–9, 70
Egypt 16, 24, 128–31, 148–9, 167, 170,
  182, 186
'Egyptian days' 51
embryology 47, 196–200
Ephrem Syrus 13, 17, 19, 55, 56, 68, 69,
  70, 148–9, 179, 183–4, 193, 195,
  201, 202, 203, 207–8, 215, 216
Epiphanius of Cyprus 5, 18, 56, 63–4,
  66, 115, 130, 131, 171, 172, 179,
  182–4, 185–6, 188
  Ancoratus 172
  On Weights and Measures 66
  Panarion 171, 182–3, 185–6
  treatise on the Twelve Stones 18
Epiphanius scholasticus 184
Epistle of Barnabas, the 46, 67, 222–3
Eusebius 57, 59, 62, 91, 124, 125,
  164–5, 171, 174, 177, 179, 181,
  183, 184, 189, 192, 226
Eustathius 205
Eve 7, 45, 70, 136–7, 142–3, 176,
  192–3, 207–8
Ever-New Tongue, the 168, 172
Expositio quomodo se habeant generationes 173

filioque clause 36–8
flight into Egypt 5, 7, 45, 128–9, 142–3,
  182–3
Fursa, St 10, 99

Galen 47, 48, 50, 51, 54, 57, 112,
  196–200
Gausbertus 2
Gildas 8, 10, 59, 65, 72, 115, 181,
  217
Gilbertus Anglicus 54
Greek 3–4, 8, 11, 12, 14, 15, 17, 18,
  20, 29, 34–5, 39, 51, 66, 87–8, 90,
  92, 93, 111, 114, 166–7, 172, 175,
  177, 179, 181, 186, 193, 220, 221,
  226, 227
Gregory of Africa 33
Gregory the Great, pope 28, 31, 81, 167
Gregory of Nazianzen 50, 97, 164, 170

Gregory of Nyssa 37, 38, 50, 217, 219
Gregory of Tours 92

Hadrian of Canterbury 2, 3, 34, 52, 101,
  115, 163, 217
Hagia Sophia 49
Heahfrith 9, 11, 99, 177
Hegesippus 171
Heraclius, emperor 32, 33, 49
Hermeneumeta Ps-Dositheana 18
Herod 5, 7, 83, 126–9, 140–3, 172,
  179, 181–2, 184–5, 190, 195,
  204–5
Hesychius of Jerusalem 62, 67, 174, 182,
  204
Heidelberg 96
Hilary of Poitiers 194, 221
Hild 9, 212
Hippocrates 47, 52, 196, 199
Hippolytus of Rome 57, 169, 171, 177,
  184, 211
Homer 45, 116
Horace 73, 92
Hydatius 57

Ibas of Edessa 41
indiction 28–9
Insular minuscule 10, 110
Ireland 16, 99, 170
Irenaeus 56, 194, 202, 203, 207, 223
Irish, the, and their scholarship 1, 10, 11,
  16, 17, 20, 26–7, 74, 77, 97–9,
  120–1, 124–5, 163, 168, 169, 177,
  178
Isaac 168, 171, 218
Isidore of Seville 65, 75, 76, 95, 96–7,
  164, 167, 202, 216, 223
itineraria 9, 90

Jacob, the patriarch 45, 69, 138–41,
  146–7, 201–3
Jacob of Sarug 56, 169, 179, 208, 225
James, the Lord's brother 122–3, 168,
  170–1, 226
Jarrow 2, 27

Jerome 26, 91, 92, 96, 97, 183, 188, 222, 224
Jerusalem 5, 7, 45, 126–7, 146–7, 177, 185, 194, 213,
Jesus 5, 7, 18, 24, 26, 38, 45, 46, 54, 67, 69, 121–57, 166, 201, 202, 206–7, 210–11, 213, 216–17, 219, 220, 224
Jews and Jewish learning 25, 41, 44, 45, 46, 68, 122–3, 126–7, 132–3, 136–7, 140–1, 148–9, 168, 172, 190, 194, 202, 205–6, 207, 209, 213, 216, 219
John the Baptist 5, 7, 22, 64, 132–3, 142–3, 144–5, 172, 188
John of Beverley 50
John Chrysostom 39, 56, 177, 193, 209, 212, 219
John Philoponus 49
John the Syrian 92
Joseph, the patriarch 45, 66, 148–9
Joseph, St 120, 121, 128–31, 142–3, 184, 185–6
Josephus 53, 57, 59, 169–70, 172, 181, 188, 192, 193
Joshua 213
Jubilees, book of 168–9, 170, 177
Julian the Apostate 48, 197
Julian of Toledo 25, 38, 177
Julius Africanus 24, 59, 173, 177
Junilius 43
Justin II, emperor 2, 60, 95, 160–1, 229
Justin Martyr 44
Justinian, emperor 5, 21, 25, 28, 32, 40, 49, 58, 72, 95, 160–1, 216–17, 229
Juvencus 72, 204

laterculus 1
Latin 8, 14, 18, 66, 74–85, 90, 92–3, 111, 114, 119, 165
law, Roman 13, 165, 216–17
Leiden glossary 73
Leo the Great, pope 31, 62, 95, 98, 203
Libanius 39, 68
liber pontificalis 220

liturgy, 18, 36, 216, 218–9
Lorsch, 96–7, 112

magi, the 5, 7, 62, 126–9, 140–1, 179, 184–5, 203, 204–5
Malalas, John 1, 2, 5, 7, 14, 18, 20, 21, 23–6, 28, 56, 57–60, 68, 87–8, 90, 114, 164–92
  Chronographia 2, 5, 21, 24, 56, 57–60, 114, 119, 162, 164–92, 225–9
Mansuetus of Milan 37
manuscripts
  Basle O IV.17   194
  Berlin, Deutsche staatsbibliothek, lat. fol. 416   105, 107
  Brussels, Bibliothèque royale, 20979   163
  Cambridge, Corpus Christi College 286   224
  Cividale, R. Museo Archaeologico, s.n.   105
  Epinal, Bibliothèque municipale 72 (2)   110
  Leiden, Bibliotheek der Rijksuniversiteit, Voss. Misc. 11 2   111–13
  London, BL, Cotton Augustus II.2   102
  London, BL, Cotton Claudius B.iv   208
  London, BL, Cotton Tiberius A.xv   43
  London, BL, Egerton 609   65
  London, BL, Royal 2.A.XX   18
  Lucca, Biblioteca capitolare, 490   11
  Milan, Biblioteca Ambrosiana, E.147 sup.   224
  Milan, Biblioteca Ambrosiana, H.78 sup.   106
  Monte Cassino, Archivio della Badia 150   162
  Montpellier, Ecole des médécines 362   194
  New Haven, CT, Yale University Library, s.n. 107
  Oxford, Bodleian Library Auct. D II 14   162, 224

Oxford, Bodleian Library Baroccianus
   182 58, 166, 180, 182, 187, 188,
   191, 229
Oxford, Oriel College 42   19
Paris, Archives nationales K2   102
Paris, BN, lat. 10837   162
Paris, BN, lat. 11411   52
Paris, BN, lat. 12214   108
Paris, BN, lat. 13246   109
Paris, BN, lat. 16361   1
Rome, Biblioteca Vallicelliana, B 24
   101
Rome, Biblioteca Nazionale Vittorio
   Emanuele, Sessoriano 13 (2094)
   106
St Gallen, Stiftsbibliothek, 44   52
St Petersburg, Public Library, Q. v. I.
   6+7+8+9+10   106, 107, 108
Treviso, Archivo notarile, s.n.   100
Troyes, Bibliothèque municipale
   504 100, 106, 107
Turin, Biblioteca nazionale, F.III.16
   89
Vatican City, Biblioteca Apostolica
   Vaticana, lat. 1342   100
Vatican City, Biblioteca Apostolica
   Vaticana, lat. 3835   101
Vatican City, Biblioteca Apostolica
   Vaticana, lat. 5750   224
Vatican City, Biblioteca Apostolica
   Vaticana, lat. 5765   108
Vatican City, Biblioteca Apostolica
   Vaticana, Pal. lat. 277 2, 74–85,
   94–111, 119, 163, 182
Vatican City, Biblioteca Apostolica
   Vaticana, reg. lat. 316   170
Vienna, Nationalbibliothek med. gr.
   1   109
Wolfenbüttel, Herzog August
   Bibliothek, Aug. 2°. 36   108
March 25, events of 5, 6, 29, 55, 122,
   123, 166, 167–70, 197
Maronite chronicle 185
Martin I, pope 33, 34, 42
martyrologium Hieronymianum 171, 188

martyrology of Tallaght 171, 188
Marutha 201
Mary, the Virgin 6, 8, 45, 69, 120–1,
   128–9, 136–7, 180, 183, 186,
   192–3, 195
Maximus the Confessor 33–4, 39, 43, 50
medicina de quadrupedibus 52
medicine 13, 47–55, 114, 136–9, 194
Meletius 50, 51
Methodius 195, 208
Miles of Susa 18
millenarianism *see* apocalypticism
miraculum S. Anastasii 63, 91
monotheletism 32–3
Moses 7, 24, 45, 124–5, 142–3, 170,
   175–6, 195, 205–6, 213
Muslims 33, 34, 48, 53

Narsai 40, 56, 69, 70, 176, 207, 213
Nemesius of Emesa 222
Nemesius of Remesiana 50
Neoplatonism 46
Nestorius 39
Nestorians and Nestorianism 12, 40, 42,
   43, 67, 191, 211
Nicomachus of Gerasa 46
Nisibis 68–9
Northumbria 2, 3, 20, 27, 163, 178
Novatian 183
numerology 7, 23, 46–7, 136, 137, 194,
   196, 200

Old English 14, 15
ordines Christi 7, 69, 98, 146–9, 214, 215
Oribasius 48, 54, 55, 57, 197–9
Origen 44, 184, 221
Orosius 181

passio S. Anastasii 18, 89–90, 92
Paul of Aegina 49, 52, 55
Paul, St 6, 23, 29, 203, 205, 209, 212,
   217
Pelagia the Harlot 92
Persia 18, 19, 26, 49, 67–8, 127, 128,
   129, 179, 205

Peter, St 33, 140–1, 152–3, 202–3, 212, 222
Phalech 5, 6, 7, 24, 88, 122, 123, 172
Philo Judaeus 169
Philoxenus of Mabbug 222
phlebotomy 50–1
Phlegon of Athens 189
Plato 46, 47, 51
Proba, Faltonia Betitia, 8, 56, 70–1, 86, 208
Procla 64, 132, 133, 189
Procopius of Gaza 24, 67, 170, 173, 205
Prosper of Aquitaine 188
Prudentius 73
ps-Athanasius 176, 177, 208–9
ps-Jerome 214
ps-Matthew 183

questiones sancti Isidori 74

Ravenna, 77, 78, 85
Reculver cross 19
Resurrection 6, 7, 134–5, 138–9, 144–5, 150–1, 152–5, 209, 220
rhetoric 14, 23, 114, 163
Rituale ecclesiae Dunelmensis 208
Rome 1, 2, 3, 8–9, 11, 13, 16, 19, 28, 33, 34, 37, 38, 39, 43, 47, 48, 61, 77, 84, 87, 88–9, 90, 99, 100, 115, 130, 131, 167, 169, 177, 186, 220, 225
Rufinus 171

Sahdona 210
S. Anastasius *ad aquas saluias* 9, 63, 88–9, 90–1
S. Maria in Capitolio *see* Aracoeli
S. Saba 43
Saltair na rann 170, 176
Scela na esergi 209
Sedulius, Caelius 8, 56, 70–1, 84, 115, 163–4, 193, 194, 204, 206, 211, 215, 216, 217, 218–20
Sergius, pope, 18, 220
Servius 164

Severian of Gabala 50
sex aetates mundi 23, 27, 138–9, 175, 177, 222–3
Sextus Placitus Papyriensis 52
Sidonius Apollinaris 72–3
six (the number) 23, 46, 197, 200, 214
Solomon and Saturn 208
Southumbria 15, 20, 27, 71, 99, 115, 163
'Sphere of Pythagoras', the 51, 52, 55
Stephanus of Alexandria 49
Stephen of Ripon 16
Suda, the 44, 186
Suetonius 164
Sulpicius Seuerus 27, 191, 211
Sybil, the 18, 130, 131, 167, 186
Syria and Syrians 5, 12, 25, 26, 40, 41, 45, 50, 62, 67, 78–9, 92, 168, 176, 192, 201, 202–3, 205, 210, 213,
Syriac 14, 15, 16, 18, 37, 57, 66, 92, 114, 162, 172, 173, 182, 183, 185, 193, 195, 206, 215, 216

Talmud 45, 68
Tarsus 13, 88
Tatian 60
Te Deum 211
Tertullian 195
Theodore of Mopsuestia 6, 39–40, 41, 42, 43, 44, 45, 56, 63, 65–6, 83, 162, 164, 169, 172, 178, 179, 191–2, 195, 210–11, 220
Theodore, pope 33
Theodore Spoudaios 34
Theodore of Tarsus 2, 3, 6, 11, 13–15, 16, 18–20, 28, 29, 31, 35, 36–7, 39, 41–2, 43, 47, 49, 50, 51, 52, 63, 77, 86, 88, 90–1, 97, 101, 110, 114–15, 163, 168, 201, 210, 212, 217, 220
Biblical Commentaries 12, 16, 43, 47, 52–4, 66, 115, 163, 164, 168, 175–6, 179, 206, 209
Canones Theodori 6, 47, 52, 53, 217
Penitential 3, 11–12, 13, 35, 115, 201

poems 3, 11
teaching at Canterbury 3–4, 11–12,
    14, 19, 20, 55, 72–3, 86, 110, 115,
    165, 175, 217, 226
Theodoretus 57, 170, 205
Theodosius, emperor 57, 160–1
Theodulf 10
Theophilus 56, 57, 120, 121, 124, 125,
    164, 207
'Three Chapters', the 32, 40
Tiberius, emperor 5, 7, 28, 130–5,
    156–7, 187, 190, 192
Timotheus 56, 120, 121, 124, 125, 130,
    131, 164, 174
Titus, emperor, 95, 156–7, 225–6
Tobias of Rochester 3, 14, 17, 116
typology 6, 7, 43–5, 61, 66, 70, 128,
    129, 136, 137, 192–3, 221

uncial 99–103

Valerian, emperor 30, 158–9, 227
Varro 73
Vergil 45, 71, 73, 86, 93, 105, 115,
    164, 208, 220
vernal equinox 29, 122, 123, 167–9
Victor of Capua 162
Victorius of Aquitaine 30–1, 169, 188
Virgin, the, *see* Mary
Vitalian, pope 13, 34
Vitellius, emperor 30, 156–7, 225

Weissenburg 112
Wetadun 50
Wihtfrith 9, 73, 99, 177
Wilfrid, Archbishop of York 9, 16, 178,
    212
William of Malmesbury 9, 19, 165
Willibrord, St 163
World Week 23–5, 67, 152–5, 174–5,
    222–3